OTHER INSIGHT GUIDES TITLES

COUNTRY/REGION

ASIA
Bali
Burma
Hong Kong
India
Indonesia
Korea
Malaysia
Nepal
Philippines
Rajasthan
Singapore
Sri Lanka
Taiwan
Thailand

PACIFIC
Hawaii
New Zealand

NORTH AMERICA
Alaska
American Southwest
Northern California
Southern California
Florida
Mexico
New England
New York State
The Pacific Northwest
The Rockies
Texas

CARIBBEAN
Bahamas
Barbados
Jamaica
Puerto Rico
Trinidad and Tobago

EUROPE
Great Britain
France
Germany
Greece
Ireland
Italy
Spain

MIDDLE EAST
Egypt
Israel

AFRICA
Kenya

GRAND TOURS
Australia
East Asia
California
Canada
Crossing America
Continental Europe

GREAT ADVENTURE
Indian Wildlife

greece

Directed and Designed by Hans Hoefer
Edited by Karen Van Dyck

APA PRODUCTIONS

THE INSIGHT GUIDES SERIES RECEIVED SPECIAL AWARDS FOR EXCELLENCE FROM THE PACIFIC AREA TRAVEL ASSOCIATION.

GREECE
First Edition
© 1988 APA PRODUCTIONS (HK) LTD
Published by APA Productions (HK) Ltd.
Printed by APA Press Pte. Ltd.
Colour Separation in Singapore by Colourscan Pte Ltd

APA PRODUCTIONS
Publisher and Chairman: Hans Johannes Hoefer
Marketing Director: Yinglock Chan
General Manager: Henry Lee
Administration Manager: Alice Ng
Editorial Director: Geoffrey Eu
Editorial Manager: Vivien Kim
Executive Editor: Adam Liptak
Projects Manager [German Editions]: Heinz Vestner

Project Editors
Helen Abbott, Diana Ackland, Mohamed Amin, Ravindralal Anthonis, Roy Bailet, Louisa Cambell, Jon Carroll, Hillary Cunningham, John Eames, Janie Freeburg, Bikram Grewal, Virginia Hopkins, Samuel Israel, Jay Itzkowitz, Phil Jarratt, Tracy Johnson, Ben Kalb, Wilhelm Klein, Saul Lockhart, Sylvia Mayuga, Gordon MaLauchlan. Kal Müller, Eric Oey, Daniel P. Reid, Kim Robinson, Ronn Ronck, Robert Seidenberg, Rolf Steinberg, Sriyani Tidball, Lisa Van Gruisen, Merin Wexler.

Contributing Writers
A.D. Aird, Ruth Armstrong, T. Terence Barrow, F. Lisa Beebe, Bruce Berger, Dor Bahadur Bista, Clinton V. Black, Star Black, Frena Bloomfield, John Borthwick, Roger Boschman, Tom Brosnahan, Jerry Carroll, Tom Chaffin, Nedra Chung, Tom Cole, Orman Day, Kunda Dixit, Richard Erdoes, Guillermo Garcia-Oropeza, Ted Giannoulas, Barbara Gloudon, Harka Gurung, Sharifah Hamzah, Willard A. Hanna, Elizabeth Hawley, Sir Edmund Hillary, Tony Hillerman, Jerry Hopkins, Peter Hutton, Neil Jameson, Michael King, Michele Kort, Thomas Lucey, Leonard Lueras, Michael E. Macmillan, Derek Maitland, Buddy Mays, Craig McGregor, Reinhold Messner, Julie Michaels, M. R. Priya Rangsit, Al Read, Elizabeth V. Reyes, Victor Stafford Reid, Harry Rolnick, E.R. Sarachchandra, Uli Schmetzer, Ilsa Sharp, Norman Sibley, Peter Spiro, Harold Stephens, Keith Stevens, Michael Stone, Desmond Tate, Colin Taylor, Deanna L. Thompson, Randy Udall, James Wade, Mallika Wanigasundara, William Warren, Cynthia Wee, Tony Wheeler, Linda White, H. Taft Wireback, Alfred A. Yuson, Paul Zach.

Contributing Photographers
Carole Allen, Ping Amarand, Tony Arruza, Marcello Bertinetti, Alberto Cassio, Pat Canova, Alain Compost, Ray Cranbourne, Alain Evrard, Ricardo Ferro, Lee Foster, Manfred Gottschalk, Werner Hahn, Dallas and John Heaton, Brent Hesselyn, Hans Hoefer, Luca Invernizzi, Ingo Jezierski, Wilhelm Klein, Dennis Lane, Max Lawrence, Lyle Lawson, Philip Little, Guy Marche, Antonio Martinelli, David Messent, Ben Nakayama, Vautier de Nanxe, Kal Müller, Günter Pfannmuller, Van Philips, Ronni Pinsler, Fitz Prenzel, G.P. Reichelt, Dan Rocovits, David Ryan, Frank Salmoiraghi, Thomas Schollhammer, Blair Seitz, David Stahl, Bill Wassman, Rendo Yap, Hisham Youssef.

While contributions to Insight Guides are very welcome, the publisher cannot assume responsibility for the care and return of unsolicited manuscripts or photographs. Return postage and/or a self-addressed envelope must accompany unsolicited material if it is to be returned. Please address all editorial contributions to Apa Productions, P. O. Box 219, Orchard Point Post Office. Singapore 9123.

Distributors
Australia and New Zealand: Prentice Hall of Australia, 7 Grosvenor Place, Brookvale, NSW 2100, Australia. **Benelux:** Uitgeverij Cambium, Naarderstraat 11, 1251 Aw Laren, The Netherlands. **Caribbean:** Kingston Publishers, 1-A Norwood Avenue, Kingston 5, Jamaica. **Central and South America:** Mexico and Portugal: Cedibra Editora Brasileira Ltda, Rua Leonidia, 2-Rio de Janeiro, Brazil. **Denmark:** Copenhagen Book Centre Aps, Roskildeveji 338, DK-2630 Tastrup, Denmark. **Europe (others):** European Book Service, Flevolaan 36-38, P. O. Box 124, 1380 AC Weesp, Holland. **Hawaii:** Pacific Trade Group Inc., P. O. Box 1227, Kailua, Oahu, Hawaii 96734, U.S.A. **Hong Kong:** Far East Media Ltd., Vita Tower, 7th Floor, Block B, 29 Wong Chuk Hang Road, Hong Kong. **India and Nepal:** India Book Distributors, 107/108 Arcadia Building, 195 Narima Point, Bombay-400-021, India. **Indonesia:** Java Books, Box 55 J.K.C.P, Jakarta, Indonesia.

Israel: Steimatzky Ltd., P.O. Box 628, Tel Aviv 61006, Israel (Israel title only). **Italy:** Zanfi Editori SRL. Via Ganaceto 121, 41100 Modena, Italy. **Japan:** Charles E.Tuttle Co. Inc., 2-6 Suido 1-Chome, Bunkyo-ku, Tokyo 112, Japan. **Kenya:** Camerapix Publishers International Ltd., P. O. Box 45048, Nairobi, Kenya. **Korea:** Kyobo Book Centre Co., Ltd., P.O. Box Kwang Hwa Moon 1 658, Seoul, Korea. **Philippines:** National Book Store, 701 Rizal Avenue, Manila, Philippines. **Singapore:** MPH Distributors (S) Pte. Ltd., 601 Sims Drive #03-21 Pan-I Warehouse and Office Complex, S'pore 1438, Singapore. **Spain:** Altair, Balmes 69, 08007-Barcelona, Spain. **Sri Lanka:** Lake House Bookshop, 100, Sir Chittampalama, Gardines Mawatha, Colombo 2, Sri Lanka. **Switzerland:** M.P.A. Agencies-Import SA, CH. du Croset 9, CH-1024 Ecublens, Switzerland. **Taiwan:** Caves Books Ltd., 103 Chungshan N.Road, Sec. 2, Taipei, Taiwan, Republic of China. **Thailand:** Far East Publications Ltd., 117/3 Soi Samahan, Sukhumvit 4 (South Nana), Bangkok, Thailand. **United Kingdom and Ireland:** Harrap Ltd., 19-23 Ludgate Hill, London EC4M 7PD, England, United Kingdom. **Mainland United States and Canada:** Graphic Arts Center Publishing, 3019 N.W. Yeon, P.O. Box 10306, Portland OR 97210, U.S.A. (The Pacific Northwest title only); Prentice Hall Press, Gulf & Western Building, One Gulf & Western Plaza, New York, NY 10023, U.S.A. (all other titles).

French editions: Editions Gallimard, 5 rue Sébastien-Bottin, F-75007 Paris, France. **German editions:** Nelles Verlag GmbH, Schleissheimer Str. 371b, 8000 Munich 45, West Germany. **Italian editions:** Zanfi Editori SLR, Via Ganaceto 121 41100 Modena, Italy. **Portuguese and Spanish editions:** Cedibra Editora Brasileira Ltda, Rua Leonidia, 2-Rio de Janerio, Brazil.

Special Sales
Special sales, for promotion purposes within the international travel industry and for educational purposes, are also available. The advertising representatives listed below also handle special sales. Alternatively, interested parties can contact Apa Productions, P.O. Box 219, Orchard Point Post Office, Singapore 9123.

Advertising Representatives
Advertising carried in Insight Guides gives readers direct access to quality merchandise and travel-related services. These advertisments are inserted in the Guide in Brief section of each book. Advertisers are requested to contact their nearest representatives, listed below.

Australia and New Zealand: International Media Representative Pty. Ltd., 3rd Floor, 39 East Esplanade Manly, NSW 2095, Australia. Tel: (02) 9773377; Tlx: IMR AA 74473.
Bali: Mata Graphic Design, Batujimbar, Sanur, Bali, Indonesia. Tel: (0361) 8073. (for Bali only)
Hawaii: HawaiianLMedia Sales; 1750 Kalakaua Ave., Suite 3-243, Honolulu Hawaii 96826, U.S.A. Tel: (808) 9464483.
Hong Kong: C Cheney & Associates, 17th Floor, D'Aguilar Place, 1-30 D' Aguilar Street, Central, Hong Kong. Tel: 5-213671; Tlx: 63079 CCAL HX.
India and Nepal, Pakistan and Bangladesh: Universal Media, CHA 2/718, 719 Kantipath, Lazimpat, Kathmandu-2, Nepal. Tel: 412911/414502; Tlx: 2229 KAJI NP ATTN MEDIA.
Indonesia (excluding Bali): Media Investment Services, Setiabudi Bldg. 2, 4th Floor, Suite 407, Jl. Hr. Rasuna Said, Kuningan, Jakarta Selatan 12920, Indonesia. Tel: 5782723/5782752; Tlx: 62418 MEDIANETIA.
Malaysia: MPH Media Services, Lot 2 Jalan 241, Section 51A, Petaling Jaya, Selangor, West Malaysia. Tel: (03) 7746166; Tlx: MA 37402 JCM.
Philippines: Torres Media Sales Inc., 21 Warbler St., Greenmeadows I, Murphy, Quezon City, Metro Manila, Philippines. Tel: 722-02-43; Tlx: 23312 RHP PH.
Thailand: Cheney, Tan & Van Outrive, 17th Floor Rajapark Bldg., 163 Asoke Rd., Bangkok 10110, Thailand. Tel: 2583244/2583259; Tlx: 20666 RAJAPAK TH.
Singapore: MPH Magazines (s) Pte. Ltd., 601 Sims Dr. #03-21, Pan-1 Warehouse & Office Complex, Singapore 1438. Tel: 7471088; Tlx: RS 35853 MPHMAG; Fax: 7440620.
Sri Lanka: Foremost Productions Ltd., Grant House, 101 Galle House, Colombo 4, Sri Lanka. Tel: (1) 584854/580971-3; Tlx: 21545 KENECK CE.

APA PHOTO AGENCY PTE. LTD.
The Apa Photo Agency is S.E. Asia's leading stock photo archive, representing the work of professional photographers from all over the world. More than 150,000 original color transparencies are available for advertising, editorial and educational uses. We are also linked with Tony Stone Worldwide, one of Europe's leading stock agencies, and their associate offices around the world:

Singapore: Apa Photo Agency Pte. Ltd., P.O. Box 219, Orchard Point Post Office, Singapore 9123, Singapore. **London:** Tony Stone Worldwide, 28 Finchley Rd., St. John's Wood, London NW8 6ES, England. **North America & Canada:** Masterfile Inc., 415 Yonge St., Suite 200, Toronto M5B 2E7, Canada. **Paris:** Fotogram-Stone Agence Photographique, 45 rue de Richelieu, 75001 Paris, France. **Barcelona:** Fototec Torre Dels Pardais, 7 Barcelona 08026, Spain. **Johannesburg:** Color Library (Pty.) Ltd., P.O. Box 1659, Johannesburg, South Africa 2000. **Sydney:** The Photographic Library of Australia Pty. Ltd., 7 Ridge Street, North Sydney, New South Wales 2050, Australia. **Tokyo:** Orion Press, 55-1 Kanda Jimbocho, Chiyoda-ku, Tokyo 101, Japan.

By Way of Introduction

This book has almost as many authors as readers. Culled from conversations at countless tavernas, from newspapers, poetry and musty travelers' accounts, and then refracted through the imaginations of at least 30 writers and half as many photographers, it is difficult to describe exactly how this book came into being. Apa Productions, a Hong Kong and Singapore-based publishing house whose innovative approach to creating travel chronicles has been honored throughout the world, has captured at a particular moment a kaleidoscope of images and text on and about Greece in this volume. As soon as you begin your reading, the kaleidoscope will be set in motion again.

Editor Karen Van Dyck (lady with short hair) and assistant editor Nelson Moe (sitting) join with the other contributors (back row left to right: Stewart, Constantine, Mazower, Vlavianos, Mackridge, Kindersley; and Cowan [second row]) to celebrate the launching of Insight Guide: Greece.

We'd like to introduce you to the team of contributors (in alphabetical order) who are most immediately responsible for bringing you *Insight Guide: Greece* in the hopes that their collective expertise will inspire you to learn and go on learning about Greece.

Katerina Anghelaki-Rooke was born in Athens and studied language and literature at the universities of Nice, Geneva and Athens. In 1962 she was awarded the First Prize for poetry from the city of Geneva. She has published seven collections of poems and a number of translations from English and Russian into Greek. She has taught modern Greek poetry at Harvard, Utah and San Francisco State. She received the Greek State prize for poetry in 1986.

David Beatty was born in London and worked for a time as a researcher on documentaries before becoming a freelance photographer traveling widely in Africa and Asia. Recently he has divided his time between India, Sri Lanka, Greece and the United Kingdom. His work has appeared in numerous publications and journals including *Illustrated London News* and *Time-Life Books*.

John Chioles's fiction has appeared with the PEN/NEA Syndicated Fiction Project; his version of *Antigone* was produced by Joseph Papp at the New York Shakespeare Festival. He teaches at the University of Athens and at New York University.

Kay Cicellis writes in English though she has lived most of her life in Greece. She is the author of *The Easy Way, Death of a Town* and *No Name in the Street* and the translator of Stratis Tsirkas's *Drifting Cities* published by Knopf.

David Constantine teaches German at Queen's College, Oxford. He has published academic books on Hülderlin and on early travelers to Greece, as well as books of fiction and poetry.

Jane Cowan was born and raised in the Midwest. The shock of her first encounter with a foreign society, as an exchange student to India at the age of 17, got her interested in cultural anthropology, which she studied at Macalester College. Her work on contemporary Greece began during an under-graduate year abroad in 1975. She continued her studies of sociocultural anthropology and ethnomusicology at Indiana University and recently returned to Grece for over two years of fieldwork and teaching. She is currently completing her doctoral dissertation on dance in a Macedonian town.

Sean Damer was born in Edinburgh. A lecturer in sociology by training, he has also done stints as a waiter, trawlerman and mountain guide. In fact, his book, entitled *The White Mountains: Travels in Western Crete*, takes advantage of his mountaineering as well as his sociological skills. He has published numerous articles and has helped prepare television and radio shows. He has spent the last year living and writing in Crete.

Markos Dragoumis, born in 1934, studied Byzantine Music at Oxford with Egon Wellesz. He is supervisor of the Melpo Merlier Center for Greek Folk Music Studies and heads the Music Department at Athens College. He teaches at the Athens Conservatory and lectures on Greek folk music and *rembetika*. He has published articles in Greek and foreign journals on Byzantine music, Greek folk music and *rembetika*.

Dimitri Gondicas studied at Princeton,

MIT and NYU and is currently a lecturer in Modern Greek and Assistant Chairman of the Committee on Hellenic Studies at Princeton University. An avid hiker, he has climbed most major mountains in Greece.

Hans Hoefer, founder-publisher of Apa Productions in 1970, set out to see the world after completing his studies in Krefeld, West Germany. With *Insight Guide: Bali* published that year, Hoefer introduced a novel approach to the field of travel literature. Acclaimed for its sensitive cultural portrayal as well as its striking photography, the *Insight Guides* series has now expanded to its 50th title covering world travel destinations, with at least a dozen more now in the works for publication in 1988.

Kerin Hope, an erstwhile archaeologist, is now the Athens correspondent for the Associated Press.

Nikos Kasdaglis was born in Cos and now lives in Rhodes; he has published many well-loved novels and a collection of short stories.

Richard Kindersley was born in London. After serving in the British Royal Service in Yugoslavia he came to Oxford in 1967 as a lecturer in Soviet Politics and Eurocommunism at St. Antony's College. He is the editor of *In Search of Eurocommunism* and the author of *The First Russian Revisionists*. Ever since his childhood which he spent in Egypt he has traveled extensively.

Julia Loomis has visited almost every village on the mainland and islands during her 25 years of visiting Greece. Although trained as a classicist she started the Modern Greek programme at Queen's College, CUNY. In 1975 she was awarded a Fulbright to teach at Salonika University. After many years in academia she is currently enjoying the relative freedom of a freelance writer and travel agent.

Michele Macrakis has been photographing Greece for seven years. In 1981 she was awarded the Fulbright (ITT) Fellowship to continue her work in Crete documenting the "works and days" of the grape growers. She has photographed for The New York Times, UPI, Reuters, Newsweek International, ENA magazine and many other publications. She has alone done portraiture work for President Karamanlis and other Greek personalities and politicians. She is currently working freelance in Athens.

Peter Mackridge is University Lecturer in Modern Greek and Fellow of St. Cross College, Oxford, and the author of *The Modern Greek Language* published by Oxford University Press in 1985. He has spent much time traveling in Greece and Turkey transcribing disappearing dialects.

Mark Mazower was born in London. He read Classics and Philosophy at Oxford and

has also studied in Bologna and Athens. His doctoral thesis on modern Greek economic history will shortly be submitted. At present he is Research Lecturer at Christ Church, Oxford where he lectures on 20th-century Balkan History.

Nelson Moe was born in Iowa. After graduating from Wesleyan University he went to Greece to teach English for a year before embarking on his study of Southern Italy on a Watson fellowhip. Although he now teaches English Literature at Naples University, his interest in Greece continues to entangle him in projects such as this guide. As Assistant Project Editor his contribution to this book is cer-

Anghelaki-Rooke   Beatty   Cicellis

Dragoumis   Gondicas   Hope

Kasdaglis   Loomis   Macrakis

tainly greater than the individual articles he wrote; many other pieces benefitted from his attentive editorial advice.

David Ricks studied Classics at Oxford and then wrote a doctoral thesis on Modern Greek literature at London. He is now a Research Fellow at the University of Birmingham, where he works on medieval and modern Greek literature.

Katy Ricks studied English at Oxford, and is now completing her doctoral thesis. She is now teaching English at a Birmingham school.

Anastasia Rubis, born in the United States to Greek immigrant parents, lives in New

York City but finds it difficult to stay away from Greece for long. Luckily she's been able to work Greece into her schedule, both during University: she spent two semesters at the College Year in Athens during her undergraduate years at Brown, and now in her career: she is advertising manager of the NTOG. In her free time, she pursues an interest in journalism and creative writing.

Lucy Rushton was born in Llanidloes, Wales, and brought up in Devon and Somerset. After doing her BA in anthropology at the University of Durham she did research in northern Greece for her D. Phil thesis on religion and identity. On a post doctoral grant

Ricks   Rubis   Rushton

Stenzel   Weil   Zinovieff

from Oxford she was able to continue her work in Greece.

Samantha Stenzel was born in Chicago, the "city of blood, meat and money." She studied English literature at the University of Illinois in Champaign-Urbana and language arts at Roosevelt University and Northwestern University in Chicago. After making Greece her home eight years ago, she became the cinema editor and a feature writer for *The Athenian* an English language magazine and contributes to a number of American and European publications including *The International Film Guide*. A good part of her formative years were spent munching popcorn in a darkened theater and her love for movies is expressed in the cinema appreciation seminars she teaches at the Hellenic-American Union of Athens.

Karen Van Dyck has been studying and translating Greek poetry since her first visit to Greece in 1977. *Insight Guide: Greece* was an exciting opportunity for her, as project editor of the book, to introduce to a larger audience the many talented writers she had met and

worked with in her own studies and their diverse views of Greece. She is currently on a Marshall Scholarship doing a D. Phil at Oxford University. Her doctoral thesis is a cultural study of Greek poetry since the Dictatorship.

Haris Vlavianos was born in Athens. He studied Economics and Philosophy at Bristol University and Politics at Oxford. He is preparing his D. Phil thesis on the policy of the Greek Communist Party during the Civil War. He has published three volumes of poetry and two books of translation. His latest translation of Ezra Pound's *Hugh Selwyn Mauberly* has just been published by 'Estia.'

Amanda Weil is a free lance photographer based in New York. She graduated from Harvard and then worked at the Whitney Museum of Art. She now splits her time between travel photography and her own studio work.

Fay Zika was born in Athens. Apart from Greece she has traveled in North and South America, Europe, Turkey, Egypt and India. She studied Politics, Philosophy and Economics at Oxford, and is now working on a Ph.D. in Philosophy at the Aristotelian University of Thessaloniki.

Sofka Zinovieff was born in London. She studied Social Anthropology at Cambridge University, and is enrolled there for her Ph.D. though she is presently living and doing fieldwork in Greece.

The publisher and the editor are also grateful to the following individuals and institutions whose assistance and cooperation were instrumental in putting the book together:

The poem incorporated into "Welcome to Greece" (page 15) is from Olga Broumas' collection, *Beginning with O* (Yale University Press) and the poem concluding "Hope Your Road is a long One" (page 95) is an excerpt of a poem by the same title written by Constantine Cavafy, translated by Edmund Keeley and Philip Sherrard (Princeton University Press).

We are also grateful to the New York and the London offices of the NTOG and to Olympic Airlines for their generous assistance. And we would like to thank the Athens office of NTOG for granting permission to reproduce their detailed and useful maps in this volume. Finally, thanks also to Gloria Maschmeyer and Clair Wills who put patient hours into preparation of the index.

— Apa Productions

TABLE OF CONTENTS

Part One
Welcome to Greece   15
   —by Karen Van Dyck
History   17–43
   —by Mark Mazower
Travelers Through The Ages   47
   —by David Constantine
The Greek Way of Life   61
   —by Jane Cowan
"Athina, My Grandmother"   84
   —by Costas Taktsis

Part Two
Hope Your Road Is A Long One   95
   —by Karen Van Dyck
The Northeast   98
   —by Fay Zika
  Mount Athos   106
   —by Haris Vlavianos
Epirus and NW Macedonia   117
   —by Nelson Moe
  Hiking in the Pindos Range   126
   —by Dimitri Gondicas
Rúmeli and the Ionian Islands   135
   —by David Ricks
Central Greece   147
   —by Julia Loomis
Athens   161
   —by Kay Cicellis

Seeing the Sites   167
   —by Kerin Hope
Islands of the Saronic Gulf   175
   —by Haris Vlavianos
  Aegina: A Place of Return   176
   —by Katerina Anghelaki-Rooke
The Peloponnese   187
   —by John Chioles
The Cyclades Islands   207
   —by Stacy Rubis
  A Hard Night on Mykonos   210
   —by Kay Cicellis
The Northeastern Aegean Islands   221
   —by Nelson Moe
The Dodecanese Islands   239
   —by Nikos Kasdaglis
    and Aliki Gourdomichalis
  Views of Patmos   248
   —by Richard Kindersley
Crete
   —by Sean Damer   256

Part Three
A Cultural ABCs   271
  Acronyms   272
   —by Karen Van Dyck
  Byzantine Church Music (an   272
  interview with Mark Dragoumis)

TABLE OF CONTENTS

Rembetika (an interview   297
  with Mark Dragoumis)
Shadow Puppet Theater   298
  —by Samantha Stenzel
Theodorakis etc (an interview   300
  with Mark Dragoumis)
Unfinished Buildings   301
  —by Karen Van Dyck
Vendetta   301
  —by Mark Mazower
Women   302
  —by Lucy Rushton
Xenomania/Xenophobia   308
Yoghurt   308
  —by Karen Van Dyck
Zorba   309
  —by Jane Cowan

Maps—courtesy of National Tourist Organisation of Greece

The Northeast   98
The Northwest   116
Rúmeli and the Ionian Islands   134
Central Greece   146
Athens and Environs   173
The Peloponnese   186
The Cyclades Islands   206
The Northeastern Aegean Islands   220
The Dodecanese Islands   238
Crete   256

Coffee   273
  —by Jane Cowan
Delectables   274
  —by Katy Ricks
Evil Eye   275
Friends/Paréa   276
  —by Jane Cowan
Graffiti and Politics   278
  —by Mark Mazower
Hospitality   280
  —by Jane Cowan
Icons and Orthodoxy   281
  —by Charles Stewart
Junta   282
  —by Haris Vlavianos
Kamáki   283
  —by Sofka Zinovieff
Language   284
  —by Peter Mackridge
Movies   287
  —by Samantha Stenzel
Namedays   288
  —by Jane Cowan
Oral Tradition and Poetry   291
  —by Karen Van Dyck
Periptera   295
  —by Charles Stewart
Queuing   296
  —by Jane Cowan

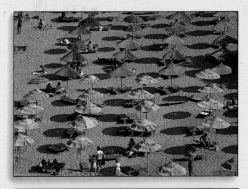

WELCOME TO GREECE

Whether you arrive in Greece by boat, train or plane, your first impression as you stretch your legs and climb down the stairs is sure to be of the sun. Glimmering on the water, reflecting off metal and glass, casting shadows, the Mediterranean sun is omnipresent. Like the flash of a hidden camera the brilliant light catches you unaware and transfixes you. From the minute you set foot in Greece you are a part of the Greek landscape—blue sky above, white sand below, the Parthenon, olive groves, a collapsing mosque, a wine festival—whatever the scene, you are in the picture as well. There is a sense that no matter how many holiday snapshots you may take, Greece will already have taken as many of you.

This country is not merely a holiday resort, ready to satisfy your every desire—it is a population of 10 million people working, eating, arguing, dancing, who will initiate you into the bustle of their everyday life, into the splendor of their mountains, ancient temples and white pebbled shores and into the fellowship of their company. When an older woman offers you a sprig of basil, the traditional gesture of hospitality, she simultaneously introduces you into her world and enters yours. This country is no escape from the everyday, it is an invitation to participate with all your senses. To dive in. A Greek poet remembered it this way:

When the Greek sea
was exceptionally calm
the sun not so much a pinnacle
as a perspiration of light, your brow and the sky
meeting on the horizon, sometimes

you'd dive
from the float, the pier, the stone
promontory, through water so startled
it held the shape of your plunge . . .

This country is no escape from the everyday, but an excuse to see it, smell it, hear it, feel it, taste it, consider it from another perspective. To roll the basil between your fingers, breathing in its fragrant greeting, and to exchange a smile with this generous woman who has invited you into her world. Just as Greece over the centuries has shaped Western civilization so, reciprocally, it holds the shape of your plunge. Greece's history would be incomplete without you and all the other travelers who have come before you. Welcome to Greece. You are a part of the story that is about to be told.

CHANGE AND CONTINUITY

In Greece the classical past overwhelms you. The visitor's first glimpse of the Acropolis seems to dissolve the intervening centuries. In a country whose language is little different from that of Pericles, whose inhabitants proudly remind you of their ancient heritage, it is easy for the newcomer to assume that a simple thread of continuity runs from the ancient world to modern Athens.

But closer acquaintance throws up new historical and linguistic surprises: a crumbling 15th-century house in Plaka offering a reminder of Ottoman Athens; communities to the south of the city where the old people, refugees from Asia Minor, still speak Turkish; suburbs to the north where you can hear Albanian. Or further afield, the roadside tents of a group of nomadic Sarakatsani shepherds, a Roman Catholic church on a Cycladic island, a Jewish cemetery in Thessaloníki.

And so the centuries since antiquity swim back into focus. For life in Greece today owes as much to the experience of those times as to the classical heritage. Her present-day inhabitants may speak the language of Pericles but many of them are descended from ancestors who did not.

Migrations and invasions: The history of Greece is the story of endless movements of people—invasions, migrations, depopulation, resettlement. Sometimes invasions were brief, like the Saracen attacks by sea in the eighth to tenth centuries. At other times they were gradual, bringing new settlers, like the Dorian tribes three millennia ago, or more recently the Slavs, both entering Greece through Epirus and moving down the west of the country into the Peloponnese.

The other side of the coin was depopulation. In the face of invasion whole populations would leave their towns and villages. The Slav invasions wiped out urban life in southern Greece. Similarly pirate raids led to the wholesale evacuation of Aegina in 896 and the abandonment of Sámos late in the 15th century. Even later, in 1821, the inhabitants of Chios fled from Turkish savagery to

Syros, bringing with them the Turkish Delight which is still one of the island's main products.

Depopulation was often a major economic headache: the strain of maintaining Alexander's empire weakened Macedon for generations. Byzantine and Ottoman rulers both tried to cure matters by mass transfers of settlers. Alternatively they welcomed newcomers, like the Albanians who were admitted to the Peloponnese in 1338 on condition they fought for the local ruler and cultivated the land he gave them.

Albanian tribes were often ready to move; their livelihood involved shifting their sheep between mountain pasture in the summer and lowland grazing in winter. Such communities covered vast distances each year. Two other nomadic groups, the Vlachs and the Sarakatsanides, also moved into Greece in large numbers. The Vlachs in particular prospered in the 18th century, and produced a number of Greece's most famous poets and politicians.

In more recent times these large movements of population have continued. At the turn of the century there was an enormous wave of emigration from the Peloponnese to the United States caused by overpopulation and economic distress. And in 1923 a compulsory exchange between Greece and Turkey led to the departure of half a million Muslims from Greece and the arrival of well over 1 million Orthodox Greeks from Asia Minor.

Continuities in daily life: In the long run people change; the endless cycle of invasion and assimilation introduces new inhabitants with new customs. But equally in the long run, daily life may change very little especially in the Mediterranean.

Take security, for example: for most of recorded history, social life in Greece has been precarious and insecure. Only our own times provide a clear exception.

The pirates who lurked in coves in the Mani in the 18th century, who, as a French traveler reported, "take prisoners everywhere, selling the Christians to the Turks and the Turks to the Christians..." were merely following in

perennial problem of highway robbery.

In a mountainous, wooded, poverty-stricken country, robbery—like piracy—was lucrative and difficult to stop. Precautions by the authorities were rudimentary. An English traveler in the 17th century noted that "... in order to insure the safety of Travelers, drummers are appointed in dangerous passages; and in Macedonia, in a narrow passe, I saw an old Man beating a drum upon the ridge of a Hill; whereby we had noticed that the passage was clear and free from theeves." In those short periods when an effective central authority held sway, it generally had such limited resources that it could do little to enforce the law. At the end of the last century the Ottoman authorities refused to permit trains to run through Macedonia at night since they could

the steps of their Homeric predecessors, who had infested just the same area. When no naval power was strong enough to control their activities, the pirates operated on a large scale. The Genoese were obliged to move the inhabitants of Sámos en masse to Chios when pirate raids made life impossible for them. And in the eighth century, Saracen raiders from North Africa left Paros such a wilderness that hunters used to sail over from Evvia after the deer and wild goats which had become plentiful on the island.

Life on the mainland was no easier. Pirate bands were likely to raid villages inshore, particularly in daylight when the menfolk of the village would be away working in the fields. For travelers by land, there was also the

not guard them against armed attack. The Germans faced a similar problem when they occupied Greece in World War II.

Local communities were left to their own devices. The cheapest security device, if not the most convenient, was a pack of dogs. More solid was a good set of walls and a defensible location. Traveling around Greece today, the visitor still notices how many towns and villages lie off the main road in foothills. Coastal settlements were often set on high ground at some distance from the shore. As conditions became more secure the settlement expanded down the slope towards the harbor or road. The town of Ermoúpolis, on Syros, illustrates this process. And in villages in the Mani the gaunt old stone fortified farmsteads are gradually being abandoned in favor of concrete bungalows along the main road.

Though life was insecure, frightening and violent, it embraced rigidly-observed codes of courtesy and honor. Today the blend is difficult to recapture. Vendettas, for example, which were common in parts of Greece, were conducted according to strict rules which changed little over the centuries. In 18th-century Epirus, as in Homeric Greece, an intended victim was immune from attack while he was farming, but was fair game the moment he picked up his weapon. In vendetta-ridden Mani, deep in the southern Peloponnese, fighting was conducted solely among the men, who were careful on most occasions to combine a maximum of disturbance with a minimum of bloodshed.

capturing them again at some future time ..."

No doubt such accounts are highly romanticized. Certainly, even if pirates kept to their word, statesmen and those in power often failed to keep theirs. A traveler in Ottoman Greece was told "... in your petty Kingdoms and States men are tryed and convicted, but our great Empire cannot be so maintained, and if the Sultan should now send for my head, I must be content to lay it down patiently, not asking wherefore ... in this country we must have ... patience even to the losse of our heads, and patience after that."

Rulers might come and go, but to the poor such patience remained a necessity for centuries. Their very existence depended upon factors outside their control. Even when their village escaped the attention of armies, ban-

Pirates, too, observed rigid codes. When a European aristocrat was ransomed by his friends in the early 19th century his captors were hospitality itself: "... Baron Stackelberg was shaved by one of the gang, a ceremony which they never omit on these occasions, and handed over to his friends. They were all pressed to stay and partake of a roasted lamb and an entertainment about to be prepared ... The robbers then wished them a good journey and expressed their hopes of

Left, an etching of the town of Ermoúpolis on Syros which was built on a hill for protection against piracy. Above, the famous Diglesi brigands before and after they were caught.

dits or the tax-man, a poor harvest raised the specter of starvation.

The past has never offered these people a "Golden Age," but always threatened starvation for the hungry citizens of Athens in the harsh winter of 1941 right back to their exhausted ancestors at the end of the Peloponnesian Wars, and back further still. The account that follows describes the changing fortunes of dynasties and kingdoms. But the history of a country involves more than a succession of names and dates. The essential backdrop is provided by the generations of nameless inhabitants whose lives involved those countless imperceptible changes which may escape our gaze but which provide the real origins of modern Greece.

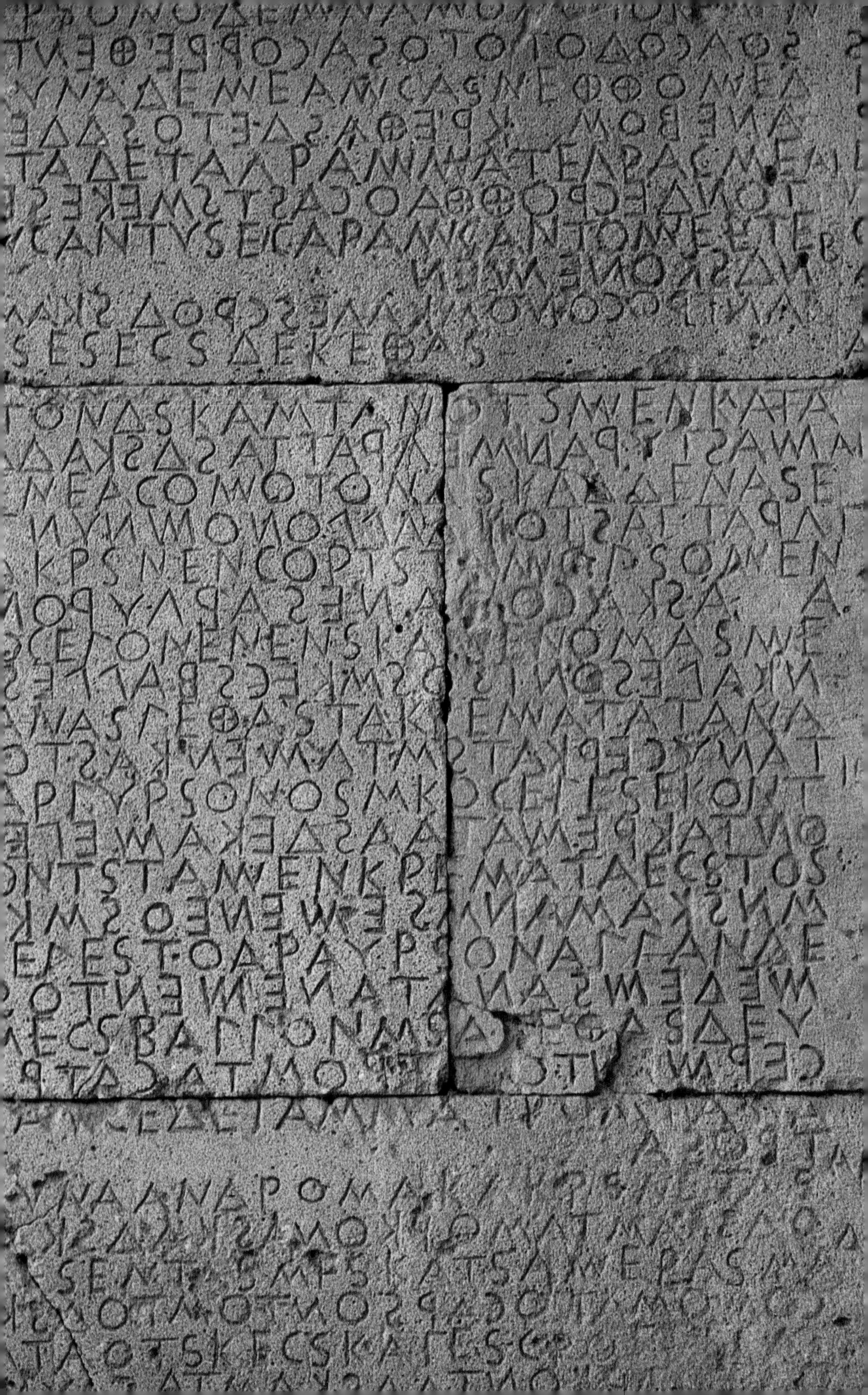

ANCIENT GREECE

One theme—the fragility of civilized life—dominates Greek history both classical and modern.

The basis for the modern way of life in Greece was laid around 3000 B.C., when settlers moved down from the northeast plains onto rockier land in the Peloponnese and islands, and began to cultivate olives and vines, as well as the cereals they had originally grown. At about the same time a prosperous civilization arose in Crete and spread its influence throughout the Aegean. The Minoans, whose rituals have filtered down to us through the legend of Theseus and his labyrinthine struggle with the Minotaur, left proof of their architectural genius in the ruined palaces of Knossos and Festos. Daring sailors, they appear to have preferred commerce to agriculture. They established outposts in the Peloponnese and made contact with the Egyptians. By 1500 B.C. their civilization had reached its zenith. Yet barely a century later, for reasons which remain unexplained, most centers of their power were destroyed by fire and abandoned. The settlement at Thira (Santorin) was annihilated by a volcanic eruption. But the causes of the wider disintegration of Minoan control remain a mystery. Only Knossos continued to be inhabited as Cretan dominance in the Aegean came to an end.

Its place was taken by Mycenae, the bleak citadel in the Peloponnese. We do not know whether the rulers of Mycenae exerted direct power over the rest of the mainland. But in the *Iliad* Homer portrays their king, Agamemnon, as the most powerful figure in the Greek forces, and this suggests that Mycenae had achieved some sort of overall authority. In its heyday the Mycenaean world contained men rich enough to commission massive stone tombs and delicate gold work. Rulers were served by an array of palace administrators and scribes who controlled the economic life of the state, exacting tribute, collecting taxes, allocating rations of scarce metals. But despite the far-flung trading links—which stretched as far as Italy and Syria—this was a conservative culture, resistant to change.

The "Dark Ages": In the 13th century B.C. this civilization, like the Cretan before it, came to a violent end. Classical myth connected the end of the Mycenaean age with the arrival of the Dorian tribes.

In fact there was no clear connection between the two events. Mycenaean power had broken down irreversibly by the time the Dorian settlers entered Greece. These invaders, like later ones, entered Greece from the northwest, down over the Pindos mountains into the Peloponnese. Probably they were nomads, which would explain their willingness to travel and their lower level of culture. They also brought their own form of Greek. Where they settled heavily we find West Greek dialects, whilst Attica, the Aegean islands and the Ionian colonies continued to use East Greek forms. In some areas the newcomers assimilated earlier populations; elsewhere they remained aloof, a governing race, and kept the former inhabitants in subjection. The hostility—at a later date—between Athens and Sparta was based in part on this division between Ionian and Dorian peoples.

The Dorian invasion coincided with the onset of the "Dark Ages." Historical evidence for the period between the eleventh and eighth centuries is patchy. But it is clear that civilized life suffered. The art of writing was forgotten. Trade dwindled and communities became isolated from one another. Building in stone seems to have been too great an effort for the small pastoral settlements that had replaced the centers of Mycenaean power. Homer's *Odyssey* is set in a simple society where even the rulers busy themselves with menial tasks, where wealth is measured in flocks and herds. Arable farming requires political stability and abundant manpower. But these are only found in the semi-mythical land of the Phaeacians, not in Odysseus' Ithaca.

Revival: In the eighth century there were signs of revival: trade spread further afield. There were contacts with civilized peoples such as the Etruscans in the west, and the Phoenicians and Egyptians in the east. Artistic influence from the east was increasingly evident in metalwork and pottery. Writing revived —amongst a much larger circle than before—with the adoption of the Phoenician alphabet.

Another Greek borrowing from the Phoenicians was equally important; this was the notion of the *polis* (city-state). In the "Dark Ages" small, isolated settlements, loosely grouped together into large kingdoms. This system survived in western and northern Greece into classical times when Thucydides

The law code of Gortyn in Crete must be read one line, from left to right, and the next, from right to left, and so on, alternately.

described how "the Aetolian nation, although numerous and warlike, yet dwelt in unwalled villages scattered far apart."

Elsewhere, however, a network of small independent states grew up. These were initially based around clusters of villages rather than one large urban center. With the population explosion of the eighth century, however, large conurbations evolved and expanded as surplus population moved from the country to the town. Land became more intensively cultivated and highly priced. In the "Dark Ages" the slump in population had caused arable land to fall into disuse. Farmers turned from sowing cereals to stockbreeding; now the process was thrown into reverse. The available land could not support such a rapidly-growing population. There is a clear parallel with the

Sparta and Thessaly both emphasized military training more than other states, and kept monarchic ceremonies after these had disappeared elsewhere.

From kings to aristocrats: In general the kings mentioned in Homer must have surrendered power towards the end of the "Dark Ages" to an aristocratic form of rule. But the aristocracy too became entrenched in power and increasingly resistant to change. As commoners settled on land and amassed wealth, pressure grew for constitutional reform. Aristotle seems to have been right in tying the demand for such reform to changes in military techniques. He noted that "when states began to increase in size, and infantry forces acquired a greater degree of strength, more persons were admitted to the enjoyment of political

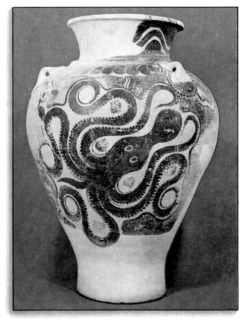

Peloponnese in the 19th century, and in both cases the outcome was the same: emigration on a massive scale. In Italy and Sicily, where formerly there had been only isolated trading posts, Greek colonies sprang up along the seaboard.

Together with the division between the new *polis* and the older *ethnos* (kingdom), a further distinction cuts across the first one. On the one hand, there were states, generally in the Dorian-speaking parts of the country, with a serf population, permanently excluded from power—like Sparta, a major *polis*, and Thessaly, an *ethnos*. On the other hand, there were states with a more broadly based citizen body, such as Athens. Athough the distinction was not always clear-cut, it is interesting that

rights." Just as the shift from monarchy to aristocracy had been reflected in the move from chariots to horseback fighting, so too the emphasis switched from cavalry to infantry, aristocracy lost ground to democratic pressure. Men would only fight in the new larger armies if the aristocrats granted them political rights.

Military power swung away from the traditional horse-breeding aristocracies—Chalkis, Eretria, Thessaly—to new powers—Corinth, Argos, and above all Sparta, where the state was protected by a hoplite army whose core was a body of citizens trained as infantry soldiers from birth. Further afield Greek technical superiority was reflected in the growing demand for Greek mercenaries to fight in Egypt and elsewhere.

Often the demand for radical reform met with resistance. The lament of the poet Theognis typified the aristocrats' response: "Those who previously did not know justice or laws, but wore goatskins on their sides, and had their pasture outside this city like deer, they have become respectable men; those who formerly were of high estate have now fallen low. Who can bear such a spectacle?" But other aristocrats, more far-sighted, often recognized the need for change. One such was Solon, elected in early sixth century Athens to introduce sweeping constitutional changes. Realizing that the city's strength would depend upon the organization of the citizen body, he opened up the Assembly to the poorest citizens and in other ways loosened the grip of the upper class. Inevitably these changes were

states. Usually they were dissident aristocrats, gaining support from the lower classes with promises of radical change—promises which were often kept, as it was in the new ruler's interest to weaken the power of his peers. In the mid-seventh century Kipselis of Corinth was supposed to have redistributed land belonging to fellow-aristocrats. Where citizenship qualifications were couched in terms of land ownership these reforms broadened the total citizen body. Indeed by Solon's time, land reform was tainted in the public eye by its association with tyranny.

But it would be wrong to regard the tyrants as great innovators. They were symptoms of social change rather than causes of it. Conscious of their own vulnerability, they resorted to propaganda expedients to stay

attacked from both sides, as Solon himself complains in a number of his poems. However they laid the foundations for the expansion of Athenian power in the next century.

Tyrants: Another symptom of these political tensions was tyranny. To the ancient Greeks the word "tyrant" was not pejorative; it simply referred to a ruler who had usurped power instead of inheriting it. In the sixth century, tyrants seized power in a number of

Far left, a black-figure vase painting of Theseus and the Minotaur and left, an earlier vase painting of an octopus. Above, a real octopus in the fish market in Iráklion, Crete.

in power. The most potent of these was the religious cult and it is from the time of the tyrants that religion comes to serve the purposes of the state. This was seen at its most cynical in late sixth-century Athens where the tyrant Peisistratos, making a second bid for power, tried to impress the inhabitants by entering the city on a chariot accompanied by a tall blonde dressed as the goddess Athina.

More generally tyrants introduced or expanded state cults and festivals, as Peisistratos did in Athens with the Great Panathenea; in fact many festivals which were later given mythical origins wer · started at this time.

Religion was not c nly important to the state as propaganda, it wis also a major economic factor. While religious festivals and games earned revenues, enormous in some cases, for their city, temples, sacrifices and other rituals were very costly. Apart from wars, temple building was probably the greatest drain on a community's resources. Thus the scale of its religious activities provided some measure of the wealth of a community. Because of this prominence, it was often in connection with religion that many technical advances were made; developments in masonry, metal-working and pottery skills in the archaic period (eighth to sixth centuries B.C.) all appear in the religious sphere.

The developing arts: Artistic developments too were pushed forward in the archaic period. Though it is the fifth century which received the most attention, the crucial innovations in pottery and sculpture had been made earlier.

began to disappear.

Greeks and outsiders: The rise of an artistic culture shared across state boundaries seemed at one point it might be paralleled by a process of political unification. People in different cities became aware of a common Hellenic culture. The historian Herodotus was a keen promoter of the idea of one Greece, and asserted that the Greeks are "a single race because of common blood, common customs, common language and common religion." The increasing prominence of interstate religious games and festivals spread this view.

But the sharpest spur to unity was a threat from outside—the rise of the Persian empire. Cyrus, halfway through the sixth century had conquered the Greek cities on the Asia Minor coast, and Persian aspirations were further

Monumental sculpture in stone was at first derived from Egypt, but by the end of the sixth century Greek sculptors had successfully broken away from the stiff poses of the pioneers towards a more expressive and naturalistic style. On vases black-figure painting gave way to red-figure in the second half of the sixth century and the greater flexibility of the technique began to open up new artistic possibilities. By the end of the sixth century the scale of public building and artistic projects in numerous city-states reflects the resources which these communities had acquired over the previous three centuries. As trade flourished artists traveled more widely. The marked regional variations in style which characterized early archaic art

encouraged by his son Darius (521 B.C.– 486 B.C.) who conquered Thrace, subdued Macedon and, after quashing an Ionian revolt in Asia Minor, sent a massive expeditionary force southwards into Greece. Athens appealed for help from Sparta, the strongest Greek city, but succeeded in defeating the Persians at Marathon before the Spartan forces arrived. This victory did more than save Attica; it also confirmed Athens as the standard-bearer for the Greek military effort against the Persians. This explains why a frieze displaying the warriors killed at Marathon (situated just over 20 miles from Athens) was placed in a prominent and highly unusual position around the Parthenon in the 440s B.C. Only now was Athens becoming a power to be reckoned with. The silver mines at Laurion only began producing enough ore to finance a major shipbuilding program from early in the fifth century. For two generations after that, Aegina remained superior to Athens as a trading force in the Saronic Gulf.

Athens and Sparta: Ten years after Marathon, when Darius' son Xerxes organized a second attack on Greece, the city-states rallied around Sparta. For while Athens had the largest navy, the Spartans controlled the Peloponnesian League, with its considerable combined land forces. Both the crucial naval victory at Salamis in 480 B.C. and the military victory on land at Plataea the following year, were won under Spartan leadership. But no sooner had the Persian menace been banished then the Greek alliance broke up. There was

East Greeks and continuing the struggle against the Persians. In fact, a good deal of anti-Spartan sentiment underlay it. The alliance was a primarily naval one, which brought out a crucial distinction between it and the Spartans' alliance—the Peloponnesian League; for whereas the latter consisted of land forces, requiring minimal financing, the creation of a navy required long-term planning and central coordination. Gradually the smaller allies found it difficult to equip their own ships for allied use, and turned instead to sending money for the Athenians to use. Athens grew in strength as her allies became impoverished.

The Persian threat had receded long before peace was officially declared in 449 B.C. By that time the Confederacy had become an

intense suspicion, especially between Sparta and Athens. Thucydides described how as soon as the Persians withdrew, the Athenians quickly rebuilt their city-walls for fear that the Spartans would try to stop them.

The development of a classical "cold war" became obvious as Athens extended her control over the Aegean. She did so through the Confederation of Dilos, formed in 478 B.C. with the professed aim of liberating the

Athenian empire whose resources were used to serve Athenian interests. Between 460 B.C. and 446 B.C. Athens fought a series of wars with her neighbors in an effort to assert her supremacy. Naval rivals such as Aegina were singled out for attack.

It was natural that enemies of Athens should turn to Sparta for help. The latent hostility of the two powers was there to be exploited by minor states. Rebels against Athenian rule on the island of Thasos had found Sparta ready to give them support. The two powers actually clashed in Boeotia and at Delphi. In 466 B.C. they concluded a Thirty Years' Peace, but this lasted only half the intended period.

In 430 B.C. war erupted again when Corinth

Left, boys running at the ancient stadium of Delphi. Above, a red-figure vase painting of dancing. Games and religious festivals expanded greatly under the tyrants between 800–600 B.C.

appealed to the Peloponnesian League for help against Athenian attack. This, the Second Peloponnesian War, dragged on for years since neither side was able to deal the deathblow to the other; Athens lacked the infantry to mount an attack on Sparta, whilst the League fielded conventional hoplite forces, unprepared for siege warfare and unable to stop food supplies reaching the city by sea. The war was conducted mostly in the countryside around Athens on a seasonal basis. The Peace of Nikias in 421 B.C. gave both sides a breathing space, but lasted only six years. Only when the Spartans got financial support from the Persians and managed to inflict a catastrophic defeat on the Athenian navy was Athens forced to surrender.

Civic breakdown: Literature and art flourished

The paradox was that city-states with imperial pretensions chose not to take the steps that might have brought success. Unlike Rome, Greek city-states did not extend citizenship to their subject territories. The Emperor Claudius rightly observed that the Greek states failed as imperial powers because they "treated their subjects as foreigners." The military strength of Athens, for example, could never keep pace with her imperial commitments. This explains the permanent cycle of conquest and revolt. The Spartans had the additional headache of a large serf population, the helots, often prone to revolt in their own province.

The first half of the fourth century seems to continue the pattern. On the one hand, there were long wars between cities, and on the

even during these incessant periods of fighting, but economic activity did not. In a world where each tiny *polis* was determined to safeguard its independence at any cost, war was endemic. Such a world carried the seeds of its own destruction. Fighting was expensive for the largely agricultural societies of the ancient world. For most cities trade was of minor consequence compared with farming, and industry still more so; in classical Athens, the largest industrial enterprise (apart from the mines) was a firm where 120 slaves manufactured shields. Athens of course had her silver mines; other states were less fortunate. But even for Athens, whose ambitions were quickly rekindled, the strain of incessant warfare took its toll.

other, evidence of prolonged economic difficulties as Corinth fell into irreversible decline and Athens struggled to recapture her previous prominence. This she failed to do. Spartan power remained supreme until 371 B.C. when Thebes defeated the Spartan army at Levktra.

The city-state system was gradually falling apart. The old form of citizen army was superseded by a more professional force, relying on trained mercenaries. Aristotle noted that "... when the Spartans were alone in their strenuous military discipline they were superior to everybody, but now they are beaten by everybody; the reason is that in former times they trained and others did not." Now things had changed.

The spread of mercenaries, in fact, reflects the economic problems of the fourth century. Mercenary service, like emigration or piracy, was a demographic safety-valve, and whereas in archaic Greece mercenaries had only come from a few backward areas, in the fourth century they were increasingly drawn from the major cities as well. This points to economic difficulties over an increasingly wide area.

As at earlier times, military changes linked up with political ones. The decline of the citizen armies coincided with a trend away from democracy in favor of more autocratic government. Power shifted from the city-states towards Thessaly, an *ethnos* state, and later still, towards Macedon, another old-fashioned kingdom.

Both regions had the advantage over Attica

pass, and after gaining control of Thessaly, defeated an alliance of Thebes and Athens at Haronia in 338 B.C. Banded together in the League of Corinth, the Greek city-states were compelled to recognize a new center of power, Macedon.

Alexander's Greece: In the "Republic" Socrates asserts ". . . we shall speak of war when Greeks fight with barbarians, whom we may call their natural enemies. But Greeks are by nature friends of Greeks, and when they fight, it means that Hellas is afflicted by dissension which ought to be called civil strife." This passage reflects three sentiments that were becoming widespread in the fourth century: first, that the Greeks were all of one race; second, that warfare between city-states was undesirable; third, that it was natural for the

in that they were fertile and not short of land. More rural than the city-states to their south, they managed to avoid the domestic political turmoil that periodically erupted in the latter. The military successes of the Thessalian tyrant, Jason of Pherae, in the early fourth century, indicated the growing confidence of these newcomers.

A little later Philip of Macedon moved southwards, secured the vital Thermopylae

Greeks to fight their enemies in the East. It is ironical that a successful concerted effort against the Persians was only made under the leadership of Macedon, traditionally a border power in the Greek world.

The rapid growth of Alexander the Great's Asian empire drastically altered the boundaries of the Greek world. The city-states of mainland Greece no longer occupied center stage. The mainland was drained of manpower as soldiers, settlers and administrators moved eastwards to consolidate Greek rule. At the same time, the intellectual and religious world of the Greeks was opened up to new influences.

The Greek-speaking world was not only expanding, it was also coming together: "common" Greek replaced local dialects in

Left, a scene from a mosaic floor in a Roman house—a man from Kos welcomes the healer Asclepius while Hippocrates sits thinking on the steps. Above, an "early owl" Attic drachma.

most areas. In third century Macedon, for example, local culture was "hellenized," and the native gods were replaced by Olympian deities.

For the first time coins became widely used in trade—something which had been impossible so long as each city had its own currency. Now the Attic drachma became acceptable in an area ranging from Athens to the Black Sea, from Cappadocia to Italy.

But there were limits to this process, for although the city-states gave up their political freedom, they clung to self-determination in other spheres. Local taxation and customs duties offer examples of this passion for independence. Likewise the calendar: in Athens the year began in July, in Sparta October, in Dilos, January!

Philosophers were debating ideas of communal loyalties which transcended the old civic boundaries. Perhaps this reflected the way in which these boundaries were being absorbed within larger units like the Hellenistic kingdoms, the Greek federal leagues and, eventually, the Roman empire. Whatever the cause, the most influential philosophical school, Stoicism, emphasized the concept of universal brotherhood and talked of a world state ruled by one supreme power. Elements of such ideas could be found in earlier Greek thought; but in its moral fervor, Stoicism was very much a product of the Hellenistic age, and it brought Greek philosophy closer to Jewish and Babylonian religious doctrines.

Macedonian weakness, Roman expansion: The expansion of Macedon curtailed the political autonomy of the city-states. The process was gradual but inexorable. In the third century they formed federations, and tried to exploit disputes between the generals who had inherited Alexander's empire. The policy had only limited success, mainly because of the paltry military resources available to the Greek leagues. Early in the second century, disputes among the city-states brought Rome in to intervene for the first time in Greek history. Within 20 years she had defeated first Macedonia, and then the Achaean League which had organized a desperate Greek resistance to Roman rule. The Roman consul Memmius marked his victory by devastating Corinth, killing its male population, and selling its women and children into slavery. As a deterrent to further resistance it was brutal but effective. Conservative factions were confirmed in power in the cities and Greece became a Roman protectorate. In 27 B.C., when the Roman Empire was proclaimed, the protectorate became the province of Achaea.

Greece — a Roman backwater: Among the educated classes it became commonplace to lament the decay of Greek civilization. Seneca, in the first century wrote: "Do you not see how in Achaia (Achaea) the foundations of the most famous cities have already crumbled to nothing, so that no trace is left to show that they ever existed?" But this is misleading. True, Greece was no longer the center of the civilized world; Athens and Corinth could not rival Alexandria or Antioch, let alone Rome. The main routes to the east went overland through Macedonia, by sea to Egypt. Thus Greece was a commercial backwater. But its decline was only relative: along the coast, cities flourished. The *polis* remained much as it had been in Hellenistic times and the Roman authorities permitted a degree of political self-rule. Philhellene emperors like Hadrian even encouraged groups of cities to federate in an effort to encourage a panhellenic spirit.

But the *polis* was no longer a political force. Hellenistic rulers had feared the Greek cities' power; the Roman, and later the Byzantine emperors feared their weakness and did what they could to keep them alive. After all, the cities were vital administrative cogs in the imperial machine. They continued to provide a social ideal for educated Greeks. Pausanias wrote of a town in central Greece "... if one may call it a *polis*, when it has no government offices and no gymnasium; they have no theater, no market, no piped water supply, but live in hovels, rather like the huts up in the mountains, on the brink of a ravine..."

This was the age of the great benefactors, like Hadrian himself, and Herodes Atticus, both of whom lavished fine buildings on Roman Athens. Since the poorer classes were permanently excluded from power, the rich were obliged to guarantee social stability by making donations—both for emergency items, like imports of food when a harvest failed, and for public buildings and facilities.

Two centuries of relative tranquility were shattered by the Gothic invasions in the third century. The invasions were successfully repelled. But the shock led to a loss of confidence and economic deterioration. Civic building programs continued on a much reduced scale. The wealthy classes became increasingly reluctant benefactors, and two centuries passed before imperial authorities and the church revived the demand for architectural skills. By that time much had changed. The emperor Constantine had moved his capital from Rome to Constantinople. Christianity had been made the official religion of the empire. The transition had begun from Rome to Byzantium.

A Coptic angel reminiscent of St. George the dragon-slayer, except that here she is a woman.

29

BYZANTINE GREECE

A revealing incident occurred in the Byzantine capital, Constantinople, in A.D. 968. Legates from the Holy Roman Empire in the West brought a letter for Nicephorus, the Byzantine Emperor, in which Nicephorus was simply styled "Emperor of the Greeks" whilst the Holy Roman Emperor, Otto, was termed "august Emperor of the Romans." The Byzantine courtiers were scandalized: "The audacity of it," they cried, "to call the universal emperor of the Romans, the one and only Nicephorus, the great, the august, "emperor of the Greeks" and to style a poor barbaric creature "emperor of the Romans"! O sky! O earth! O sea! What shall we do with these scoundrels and criminals?"

Behind this contemptuous outburst at "Frankish" presumption lies the curious fusion of cultures which made up the Byzantine tradition. From the Hellenistic world came the belief in the superiority of the Greek world, the summary dismissal of outsiders as barbarians. From Rome came a strong sense of loyalty to empire and emperor. And in the fervor which marked their belief in the moral superiority of *their* empire—which they regarded not as the "Eastern Roman Empire" but as the only true empire—is the stamp of evangelical Christianity. This strength of purpose was not easily repressed. Even after crusaders had sacked Constantinople in 1204, a Byzantine author exclaimed that: "The accursed Latins ... lust after our possessions and would like to destroy our race ... But we tread them down by the might of Christ who gives to us the power to trample upon the adder and the scorpion."

The inhabitants of this empire did not call themselves either Greeks or Byzantines; they were Romans, "Romeii." But increasingly, the mark of a *romaio* was that he spoke Greek and followed the Orthodox church. Thus the three elements were intermingled.

The end of antiquity: The real break with antiquity came late in the sixth century when Greece was first attacked and then settled by Slav-speaking tribes from the north. The invasions marked the end of the classical tradition in Greece, destroying urban civilization and with it Roman and Christian culture. An eighth-century chronicler reported that the Slavs were "subject neither to the emperor of the Romans nor to anyone else." But the empire fought back. Christian missionaries converted the pagan Slavs in the Peloponnese, and at the same time taught them Greek. The language survived but the old urban culture

did not. The disappearance of the city-states is shown by the way in which the word *polis* came to refer exclusively to Constantinople as though there were no other cities. A small urban elite studied and wrote in ancient Greek but had little impact on the mass of the population; their books were probably not read by more than about three hundred people at any one time. Monks' chronicles show how muddled people had become about the history of previous centuries. Ancient monuments were left untouched because peasants thought that they were inhabited by demons.

An archbishop, Michael Choniates, arrived in Athens from Constantinople in 1182 with a solid education and high hopes of discovering traces of Athens' former glory. He was soon disappointed. Not only was the inhabitants' knowledge of the classics lamentable, but they lived in such a primitive fashion. The unwalled *polis* had become a medieval fortress, as at Mistra near Sparta, a place of refuge for the outlying district. The civic arts were abandoned. The Greek countryside, even in periods of relative prosperity, remained under-populated, pulling in Albanian and Vlach migrants.

The weaknesses of Byzantine rule: The Byzantine empire lacked the resources to maintain tight control over its territories. It was beset on all sides—by the Italian city-states, the Slav kingdoms to the north, the Persians and Turks in the east. The Greek provinces were less vital than Anatolia, which supplied Constantinople with corn, and were ceded more readily to other powers.

Byzantium's period of glory was shortlived, lasting from the mid-ninth to mid-eleventh centuries. The prosperity it experienced under a succession of Macedonian emperors was cut short in 1071 when a new enemy, Turkoman tribes of nomads from central Asia, cut the Byzantine army to pieces at Manzikert in Anatolia. The threat from the West was soon felt too: the possibility of a Norman invasion was realized in the 12th century when the Norman ruler, Roger of Sicily invaded Greece and sacked Thebes and Corinth. But this was only a foretaste of still worse misfortune. In 1204 Constantinople itself was sacked by the crusader forces en route to the Holy Land for the Fourth Crusade. The empire was fragmented: successor states arose in Epirus, Nikea and Trebizond. Greece itself was divided into small kingdoms—the Duchy of Athens under the Burgundian de la Roche, the principality of Achaea under Villehardouin, islands to various Italian adventurers, crucial ports on the west coast retained by Venice.

Over the following half century Byzantium reemerged as Nikean rulers, the Paleologues, fought back into mainland Greece and recaptured Constantinople. But there was considerable confusion in western Greece, which briefly came under Serbian control, and in Thessaly where the Vlachs established a separate principality. Southern Greece and the islands remained under the control of the crusaders' successors until in the 14th century the Paleologues reestablished a Byzantine presence at Mistra. This political confusion gave rise to ethnically mixed populations. The Peloponnese was inhabited, according to a 15th-century author by "... Lacedaemonians,

their turn next. The occasional marriages between Ottoman princesses and Greek princes failed to negate the threat posed by this new power. By 1400 the empire had shrunk to Constantinople, Salonika and the Peloponnese. Mongol attacks on Ottoman territories in the east gave Byzantium some breathing space but no more. In April 1453 Sultan Mehemet II besieged Constantinople and took the city within two months; eight years later the rest of the mainland had succumbed too. The Aegean islands held out longer— Tínos until 1715—but mainland Greece was now part of the Ottoman empire.

The fall of "The City" reverberated throughout Europe; with it had fallen the last descendants of the Roman Empire itself. Although in the West this seemed the inevit-

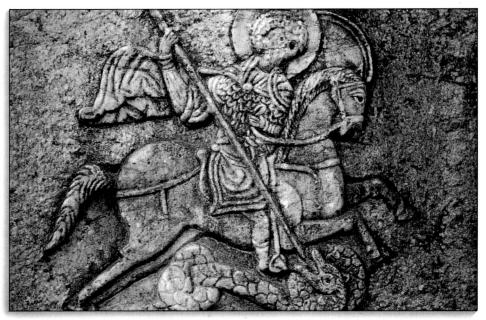

Italians, Peloponnesians, Sclavinians, Illyrians, Egyptians (i.e. Gypsies) and Jews..."

Continual fighting between all these parties was notable for one thing: the introduction of Turkish mercenaries. The Byzantine empire, like the Roman, lacked the men to do its own fighting. Turkish forces were enlisted to act as a buffer against the Serbs and the Bulgars. They were alarmingly successful, crushing the Bulgars on the Maritsa River in 1371 and the Serbs at Kossovo in 1389. The Greeks took little satisfaction from these victories. It was

Carved in stone at the Byzantine city of Mistra, a more typical version of St. George slaying the dragon from atop his horse.

able result of Byzantine decline, to the Greeks it was something more traumatic—the moment when they passed from freedom into slavery. Later generations would regard the recapture of Constantinople as the crucial mission of the Greek people. But at the time, as a contemporary folksong suggests, the prevailing reaction in the Greek-speaking world was simply one of shock:

"As an old woman was cooking fish in a pan/a voice from on high called to her:/"Stop your cooking, old woman, the Turks have taken the City"/"Not till the fish come alive and fly will the Turks have the City"/The fish came to life and flew away/And the Emir himself burst in on his horse."

OTTOMAN GREECE

The Ottoman Turks who now controlled the Balkans were the latest in a stream of nomadic tribes to move westwards from central Asia. Highly mobile, they were set on military conquest though few in numbers, and their way of life reflected these conditions.

From Constantinople the Sultan tried to maintain control of his far-flung empire with a minimum of expense. He tried to avoid the creation of rivals with local power-bases by shifting regional governors from place to place, and by rewarding Muslim officers with estates which reverted to imperial control on their owners' death. The lack of funds allotted to local police forces is graphically suggested by the fact that one of the chief means of punishing an offender was for the "Subashi"—or police chief—to quarter his officers in the offender's home. Although the Ottomans were bent upon conquest, they were less enthusiastic about maintaining or improving areas once they had conquered them. Roads soon fell into disuse, and most travelers went by sea whenever they could.

Religious tolerance was reflected in the "millet" system of government. The Turkish authorities recognized minority religions, and permitted each "millet" or religious community, a measure of self-government. The Greek Orthodox Church was granted special privileges and came to exert both religious and civil powers over Ottoman Greeks.

Under their new masters the Greeks lived in much the same way as they had done earlier. Their houses, like those of the Turks, tended to be miniature fortresses, built on two floors around a central courtyard. The restored merchant's house in Kastoria gives a good idea of the effect. Most elements of contemporary Greek cuisine were common then—from the *resinato* wine so distasteful to foreign travelers to the strong coffee which Ali Pasha, the "Lion of Ioannina" found helpful in poisoning his rival, the Pasha of Vallona. Only the potato made a late arrival—opposed by Greek priests who insisted that this was the apple given to Adam and Eve in paradise.

But autonomy did not rule out oppression. When, from the 17th century onwards, central authority weakened, local magnates were free to burden the peasantry with their own impositions. Many revolts in the Ottoman Balkans, notably that in 1805 which revived the state of Serbia, involved appeals to the Sultan for help against corrupt local landowners or bishops. Conversely, areas under direct Ottoman control, like Chios, which traditionally belonged to the Sultan's family, often enjoyed prosperity and orderly administration.

Powerful enemies continually threatened the Ottoman grip on the country. The Venetians, and later the French, were thorns in the Ottoman flesh. Within the empire the wild Albanians, the backbone of the Ottoman armies, often threatened to break loose and establish claims of their own. The resulting conflicts left Greece much the weaker.

Thus in 1537 a Turkish army carried off half the population of Corfu after an attack on the Venetian colony there, leaving the island with barely one-sixth of the population it had had in antiquity. The Peloponnese was similarly decimated, caught in a bloody tug-of-war between the same two rivals. It was ravaged by Albanian forces fighting for the Ottomans in 1715 and again in the 1770s. Further destruction came in the wake of the 1821 uprising. Greeks slaughtered Turks in Tripolis; the Turks uprooted the Greek inhabitants of Chios. Finally Egyptian troops, under Ibrahim Ali laid waste to most of the Peloponnese.

Brigands and pirates provided a perpetual undercurrent of violence in daily life, while plagues often reduced populations more dramatically than wars and made entire regions —Thessaly was especially notorious—impassable to travelers.

When, during the 17th century, the Ottoman empire ceased to expand, new strains appeared. In the hills and mountains, where the Ottoman grip had never been sure, groups of brigands, known as *Klephts* were formed. They were bandits, as proned to plunder a Greek village as a Muslim estate; nevertheless, in peasant folklore they came to symbolize the spirit of Greek resistance to the Ottoman authorities.

The rise of Greek nationalism: Perhaps more important for the development of Greek nationalism was the growth of a Greek merchant community. The Byzantine Greeks had despised commerce, leaving it to foreigners. So did the Turks, and now the Greeks, together with the Jews and Armenians, became the traders of the Ottoman empire. Commercial links with Europe introduced wealthy Greeks to European life-styles, but they also encountered European cultural and political ideas. Late in the 18th century two ideas in particular, philhellenism and nationalism, found a fertile ground among young educated Greeks.

The Turks had favored certain groups of Greeks in the hope of heading off rebellious inclinations. Senior posts in the Ottoman administration were frequently filled by Greeks, and in Constantinople aristocratic families, known as Phanariots, forged close links with the imperial court. The Orthodox Church benefitted similarly from this policy. Consequently these two powerful groups in the Greek community were badly placed to head a revolt against Turkish rule.

The French Revolution provided the political stimulus for revolt, but the ground had already been prepared by the spread of nationalist ideas among the Ottoman empire's Christian inhabitants. In 1814 three Greek merchants in Odessa formed a secret organization called the "Friendly Society" devoted

a kaleidoscopic society. Fighting the Turks was a motley crew of *Klephts*, merchants, landowners, primates and Phanariots—all as keen to further their own interests as to advance the cause of Greek nationalism. When they were not fighting the Turks they turned on each other. Ironically, the belief that this was a national struggle was held with greatest conviction by the foreign phil-hellenes—Byron and others—who came to help the Greeks. These men were influential in getting Western public opinion behind the Greeks. Thus the major powers, initially unsympathetic to the Hellenic dream, came to put military and diplomatic pressure on the Turks to acknowledge Greek independence. The turning-point came with the almost accidental destruction of the Ottoman fleet by an

to "the betterment of the nation" which rapidly acquired a network of sympathizers throughout the Ottoman lands. A number of vain attempts to secure themselves powerful and decisive backing were finally rewarded when their members organized an uprising against Turkish rule in 1821.

The struggle for Greek independence, which lasted from 1821 to 1832, was not a straightforward affair. Greek propaganda glossed over the difficulties of a nationalist struggle in

Dinner at a Greek house at Chríssa in 1801, painted by Dodwell during his travels and compiled in his book Views of Greece.

allied force at Navarino in 1827.

Count Ioánnis Kapodístrias, a Greek diplomat formerly in the service of the Russian Tsar, was elected President by a National Assembly in the same year. He encouraged Greek forces to push north of the Peloponnese, and was rewarded when the 1829 Conference of London fixed the new state's northern boundary on the Árta-Volos line. But numerous Greeks were dissatisfied with his administration and suspected him of aiming at one-man rule. In 1831 he was shot by two chieftains of Maina as he entered a church at Nauplia. While the powers—Britain, France and Russia—tried to find a suitable candidate for the Greek throne, the country fell into a period of anarchy and civil war.

34

35

MODERN GREECE

The new state had a difficult birth and a sickly infancy: it was desperately poor, overrun by armed bands of brigands, beset by quarreling among various political factions. In 1834 a rebellion in the Mani resulted in Government troops being defeated and sent home without their equipment.

There were few good harbors or roads. Athens remained the squalid, provincial town that Byron had visited. Internally, conditions were worse than they had been under Ottoman rule.

Bavarian absolutism was partly to blame. Kapodístrias' death had confirmed that no Greek would accept another as his ruler. The crown of the new kingdom, which had been offered to various candidates, was eventually accepted by Otto, son of Ludwig I of Bavaria, who arrived at Nauplia in 1833 on a British man-of-war. Since he was underage, a succession of Regents ruled in his stead. They ignored widespread calls for a constitution until in 1843 a brief and bloodless uprising in Athens forced Otto to dismiss his Bavarian advisers and accept the idea of constitutional rule and parliamentary government.

Despite a poor and backward economy, the 1844 and later the 1864 constitutions endowed the country with the trappings of an advanced democratic apparatus. But politics does not function in a vacuum and Greek parliamentary politics reflected her strange situation. Rather than political parties representing different classes, there were factions grouped around individuals, valued as much for their powers of patronage as for their ideas. In the absence of class distinctions, other issues—generally of foreign policy—separated these factions. During Otto's reign the three main parties were called after the foreign power they supported—Britain, France and Russia.

The "Great Idea": The new kingdom contained less than one-third of the Greeks in the Near East. The prospect of "liberating" Ottoman Greeks, of creating a new Byzantium by recapturing Constantinople and avenging the humiliation of 1453—this was the so-called "Great Idea" which aroused enthusiasm, not least among politicians who found it a convenient distraction from domestic problems.

The "Great Idea" had roots embedded in the soil of a fervent nationalism. It was rarely a realistic policy since the Greek army was never on its own a match for the Turks; yet it survived repeated humiliations. After the defeats of 1897 and 1922 it continued to rear

its head. King George I, who succeeded the ousted and unhappy King Otto in 1863 was titled, according to the new constitution of the following year, not just "King of Greece" like his predecessor, but "King of the Hellenes."

The most prominent populist of the late 19th century, Theodore Deliyiannis, encouraged several foolhardy expeditions to Thessaly and Crete. His more far-sighted rival, Charilaos Trikoupis, realized that such a policy was unwise so long as Greece lacked the resources to sustain it. Greece was dependent on foreign loans, which gave her foreign creditors the whiphand over any foreign policy initiatives. Only economic growth would reduce such dependence.

Trikoupis, therefore, set out to encourage economic activity. Roads were improved, the Corinth canal constructed. Piraeus expanded rapidly and became one of the busiest ports in the Mediterranean. Foreign investors participated in banking and mining operations.

But despite the appearance of a few textile and food factories, industrial activity remained minimal right up to World War I. Greece was a rural nation, a country of peasant small-holders. The lack of large estates ironed out social inequalities but it did mean most farmers remained miserably poor, too poor to adopt modern farming methods. The export of currants brought prosperity for a while, but a world slump in 1893 hit the entire economy. Greece was bankrupted and hunger drove peasants to emigrate in large numbers. By 1912 numerous villages lived on remittances sent from the United States by young men who would only return for marriage or retirement.

Such domestic problems seemed to increase Greek enthusiasm for the "Great Idea." Further territory had been acquired in 1881, without fighting, as a by-product of the Congress of Berlin. When troubles in Ottoman Crete in 1897 provoked a wave of sympathy on the mainland, Greek naval forces were sent to the island while the army marched northwards—only to be checked by the Turkish forces who pushed back down into Greece. This defeat was humiliating for the Greeks, but it proved only to delay the future enlargement of the kingdom.

In Crete and Macedonia Ottoman rule was crumbling. But the rise of the new Balkan nations—Serbia and Bulgaria—added a new complication to Greek ambitions. Macedonia was a melting-pot of different racial groups (which is why the French call a fruit salad a *macedoine*), whom each of the neighboring states claimed as her own.

Within Greece, political changes had often been forced through by military uprisings. This had happened in 1843 and 1862. In 1909 it occurred again. Junior army officers staged a revolt against the political establishment. At their invitation a new politician with a radical reputation, Eleutherios Venizelos, came over from Crete to form a government. A consummate diplomatist and a man of great personal charm, Venizelos channeled the untapped energies of the Greek middle-class into his own Liberal Party, which dominated Greek politics for the next 25 years. With foreign assistance he built up the army and navy into efficient fighting units.

There was barely time to consider what burdens the new territories would impose on the Greek state before the country was embroiled in World War I. In fact the country was almost continuously at war for a decade. The legacy of this disruption was a bitter one: financially the country was crippled, politically it was divided.

Venizelos and King Constantine quarreled over whether to bring Greece into the war. The Prime Minister wanted Greece to give the Entente active support, while Constantine insisted on keeping the country neutral. The quarrel raised vital constitutional issues: who had the final say over foreign policy—the King or parliament? The dispute reached the point of open civil war which ended in 1917 with Constantine being forced to leave the

A decade of wars: When the Balkan Wars erupted in 1912, Greece was strong enough to wrest southern Macedonia from the Ottoman forces and then to defend her gains, in alliance with Serbia, from a hostile Bulgaria. The full gains from the fighting of 1912–1913 included—in addition to Macedonia—Epirus, Crete and the east Aegean islands. Greece's area and population were doubled at a stroke.

Preceding pages, Panagiótou Zographóu's illustration for Makroyiánnis' book about the Greek War of Independence. Above left, Ioánnis Kapodistrias, a statesman who played a prominent role in the Greek struggle for independence; and right, colored lithography entitled "A Great Musician" from the satirical newspaper *New Aristophanes* (Athens 1888–1895).

country and Greece entering the war.

Venizelos had hoped that the Entente powers would reward Greece for her support with new territories. Smyrna and its rich hinterland in Asia Minor had been promised by the British to Greece during the war, and in 1919 Greek troops were invited to occupy the province and place it provisionally under Greek control. It began to look as though the "Great Idea" might at last be realized.

But in Greece in 1920 the Liberal Party was surprisingly voted out of power and succeeded by a Royalist Government. The fight against the Turks continued, however, invigorated by the myth that Constantine had been divinely named to lead the Greeks into Constantinople. Encouraged by the Allies, Greek forces advanced inland from Smyrna against the Turkish Nationalists, led by a rebel general called Mustafa Kemal. Spirits were high, but the long march over hilly, waterless country weakened the Greeks and stretched their lines of communication. In September 1922, only 50 miles from Ankara, the Nationalists finally pushed back the Greeks. Their retreat turned into a rout. As Greek soldiers and civilians fled from the Turkish army, Smyrna was surrendered without a struggle.

The 1923 treaty, which finally ended the war between Greece and Turkey, fixed the boundaries between the countries which hold today (with the exception of the Dodecanese islands, at that time held by the Italians). In addition, a massive population transfer was agreed: half a million Muslim inhabitants of Greece

of singing—a melancholy vocal line over violin and bouzouki swept the Athenian cafes.

After the "Disaster" of 1922, King Constantine was forced to leave Greece a second time, and a parliamentary republic was established. It lasted only 12 years, a succession of short-lived coalitions and minority governments, broken up by military dictatorships and abortive coups d'etat. Governments regularly altered the electoral system to keep themselves in power. The only period of stability—Venizelos' years in power from 1928 to 1932—was terminated by the shock of the international economic depression. In 1933 the Liberals were succeeded by the royalist Populist Party, whose timid and uncertain leaders only half-heartedly supported the Republic. Apart from the constitutional

10 SALONIQUE — Quartier Vardar, Groupe de Réfugiés - Vardar district, A groupe of Refugees

moved to Turkey in exchange for over 1 million Orthodox Greeks. The Greek presence in Asia Minor, which had endured for over 2,000 years, was thus ended.

The interwar years: Buffetted and impoverished by 10 years of war, the nation now faced the huge problem of absorbing these impoverished newcomers into an already crowded country. The economy benefitted from this new source of cheap labor, and it was in the interwar period that Greece began to industrialize. But the arrival of the refugees also increased social tensions. Over half a million refugees settled in urban areas, often in squalid shanty towns outside the large cities, searching for poorly-paid jobs. With them they brought their music, and the Smyrna style

issue, little separated the two parties. In matters of economic and social policy both were equally unimaginative. Both ignored the signs of growing inequality and class conflict.

Lacking popular support, parliamentary government remained vulnerable to military pressure. In 1935 this led to the restoration of the monarchy. The following year the King dissolved Parliament and offered the premiership to an extreme right-wing politician, John Metaxas, a former senior army officer and a fervent royalist. Later the same year, Metaxas responded to a wave of strikes by calling out the army and declaring martial law.

Metaxas' dictatorship was run along totalitarian lines. But although people had become dissatisfied with the instability of parlia-

38

mentary rule, they did not greet the alternative with great enthusiasm. "The First Peasant" (as Metaxas liked to be called) never succeeded in digging solid foundations for his longed-for Third Hellenic Civilization.

World War and resistance: Metaxas had tried to steer a middle course in foreign policy between Britain and Germany. The latter's increasing dominance in the Balkans had to be set against Britain's naval strength in the Mediterranean. But Germany was not the only power with aggressive designs in the Balkans. In April 1939 Mussolini sent Italian troops into Albania. Eighteen months later he tried to emulate Hitler's record of conquests by crossing the Albanian border into Greece. Metaxas could not hope to keep Greece neutral any longer. Receiving the

(Spaghetti Eaters)—as the Italians became contemptuously known in later folksongs—back deep into Albania. But in the spring of 1941 Hitler sent German troops south to pacify the Balkans in preparation for his invasion of the Soviet Union.

Britain had sent reinforcements to support the Greeks, but poor coordination between the two Allies allowed the Germans to advance unchecked as far as Salonika. German victory was swift. Their invasion of Greece began on April 5; on April 30 they appointed General Tsokaloglu, who had signed an armistice with them, as a quisling Prime Minister.

Greece was occupied by German and Italian forces until late 1944. Their hold over the countryside was often tenuous, but firm in the towns. It was the towns which suffered

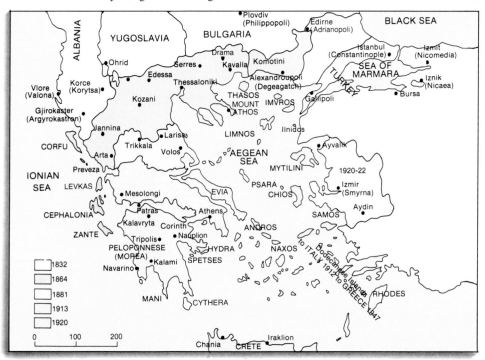

Italian ambassador in his dressing-gown, he listened to a recital of trumped-up charges and responded to the Fascist ultimatum with a curt "No!". Or so the story runs—a story commemorated every year on October 28 by "Ohi" ("No") Day.

Fighting on their own in the mountains of Epirus, the Greek forces were remarkably successful and pushed the "Makaronades"

Left, a group of refugees in Salonika after the Asia Minor disaster of 1922. Above, a map of Greece's modern history showing different emancipations.

most from the shortage of food, notably in the terrible winter of 1941–1942. It was also from the towns that the Germans—against Greek and to some extent Italian protests—deported and eventually exterminated Greece's old and varied Jewish communities. King George and his official government had left the country in 1941 and passed the war under British protection. And when an organized resistance movement did eventually emerge in the hills, most pre-war politicians remained in the towns—on the sidelines.

The earliest and most important group was

known as the National Liberation Front ("EAM" in Greek). This was organized by the Communist Party, but rapidly attracted a broad base of support, including many Greeks for whom patriotism and anti-royalist feeling were alone sufficient motivating forces. Numerous other groups also sprang up. Drawing on the *klepht* tradition of mountain resistance, these groups would make occasional forays down into the plains. Clashes between different groups were unfortunately common.

The dominance of EAM meant that when the British began to establish contacts with resistance groups in 1942, they found military considerations colliding with political ones. EAM, with over 1 million supporters, was well placed to pin down German troops. On the other hand, the British suspected that EAM

trusted the Allies' intentions and refused to lay down their arms. The Allies feared the specter of a communist rising and tried to find moderate politicians to whom they could hand over power. But these politicians were reliant upon a heavily right-wing militia to keep order. It was in such circumstances that the King returned to Greece in September 1946 after a bitterly disputed plebiscite. Inflation was soaring, the black market flourished and violence spread rapidly through the country as old wartime scores were settled.

As Greece slid into open civil strife, she became a crucial stage in the rapidly evolving Cold War. The Government survived on Allied loans and politicians became adept at exaggerating the communist threat as a means of extracting further American support.

intended to set up a communist state in Greece after the war, and they therefore armed other groups as a counterweight. EAM, for its part, feared that Churchill wished to restore the monarchy in Greece without consulting the Greek people. This fear was amply justified. Churchill had little sympathy for the guerrillas, whom he described as "miserable banditti," and supported the monarchy with fervor.

Into the Cold War: In autumn 1944, the German forces retreated, to be replaced by British troops. First Britain and then, after March 1947, the United States found themselves with the task of reintroducing civilian rule. The climate of suspicion made this almost impossible. Resistance forces mis-

In fact, the official Government forces had to abandon control of large parts of the countryside to the rebels. When Kenneth Matthews, a BBC correspondent, was captured by guerrilla forces, he found an entire alternative government operating in the mountains of the Peloponnese.

Greek Government forces, with American provisions and advice, eventually defeated the rebel army in the mountains of northwest Greece in October 1949. But victory was not achieved without the mass detention of suspected left-wing sympathizers and the forced evacuation of entire villages. The violation of civil rights and the emergence of a powerful security service apparatus did not end in 1950. Once more domestic politics was polarized: the old pre-war split between royalists and republicans gave way to one between Left and Right.

Greece looks West: Democracy had weathered the civil war—but only just. In the following decade a certain stability seemed to have been achieved, with only two Prime Ministers, both conservatives, in power between 1952 and 1963. Yet this stability was precarious, relying on a policy of outlawing the Communist Party and discouraging opposition to the regime. Anyone with a suspected left-wing past found life difficult.

Greece had joined NATO in 1951, and the pro-western orientation of her foreign policy secured financial support from the United States. However, the relationship was not straightforward: when the Cyprus dispute of any general economic expansion were felt. This occurred in the 1950s and 1960s. Greece—like Italy and Spain—experienced, an "economic miracle" which transformed the country.

Electrical power became widespread, communications improved. As roads opened up new horizons, young Greeks went to meet them. Athens mushroomed outwards, a chaotic sprawl of concrete apartments, until it contained almost one-third of the country's entire population. Many young men left for West Germany to meet the sudden demand for labor. In many ways life was changing for the better. And not just materially.

For women, the old life had been harsh and limiting. As they left the village for the city they slowly found a new freedom. In the Mani, one of the most conservative areas

flared up in 1954 Greece refused to take part in NATO maneuvers. This foreshadowed the problems that later governments would have in defining Greece's role in Europe. The quarrel over Cyprus was resolved—for a time—when the island was created a republic in 1960. And Greek links with the West were strengthened by her entry into the Common Market as an Associate in 1962.

A troublesome "miracle": Greece's close dependence on international economic conditions could work two ways: it made for great vulnerability but it also meant that the benefits

Left, many young women left their homes and villages to fight in the mountains with the Resistance during the Civil War. Above, anti-dictatorship posters.

of Greece, so many young women left the region that men had to rely increasingly upon Athenian marriage brokers to find a suitable bride. The days when it was left to the woman to carry stones from the quarry or to bring water from the well were coming to an end. A new pattern was emerging of ghost communities, inhabited for most of the year by local farmers and a few old people, which filled up suddenly in the summer months as workers and their families returned from Athens to holiday in their native village.

The old forms of political control which had operated best in small rural communities began to lose their effectiveness. A new urban middle class arose which regarded the conservative political elite as culturally backward,

Modern Greece 41

rooted in the rhetoric of the Cold War, lacking a vision of Greece as a modern state.

The 1961 elections saw the resurgence of the political center, under the leadership of a former Liberal, George Papandreou. The contest was bitterly fought. When the results were announced in favor of Karamanlis, Papandreou alleged that police and rural gendarmes had been used to intimidate voters, and that the result was fraudulent.

Public disquiet at possible links between the ruling party and extreme right-wing violence increased in May 1963 when a left-wing deputy, George Lambrakis, was assassinated at a peace rally in Salonika. Shortly afterwards Karamanlis resigned and in elections held at the end of the year, Papandreou's Center Union party won power. This was the first

officers to make contingency plans for military intervention. But these plans were preempted when a group of junior army officers, working according to a NATO contingency plan, executed a swift coup d'etat early on the morning of April 21, 1967. Martial law was proclaimed, political parties were dissolved. The Colonels were in power.

The Colonels: The junta was motivated by a mixture of self-interest and hazy nationalism. This combination was certainly not new; on a number of occasions in the interwar period army officers had used the rhetoric of national salvation to head off a possible purge in which they feared they might lose their jobs.

In their policies and attitudes, too, the Colonels drew on earlier traditions. With peasant or lower middle-class backgrounds,

centrist ruling party for over a decade.

The way now seemed open for an extended period of centrist rule. But although conservative politicians were prepared to surrender power, right-wing groups in the military regarded the new government as a threat to their own interests.

When Papandreou demanded a reshuffle of senior army officers he found his own defense minister and the young king, Constantine II, opposed to him. The King tried clumsily to bring down the Center Union Government, but when Papandreou agreed with the main conservative opposition to hold elections in May 1967, Constantine was faced with the prospect of a further Center Union victory. He held a series of meetings with senior army

they symbolized a provincial reaction to the "miracle's" new world of urban consumers. Thus they laid great stress on the need for a return to traditional morality and religion. They closed the frontiers to bearded, long-haired or mini-skirted foreigners—at least until they realized the implications for Greece's tourist trade. They prevented Greeks from reading such subversive literature as Greco-Bulgarian dictionaries. They wanted the country to "radiate civilization in all directions" by establishing a "Greece of the Christian Greeks" which would make Greece

A rally in Salonika supporting the socialist Prime Minister Papandreou just before he was re-elected in 1985.

once again "a pole of ideological and spiritual attraction." This was the old dream once more: an escape from the dilemmas of the modern world in a fantastic fusion of classical Athens and Byzantium. Perhaps because of the harsh censorship of intellectual activity and the suppression of any dissent, there was little active opposition to the regime.

The first signs of widespread discontent coincided with the economic downturn of 1973. The leaders of protest were students, whose occupations of university buildings in March and November were brutally broken up. Increasingly the regime was proving incapable of dealing with ordinary problems of government. In the bloody aftermath of the November student sit-in at the Athens Polytechnic Colonel Papadopoulos, the regime's figurehead, was deposed by army units and power switched to a more sinister figure, Dimitrios Ioannides, commander of the military police.

In the end it was the Cyprus problem which toppled the junta. A foolhardy Greek nationalist coup—supported from Athens—against Archbishop Makarios, the President of Cyprus, led the Turks to land troops in northern Cyprus. Ioannides ordered Greek forces to retaliate, but mobilization had been so chaotic that local commanders refused to obey his orders. Pressure grew for a return to civilian rule. An invitation was extended to the former Premier, Karamanlis, to return from his exile in Paris to supervise the restoration of parliamentary democracy. On July 24, 1974 Karamanlis returned to Athens.

A new start for democracy: The transition to democracy proceeded remarkably smoothly considering the enormous problems which Karamanlis faced. Aware of his own vulnerability, he moved slowly in dismissing collaborators of the regime. At elections held in November 1974, Karamanlis' New Democracy party won an overwhelming victory, though there were indications that many people had voted for Karamanlis simply as a guarantor of stability.

Karamanlis himself was well placed to make any necessary political reforms, since a referendum the month after the elections produced a decisive vote for the abolition of the monarchy, which had been compromised by the King's actions before and during the junta. In its place Karamanlis created a presidency with sweeping powers. It was widely believed that in the event of a swing to the Left, Karamanlis would resign his parliamentary seat and become President.

Signs of such a swing were evident after the 1977 elections in which Andreas Papandreou's Panhellenic Socialist Movement ("PASOK")

made large gains. The younger Papandreou, George's son, represented a new, post-war generation—at home with the "miracle" and its fruits. With his background as a professor of economics in the United States, he was well placed to lead a party of technocrats. At this time he still had a reputation as a radical and he vehemently attacked Karamanlis' policies, taking a more belligerent stand over relations with Turkey, and threatening that a PASOK government would take Greece out of both NATO and the EEC subject to popular referendum. The future was to show that Papandreou's promises were an unreliable guide to his actions in power. Nevertheless support for PASOK was evidently growing and in 1980, a little over a year before the next elections Karamanlis resigned as Prime Minister and was voted in as President by Parliament.

After PASOK's victory in the October 1981 elections, based on a simple campaign slogan of "Allagi" ("Change"), Papandreou took office and formed Greece's first ever socialist government. His significance lies not in his socialism, which has been rather muted, but in his remarkable success in articulating the attitudes of his generation. In the 1960s he brilliantly blended the rhetoric of the Left with the social optimism of Kennedy's America. Twenty years later he has grown older together with his voters. Now he is plumper, more paternal. The rhetoric still culls votes on the Left, but it is a middle-aged, middle-class Left who seek economic security, stability, a "better future" for their children. This slogan, accompanied by images of a little girl, who symbolized a vague appeal to classless desires for peace and prosperity, won PASOK the 1985 general election.

Events since 1974 suggest that for the first time in her history Greece may have evolved a stable three-party system: New Democracy (conservative), PASOK (socialist), KKE (communist). Minor parties have come and gone, but these three parties dominate the scene. The crucial question has always been: can Greek parties outlive their leaders? Until recently the smallest of the three, the KKE was unique in having done so; now New Democracy too has weathered several changes of leadership. What of PASOK, whose increasingly centrist policies have been pepped up with the popular appeal and charisma of Papandreou himself? There are intriguing parallels between the present Premier and Venizelos, the Liberal leader both indulge in radical rhetoric but moderate action. Both founded new parties, modern in their context, on the strength of their own personalities. Will PASOK go the Way of the Liberal Party, falling into decline when its leader quits the stage?

A

JOURNEY

INTO

GREECE,

BY

George Wheler Esq;

In Company of

Dʳ SPON of LYONS.

𝔍𝔫 𝔖𝔦𝔯 𝔅𝔬𝔬𝔨𝔰.

CONTAINING

I.   A Voyage from *Venice* to *Constantinople*.
II.   An Account of *Constantinople* and the Adjacent Places.
III. A Voyage through the *Lesser Asia*.
IV. A Voyage from *Zant* through several Parts of *Greece* to *Athens*.
V.   An Account of *Athens*.
VI. Several Journeys from *Athens*, into *Attica*, *Corinth*, *Bœotia*, &c.

With variety of Sculptures.

LONDON,
Printed for *William Cademan*, *Robert Kettlewell*, and *Awnsham Churchill*,
at the *Popes Head* in the *New-Exchange*, the *Hand and Scepter* in
Fleetstreet, and the *Black Swan* near *Amen-Corner*.
MDCLXXXII.

TRAVELERS THROUGH THE AGES

The Ancient Greeks had a strong sense of their own identity. From the Homeric age until at least the disintegration of Alexander's empire Greeks were conscious of themselves as a people distinct from all others. These others they called barbarians. 'Barbarous' first meant only that—non-Greek. The word was probably imitative of unintelligible foreign speech. It was in their common language and in their common culture that the Greeks, however various and however widely distributed, knew themselves to be Greek.

According to myth, the goddess Athina chose the land of Greece for her favorite people because of its ideal location between the frozen north and the torrid south. Later civilizations, particularly northern ones, have believed that myth wholeheartedly. The Greeks, it was thought, were Nature's favorites.

Greek poets have always celebrated their peculiarly blessed zone of the earth. The end of the Ancient World has been likened to a huge shipwreck. Bits came ashore, bits of a whole sense and vision, the names of cities, mountains, rivers, plains and islands. No geography has ever been so resonant. We learn a few epithets from Homer, and we have discovered that they were exact and telling: windy Troy, sandy Pylos, Mycenae rich in gold. And in Pindar, Sophocles and Euripides there are brilliant glimpses of places within and around the limits of the Greek world: of Mount Tmolus and the golden Pactolus in the east, of Etna in the west (where the Titans were confined), and of Kolonos, Thebes, Cithaeron and Delphi at the center. There were extraordinary travelers among the heroes of Greek myth and legend: Odysseus, who was ten years getting home from Troy; Heracles, whose labors took him north into the land of the Hyperboreans and west to the Garden of the Hesperides; Jason, who sailed to Colchis on the Black Sea after the Fleece.

Finding reality in the myth: The Greeks had a strongly mythical and religious sense of the places in their world; and this sense, or something like it in intensity, survived them and has inspired or colored the vision of travelers in their country ever since. It should excite the traveler to know, that places of terrific mythical resonance really exist. They are not *beyond* the zone, in a nebulous otherwhere, but actually within it, substantial and real. Helicon, Parnassus, Olympus are real mountains and can be climbed—which affects the imagination very curiously, as an excitement but also, almost, as an offense. The Aheron still flows and meets the Cocitus by the hilltop Nekromantion of Persephone and Hades, just east of Parga. Parga was a fishing village and is now a holiday place. It is one street thick, and on that one street you will have trouble buying anything as necessary as bread. But there are many travel agencies, and they all offer the same thing: day trips by boat to the entrance to Hades.

The Ancients sited many of their myths very precisely indeed. Citizens of Athens, Corinth or Thebes constantly saw with their own eyes places their divinities and heroes had operated in. Travel was difficult, but people *did* travel, they went about their ordinary business in a country the myths had illuminated. The everyday and the mythical seem to coexist very easily in Greece. Judging from the leaden tablets unearthed at Dodona, they were often very ordinary men and women who made their way to the sanctuary and oracle there. The questions they put to Zeus through his priests, who, as Homer says, "sleep on the ground with unwashed feet," were often very mundane ones: "Whether it will be alright to buy the small lake by the sanctuary of Demeter?" "Whether it is good and possible to sail for Syracuse at a later date?" "Whether I shall be successful in my craft if I migrate?" The answers were given in the rustling of the leaves of the sacred oak.

The mythical and religious sense of place coexisted, from quite early on, with a concern for topographical accuracy. Scholars and travelers in the 18th century made the important discovery that Homer had sited his story precisely. When Lady Montagu sailed through the Dardanelles it gave her great pleasure, so she wrote to Pope, to check Homer's descriptions for herself and to find them exact. Others actually used the *Iliad* for their archaeological researches on the plain of Troy. Schliemann, in the 1870s, was only the most maniacal, credulous and fortunate of a long line. When travelers and critics called Homer a "truthful" poet, "a painter after Nature," they meant not just his depiction of human passions but also his eye (blind though he was) for the landscapes and topography of the real world. This led to some partial and *interested* readings of the texts, but in its day it was a justifiable and fruitful corrective. It rescued the poems out of a timeless classicism and located them where they belonged, in real time and place.

Travelers were on firmer ground when they took the historian Herodotus, the geographer Strabo and the tourist-cum-topographer Pausanias as their guides. The latter two particularly are frequently referred to at great length in the early modern travel literature of Greece. Quite simply, until the modern tradition itself became established, travelers in Greece seeking to locate places famous in antiquity *only* had ancient testimony to go on. Not only particular monuments—the Temple

and enhances the glamor of places), let us say that the texts worked in a dual way: they located the sites and aroused what Dr Johnson called "local emotion." The knowledge the travelers had or gained was, in varying proportions and intensity, both factual and imaginative. Most often, of course, the "local emotion" felt by a traveler at some important site in Greece would be very different from what we may suppose an Ancient Greek to have felt. The modern response is almost inevitably a sentimental one; its most characteristic coloring is nostalgia.

The "good old days": Nostalgia for Greece increased as the value of Ancient Greek Civilization increased in the eyes of later nations. Early modern travelers came to Greece from countries—England, France, Italy—whose

of Olympian Zeus in Athens, for example, or of Artemis at Ephesus—but even entire sanctuaries and cities of the very greatest importance—Delphi, Miletus, Sparta—had vanished if not from the face of the earth at least out of all local ken, and could only be located and identified by following ancient directions (converting stadia into miles, allowing for changes in the landscape) and searching hopefully for telling inscriptions.

The Ancients themselves then were the best guides available to travelers when Greece in modern times began to be explored; and, not making any hard and fast distinction between poets on the one hand and topographers or historians on the other (Homer was thought to be accurate, Herodotus honors the myths

cultures were deeply indebted to the Classical World, and naturally, in varying degrees, they brought that influence with them and it affected their responses. In Europe by the late 18th century, in Germany especially, with some writers, nostalgia was almost literally what the component elements of the word imply—a sickness, an ache—because by then in their eyes the excellence of Greece, the absolute supremacy of her achievements over those of every later age, was crushingly evident.

It is worth noting that nostalgia for Greece,

A statue of Odysseus found in a cave in the south of Italy. For the Western world he is the archetypal traveler.

though not to the same degree, already existed in Roman and Alexandrian times. Both those ages were, in some respects, backward-looking to a civilization which they thought superior to their own. European travelers of the 17th and 18th centuries found in Roman and Alexandrian sentiment towards Ancient Greece a precedent and an authority for what they, more intensely (the gap having widened) felt themselves. They would quote Cicero's lament for the decline of Athens at the appropriate moment in their own accounts. And Pausanias, though not himself sentimental, provided *material* for sentiment, because when he traveled, in the second century, much had already been lost. Many of the monuments and sanctuaries he described were already in ruins or had lost importance. His whole undertaking, which was to write a travel-guide to Greece, may be objectively called a sentimental one, whether he himself felt sentimental towards the sites or not. When 1,500 years later, travelers arrived looking for Rhamnus or Orchomenus with Pausanias in their hands, they measured a further or perhaps a total loss, and felt, if they were that way inclined, a compounded longing.

Once the tradition of travel in Greece had become established each new explorer could refer to and perhaps correct his predecessor's works on the spot; but he would not, for that, forget the ancient texts. The classical authors themselves continued to direct and influence travel in Greece throughout the18th and 19th centuries, and perhaps they do so still. It was *by* the light and *in* the light of classical literature that the travelers saw the famous localities of Greece; and in Roman and Alexandrian works the moderns discovered the beginnings of their own nostalgia.

Looking for the "real" Greece: Serious exploration of Greece did not get underway until the late 17th century. There were many practical deterrents, not the least of which being the fact that nearly the whole of Greece, from the late 15th century onwards, was Turkish territory; but also, just as important, the cultural incentive was lacking still in those countries from which, later, the travelers would come. Medieval Christian Europe, though it took a great deal of its learning from Plato and Aristotle, had no wish to visit Greece—unless as crusaders and robber-knights to carve out feudal domains there. A confidently Christian culture had no reason to turn with any sentimental or nostalgic interest towards the land of Greece. Geography then was more figurative and symbolic than empirical, there was no impulse from that discipline to map Greece or any other remote country accurately.

The *Mappa Mundi* (of about 1290) in Hereford Cathedral illustrates this very well. The world is disposed there almost entirely figuratively: Jerusalem at the center, the River of Death all around the circumference. If you look on that map for information about the classical lands you find some very strange shapes and locations. Greece herself has no general designation, unless the word *ICAYA* (Achaea) is meant as one. Famous ranges and rivers are hopelessly misplaced, and there are some notable confusions: Athos appears as Atlas, Delphi as Dilos. Thasos and Patmos have drifted north into the Black Sea. The Peloponnese is drawn as a rounded lump and labeled: *INSULA*. The Chersonese peninsula in Thrace has the shape which clever etymologists deduced for it from the name of its chief city Cardia: the shape of a heart.

Two-and-a-half centuries later, even among the learned, the degree of knowledge was scarcely higher. Martin Crusius, for example, a German scholar writing in the 1550s, asked a correspondent in Greece whether it was true that Athens no longer existed. The trade-routes passed the city and Piraeus by. Ships rounding the Peloponnese crossed to Smyrna through the islands. On the first modern maps Athens occurred as Stines—which is what the Franks heard when the Greeks said "Stin Athina" (in Athens)—and by that misnomer all connection with the ancient city was effectively severed. In Holland and Germany in the 16th and 17th centuries scholars did write geographies of Greece, but entirely bookish ones, entirely on the basis of classical texts. The author of one of them indeed, Christoph Cellarius, was renowned for having taken only one short walk throughout the 14 years of his professorship in Halle. Such works prove the reverence Renaissance learning had for Greece, and at the same time a nearly medieval indifference to empirical knowledge. The shift that then took place is exemplified by Joseph Pitton de Tournefort who set off in 1700, funded by the King's Academy, to see for himself whether what the ancient geographers and botanists had written was true or false. It needed a cultural incentive to send travelers to Greece, and the Renaissance supplied that; but also a shift in the manner of apprehending the world, a shift towards belief in the value of autopsy and empirical enquiry. A lull in the wars of the Turks and Venetians, after the Turkish victory at Candia (Iráklion) in 1669, made trade and travel easier. Travel for pleasure or for scientific purposes was of course greatly facilitated when the trade routes and commercial contacts were secure.

The "Hellenic Ideal": Greece is not just any foreign country but the still surviving site of an excellent and—for the West—a supremely influential civilization. True, there is more to Greece than her classical past; and having such a past, and having had so much outside passionate attention directed at it, has not always been an advantage; but, for better or for worse, Greece even today is the real location, able to be visited, of achievements by which our sciences, our politics and our arts have been massively influenced. Greece, so far as the West is concerned, cannot be neutral ground. The first travelers, or those of them at least who set out deliberately to see Athens, Elfsis or Dilos, were not impartial. Even the most reasonable and "scientific" among them had ideas and ideals in mind when they set out which colored their perceptions when they got there. Fortunately, the "Hellenic Ideal" is a

her excellent past increased, and what was learned of Greece and brought back by the travelers further fueled that interest. This is most apparent in the 18th century. Travel literature altogether was an important and popular genre. Within it, accounts of Greece had a wide circulation, often went through several editions, and were very quickly translated. Furthermore, book-sellers, knowing the market, engaged hack-writers to plagiarize and excerpt from the best available accounts and to compose compendium volumes out of them. *The Travels of the late Charles Thompson Esq.*, for example, was put together in this way (in 1744), and was very well received. Though inauthentic and uninspiring it makes a serviceable book. Its fabricator cannibalized Tournefort, Wheler,

many-faceted thing, and the company of travelers who might all be called Hellenists had very various interests and aspirations. We need not enumerate these. The point is: the earliest travelers *were* interested, they came with ideals and presuppositions, with a disposition to be affected each according to his bent.

These particular inclinations were contained within a more general attitude: admiration, admiration of the past. Modern Greeks have never had an easy time of it, being expected by Western Hellenists to live up to their glorious past. Admiration has its obverse disappointment, which may turn hysterical and even vengeful.

Opening up: Greece was opened up to the West as scholarly and sentimental interest in

Pococke and others into one rather stodgy summary of researches to date. Greece, from the late 17th century onwards, was very marketable in England, France and Germany.

The best among the early books on Greece were written, naturally enough, by men who traveled there and who, back home again, related what they had learned. Spon, Tournefort, Wood, Chandler, were deliberate travelers who made their discoveries known to an interested public. Their undertakings were in that sense purposeful. But, especially at the beginning, much information about Greece

An engraving of a Turk and a Greek from Tournefort's *A Voyage into the Levant* published in 1718.

50

and much assistance in the exploration of Greece was supplied by people who happened to be there on other business. Such figures occur passim in the published accounts, and travelers were much indebted to them. They were, for example, Capuchin priests who, being residents of Athens, accommodated the first European travelers in their own religious house, showed them around the still visible monuments and supplied them surreptitiously with maps.

One of their number, le père Jacques Babin, based at Negropont (Euboea) but visiting Athens, wrote the very first modern account of the city—*Récit de l'état présent de la ville d'Athènes* (1674). This brief but curiously moving work (we witness in it a man opening his eyes to beautiful things around him, we hear the first accents of true admiration) was sent to Jacob Spon in Lyons. He edited it, and in so doing was inspired towards his own journey. An armchair traveler, Guillet de Saint-Georges, with whom the authentic Spon was later in controversy, got most of the material for his immensely successful *Athènes ancienne et nouvelle* (1675) from Capuchin priests in Patras and Athens.

Some early travelers: All the early travelers were glad to make use of contacts on the spot and even to supplement their own accounts with eyewitness reports of places they were not able to visit themselves. Merchants were particularly useful in this respect, if they were intelligent observers and had some interest in classical things, since their business took them traveling. Consuls even more so, being in one place for a length of time. Consul Giraud, for example, who served first French and then British interests in Athens, for some 30 years, offered hospitality to travelers and showed them around the sights. He also engaged in scholarly researches, which Spon made grateful use of. A most powerful figure at this time was the French Ambassador in Constantinople, the extravagant Marquis de Nointel. He considered it part of his diplomatic duty to travel through Greece, his domain, with a large entourage and much ostentation, collecting and recording curiosities and antiquities as he went. A Flemish painter in his party did drawings of the Parthenon frieze which, though crude, are of great value still, since they were done before the bombardment of 1687 in which much was damaged. When Spon and Wheler arrived in Greece they were entertained by Nointel, who gave them not only inspiration (he showed them the memorials of his own tour) but also protection and practical information for their further journey.

The researches done and passed on by men who were in Greece in some professional capacity—diplomatic, commercial, religious—were important, but it was the travelers, particularly Spon and, later, Chandler, who published them. An exception was Pierre-Augustin Guys of Marseilles, a most engaging man. He was a merchant who spent nearly all his working life in Greece and loved the land and its people and its classical past with passion. He was both a wealthy and a well-read man, a correspondent of Winckelmann and a devoted admirer of his aesthetic works. Indeed, as he traveled Greece, pursuing his commercial interests, he saw her landscapes, her people, climate, customs, with a vision as sympathetic and passionate as Winckelmann's, who never went there. He was unusual in his day, for instead of dislocation and discrepancy he saw continuity, survival and connections wherever he went in Greece. By insisting on continuity, by refusing to think of the modern Greeks as hopelessly cut off from their heroic past, he contributed, in a small way, to that raising of expectations and of confidence by which, finally, the Turks were driven out. M. Guys was given the freedom of the city of Athens for his sympathetic depiction of contemporary Greece.

Spon and Wheler were in Greece in 1675–1676 and their explorations and their separate publications constituted the first coherent survey of the land for modern Europe. Spon especially wrote as a scholar and a Hellenist, Wheler followed him as well as he could. When he entered the church in 1685 he gave his souvenirs, the bits and pieces of marble he had brought back with him, to the newly-founded Ashmolean Museum, which already housed the Arundel collection. Spon, for his part, had copied thousands of inscriptions. It is worth remembering that from the start journeys to Greece were undertaken with the intention of bringing things back—information, of course; copies of inscriptions; but also anything readily movable. Wealthy collectors in England and France had their agents in Greece buying, begging and stealing whatever they could, for shipment home, to adorn their country houses and private cabinets. It was many years before anyone criticized this business. Byron was among the first to find it outrageous. The reasoning was very simple: the Greeks were degenerate and the Turks, their masters, were barbarians who would deface as a matter of religious duty whatever statuary they came upon. Therefore it was the duty of civilized western travelers to rescue the precious relics.

The travelers recorded numerous instances of Greek neglect and Turkish maltreatment of ancient works—an architrave used in a cowshed here, a sculpted head used for target-practice there—and felt wholly justified in removing whatever they could.

Recording the visits: The first journeys to Greece were, in some cases, extensions of the Grand Tour beyond Italy. Spon, who perhaps always intended to go, made up a party with Wheler and two other English gentlemen when they met in Rome. Wheler had been traveling through France to complete his education with his Oxford tutor. He had money, Spon had the scholarship and enthusiasm. They were an interesting combination at the very outset of the tradition. Both professed Protestantism (Spon went into exile for it after his return), but Wheler, Church of England, although the younger man, was much more hidebound and hectoring.

largely on Wheler's funds. Tournefort in 1700 and the *abbé* Fourmont in 1728 were sent and financed by the French Crown. For serious exploration some such backing became increasingly necessary, and in France and England at least there were public bodies and a few wealthy private individuals who were willing to provide it. National pride was a factor certainly, but also a sense of social and cultural responsibility, and of noblesse oblige. The early exploration of Greece coincided with the opening of the first public museums and galleries.

Tournefort, primarily a botanist, was a man of the broadest learning, an excellent traveler, wide-awake, good-humored, resilient. He took in classical sites en route, so to speak—not incidentally, but as part of a whole interest.

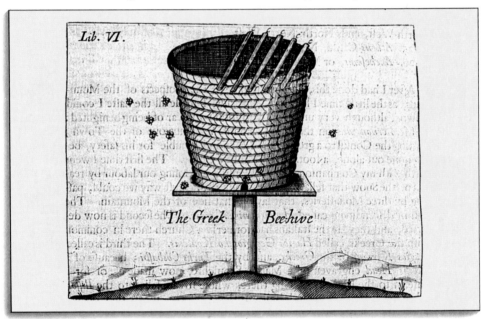

Quite simply, he preferred Restoration England to Greece, even to Periclean Athens as the imagination of a Hellenist might recover it. He was not a very open-minded man. We may recognize his type even today: the man who travels to confirm his prejudices, and who is profoundly relieved to get home again unchanged.

Spon was the better traveler. True, he was disposed to feel in a certain way; but he was alive and awake on the spot to the places themselves. He was consequential in his passion for Greece. His travels, despite Wheler's assistance, impoverished him. When he went into exile he was penniless. He died in a pauper's hospital.

That first enterprise was a private one,

His book *Voyage du Levant* (1717) is perhaps the best of the early accounts for any reader whose interest in Greece is a general one. He gives the ancient and present state of places, what they produce and pay in taxes, how they are administered, how the people live, where the best harbors are. He exerts himself—climbs a high hill to have a good vantage-point, enquires diligently of the *papas* (the priest) and village elders who might be able to inform him. Later accounts constantly refer to Tournefort as an authority and point of orientation.

Cultural expeditions: When the London Society of Dilettanti sent their expedition to Greece in 1764 it was with a more specific, more particularly Hellenist intention. Cultural demands had altered, and the Society, founded in 1731 chiefly for convivial purposes, was by the middle of the century beginning seriously to respond to them. In 1751 they had taken up two energetic individuals, the architects James Stuart and Nicholas Revett, who had made their own way to Athens and were measuring and drawing the monuments there. The Society financed the gradual publication of their work —as the *Antiquities of Athens*—and conclusively promoted the Greek style of architecture and furnishings by doing so. In 1764 then, directed by Robert Wood, they sent a party to Greece and Asia Minor specifically to locate and describe the ancient remains.

Chandler's account of the tour (in two volumes, 1775 and 1776), may be set alongside Tournefort's as the century's best. Its appeal is rather different, just as the journey

in Greece. In his two books he consolidated that tradition. To an extraordinary degree he worked as a compiler, editor and generous critic of other travelers and their accounts. Characteristically, he often begins a chapter on a particular place with a quotation from Pausanias, setting his own observations against that to indicate what has altered and been lost. Then, where appropriate, he will adduce reports by his predecessors—by Wood, Pococke, or, very frequently, Wheler— and comment on them.

With Chandler's expedition the archaeological exploration of Greece was put on a professional footing. He consolidated the tradition to date, and his publications, together with others under the auspices of the Society, made a firm scholarly basis for

it describes was different in character and aims. Chandler knew what he had to look for, and what it was his duty to report. Though his tone is throughout reasonable, *un*enthusiastic, and his prose style deliberately plain, he was nevertheless writing in the service of a love and admiration of Ancient Greece so assured in himself and in the Society he represented as to need no special pleading.

By 1764, when Chandler and his party sailed, there was already a tradition of travel

serious-minded successors in the next century to build on.

Travel practicalities: The tradition of Greek travel literature is a very rich one and this is only a cursory survey of it. Spon and Wheler, Tournefort, Chandler, being very distinctive figures, will have to serve also a representative function. I shall make further use of them now, as I try to give some sense of the real experience, of the practicalities of travel in Greece, in the years before it became an easy matter.

The starting point was very often Rome. The wish to go further than Rome increased with the sense that the classical world was in fact more purely represented by Athens. We may think this self-evident, but the discovery

Left, 18th-century travelers' accounts contain a wealth of information about local customs, dress and even bee husbandry. Above, a woodcut of Greece made in 1545.

of Greece, the recovery of Greece from concealment under Rome, took a long time. The Society of Dilettanti were themselves great movers of the process by which the status of Greece ascended at the cost of Rome. Rome was full of classical works—of noble buildings and, in galleries accessible to respectable travelers, of statuary. Most of the statues were Roman copies of Hellenistic copies of truly classical originals; but this was not known and could not be known, since the originals themselves has not yet been brought to light. When, finally, the Parthenon marbles were seen close to, connoisseurs used to the Apollo Belvedere suffered a severe shock. Travel to Greece, even though great works of art there (since few of the travelers were also excavators) were not often to be seen, was part

all a passage, from Venice, with the Italian ambassador. Such influence was of crucial importance. Spon and Wheler were fortunate in having Nointel's protection, and both traveled under French passports issued by him in Constantinople. The Turks, whose territory Greece was, were notoriously difficult to deal with. It happened that in the 1670s Nointel was in high favor with the Porte, and his English counterpart, Sir John Finch, was not. To travel at all Westerners needed permission, written permits issued by the Sultan himself or by local Agas; but in remoter areas these might be valueless—in parts of the Peloponnese and Asia Minor the word from Constantinople was disregarded and, to make matters difficult for travelers passing through, local potentates were often in conflict with one

of the process by which, very slowly, Greece, in the modern culture of Western Europe, triumphed over Rome.

In Rome, by the middle of the 18th century, travelers would meet with others who had come from Greece. Winckelmann, who, despite attractive offers, never made the journey himself, was in dealings with men who had been there and in his official capacity as Papal Antiquary he got to see shipments of finds as they arrived from Greece and Asia Minor for restoration, alas, and "completion" before going on to the markets of London and Paris. It was in Rome that Spon and Wheler made up their party for Greece. A third member, Francis Vernon, had diplomatic contacts and was able to get them

another.

Misconceptions: Neither the Turks nor the Greeks had any understanding of what the travelers were about. If the travelers' interests were archaeological they met with great incomprehension and mistrust. One energetic Turk, seeing a party inspecting the drums of a column, set to pulverizing the marble with cannon balls in the belief that gold, at least, must be contained therein. Stuart and Revett,

Stuart and Revett meticulously drafted reproductions of classical ruins such as this one of the temple of Corinth. Two hundred years later their *Antiquities of Athens* is still an indispensable reference book.

when they needed to erect ladders and scaffolding, met with objections from Turkish pashas who feared that from that height the Westerners would spy into their harems.

It was also frequently the case that places the travelers wished to explore were of military importance to the Turks. The Acropolis of Athens was a Turkish citadel, the Parthenon was a store for powder and ammunition. It suffered accordingly when Morosini bombarded it. Drawing and measuring, which a traveler would naturally want to do, were extremely suspicious activities in Turkish eyes. Francis Vernon, examining the Theater of Dionysus under the Acropolis, was fired on, and only escaped through the intervention of Consul Giraud. The Capuchin maps were drawn surreptitiously, which partly explains their inaccuracy, and circulated likewise.

In time the travelers produced their own maps. We know that Chandler in the Troad in 1764 had with him a map, done by a Frenchman, which Wood had with him in 1726. Their reliance on one another, and on the ancient authors was very great. But how many books could they actually carry with them? Wood tells us that he and his companions took "a library, consisting chiefly of all the Greek historians and poets, some books of antiquities, and the best voyage writers." But they were perhaps unusually well-provided for, since James Dawkins, one of their party, was a very wealthy man. Spon and Wheler received the newly-published *Athènes ancienne et nouvelle* (by the impostor Guillet) just as they were sailing from Venice. They were able then to check its descriptions on the spot, and found them, in Vernon's phrase "wide from Truth."

A party would hire guides and interpreters and enquire locally, once they had established the area of their interest, whether any ruins were still apparent in it. The same employees would procure them food, and accommodation (often of a very wretched, flea-ridden kind). In many districts the travelers needed more than guides: they needed armed guards. Bocher, traveling alone, was murdered. James Stuart was two or three times set upon and robbed. The roads at the back of Smyrna were infested with bandits, and travelers there did well to join with caravans of merchants who had janissaries riding with them. These difficulties should be borne in mind when we evaluate the travelers' achievements. They could not always go where they pleased or see what they wanted to see. Chandler's party were deterred from climbing Parnassus by the menacing behavior of some Albanian soldiery camped near them at the spring; they kept clear of Rhamnus because the local

Turks there "bore a very bad character."

Other hardships: We should mention the sea's dangers too. Spon and Wheler, crossing from Constantinople, were tossed to and fro for 37 days. Vernon was taken by pirates and stripped of all he possessed (he escaped with his life—only to lose it a few months later, in Persia, in a quarrel over a penknife). And had Chandler sailed home in the *Seahorse*, as he intended, he and his party would very likely all have been drowned off Scilly when that ship went down.

Sir Giles Eastcourt, the fourth member of Spon's party, died on the road to Delphi near Návpaktos. Wood's friend James Bouverie died at Magnesia on the Maeander. Plague was endemic still in many areas. It had a high season in the summer months. The Turks, with their fatalistic view of things, allowed it to carry them off in great numbers. The Franks were more circumspect and withdrew into isolation if they could. Chandler and his companions spent three months holed up in a village above Smyrna, the town itself being too dangerous to enter.

A certain piety entered the tradition. Earlier fates were remembered and commemorated. Tournefort got the whole story of Vernon's death from the English Consul in Isphaham, and recounted it. Chandler searched for and found the names of Eastcourt and Vernon where they had scratched them on the south wall of the Theseum (they are still there and can still be read).

The journeys were often dangerous and—what with mosquitoes, heat, dirt and wolfish dogs—must almost always have been uncomfortable. Though some of the travelers were born adventurers, for others it was only an interlude, perhaps the only escapade of their lives, and they returned to Oxford common rooms and quiet country living with a few mementos and a fund of stories. They had many high moments to remember.

The "travel experience": Discovery, that is the essence of the experience of early travel in Greece. For those travelers seeking to identify, after a lapse of nearly 2,000 years, a particular site famous in antiquity, the satisfaction when they were successful must have been very great indeed. They weren't excavators, they didn't dig their way through to treasures like the Mask of Agamemnon or Helen's Gold; but, knowing their texts, they brought to such places as Marathon, Mistra or Delphi considerable reverence and a willingness to be moved. They were in a landscape such as they had not seen before; not only the botanists among them were excited by the flowers and shrubs, by their vivid colors and rich scents. Again and again they saw scenes that painters in the 18th and 19th centuries loved to depict: ruins among olive trees, broken columns on a headland against the sun, animals grazing in fields littered with marble. And their interest was not always antiquarian. Guys says rather pointedly of Spon that looking for Ancient Greece he found only stones; Guys himself, then, as a corrective, looked to the people and their present lives. True, he saw them through a veil of Homer and Theocritus. But perhaps our perceptions are always colored. The first Western painters in Greece saw the landscape through a haze of Claude Lorraine. Our view is harsher now and more historical, but the 18th-century images are still appealing. Indeed, at times in certain places they are quite compelling.

Enormous changes, some of them irreparably damaging, have occurred in the experience of travel in Greece. Large areas are going to perdition as rapidly as money will permit. We may look even *more* to the past, in horror at what is being done in the present. Out of that past things have been brought to light—out of the earth, out of the sea—which the early travelers never saw the like of, though perhaps the poets of their day imagined them: the great bronzes in the National Museum, for example, the gold of Mycenae, the palaces on Crete. Some sites have undergone marvelous resurrections. On Dilos, at Delphi, Olympia and Athens there is now infinitely more to be seen. Chandler discovered Olympia, Spon and Wheler Delphi, but having identified those sites they saw very little. When we see the richness of Dilos nowadays we can scarcely believe that by the early 18th century it was thought nothing there merited a visit.

We have more knowledge nowadays, the museums are richer, the sites more extensive. On the other hand, it may not be easy in present-day Greece to get a sense of what early travel was like. Out of season, and out of the way, is best: at Dion, for example, under Olympus, or at Gortyn in the center of Crete (where the road runs through what was the ancient city). And of course when you least expect it there are places where a few yards of old walling, or the remains of old irrigation channels, or ledges and niches in a goatherd's cave, will suddenly bring the whole experience upon you with a rush.

In Turkey, in old Ionia, there are some potent reminders. Ephesus, for example, ends in a marsh. There you may see fallen pillars, broken architraves and beautiful carvings sinking among the bulrushes. The Temple of Artemis, one of the Seven Wonders of the Ancient World, lies (what little is left of it) on swampy waste land, on a patch that serves as village green, football pitch, grazing ground

and rubbish tip. The precinct falls away into a pond that looks malarial, and there blocks and drums of the temple, swarming with terrapins, emerge and sink according to the season. Selçuk was built out of the ruins of Ephesus. Dressed stones, portions of columns and many ornamented blocks bearing inscriptions were quarried from the public buildings and the temples of Ephesus for the castle walls, and even in the poorest houses, in some wretched slums, you may suddenly spot the glimmer of fractured marble. Your guesthouse in Selçuk might well have a Corinthian capitol as a seat in the shade by the door. The Roman aqueduct still steps through the town and anyone inclined to can copy the inscriptions embedded topsy-turvy in its pillars. Such details are the stuff on which the nostalgic imagination of the early travelers fed.

Teos, among thorns and holm-oaks, entirely deserted, is in that sense a classic site. The fields the peasants plow there are almost choked with sherds. Priene on its hill looks across to Miletus—over what was the sea, over what is now a dusty plain. And at Pergamum something barbaric has been done, something at least as shocking as the things the early travelers were affronted by. You get to the Sanctuary of Asclepius, God of Healing, through barbed wire, past soldiers with submachine-guns. You are forbidden to take photographs of the famous view from the theater because that famous view is now, largely, of a military camp. The Sacred Way, which used to link the Sanctuary with the Acropolis, is severed by wire now and blocked by a row of neatly parked tanks.

I have been writing here about the beginnings of western travel in Greece, and I make no secret of my sympathy with those first explorers. Their interest was predominantly Hellenist. In what other spirit would they have gone? True, others were in the country for quite different purposes—commercial, diplomatic, military—but they are not the ones who wrote accounts. The documentation of early travel in Greece is very much colored by the travelers' perception of that land as supremely important for their own and their national culture. I doubt if any traveler can be quite rid of that sense even today. There is something compelling about the old images still. Myths are as necessary as they ever were, and some myths are more productive than others. We all know what the worst are: in Greece, still, we can glimpse some of the best.

For the early traveler classical sites were often difficult to locate; ruins were more likely to be piles of rubble than the reconstructed temples that greet the visitor today.

Themiſtocles for his Meat, as *Lampſaca* was for his Wine, and *Magneſia* for his Bread.   Although *Strabo* here brags to be ſo exact in his Geography ; yet he and *Ptolomy* do not agree concerning the Bounds of *Ionia* and *Caria*.   For *Ptolomy* makes the *Meander* to part *Ionia* and *Caria* ; and alſo placeth *Pyrrha, Heraclea,* and *Miletum* in *Caria :* whereas *Strabo* makes this part of the *Meander* to be in *Ionia* ; and alſo placeth *Pyrrha, Heraclea,* and *Miletum* in *Ionia* ; as alſo, *Myuns :* about half a Mile beyond which begins *Caria,* at a little Village called *Thymbræa.*   But both of them put Mount *Latmus* between *Heraclea* and *Miletum* ; and ſo far agree in the *Topography,* or Order of placing them. However the queſtion, *viz.* Whether *Palatſha* we were now ſpeaking of, be the antient *Miletum,* or *Pyrrha,* muſt remain ſtill in doubt.   For *Pliny* placeth *Miletum* at ten *Stadia* diſtant from the Mouth of the *Meander* ; but yet placeth *Mons Latmus* after it.

About five in the Afternoon they parted from *Palatſha,* and about two hours after came to a *Greek* Village, where they lay ; from whence two hours more in the Morning, brought them to the bottom of a Bay, which they call the *Gulph of Samos* ; perhaps formerly *Latmicus Sinus :* going on ſtill by the Sea-ſide, they found the Ruins of a vaſt Structure, called by the *Turks, Jotan.*   Dr *Pickering* was of opinion, That it was the Sepulcher of *Mauſolus,* built by *Artemiſia* to the Honour of her Husband at *Halicarnaſſus,* and one of the Seven Wonders of the World.   For it is yet moſt ſplendid in its vaſt Ruins, built of white Marble, and adorned with Pillars of all Orders ; of which two only were entire of the *Ionick* Order, with an Architrave on them.   But I believe the Doctor was ſhort a great way, in his Conjecture of that *Mauſolum,* as will appear further.   I ſuppoſe it to be only the Ruins
of

JOTAN.

THE GREEK WAY OF LIFE

Imagine that you are a guest in a Greek family house on a Sunday afternoon; you have just finished an immense and leisurely dinner, and though your head floats with a pleasantly sleepy retsina high, the weight in your stomach keeps you earthbound. Buoyant dinner repartee subsides as appetites are sated, and someone lazily flicks on the television. A low clarinet wails plaintively, and as the picture focuses, you perceive a dozen human forms clasping a chain of kerchiefs and gravely circling a green hilltop: women shapeless in weighty layers of embroidered frocks with wide bronze belts and men in white skirts and tights and pom-poms on their shoes. The camera coyly keeps a discreet distance, as if catching the dancers unaware at their customary Sunday afternoon dance, so you cannot yet discern their shy smiles or the identical chorus line of factory-made shoes. "Epirots," your hostess remarks off-handedly, "how do you drink your coffee?"

"Our Greek Folk Songs" is broadcast nationwide every Sunday afternoon on the state-run television. With the traditional Sunday afternoon dancing now mostly a picturesque memory, the broadcast makes a peculiarly appropriate substitute. Electronic impulses transmit the deep-voiced clarinet, the distinctive costumes, the alpine vista, the ponderous "Berati" dance, but the "Epirotness" which these symbols evoke is oddly tamed. In the mid-1980s, regional consciousness verges dangerously upon a sentimental "*folklorismös.*" It often seems a parlor game of a regional trivia shorn of its divisive power: knowing that Kalymnians wrap *dolmádhes* in cabbage—not grape—leaves, that potatoes in the "village salad" signal a Cycladic chef, that the novelist Kazantzákis hails from Crete and the popular singer Kazantzídhis, beloved of immigrants and workers, from Asia Minor.

But regionalism was in earlier days hardly a matter of songs and salads. Of neighboring Italy, in the early days of its nationhood, D'Azeglio remarked ruefully that "now that Italy had been created, it was necessary to invent the Italians." And was Greece so very different? The travel-writer Patrick Leigh

Fermor once described the Greek world as "an inexhaustible Pandora's box of eccentricities" and doubtless an extreme topography has nurtured great variety in a relatively little land. Vlach-speaking shepherds in the Macedonian mountains had little contact and little enough in common with shipbuilders of Chios or Jewish merchants of Ioannina. Though not all communities were equally isolated by terrain, they tended to be introverted socially. *Xénos*, the "foreigner-stranger-guest," is in Greece an elastic designation, and brides marrying in from the next village forever remained

"strangers" in their husbands' village.

It was not just the land which came between them: but differences in language, culture, religion, education, class. At the same time, that Kutsovlach shepherd was typically polyglot, speaking his own romance language with his kin, Greek with the cheese-merchants, a smattering of Albanian and Macedonian with the villagers he encountered on his treks with the sheep, and enough Turkish to outwit the odd Ottoman official. Under the tolerant Ottomans, a plethora of religious and ethnic communities thrived: Greek-speaking Orthodox, Macedonian-speaking Orthodox, Bulgarian-speaking Muslims, Romaniot and Sephardic Jews, Turkish farmers, Gypsies, Francolevantine Catholics in the Cyclades,

Protestants converted by American missionaries in Asia Minor, Orthodox Albanian shepherds, crypto-Jewish Muslims of Salonika and Smyrna ... the list goes on. From this multiplicity, the inhabitants of a newly invented, formally secular nation-state of Greece were charged with inventing *themselves* anew.

The cultural homogeneity which undeniably exists today is as much a goal and a consequence as a precondition of this new nationalism. With one eye on the past and the other on the West, official policies of the Greek state have long worked to eradicate—or at the very least, to trivialize—local variations in language, dialect and custom. Differences which seemed to threaten the integrity of the state—like the speaking of Slavic-Macedonian—have been systematic-

all the same?" they query. All roads may lead to an ever-bloating Athens, and in many regards the most vivid distinction today is between "Athens" and "everywhere else," yet Greeks continue merrily ragging the "dour" plains farmer, the "gullible" Pondios, the "dull-witted" Chiot. Stereotypes of ethnic-groups coexist with stereotypes of regions and topographies. In a society fascinated with "appearances" the stereotype of a place becomes part of its reality, and to see the mountains, the plains and the islands as the Greeks do one must set out on the journey across their cultural terrain.

In the Mountains

"The Blue Guide hardly knows the existence of scenery except under the guise of the

ally suppressed. More insidious, the traditional refusal of both the state and private investors to develop the provinces economically has inflamed a ruinous pattern of poverty, massive emigration to Athens and abroad, and a frequent sense of cultural inferiority by those who have remained in the "backwaters."

Even so, the monolithic vision of the official state, with its images of Pericles and Kolokotrónis, has always been quietly subverted from below. "The people," a categorical fiction required by the new nation, which meant—until PASOK reappropriated the word—"everybody except the Athenians," refuse to imagine themselves a lumpish mass, and remain stubbornly sure of essential differences amongst them. "Are the fingers of one hand

picturesque. The picturesque is found any time the ground is uneven." If there is any truth to Roland Barthes' wicked verdict, Greece is a veritable paradise of the picturesque. From the scrubby hills of central Greece to the soaring peaks and wide wooded vales of the majestic Pindos, the land seems in continuous undulation, and even from the plains—a "relative" term, so little do they recall the great flats of Nebraska or Hungary—the mountains seldom disappear from view. Those of a romantic sensibility, who look for the truth in the land, often claim that the irregularity of its surfaces has most forcefully shaped "the Greek character." Surely this gives too little credit to humans, who alter the land as they confront each other.

And yet, many contours of Greek experience —ways of making a living, governing and fighting—doubtless arise from this rugged topography.

The settlement of Greeks in mountainous areas has not been stable and continuous, and for many groups, is "traditional" only if we don't look back too far. Of course, some settlements are of a Byzantine or Frankish vintage. And certain tribal groups of transhumant shepherds—Sarakatsanides, Karagunides, Kutsovlachs, Arvanitovlachs — who herd their sheep and goats on mountainsides in summer and move them to the plains in winter, have probably always wandered widely across the Balkan territories. Of these, all except the Sarakatsanides built permanent mountain villages where women, elders and infants kept

the time-honored random piracy of the Aegean became altogether systematic, with pirates looting merchant ships then selling the booty at low prices to other, competing merchants, who resold the goods within the Empire. Pirates apparently did not always confine themselves to ships.

Pirates did not venture far inland, though, and in the first hundred years of Ottoman rule, when peasants enjoyed a level of justice and prosperity far above that of their counterparts in feudal serfdom in Europe, inaccessible mountaintops held fewer attractions. But as the centralized system—and the safeguards it had ensured—began to break down, Christian and Muslim peasants became increasingly vulnerable to exploitation from all sides: from their Turkish landlord anxious for profits

home fires burning when the men descended each winter with the sheep. However, other sedentary mountain villages found their raison d'être in conditions of Ottoman life.

In island and coastal regions, many towns were (and many still are) situated not at the portside but high on the crest of the mountain, even—indeed, preferably—hidden from view altogether. This town-plan was a response to the threat of pirates. In the late 16th century, when the Ottoman State began its long decline,

from maize and wheat sold to the West, from local bands of brigands who periodically helped themselves to the peasants' crops and livestock, from unruly Janissaries—the Sultan's professional army—extorting tributes for their "protection." By the 17th century, vast stretches of countryside began emptying, as disgruntled peasants fled to the cities and upwards to the mountains.

Mountain settlements multiplied, interspersed among already established villages whose inhabitants made a living (sometimes a handsome living) not only by farming and shepherding, but as itinerant stone-masons and charcoal-makers, as wandering merchants and muleteers and mountain guides to Turks and travelers, and as artisans and immigrant

Left, shepherd wearing traditional Cretan scarf. Above, two sisters tell a story.

laborers to richer regions of the Empire. Still required to pay the annual tithe to the Sultan, newly settled peasants terraced the rocky mountainsides, wresting a meager living from their flocks and gardens and small fruit orchards. Still vulnerable to extortion by brigand and Ottoman official alike, the community drew inward, socially and physically. In this setting developed the ethic and organization of village life which has come to be regarded —by foreigners, but by Greeks, too—as quintessentially "Greek."

For as much as the mountains dominate the topography, the mountain village and the mountain man dominate the modern Greek imagination. The mountain is no more a physical entity than an idea—indeed, a cluster of ideas, even contradictory, evoking both the

but so beautiful . . .

The mountain village typically comprises a cluster of houses, often with adjoining walls, circling a central church and a square. This physical arrangement reveals a moral geography, for the boundary between the "civilized" human space and an unsanctified wilderness teeming with human and supernatural dangers is marked by a ring of tiny churches and shrines. United by Orthodoxy and a common way of life, villagers were nonetheless divided into separate households. The family, rather than the individual, was— and is—the central unit of Greek society, enormously interdependent economically, socially and emotionally, and whatever the harmony or tumult within its four walls, to the "outside" the "house" stood united. Indeed,

heroic and the ridiculous. What the mountains (in the generic and the particular) mean to Greeks today recalls no mere Olympian mythology but rather, a chain of associations dense in history and sentiment—which no map or photograph or hike to the summit can easily convey.

The "traditional" mountain village: Every Easter Athens spits out its millions toward numberless villages, only to swallow them up again two weeks later, laden with baskets of olive oil, cheese, homemade bread. Every Athenian, every Salonikan speaks reverently of "his or her" village, and when was "his or her" village ever *not* a mountain village? The mountain village is never merely real but partakes of the archetype, the village poor in all but rocks. Ah,

the unconditional loyalty to the family and the demand that each member helps further its collective interests made friendships outside the house inevitably fragile. Tenuously bound by ties of religion and local patriotism, these families competed for scarce resources: for land, water, pasturage, and for that most ephemeral substance: honor.

Anthropologists, who have tended to study small villages, have conventionally identified "honor" and "shame" as key moral values in Greece. According to this moral code, a family could rarely be considered to have honor if its women were seen to be immodest. Since Orthodox teachings and native thought both agreed that woman was by nature sensual and seductive, social chaos was avoided by strictly segregating unrelated men and women, and defining various tasks as "male" or "female." Segregation relaxed only during feastdays and weddings. Girls and women had always to be accountable, and even so, could find themselves victims of innuendo and slander if they strayed from strict conventions of conduct. The jealous or suspicious attacked with words. "The tongue has no bone and yet it smashes bones!" In turn, male relatives were responsible to defend, and in some cases, to avenge with blood, insults to women's reputations.

Recent work suggests that the image of meek womenfolk in household purdah and domineering but protective men is both outdated and overly simplistic. Moreover, what acting "honorably" means varies from one Greek community to the next, and whether "facticity."

A Sarakatsanides feast: From the grounds of the monastery, thick with cherry and chestnut, to the encampment of Sarakatsanides it is less than an hour's walk. Yet the land itself never hints at any human presence in this high landscape, and it was on the barest trace of a path that we threaded our way along a mountainside choked with trees and brush one afternoon in August. Only Tassoula, the daughter of a family which ran a restaurant for the visitors, could read its signs. She was engaged to a Sarakatsanides policeman who had taken her once to show her off to the distant kin camped in these mountains, and she plainly found them both quaint and exotic. "Sarakatsanides women," she insisted as we wended our way through the shadows, "they

one is rich or poor, male or female. Today, to be *filótimos*, to "love honor," can mean something as vague as acting as a "good" person should, though this presupposes no small knowledge of what the community considers good. It differs from the Protestant idea of "conscience" in one crucial way: one must *be seen* to act honorably, for it is a judgement which only others—almost begrudgingly—bestow. In such conditions, reputation becomes all-important, taking on a public

Gypsies, Greece's migrant farmers, stop for a midday picnic (left); and a smile for the camera (above).

know nothing about sex. When they have their babies, they are still virgins!"

When we finally emerged from the canopy of trees, we could see a flat and treeless plateau, and upon it three huts constructed on branches, a mud-oven and a cooking fire. Tassoula shouted a greeting, which set a dog yelping, and a laughing woman in a kerchief invited our little band of four to the campsite.

We stayed the afternoon, squeezed together all eight of us on a cot of branches, thick with woven blankets and sheepskin *flokatis*, fed on stodgy and slightly sweet cheese-pies warm from the oven, talking with the women and the young girls. Eleni, 15, was on holiday from secondary school in Larissa, on the plains, where she lived in the winter months with relations who had already left the difficult shepherding life. She loved the sheep and the mountains, she confessed, but she wanted to be a secretary. Deep lines engrained her forehead and folded around her small but sparkling eyes, and only a mild case of acne and the flat immaturity of her features betrayed her adolescence.

Because it was a feast day—the Assumption of the Virgin Mary—the three Marias in this encampment of 19 souls were "celebrating," and by late afternoon, the central ground between the thatch houses filled with grimy children and many new adults. The old man—Eleni's grandfather—entered with a sheep's cape around his shoulder and a long carved shepherd's crook. Tassoula, delighting in this folkloric relic, insisted that I take her photo,

Arab, and I will ask him how love is caught. From the eyes it starts, then descends to the lips, from the lips to the heart." (The song continues on—and down—but a look of panic from the girls and it faltered there.)

An ancient truck lurched up an invisible road and screeched noisily behind the huts, and the dance dissolved in excitement. The driver, yet another young man, was greeted with raucous hoots and cheerfully complied with the dancers' now insistent demands to turn on the "kaséta." He turned the volume up "full." The music, sizzling with static, gashed at the green tranquility of the hill, but even this frantic distortion could not quite block out the thumping base which signaled when to move our feet and our bodies. When we tired of dancing, we sat on the ground, mugged for the

the crook laid across her shoulders.

Three youths soon followed, dusty and smelling of sheep and Turkish tobacco. We discovered then the bittersweet twist to the celebration, for these three cousins were soon to be inducted into their army service. Amongst much giggling, the central ground became a dance floor, but as we had no music, we sang. The youths wrapped their arms across each other's shoulders, and in voices deepened with exaggerated bravado, started the simple tune, "I'll become a swallow, and fly to Arabia . . ." The girls, hand in hand, echoed the verse, slightly out of time and out of tune but suitably shrill in feminine contrast. We circled, stepping grandly if somewhat out of kilter, "I'll fly to Arabia, and marry a black

camera and the young men sang us a song in praise of King Constantine, and another about the "boys of '21" (*eighteen* twenty-one!), lazily tapping and strumming the beat on a milk can.

The myth of the mountain man: The mythology of the mountains is emphatically masculine. Greeks are inclined—like the romantics among us—to see in the mountain man an embodiment of alpine virtue: in his "craggy" face they discern a "harsh" pride, a "rugged"

The post-dictatorship generation: rebels without a cause? Caught between the East and the West, the Greek youth struggle for a new identity.

individualism, a moral "purity" as pristine as the mountain springs. To the ferocious clans of the Mani and Crete which always kept the Turks at bay, and the Souliot women who danced into the abyss rather than submit to the finally victorious Turks, they reserve their highest praise. In the figure of the *Klepht* they celebrate a more pugnacious heroism. Scholars protest that the *Klepht*—which means "thief"—was seldom more than a self-serving outlaw, preying on landlord and peasant alike, intent on building a local empire in the time-honored Balkan style combining coercion of the weak and spoils to his own minions. But in the national mythology, the *Klephts* became symbols of resistance to the "hated Turkish oppressor." If the myth glorifies a selfless klephtic patriotism, surely the Greeks do not fail to relish the cunning which turned patriotism to personal advantage.

On the slopes of Crete's Mount Ida, shepherds steal each other's sheep to prove their honor and daring, and insist that their way of life upholds a Greek ideal degraded by morally slack, soft-palmed Athenian bureaucrats. And 40 years ago, during the German occupation, resistance fighters lived like klephtic heroes, in small wandering bands and attacked from the mountains. The great rebel leaders, the *kapetans*, absorbed that heroic aura and held control of a newly democratized, mountainous "Free Greece" long after the Germans were ousted. To many, the *kapetans* resuscitated a dream of a Greece liberated from foreign domination—not Turks this time, but Germans and Brits and Americans. The image lives, but the dream died.

Of Vlachs and empty mountains: There is an underside to the myth of mountain man. The word *Vlachos*—both the ethnic label of many of Greece's transhumant shepherds, and the simple occupational term for "shepherd"—holds a hint of scorn. It is the Greek equivalent to the term "hill-billy" and draws on the same imagery. Moreover, *vlachos* sounds almost like *vlakos*, "idiot," and though Greek ears keenly distinguish *chi's* from *kappa's*, the phonic resemblance is gleefully savored. *Vlachi*—the lot of them—are the butt of countless jokes, which portray them as brawny but dull and silent.

This underside reveals less about ethnic slurs than about a vaguely guilty disdain for a whole way of life. As people have out of hunger and hopelessness gradually abandoned the mountains for Athens and Chicago and Vancouver, they have learned to reject that life, even to see that once "heroic" shepherd as uncouth, unlettered, slightly ridi-

culous. The conditions of contemporary life in a developing nation-state make the mountain life less rewarding than ever: social services do not reach them, national borders once open are now strictly patroled, shepherds clash with mountain farmers over land-rights as grazing lands shrink, and Athenian bureaucrats uneasy with wandering shepherd communities invent endless rules and regulations to control them. And even if the land could support the huge flocks and fortunes of the past, the children won't stay. They are looking for cleaner, more secure, more prestigious jobs in the towns.

On the lower slopes, some villages survive by combining small-scale shepherding and livestock raising with the growing of high-quality tobacco and cereals, and by cultivating orchards which thrive in the cooler climate: peaches, apples, pears, cherries, walnuts and chestnuts. If they happen to ,be beautiful—like old stone-built villages—and not too hard to find, they might attract tourists, and sell them sweaters and weavings and souvenir hand-carved shepherds' crooks. The socialist government has tried to encourage cottage industry and collectives; a valiant gesture, but after decades of neglect, it is too little, too late. Perhaps they will be discovered by wealthy urbanites willing to renovate a crumbling house as a holiday retreat. (Indeed, the landscape between villages, once empty, is now dotted with alpine pre-fabs and magnificent concrete eyesores.) All too many villages are hardly more than "old people's homes," with too few children to support a school (to say nothing of a doctor), where the only weddings are those of the children of urban migrants returning for a "traditional" celebration in their parents' beloved village, and where Gypsy musicians complain that celebrations have become "cold" things. At the funerals—far outnumbering weddings—old women lament not only their dead kin but the empty houses of this high place, "forgotten by God."

In the Plains

The plains—the *kambi*, as Greeks call them—hold no hallowed place in the national mythology. Marshy and malarial, muggy in summers and muddy in winters, they have seldom inspired the poets, who find few metaphors in their flatness. So absent among the rocks and mountains and sea and sun of the tourist board posters, we are almost surprised that plains exist here. Redeemed at times by the curiosities of human architecture (the abundance of windmills on Crete's Lassithi Plain) or by the surprise of mountains (Mount

Parnassus rising from the Boeotian plains) the *kambi* arouse our respectful interest, not our passions.

Yet the plains—flat, rolling, and if we stretch the term, sloping patches of plateau—have been among the most coveted of spaces in Greece. Certainly the Ottomans recognized their value. As their empire expanded in the 15th century, they awarded a parcel (*timar*) of this most fertile of Greek land to each loyal warrior (*spahi*). In return for defending and managing (not owning) this land (since all land belonged to Allah, and was overseen by his earthly representative, the Sultan), he was allowed to collect a set tithe from Muslim and Christian peasants who retained firm rights to cultivate it. It was a system designed to prevent a strong landed aristocracy (of the sort which

never recognized as legal by the Ottoman state, enriched the landlord but made the sharecropping peasant poorer and less secure, sometimes ending a harvest season with barely a third of what he and his family had produced. Forced to borrow from the *chiflik* owner to buy food and tools, the peasants also found themselves perpetually in debt, and thus, like serfs, bound to the land.

Those who did not escape endured poverty and upheaval. Many such peasants joined in the early 19th-century struggles for national independence in the hope of acquiring a bit of the ousted Turks' lands. As it happened, some land fell into the hands of equally powerful Greek landlords, while other properties reverted to the state. Many families acquired small pieces by "squatting" while formal

wreaked havoc in a deteriorating Byzantium) and as long as it worked, the peasants fared reasonably well. As it began to break down in the face of pressures from the West as from within the Empire, peasants suffered.

From the 16th century onward, the *timar* system gradually gave way to that of the infinitely more oppressive *chiflik*. The Ottomans had initially introduced the *chiflik* —a large track of land under hereditary ownership—as a way of putting previously unused land under cultivation, but this relatively minor form of landholding gradually became dominant, coming to include formerly *timar* lands and expanding to the fertile plains areas of the Peloponnese, Thessaly, Macedonia and Thrace. These *chiflikia*,

redistribution of Turkish *chiflikia* proceeded fitfully. In 1905 and 1910, the government's failure to redistribute *chiflikia* of the rich Thessalian plains, annexed to Greece in 1871, resulted in peasant revolts, bloodily repressed. Anxious to stave off a serious social revolution, Venizelos in 1909 launched a program of radical reform, including land reform; but this faltered in mid-course when Greece became embroiled in the Balkan Wars. The 1923 exchange of populations between Greece and Turkey—the aftermath of the Asia Minor catastrophe—forced the government's hand, and thousands of the 1.5 million Greek-speaking refugees were resettled in Macedonia and Thrace, on *chiflikia* and in houses and villages abandoned by the Turks. Major land-reform was completed only when Metaxas, a bizarrely populist-fascist dictator, came to power in the 1930s.

A continuity of uncertainty: The major way of making a living on the plains has always been farming. Despite the richness of much of this land, most farmers have remained poor, especially in relation to their European counterparts. This is less a consequence of peasant fatalism, familism, and superstition than of a complex combination of factors, including historical patterns of land ownership, Greek state policies, patterns of economic interdependence between Greece and the West, and various commercial priorities and practices over which the farmer had no control.

A chronic problem of Greek agriculture has

pattern established in the 16th century— where Europe looked to Greece for cheap agricultural goods (and cheap immigrant labor, one might add) while requiring Greece to import manufactured goods—has not fundamentally changed.

Historical conditions have also quite literally "shaped" agricultural lands. Large farmsteads are rare; rather, farmers have traditionally clustered their houses in a village and walked out daily (and today, ride out on donkeys or tractors) to scattered fields. Inheritance practices, though varying somewhat among localities, have generally ensured that a father's fields, and those his wife had brought as part of her dowry, would be divided equally among all his children, with daughters awarded their portion—or its

always been too many farmers for the land to support. Small plots and inefficient farming methods made life on the land quite marginal, yet few alternatives outside of emigration to America existed in the 19th and early 20th century. The nascent handicrafts industry had already been wiped out by the cheapness of English mass-produced goods and the rich Diaspora Greeks who controlled most of Greece's private capital were reluctant to invest in industry, which has remained underdeveloped to the present day. Indeed, the

Greek salads with feta, olives and lots of the local baker's bread for dunking are a welcome meal any time of day.

equivalent in livestock, a house, or cash—as a dowry at marriage. Since fields varied in fertility, protection from wind and access to water, it has not been uncommon for even small parcels to be subdivided, and then re-subdivided, with each generation.

The system is not as mad as we might think. It is surprising to learn, accustomed as we are to thinking that only massive fields and mono-cropping make sense, that a handful of tiny plots, growing varied produce, may provide the farmer a real stability in areas where rain is unpredictable and soil fertility marginal. "A little bit of everything" can be better than a big crop that fails... Indeed, farmers throughout Greece make a virtue of the fragmentation caused by both social custom and the land's own irregularity, expertly nurturing even tiny and awkwardly situated pockets of arable land. Farmers' ingenuity is especially remarkable in mountainous locales, where (inheritance practices aside) an uneven terrain precludes large fields. Instead, neat, narrow terraced gardens hug the mountain slopes.

Yet, the land's progressive fragmentation has sometimes reached ludicrous proportions. Tales abound of single trees—an olive tree, say, or walnut tree—in which 15 households of second- and third-cousins own shares. Ironically, such a tree often goes unharvested: trying to gather all 15 representatives (some of whom have now moved to Athens, others to Australia) to harvest together is a logistical nightmare, and those who could be present are

owners search for extra hands at harvest time. Along with impoverished tourists and local day-laborers, Gypsies figure importantly in this migrant labor force. Though wages are often low, such seasonal work allows them to preserve their independence. While their Romany-speaking compatriots (perhaps 100,000 or more live in Greece) survive as musicians or peddlers, these Gypsies move across the land with the harvests, setting up roadside encampments of trucks and tents.

Like peasants everywhere, Greek farmers were—and are—perpetually vulnerable to all manner of disaster: drought and pestilence, crop failures, fluctuations in the price of agricultural produce internationally and locally, the whims of changing governments. Indebtedness—to the grocer, as to the state-

unwilling to risk "misunderstandings," like accusations of filching, from those who cannot. On the ground, plots become so small, and so scattered, they cannot support a family. Disputes over the boundaries of agricultural fields have consequently always been rife in farming villages, and indeed, a site on which competition between families is vented. A farmer who would never dream of stealing his neighbor's wallet will plow a few inches into the neighboring field, and congratulate his own cunning when the neighbor fails to notice.

The large agricultural estate—whether an Ottoman legacy or a more recent conglomeration—can be found, too. From Nauplia's citrus groves to Naoussa's peach orchards and Thessaly's fields of cotton, estate

controlled Agricultural Bank (established in 1929) which they approach for loans—has been the rule. Farmers once dependent on the *chiflik* owner have now become dependent on the state.

Indeed, one of the basic themes in farming life is the confrontation between the farmer and the state bureaucracy. Traditionally, the only place more crowded than the land was the civil service. When the state apparatus was being developed after 1830, politicians and lawyers with "pull" handed out endless minor clerkships to their constituents fleeing rural poverty. (By 1880, Greece had seven times as many civil servants per 10,000 as Britain.) Thus was created a bloated bureaucracy of barely literate peasants, mostly from the then-politically dominant Peloponnese. Even today, if you talk to plains farmers from the north (and since most such farmland is in Thessaly, Thrace and Macedonia, their attitudes reveal a double antagonism: north vs. south, farmer vs. functionary), they are scornful of the southerners who—until recently—seemed to occupy with all the self-importance they could muster the bulk of the clean and comfortable civil posts: doctors, teachers, lawyers, administrators, policemen. *Palioelladhítis!* the farmers sneer, punning wickedly, for the term remarks not only on such a man's origin in "Old Greece," the still-shrunken nation before the northern provinces were annexed after 1871, but also on his depravity. To call someone a *palioánthropo* is to call him a "dirty old man," a lech, a dis-

to process even the most routine applications without the immediate superior's approval; while he, in turn, checked with *his* superior, and as requests climbed, so did the piles of paper. Moreover, unless the farmer had some moral claim on him—as a relative, godparent, or co-villager—the bored civil servant offered him only the most perfunctory assistance. Understandably daunted by this state of affairs, farmers turned to those they considered to have "means" (*mesa*) to intervene at higher levels and push through their modest requests. The local politician, the ambitious lawyer, the doctor with connections "helped" the less powerful, obliging them to return the favor (their votes or their custom) afterward. Born of such conditions, patronage became endemic. Providing individualistic solutions

honorable parasite, but then, northerners are fond of saying that the poor but powerful southerners are parasitical on the north's wealth. "The civil service is a big cow," they explain, "and we Macedonians, we are the grass she eats and eats. When she is finished, the politicians milk her dry, and she is so happy, she drops a great load of shit on us!"

To farmers, the impersonal bureaucracy was just as arbitrary as any Ottoman official, and infinitely less responsive. Its hierarchical character has meant that petty clerks refused

to systemic problems (and obstructing the requests of the "uncooperative"), patronage thwarted collective action among farmers, at the same time as it ensured that they remain politically and socially docile. Yet resentment to the system grew as well, and it was in no small part PASOK's pledge to make war on *rousfeti*, "string-pulling," that landed its election victory in 1981.

A Macedonian "Coffee-Bar-Disco": In southern Macedonia, in the melodious-sounding region of Roumlouki, a refugee village of 800—laid out in the typical manner of such "new" villages, with individual houses plunked onto individual plots in symmetrical rows—sits on the crevice joining mountain to plain. Looking backwards, westwards, that is, you see only

Left, a happy farmer during harvest. Above, workers enjoy a mid-morning snack.

green mountain rising. Looking eastward—as all the houses do—to the sea, invisible yet present, you see an endless, hazy flatness. Once a *chiflik*, cultivated with tobacco, it is now covered with peach orchards and fields of wheat.

The village is described by one travel guide as "insignificant"; presumably it cannot compete with the spectacular ancient ruins found nearby. And although it is in summer deluged by busloads of tourists, in winter it supports only one young archaeologist and one bored archaeological guard. Oblivious to its fame, the village carries on in its quite ordinary way. Like many in the area, it is ethnically mixed: half "indigenous Macedonians," wiry and taciturn with an accent both thick and abrupt; and half "Pondi," refugees from the

queen, is 15, chubby and wants to be an actress, and she is the only girl (except for me) in the "Paradise," a bleak, chilly coffee-bar in the upstairs of a two-story concrete cavern. She chatters gaily while her 17-year-old brother, Yannis, on whom she dotes, and who is now "chaperoning" her, slouches gloomily at the next table. Since it is winter, the young men aren't sitting on top of tractors or ladders wedged into peach trees, spraying fertilizer and pesticide; instead they're sitting here, not playing cards, not arguing politics (like their fathers), just sitting, smoking, waiting for something to happen.

Amalia's mother, Stavroula, grew up here, a child of Pondian refugees, but her father, Yórgos, was born of refugee parents hailing from Bursa, who were resettled in 1923 in a

Black Sea. Pondi are a remarkable people: literate, progressive,. solidaristic, they still write plays and T.V. serials in their distinctive dialect, while their rhythmically subtle, exhilarating dances are popular throughout the northern countryside. Yet they remain the scapegoats of Greek national humor. The village's Macedonians, though poorer, consider their indigenous status—*dópyi*, "of this place"—a source of an irrefutable moral superiority, and view these interlopers with their strange language "Turks." Though their children study and court and sometimes marry each other, those beyond middle-age stick mostly with their "own people," eyeing each other warily from across the coffeehouse.

Amalia, namesake of Greece's first Bavarian

village near Veria. Yórgos' father was a cloth merchant before the 1922 catastrophe, and could never accustom himself to the farming life. Yórgos, on the other hand, loved to make things grow, but with the devastations of the wars and the uncertainties of farming, he decided to leave the land in 1953, to work in a Germany plastics factory. When he came back in 1963, he married, and opened a small cafe in Veria. But, nostalgic for the "clean air" of the countryside, he made frequent visits to his wife's village, planting peach trees on land she'd inherited from her father, until he decided, in 1982, that they should move there permanently. They opened a small grill on the road at the bottom of town, which a stalwart but always exhausted Stavroula manages.

They began to build a "villa" on the plain. Still in mid-construction, it is a huge damp concrete mansion with marble floors and no toilet.

If it weren't for the "Paradise," Amalia would be miserable. The girls her age never go there—their fathers are too strict, or they're cramming for university entrance exams, so they can escape this place—which just proves her theory that people here are "bad," that they have nothing to do but gossip! Sometimes, Amalia visits her aunt, whose house in the long empty spaces of winter is a gathering place for neighborhood women, and one of them always reads the residue in her coffee-cup, for a laugh, telling her who she'll marry (see "Coffee" in Cultural Dictionary, page 273), while Amalia protests she's not interested in marriage.

Roumlouki plain, until the music shifts. An electric piano thumps out a fast 5/8 rhythm, and teenage stars of the local folk dance troupe, showing off the fancy improvisations they've been learning, lead a long line of pressed bodies through the taut, tiny movements of *tik*.

The changing face of the plains: On a drive through the towns and farming villages of the plains, one is struck by the amount of new house construction and farm machinery. Indeed, with tractors and earthmovers and ubiquitous mud, the scene often evokes a real estate venture before landscaping. Post-war economic aid certainly helped rebuild the countryside. But the noticeable bourgeoisification of the wealthier farming villages has also depended on the surplus of farmers emigrating

She won't have to stay here forever. Her parents have already built her a flat in Veria— her "dowry" house. They don't really want her to marry a farmer; a bank teller would be nice, or some decent fellow with his own shop. Like the one with the record store who makes the "pirated" tape copies for the "Paradise Disco," where every Saturday night, teenagers from the surrounding villages gather to primly sip beer and whiskey, and smoke and watch each other. There, strobes throbbing, Madonna crooning in her little-girl voice, you'd never know you were on the edge of a

Tobacco is mainly cultivated in the northern plains. Left, a woman prepares a bunch for drying. Above, a close-up of tobacco leaves.

(alone or with their families) to Germany and Australia in the 1950s and '60s, or to the oil-rigs of Saudi Arabia in the '70s. The village prospered from the handsome remittances sent back to their families; at the same time, relatives and neighbors were often able to rent or sharecrop the fields left behind.

It is one of modernization's contradictions that mechanized farming has, in a pattern familiar from the Third World, frequently marginalized women, whose farming skills and labor are rendered obsolete. While women have by no means left the land completely, many find themselves imprisoned in a domesticity their mothers never knew. They remember the drudgery of farming in the pre-tractor era with little fondness, yet the oft-heard remark that such a housewife "just sits" reminds them of their economic dependency on their husbands. It also betokens a loss of status and power, for men are skeptical when "the little housewives" (*nikokyróules*) start talking "*feminisimós*." "It's men who are oppressed," they protest, "we work so you can eat." High inflation and rising material aspirations mean that most families want the woman to bring in wages, but opportunities in farming villages are limited. A woman might earn a little extra by contracting with large garment companies to do piecework at her own sewing machine, a practice which alleviates the problem of finding childcare but denies her a secure income and most social security benefits. Other women work in family shops or small enterprises.

Some farming villages look more affluent, and some farmers are no doubt wealthier than before. Yet farming life is still perceived as dirty, exhausting and unpredictable, and the horizons of village life limited by few jobs and a dearth of entertainment and cultural life. The farmers' children tend to marry out, and the migratory current still flows towards the cities. It remains to be seen whether PASOK's "decentralization" scheme—bringing small hospitals, day-care centers, adult education and greater administrative autonomy to the countryside—and the increasingly unlivable conditions of Athens, can turn the stream.

In the Islands

"Little sea, who has drowned
The young girl's husband,

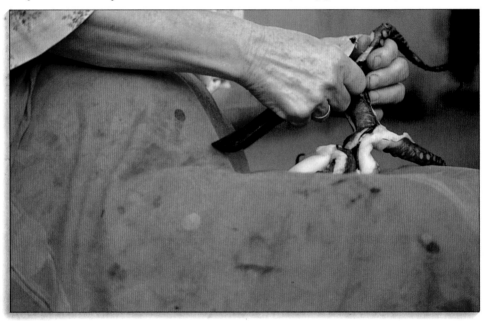

It is partly in response to the village's limited work opportunities that parents want an urban bridegroom for their daughter, and a professional job for their son. Here, women with no special skills may find jobs in light industry—cutting or stitching in garment workshops, or stuffing sliced pears into cans. In a gesture which promotes—not just anticipates—this move, the "dowry" flat is now likely to be bought or built in Athens or Salonika, or in one of the larger plains towns, like Serres, Katerini, Tripoli. Often, instead of a flat, parents fund a daughter's education—from beautician's training to a law degree—which will guarantee her greater financial security and a higher status bridegroom, to boot.

Bring back my love, my little bird.
The girl is young,
Black does not become her,
My little sea.
— (*Thallasáki*, Kalymnian song)

When the foreigners began to descend on the islands, first in dribbles and then in droves, it was perhaps their worship of the sea which first amazed the island inhabitants. But tourists, who appear in the summertime, are to the sea only fair-weather friends, lured by her tranquil visage, azure and clear and benign. They lie dreamily on the sands, courting the sun for a golden-brown color eschewed not so many years ago by the island aristocrats as a mark of a common laborer, in a state of public undress unimaginable to the sartorially puritanical natives. The tourist encounters the sea playfully, teases her edges (for in the Greek vernacular, the sea is a "she") and leaves her at the holiday's end. The tourist comes to the island for the sea, by way of the sea. The water is both a presence and a boundary, wetly delimiting the spaces of work and leisure, duty and pleasure.

If the tourist regards the island as a temporary escape and the sea as soothing and benevolent, the perspective of those who live, and who have lived for generations, on the island, is rather different. In the early days of tourism, islanders seldom knew how to swim, and children who ventured too far into the waters were regularly snatched by shrieking

Geologically, the 1,425 isles in Greek territorial waters are born of the meeting of sea and mountain, for the isles are merely the crests of now submerged mountain ranges. About one tenth of these are inhabited, some by a few monks and goats. It is tempting to stretch the comparison, for the individuality of each island in its architecture, costume and dialect is striking, and would seem to suggest an isolation reminiscent of high mountain villages. Yet this individuality is not a simple matter of remoteness. To the contrary, there has always been frequent and intense contact among clusters of islands, and within each island group—the central Cyclades, the eastern Dodecanese, the northerly Sporades and the Ionian Islands of the western coast —songs are traded, wives are sometimes

mothers who had no reason to romanticize the sea. To them, the sea was no less treacherous for her beauty. "There are three things to fear in the world," goes an old proverb, "fire, woman, and the sea." Death by the sea is both a memory and an expectation to those who live, winter as in summer, at her edge. They know the winter squalls, the convulsions of rain and wind that erupt without warning and toss fishing *caïques* like so many toy boats in a bathtub. The sea gives life with her fish and her sponges, but also takes it back.

Left, a woman cleaning an octopus. Above, octopus hanging out to dry.

sought, house styles remain familiar. Rather, embedded in the houses and faces and words of each island is its own particular history of labor, ecology and foreign domination.

The pre-modern economy of the sea— piracy and plunder, shipbuilding and manning vast merchant fleets, sponge-diving and trade—made the islands until this century among the richest and most coveted territories in the Mediterranean world. The Ottomans held a much more tenuous and intermittent control on the islands than on the mainland. European principalities, from the "Hospitaler" Knights of St. John to the Venetians, the Genoese, the French and the British, sought through political control and trading privileges to exploit the strategic position and trade of particular islands. Though the object of the European principalities was to extract wealth passing as merchandise through the islands, some wealth stayed on the island, concentrated in the hands of an indigenous elite. This local elite owned land (as in the Ionian Islands) or ships and shipyards (on islands spread from Hydra to Chios), and often cooperated with the Europeans on mutually profitable terms. At the turn of the century, many islands had a clear class hierarchy.

On islands blessed with good soil and adequate water resources, some inhabitants lived then, as today, as farmers, and farmed very much as their compatriots did on the mainland. Grapes, melons, figs, tomatoes, oranges and lemons thrive in the arid summer

pensions when they return home to retire) and on the development of tourism. The elegant mansions which rise along the hill encircling the Simi harbor mutely witness to the incredible wealth of the sea traders and shipbuilders, and renowned sponge divers, but they are empty now, mausoleums, mute testimonies to a way of life which collapsed when upstaged by a steamship economy. The wealthy pulled out their money and moved—to Athens, to Tarpon Springs, Florida, to Argentina. On the skeleton of this affluence a new prosperity is being built. For it is the stark and lovely grandeur of these abandoned houses and harbors which tourist agencies translate as "picturesque" and which draws the concrete-weary foreigners.

A Kalymnian close-up: If you happened to be

heat of many islands, and beans and onions can be coaxed to grow as well. On luxuriant Corfu, tenant farmers labored on the estates of local aristocrats in a system not so different from Turkish *chiflikia*, while in the pre-independence Cyclades, the rocky hills were shared, as in Tinos, between the islanders and a powerful monastery. The significance of farming varied greatly, yet even the most desolate islands usually supported a few vineyards and olive trees.

In many ways, the distinctiveness of each island is a legacy which speaking in the present tense obscures. The island economies of the present, for all except those blessed with fertile land and plenty of water, depend largely on the remittances of island migrants (and their

in Kalymnos in November 1984, you would have seen the twisted wreck of a motorscooter and a tractor, entwined in grotesque metallic embrace, standing like a civic sculpture of some patriotic local hero on the central quay. The authorities put it there as an "example," the crumpled outcome of yet another act of suicidal swagger. The death of two men and the crippling, and maybe eventual death, of a third resulted, or so a shocked and grieving town whispered to each other, when the severely short-sighted (and un-bespectacled) young driver of the motorscooter decided on a very fast late night ride. His friend clutching him from behind, he roared up a dark road in a braggadocio of blind speed (so to speak) and crashed headlong into a tractor coming the other direction. It was a tragedy—but all too typical, for the rate of motorcycle deaths, of both passengers and unwary pedestrians, is horrifyingly high in Kalymnos. Driving a motorcycle very fast was just a new manifestation of a very old code of male bravado.

The Kalymnians like to think of themselves as wild and fearless, rather like their own harsh mountains, and they scorn the soft life of the farmers of verdant Kos, who they sneeringly dub *Kotes*, or "hens." But the tradition of swagger is almost certainly derived from the sponge-divers, who pushed themselves relentlessly in quest of wages and prestige, and profits for their captains, and who daily faced death (in the form of the "bends") in the sea.

The sponge industry is much diminished now, but there are other ways that Kalymnians

sponge-diver who disembarks the Athens steamer in a coffin. It is also thrown on a dare. Very much in the tradition of noise-makers everywhere else in Greece, the thunder and crack of dynamite marks the beginning of Easter. On Easter day several years ago, an accidental explosion, with the power to shatter windows of the harbor shops, killed four young men, but though local businessmen and politicians circulated pleas to stop the madness, the mourners were among the most adamant that the Easter "tradition" must continue. It still goes on.

Fewer men dive for sponges now, though many sign onto the merchant fleets for a few years in the island male's rite of passage, drinking and whoring and spending lavishly in the raucous pattern of sailor life, until they decide

 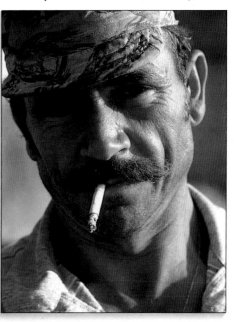

show their *andrismos*, the Greek version of "machismo." Becoming summer *kamáki* (see pages 283–284) is popular among the less imaginative, but this is not unique to Kalymnos, and anyway, tourism is not well developed here. Others show prowess with more dangerous feats. Throwing dynamite off the mountain tops announces, and honors, the Kalymnian who perishes tragically at sea; it is also thought the only seemly tribute to the old

Left, loading fish onto a ferry for transport from the island of Kastellórizon to the island of Rhodes. Above, an empty *kafeneion* in the late afternoon light and a fisherman smoking a cigarette.

it is time to come home and get married. From the 1950s onward, hundreds of men also left for periods of five to 25 years abroad, building highway bridges from Ohio to Florida or sweating in factories, of Darwin, Australia, a city so full of Kalymnians the Australian-Greek taxi-drivers simply call it "Kalymnos." Sometimes these men married a Kalymnian bride and returned abroad with her to raise a family (reemigrating to Kalymnos again a generation later). Just as often, though, men emigrated alone, with cousins and compatriots, leaving the daily management of the island to the women, as their fathers and grandfathers had done before.

The myth of the island woman: In the mythology of the land, the mountain man finds his apogee in the island woman. Mainland Greeks contrast their own heroic traditions of the "masculine" mountains with the "femininity" of the islanders. Island dances are soft and undulating, like the sea, and very quick, they insist, while theirs are upright, rigid and proud, like warriors dancing on mountain peaks. (They forget the low, quick, sweeping *zonarádhiko* of Thracian hills.)

The music, too, is "sweet." In this, they have given a sexual nuance to what is probably more accurately the difference between a refined urban sound and a raucous, rustic style. Never mind that the ubiquitous electric piano has infiltrated the *nisiótika* of popular cassettes—it cannot destroy the lightness of that most popular and familiar genre of island music, a music developed in a network of

the Cyclades and Dodecanese.

The "femininity" which mainlanders attribute to the islands is no doubt intertwined with their suspicion that women actually run things there. And indeed, the seasonal exodus of men as they followed the ships, the fish, the sponges or the factory job in Mannheim or Melbourne, has given many an island a strikingly female character. If tourism has enabled many men to return, the "feminine" quality is still perceptible in the way women dominate neighborhood spaces. "A man is a visitor in his own house," Greeks say, and islanders with even more reason, and men are shooed out of the house every morning so women can get on with their chores. Mainlanders slyly insinuate that island women not only dominate their men, but cuckold them—

wealthy Aegean port cities, including the sophisticated Greek-dominated Asia Minor cities of Smyrna and Constantinople. This style uses an ensemble of stringed instruments: a dolorous, hauntingly human-voiced violin; a santouri—hammer dulcimer of the Orient—whose resonating strings create a waterfall of sound; and the long necked and deep throated voice of the Turkish *ud* (in Greek, the *úti*), or its smaller substitute, the strummed *laúto*. (The reedy island bagpipe, the *tsambúna*, goes unmentioned.) Island songs, with an almost courtly and Venetian chivalry, celebrate love, courtship, beauty: from the Cretan verse-romance *Erotokritos* whose verses still tunefully resound throughout the Aegean, to the improvised teasing couplets, the *pismatiká*, of

after all, how do they manage while their husbands are away months and years at sea? Tales of bored housewives and exhausted island-bound lovers proliferate even on the island, though their veracity remains quite unverifiable.

Yet on some islands, the family of an unmarried girl guards her reputation against slander ("better your eye come out than your name," the proverb warns) with a vehemence rarely found these days on the mainland. On Kalymnos, for instance, coeducation in secondary schools was long resisted; it is only a few years since island teenagers began to take classes together, and some parents are skeptical that the camaraderie of these mixed student *parées* can really be innocent.

Consequently, an explicit moral and religious conservatism accommodates a tradition of feisty women with most peculiar results: the same community which, pleading local "custom," petitions the bishop to negotiate a Kalymnian exemption from Greek law, giving them permission to marry daughters off at 14 —before they lose their hallowed chastity— amiably tolerates the 25-year extra-marital liaison of a lusty yet commendably fastidious "housewife."

This last word translates badly. *Nikokirá*, "house-mistress," though an entirely ordinary title, holds no slur, and all the more so in the Aegean, for here, houses belong to women. If mainland brides used to move in with their mother-in-laws on many Aegean islands, the mother still gives her house to her oldest

foreigners skip down her stairs on the way to the beach and struggle back up after a bout in the disco. They may pass in the hallway, but in many ways their worlds remain quite separate. She sells postcards in the family tourist shop, while her husband works on the construction crew of a new hotel. She watches "Dallas" as she crochets another doilie for her daughter's trousseau. She worries about her son becoming a *kamáki* and about her daughter passing her university examinations. "Tourism is good. It brings money," she hears everyone say—and she says it, too—but sometimes she wonders.

In the City

Viewed from the heights of Pendeli which flanks the city to the east, Athens resembles—

daughter when she marries, moving herself (and her husband) to smaller quarters: a tiny flat in the basement, a shed on the edge of the property, a rented room nearby. Second and third daughters, who once could expect little in the way of dowry, now almost always get a house as well.

Today, now married, that island daughter probably shares a room or two of this house with strangers. Like innumerable island houses, hers hangs a scrawled sign: "ROOMS. CHAMBRES.RAUME" and, summer after summer, countless sleek blonde and sleek

as the novelist John Fowles put it—a mass of dice scattered across the Attica plain. Block after block of more or less identical six-story cement "multiple dwellings" (as they are known in Greek) do not make it the most beautiful urban center in Europe. Moreover, the rapidity with which the city was thrown up effectively postponed questions of urban planning, zoning, and the siting of local parks to some later date. With close to 4 million people living in its greater area, Athens is today a concrete matter of fact.

Planners and politicians are attempting to make it more attractive by protecting those few houses still standing which possess any

Left, musicians serenade a newly-married couple. Above, tourist portrait painter: who's looking at who?

architectural merit and by converting certain side streets into pedestrian walkways or turning the odd vacant lot into a playground for children. It may be a question of too little too late, but a good many political points are nonetheless scored for trying to make Athens more livable.

Of course none of this ever stopped people from both visiting and enjoying the Greek capital. Beneath its horrific architectural visage Athens conceals a palpably human heart. Nowhere better than here does the ancient formulation, "Man is the measure of all things," ring true. More than just a heart, Athens has soul and some districts, such as Athinás Street around the meat market or Plaka on a hot night, are downright funky.

What makes Athens attractive are its temperamental inhabitants. Clicking their worrybeads, making funny gestures with their

It should be kept in mind that Athens, as sprawling urban metropolis, is a very recent, and unforeseen development. The city was suddenly transformed, increased by onequarter practically overnight, in 1923 with the influx of Greek refugees from Asia Minor. These newcomers were exceedingly poor, in many cases arriving from Turkey with just the clothes on their backs. At first they were settled in makeshift barracks around the city in areas such as New Ionia or New Smyrna, names which recall their land of origin. Thus the trend of urban expansion was founded and other characteristics such as inner city poverty, the dark underworld of petty criminals (*manges*) and *rembetika* music (see pages 297–298) came to form part of the capital's image.

hands; by turns provocatively rude or unexpectedly friendly, arguing and laughing —it is enlivening to walk among these people. Athenians do not hesitate to show their feelings and it often seems that emotional states constitute a more powerful communicative device than words. After a few days visitors who expected to remain casual observers find themselves expressing long-forgotten feelings, exercising new facial muscles and vocal chords; unexpectedly at ease and unselfconscious. Aristotle described these as the effects of watching good drama and labeled them catharsis. In modern Athens catharsis is always on offer, only there is no strict demarcation between audience and actors and the drama never ends.

Athens has mushroomed in the last 60 years, a period which saw the city's population soar from 453,000 in 1920 to 3,027,331 in 1981. That is a 568 percent increase over a stretch of time when the population of the country as a whole rose only by 93 percent. Clearly there has also been a significant movement from the countryside into the city. All roads lead to Athens.

The sheer density of people makes for monumental traffic jams twice a day and four times when there is late shopping. Automobiles are a prime cause of smog (the socalled *néfos*) which chokes the city during windless periods. This smog also mixes with atmospheric humidity to form an abrasive acid which has been dissolving stone monuments that have stood for millennia in the city. Recently a restricted area was drawn around the city center in order to alleviate the problems of traffic and smog. On alternate days private cars with even and odd license plate numbers are allowed to circulate within this exclusion zone. This is great for taxi drivers but there are not enough cabs to cope with the rush-hour demands. Be prepared to accept a jitney-like arrangement where other people share stretches of the ride with you.

License plates serve another controlling function as well. If you notice the police unscrewing number plates from parked cars this is not a practical joke. It is the only means they have of ensuring that traffic violators will come to the station and pay their fines.

For the average Athenian these inconve-

Urban attraction: While the disadvantages of the metropolis are all too apparent to the casual observer, the benefits which Athenians enjoy are perhaps less obvious. There are more doctors, medical specialists, and hospital beds than in any other region of Greece. Educational opportunities are also superior. There are more schools, teachers and university places per capita in Athens. And when the studying is finished, there are jobs. Furthermore Athenians are often more highly paid than workers in other parts of the country.

Greece as a whole may be underdeveloped industrially, but 50 percent of the nation's industries (employing 10 or more people) are located in or around the capital; everything from chocolate factories and breweries to the massive dockyards and refineries sited

niences do not in the least detract from the desire to remain in the capital. Athens is electric. "It breaks your nerves," a friend confided over what must have been our fifth coffee of the day. Apparently once one is accustomed to the crowds, the excitement, the movement and, in contradistinction to the village or provincial town, the anonymity, it is difficult to contemplate living elsewhere in Greece.

Two kinds of self-service: Italian style and old Athenian. The one on the left sells ice-cream and Greek doughnut, *loukoumádes*; the one above sells *kouloúri*, the favorite Athenian breakfast.

along the coast at places such as Pérama, Scaramánga and Elefsina. The drive from Athens to Corinth is virtually a tour of Greece's industrial heartland.

Those who hold a high school diploma are eligible for a number of prestigious civil service positions which could mean anything from working for the electric company to serving as a government advisor. Such positions are desirable because salaries are inflation-indexed and hiked every year; best of all they are secure for life and include a pension scheme. This permanence and security are highly prized in a society which is emerging from a primarily agrarian mode of existence (up until 1960 more than 50 percent of the population were living on the land).

Whereas in former times it was hoped that a son would work his father's fields and flocks, such a proposition is now scoffed at by young men in villages. Supreme admiration is no longer accorded the rugged, autarchic shepherd able to provide his family with goats' milk, cheese, meat and other basic needs. The image of the educated civil servant or professional has usurped earlier ideals, office workers do not dirty their hands or sully their clothes, and some civil servants will allow the fingernail on their baby finger to grow extra long as evidence of their non-manual employment.

Education is thus consummately valued as it facilitates upward social mobility. In this striving for knowledge and in the fascination for foreign goods and ideas—for which the

Some go to work as teachers in the private tutorial schools (*frontistiria*) which one sees all around Athens. These institutions help students to cram for the State University entrance exams. Many talented students go abroad to study and, aware of how limited their opportunities for research or employment would be if they returned to Greece, they remain abroad. Who can blame them when by some estimates, there are more lawyers in Athens than in the whole of France.

In the view of villagers, the move from the country to Athens is one which is likely to secure employment, relative financial prosperity, and prestige. Though in which order it is not exactly clear. In any case it is not easy to move back to the village except for holidays or retirement because this would mean re-

Greeks have a word, *xenomania* (see xenophobia/xenomania in Cultural Dictionary)—one may discern many symptoms of the "developing country" syndrome. People are engaged in the effort to secure white collar employment which they associate with an image of modernity and sophistication. Yet Greece has neither the industrial base nor the GNP to support such aspirations at present. In relation to GNP there are twice as many students pursuing higher education in Greece as in the United States. Granted that most businesses originate in family enterprises no real demand has arisen for managers at the executive level. Thus many of those who complete courses of higher education end up in positions which under-utilize their talents.

adapting to village life which pales after a stretch of time in the city. Athens is the center of Greek political, commercial and cultural life. More than 17 major newspapers are printed every day in the capital accounting for 90 percent of national circulation. National television, which is government-sponsored, also emanates from Athens, a fact apparent in the advertisement of products designed for the city dweller or in the promotions for Athenian stores not to mention the weather reports which concentrate on conditions in the capital. Living in this city one feels oneself to be connected to the navel of the hellenic world. It is difficult to cut the cord.

East meets west: Athens is the primary point of entry into Greece. In 1981 close to 2 million tourists, over half of all those arriving by air in Greece, landed at Athens' Hellenikon Airport. In this and in other respects Athens is the main interface between Greece and the rest of the world. Here, villagers from outlying rural areas will probably encounter European and international culture for the first time. This is also the place where most Europeans will form a first impression of Greek culture.

It is said that approached from the east Athens is the first European city, and approached from the west, it is the first oriental city. This interplay of east and west may be put to use in making sense of the cityscape as well as the types of people living and interacting within it. On the western pole, ideally speaking, is Syntagma Square bounded by the offices of international airlines, deluxe hotels

and the House of Parliament. Syntagma bears a smart western look; Gucci, St. Laurent and Chanel vie for the allegiance of the heart in this zone where English is the *lingua franca*. Visitors from rural Greece are totally awed should they stray into this area. Yet they feel slightly uncomfortable for there is nothing here to which they may readily relate. One humble man from a Cycladic island expressed alarm at not being able to tell who was Greek from who was not.

Left, Athens is a bustling city full of Greeks from all over Greece and foreigners from all over the world. Above, star wars have reached even Greece's smaller cities.

Less than a mile away is the opposite pole, Omonoia Square. Here one may savor a Turkish coffee in some of the largest coffee houses (*kaffaneio*) to be found anywhere in the country. Try the "Alexander the Great" or the "Neon." Women are served but one cannot help noticing that they form a distinct minority in these male domains. Omonoia is filled with hawkers and small merchants who peddle anything from wristwatches to rice pudding. At night men appear wheeling large copper samovars with a warm drink called *tselépi*; a creamy, slightly gingery concoction said to be the perfect antidote for an oncoming cold. Here, it is the tourist's turn to feel foreign.

Omonoia and Syntagma are representative of two extremes of Athenian, one could even say Greek, identity. These two styles, the traditional and the modern, are to some degree apparent in every individual in what amounts to a cultural bi-polarity. As a hypothetical illustration, if a *romaios*, that is a Greek of traditional leaning, needs to go from Plaka to Omonoia he would possibly choose a course so as to pass the main church of Athens, the Mitropolis, then proceed through a district of small shops selling cloth, jewelry, household and religious objects; that is if it is decided against dropping down to Athinás Street which is itself practically a full scale bazaar. The more progressive Greek, the hellene, would probably take a course so as to pass through Syntagma and then proceed down Stadíou Street past numerous cinemas showing subtitled foreign films, department stores and neat shopping arcades. At one point there is a museum of folk art with a statue of Kolokotrónis, the hero of the Greek War of Independence, standing before it. For the hellene, Greek traditionalism is a strange sign of backwardness and an embarrassing indication of eastern influences. It belongs in museums.

In the different routes which they might choose, the imaginary hellene and *romaios* confirm two very separate experiences of the capital—and life in general. This mixture of east and west may possibly account for the popularity of Greece as a holiday spot, and the attractiveness of Athens in particular. One explores and lives out romantic fantasies linked with the east, but in a constrained fashion. There is always the familiar, western aspect of the city to fall back on.

"ATHINA, MY GRANDMOTHER"

One of Greece's best contemporary writers, Costas Taktsis, has written a collection of short stories entitled *Athina, My Grandmother*. The title suggests how a huge industrial city like Athina has managed not to alienate its inhabitants: Athina is both the name of Taktsis' grandmother and the name of the city he loves. No matter how polluted and noisy Athina may get—she is bloodkin; all her contradictions and bad habits are tolerated, and even appreciated. Taktsis' story of being brought up by Athina in an Athina that is growing up around him plays on the contradictory feelings of pride and melancholy which most Athenians have for their city. The last few pages, in particular, give an insider's view of this quickly expanding capital.

I am an Athenian, and indeed one of the few fifth generation Athenians. For the last forty or so years I've watched Athina change—for the worse. It's one thing to learn something from books—*"Perhaps Socrates and Phaedris once sat here, where we are standing now"*— and quite another thing to know it first hand, so you can say: *"Do you see that busy avenue swarming with cars and exhaust? When I was a child it was a trash-filled ravine with a thin stream which watered the few surviving plane trees."* What I want to say is that I see Athina over time, in a way which would be impossible for provincial folk or foreigners, and with this same temporal perspective I see myself... As the years pass I begin to feel not simply Athenian but also as if I am a small piece of Athina, like some microscopic archaeological monument in motion. Sometimes in the evenings when I go out on my terrace to water my flowers—geraniums, jasmine, basil and hibiscus—and I see the provincial folk and tourists hanging from St. George's bell tower to get a good look at Athina, I have the strange and overprotective sense that I am, even if they don't know it, a postcard like the ones they buy to send back home.

I have lived in many cities. A few of them— Sydney, New York—I love dearly, and I would gladly see them again for a bit, even if only once every five years. But more than anywhere else I would like to live out my life here in Athina, and when the time comes I'd like to die here. And unless something unexpected happens my wish will come true: I'll die someday when the population reaches five million (five-and-a-half million, in high tourist season). By then, I sometimes think, nothing will be left of my Athina, the Athina I loved. But something inside of me tells me that I may in fact be wrong. Because—unless something earthshattering happens—for a long time, forever I hope, there will still be the Lykavitos and Philopappov hills. By then of course they will have become 'protected' by some tacky public or state organization, and they will have been fenced off with barbed

wire. But children and lovers will always find an opening, a hole just big enough to squeeze through. No matter how polluted the air gets the Athenian honey autumn won't change much, nor the gentle Athenian winter, with its kingfisher days, nor the intoxicating spring, nor the narcotic summer, with its rare light breezes. Even if the Saronic Gulf gets dirtier there will always be a few clear swimming spots. People in the meantime may have gone to the moon to find jobs but the magic of the moon when it pokes up from behind Imettov peak will always be the same....

Two or three times recently late at night I let my car drive me to Saint John of Rendi. In between the factories that spit up infected vapors and the workers' apartment blocks there are still a few cabbage patches... Driving back I passed the Kerameikou cemetery where I played as a child. Once I couldn't resist the temptation: I left the car in front of the new Kitsch Christian Church and walked up to the railing. I glued my eyes to the spot where the memorial tomb of Fgesus was, and suddenly, I swear, I saw my grandmother, god rest her soul, quite alive watching me with a look of gentle reproach, as if to say: "So there you are, at least you didn't turn out worse" and then she disappeared. Thanks to her, no matter what my identification papers claim, I am Athenian. Thanks to her I love Athina. Some say the way she's ended up she's the ugliest capital in the whole world. I don't know, nor does it concern me. Beautiful or ugly, for me she's unique. She's the city in which I was born, in which I have lived and in which my grandmother died. Naturally I have to admit that from some vantage points—just like Athina the city—she was a monster, and she put me through hell a great portion of my childhood and adolescence but what can I say? She's the only woman ... I ever loved.

All Greek males must do a two-year compulsory military service. Although some consider it a right of passage most, like this young man, resent the endless hours of sitting around.

HOPE YOUR ROAD IS A LONG ONE

In this section our writers will take you on ten individual journeys, each writer to the part of Greece he or she knows best. Starting in the northeastern corner near Turkey and Bulgaria and traveling in a zigzag fashion down to Crete, you'll find the history, geography and local culture of each area covered in detail. Whether you are browsing through these pages in order to conjure up visions of what lies ahead or in order to bring back memories there are plenty of pictures, anecdotes and information to spur you on. The ten sections have been loosely designed as two-week itineraries, but of course the longer you stay, the better. As the Greek poet from Alexandria once wrote:

As you set out for Ithaka
hope your road is a long one,
full of adventure, full of discovery.
Laistrygonians, Cyclops,
angry Poseidon—don't be afraid of them:
you'll never find things like that on your way
as long as you keep your thoughts raised high,
as long as a rare sensation
touches your spirit and your body.
Laistrygonians, Cyclops,
wild Poseidon—you won't encounter them
unless you bring them along inside you soul,
unless your soul sets them up in front of you.

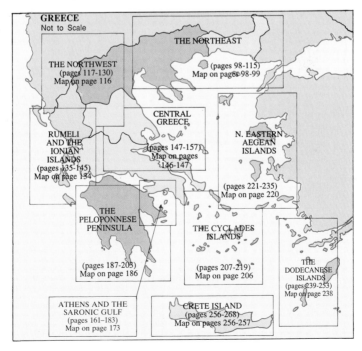

THE NORTHEAST

Salonika stands about halfway between the Ionian Sea to the west and the Evros River to the east. It is the second largest city of Greece and is often referred to as the co-capital with Athens. A line projected north of Salonika reaches the tripartite border between Yugoslavia, Bulgaria and Greece. This line also divides the Northwest of Greece, comprising Epirus and Western Macedonia, from the Northeast, including Eastern Macedonia and Thrace.

The history of the Northeast is dominated by the movement of tribes, races and nationalities across its territory. The local Macedonian and Thracian populations were subject to constant invasion and flux. On his way to fight Athens and Sparta, the Persian Xerxes marched countless troops across the north Aegean land route, while his fleet followed along the coast. It was from here that Alexander the Great set off to conquer the East, and here that the Romans established the Via Egnatia stretching from the Adriatic coast to the Hellespont (Dardanelles). Later, the disintegrating Byzantine Em-

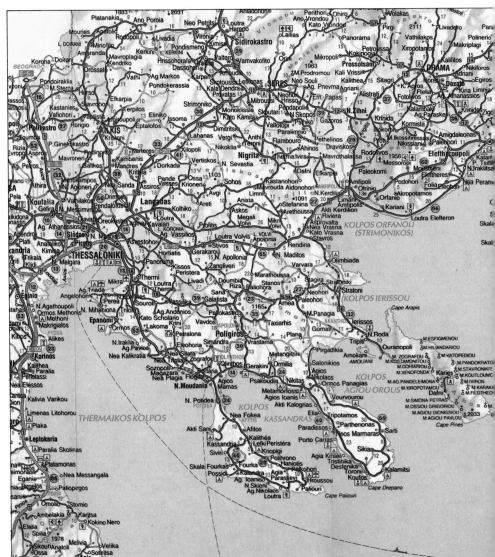

pire would face continuous incursions from the north due to Slavic expansion. And the Ottoman Turks, advancing from the east, would make a circle across the Balkans, conquering the Macedonian and Thracian lands before closing in on Constantinople.

The sea provided an important access to the Northeast, despite the fact that the coast is tucked away at the northeastern-most corner of the Aegean. Odysseus, leaving Troy for his return journey to Ithaca, drifted to the land of the Kikones, the ancient site of Maronia. Southern Greek cities, especially Athens and Chalkis, began their colonization of the

Chalcidice peninsula via the sea as early as the seventh century B.C. Later, when Salonika became the second largest city of the Byzantine Empire, Venetians, crusaders and other seafarers skirted the coast to and from Constantinople.

The Northeast does not offer the traveler the magnificent large-scale archaeological sites and stunning temples of Central and Southern Greece. However, its proximity to other Balkan states and its rather late acquisition by Greece give it greater ethnic variety and more unspoiled natural beauty. Both these features are rapidly changing due to modernization and integration into a

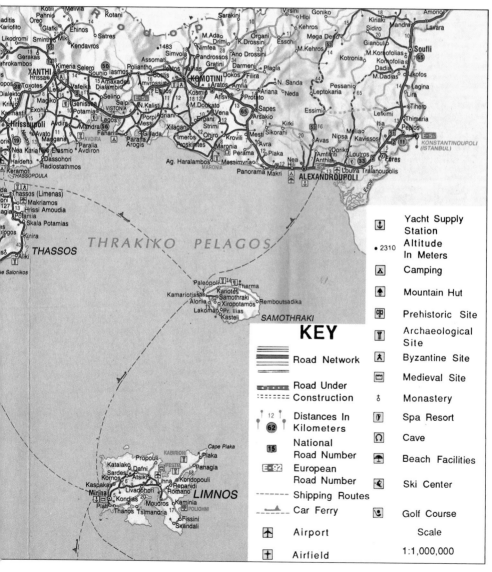

more uniform national culture. The northern frontier is flanked by the wooded edges of the Balkan mountain ranges. Rich plains stretch from west to east crossed by four major rivers. River deltas, lagoons and lakes form protected wetlands with a rich variety of birdlife. The coast is tamer than the more rugged coastline of other parts of Greece, and therefore offers excellent beaches. The sites themselves fall into two categories: either they are too bare to astound, or they are palimpsests where different layers of civilization can be read one after another. One of the best examples of the latter category is **Salonika** itself.

Salonika: To the visitor approaching it by sea, the modern city presents the solid facade of apartment blocks characteristic of many Mediterranean seaside cities. At the beginning of this century, the same view was marked by elegantly rising minarets, which were destroyed either by the Great Fire of 1917 (which turned nearly three quarters of the city to ashes), or by Greek nationalism retaliating for previous Turkish desecration of churches. Behind today's high-rise facade, encircled by the Roman and Byzantine walls, and scattered in the midst of main traffic arteries and pedestrian alleys, lies the city's historical wealth. Roman ruins, Byzantine churches, Turkish buildings and Jewish tombstones are hidden away behind the greenery of piazzas or the colorful houses of the old Ano Poli (upper town).

Thessaloníki was founded in 315 B.C. by the Macedonian king Kassander, who named it after his wife. It was not an important city during the rise of the Macedonian Empire in the fourth century B.C. Today its **Archaeological Museum** houses Macedonian, Hellenistic and Roman finds from the whole region, including the notable Sindos and Vergina collections. The latter comprises the magnificent treasures of what are alleged to be Philip II's royal tombs.

Macedonian sites: These are situated at some distance from Salonika. **Philippi**, north of Kavala and founded by Philip II himself, has little that is Macedonian to show for it developed in later Roman times. **Vergina**, on the way to Veroia, was the capital before Pella and remained the royal cemetery. The tombs of Philip of Macedon, discovered in 1977, are closed for further excavation. But there are other tombs and a half-standing palace

Preceding pages: little girls during an Easter Epitáphios procession; fishing boats i Kalymnos; the town of Kastráki in Thessaly; oliv trees in Crete sunrise at Cape Soúnion; and Edward Lear's watercolor of Salonika.

situated in a pleasant landscape. **Dion**, at the foot of Mount Olympus further south, was founded by Macedonian kings as a place of worship to the Olympian Zeus and, most likely, as a Macedonian showcase to the rest of Greece. Races, sacrifices and a nine-day festival were held here. Alexander the Great came to sacrifice to Zeus before setting off on his eastward campaign. The town remained prosperous through Roman and early Christian times.

Pella, on the road to Edessa, is the most outstanding site. The rather small scale of its revealed grounds, and its location right by the side of the road, give it a humbleness which doesn't correspond to its past glory. Standing in the courtyard of the **House of the Lion Hunt**, surrounded by graceful Ionic columns and the exquisite floor mosaics that have survived (some on site, some in the local museum), one cannot help but sense that here stood the imperial court which became master of the Greek world in the fourth century B.C. It is here that Philip of Macedon planned the conquest of Greece. And here his son, Alexander the Great, trained at arms and was taught by the philosopher Aristotle in preparation

for a brilliant though short-lived career as conqueror of the East. With the Roman conquest of Macedonia in the mid-second century B.C. the city lost its importance to Salonika. Visitors will find the mosaics unforgettable, and will be impressed by the powerful effect of expression and movement produced by the juxtaposition of colored pebbles. It is rewarding to compare them with the fine examples of Byzantine wall mosaics in Salonika.

City tour: Salonika gained renown as a Byzantine city. It has yet no Byzantine museum, but an interesting exhibition outlining the city's history is housed in the **White Tower** by the waterfront. This is the city's landmark. Built in the 15th century, it served as a prison under Ottoman rule. In 1826, it was the site of a massacre of multinous Janissaries, the Sultan's guard, which earned it the name of "Bloddy Tower." The memories of this event were brushed away with a coat of whitewash and a consequent change of name. Today this name is misleading, for the tower is no longer white. The steps going up in a spiral around the inner wall are flanked by small deep-set windows which frame partial views of the city and gulf. One can then assemble the different

eft, a quiet oment along e Salonikan aterfront. elow, fisheren wind in eir nets in avála.

pieces into a single panorama from the battlements.

It is possible to visit both the Archaeological Museum and the White Tower in one afternoon, especially as they close at 7 p.m. and 9 p.m. respectively. If you haven't acquired the Greek habit of taking a nap after lunch, this is a good time to visit the museums as everyone else is asleep. Churches close between 1 p.m. and 5 p.m.

The Roman ruins are distributed along the two main avenues leading to the waterfront: the **Forum** and **Odeon Galerius Palace Complex** along Dimitriu Gunari Street. Caesar Galerius built this complex at the beginning of the fourth century, when he chose Salonika as his seat of residence. He was famous for his ruthless persecution of Christians, including the martyrdom of St. Demetrius, patron saint of the city. The palace ruins are scattered in the midst of busy **Navarinu Square**, lined with *tavernas*, snack bars and ice-cream parlors. The triumphal **Arch of Galerius** was built to commemorate the emperor's victory over the Persians: relief panels at its base depict scenes from the campaign.

Churches: Undoubtedly the most important building in the complex is the **Rotunda,** or **Church of Saint George**, one of the few surviving examples of circular Roman architecture. Damaged in the 1978 earthquake, it is closed for restoration. Galerius intended it for his mausoleum, a function it never fulfilled as the emperor fell in battle and his enemy did not return the body to Salonika. With the spread of Christianity, it was soon turned into a church and decorated with glorious wall mosaics which only partially survive around the upper part of the interior. The Rotunda is flanked by a half-standing minaret from the days when it served as a mosque. It dominates the views down to the sea from above and up to the **Chain Tower**, from the seafront marking the northeastern corner of the Byzantine fortifications.

Another early Christian building is the tiny **Church of Ossios Davíd**, tucked away in the old part of town up the hill. It was allegedly built by Galerius' daughter, Theodora. If you speak a bit of Greek, you can ask the church's caretaker to tell you the legend of Theodora's secret baptism while her cruel father was away on one of his campaigns. The unique fifth-century mosaic in the apse is one of

the earliest samples of its kind. Its outstanding beauty derives from the *naif* depiction of Ezekiel's vision, the rare representation of a youthful Christ, the fine colors and elaborate symbolism.

From Ossios Davíd one can continue a visit to the city's important Byzantine monuments by following one of two paths: one goes back down the hill to the major fifth- to eighth-century basilicas, while the other makes a long semi-circle across the old city past 14th-century churches.

The early Christian basilica was a plain rectangular building. In a sense, its plan derives from the classical Greek temple, replacing the exterior colonnade with walls. Both the fifth-century **Ahiropiitos Church** and the heavily restored **Church of St. Demetrius** are such examples. Both have been badly damaged by fire and the surviving mosaics must be sought out: in the first under the arches, in the second above the pillars on the east and west sides of the church. The crypt in St. Demetrius is supposed to mark the site of the Roman bath where the saint was martyred. The **Church of Ayia Sophia** (Holy Wisdom) shows a first attempt to convert the basilica into a domed structure. The inside of the dome, which represents the heavenly vault, is covered with a surprisingly well-preserved large-scale mosaic depicting the Ascension; the inscription of "Ye men of Galilee, why stand ye gazing up into heaven?" is illustrated by the corresponding scene of the twelve apostles, two angels and the Virgin Mary, separated by trees and gazing up at the "Pantocrator," the Almighty Christ.

The great controversies: During the Byzantine period, Salonika lived through two major theological debates. The Iconoclast Controversy raged in the eighth and ninth centuries when excessive worship of icons led to an equally extreme reaction against them. The Ossios Davíd mosaic was covered with cowhides to save it from destruction, while the original mosaic of the Virgin in Ayia Sophia's apse was destroyed and restored after this storm had passed. The focal point of this controversy was Constantinople, while the 14th-century Isihast Debate centered in Salonika itself. Isihasm (from "isihia" meaning peace) was propounded by the monks of Mount Athos, and claimed that "by holding the breath, by making the spirit re-enter into the soul, and by gazing fixedly upon the

navel they could attain to the vision of the uncreated light which shone on Tabor." This creed was ridiculed by the Calabrian monk Barlaam, leader of the Zealot opposition. A struggle ensued which was at least as social and political as it was theological. Isihasm's major theorist, Gregory Palamas, was Archbishop of Salonika; his reliquary is kept in the city's Cathedral.

If you take the second walk from Ossios David, you cross the charming **Ano Poli**. A 20-minute walk from the downtown center takes you to this part of town which still lives like a village; in the summer, women chat and knit sitting on their doorstep while children play in the streets. The greengrocer's cart has been replaced by a small truck, but still goes from door to door every morning. And men come from the suburbs on their donkey selling blocks of lime for a new coat of whitewash. Here and in the Acropolis, the highest part of town enclosed by fortifications, you can find good *tavernas*. In the 14th century the hill was covered with small monasteries of which only some of the chapels survive. The **Church of St. Nicholas Orphanos** has exquisite frescoes. The **churches of St. Elias** and **St. Catherine** represent interesting develop-

ments in the cross-in-dome architectural form, which culminates in the **Church of the Holy Apostles**. The latter's fine mosaics with scenes from the life of Christ are so high up that they can only be appreciated with a pair of binoculars.

Other influences: Salonika was conquered by the Turks in 1430, just 23 years before the fall of Constantinople. Churches were conveniently turned into mosques by plastering over the interior decoration and building minarets on their side. Fifteenth-century Ottoman monuments develop the style of elaborate dome constructions of late Byzantine churches. There are two mosques of particular interest: the graceful **Alaja Imaret**, now turned into an exhibition hall, and the **Hamza-bey Jami**, now the Alcazar movie theater. Drapers and goldsmiths sell their wares as they did long ago in the **Bezesten**, a six-domed covered market. The **Yahoudi**, once a Turkish *hamam* (public steam bath), now shelters an open-air flower market and a small fish *taverna* which is recommended. Around it spreads today's central market area, displaying a colorful array of mounds of fresh fruit and vegetables, fish and meat, heaps of olives, sweets and spices, wooden utensils and

straw baskets. A more contemporary Turkish monument is the house where Mustafa Kemal was born, today the Turkish consulate. Later known as Atatürk, he was the leader of the Young Turk Movement that overthrew the Sultan and founded the Turkish Republic in 1928.

A small trace of another cultural influx remains today. Nearly 20,000 Jews, banished from Spain in the 15th century and speaking Ladino, came to settle in Salonika under tolerant Ottoman rule. By mid-16th century they formed the city's prosperous majority. But the fire of 1917 destroyed most of the area where they lived near the western seafront, and almost the entire community was tragically deported to the death camps of Poland during the World War II. Several tombstones with Hebrew inscriptions from the old Jewish cemetery, now the University Campus, are scattered amongst the city's paving stones.

Contemporary things: Modern Salonika spreads far beyond the old city walls. The University gives it a bustling student life which gathers at the bars near the seafront and White Tower at night. The International Fair held every October makes it an important trade center for the Balkans. Along the eastern quay, modern apartment blocks are interspersed with grandiose old mansions. One of them, now the **Folk Art Museum** offers an exhibition on ethnic differences in Northern Greece.

Further along, the suburb of **Kalamaria** provides good seafood restaurants right on the sea. **Panorama**, an affluent suburb to the northeast, affords views which justify its name and features delicious triangular cream pastries, called *trigona*. On a clear day, look out far to the south as you sip coffee by the waterfront or pause on the sinuous uphill pathways of the Ano Poli; you may see the massive form of Mount Olympus blocking the entrance to the bay, a link between modern Salonika and the ancient Greece.

Going east: Many roads lead east out of Salonika. One of them first leads north to the town of Kilkis and the shore of the Greek half of Lake Doiran, then up the mountains to the Rupel Pass (the only access route to Bulgaria), and further east to Serres. This route is also followed by the railway. Greek trains are very slow, but provide a good and inexpensive way to travel if you have time to spare and

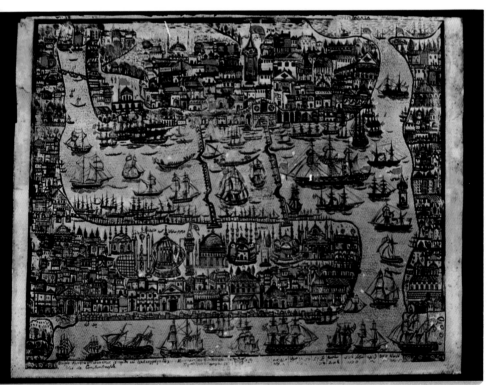

MOUNT ATHOS

What can I do for you if you wear the shameful garment
of the flesh and have not laid bare your mind and made
naked your soul, if you remain covered in darkness and
do not have the strength to see the light?
—Seymeon the Mystic

From the northern seaboard of Greece three long arms of land known as Chalcidice reach into the Aegean. At the extreme end of the third and most easterly arm, the mountain which has given the peninsula its name—**Mount Athos**—rises in solitary magnificence. The fame of Athos rests on its large monastic community; these saints and humble monks have earned it the epithet "holy," now an intrinsic part of the name: Agion Oros, the Holy Mountain.

In the beginning: The history of the monastic settlement begins with the advent of hermits in about the mid-ninth century, roughly a hundred years before the foundation of the first monastery. St. Peter the Athonite, perhaps the most famous of the early monks, is supposed to have lived in a cave for fifty years. The first monastery, the Great Lavra, was founded by St. Athanasios in A.D. 963. He was a friend and councillor of the first historical benefactor of the Holy Mountain, Nikephoros Fokas. Thereafter, the foundations multiplied under the royal patronage of the Byzantine emperors who supported the building of the various settlements with imperial resources, in the form of money, land and treasures.

Thus all the monasteries share a rich heritage. The names of Byzantine emperors are still commemorated in their churches and imperial charters are zealously guarded in the library of each monastery.

The monasteries are divided into two categories: Coenobite and Idiorrhythmic. In the Coenobite monasteries all monks keep to strict regulations under the direction of an abbot or *Hygumen*. Property is divided and meals are eaten in common in the *Trapeza* or refectory. In the Idiorrhythmic monasteries (which include the three largest: Lavra, Vatopedi and Iviron) there is no property in common,

and each monk provides his own food and clothing from his own resources. All monasteries are Greek except for the Russian Pantaleímon, the Serbian Chilandari and the Bulgarian Zografou, and they all, with the exception of Vatopedi keep the old Julian calendar, thirteen days behind the rest of Europe, and Byzantine hours which commence at sunset and therefore vary every day.

The monasteries, however, form only one part of this "holy" community. A great number of monks prefer to live in smaller monastic establishments, the *sketes* and *kellia* dotted around the peninsula. The *kelli* or cell is a single building containing a little chapel inhabited by a smaller number of monks. The *skete* is a small monastic village composed of a few cottages clustered round a central church. Both *sketes* and *kellia* are dependent on one of the twenty monasteries. There are also monks who choose to live like hermits, following the traditions of St. Peter the Athonite, in an *Isihasterion*, a rough unadorned hut or a cave, perched precipitously on a cliff's ledge. The hermits live in great poverty and are rarely seen.

If Athos continues to exercise a singular compulsion over the hearts and minds of others, this is not because of the scenery, spectacular though it is, nor on account of its being one of the richest museums of Byzantine art and culture. Ultimately it is because it lays claims to represent the highest form of spiritual life known in the Orthodox and indeed in the entire Christian tradition. Through the pursuit of a discipline demanding scrupulous attention to both outer action and inner prayer, the monk aspires to purify his body and soul from various alien attachments by which he is bound, and thus traverse the road that leads, by way of ascetic practice and the higher forms of contemplation to his "deification."

All visitors to the Holy Mountain will recognize that they themselves have also traversed a road that leads to a very different realm, a realm which by ordinary human standards may even be conceived as divine by those with a strong sense of religiousness. Thus the description of Athos by one of its poets as the "domain and garden of the Holy Virgin" strongly echoes the feelings of most men who have had the fortune, and the luck to be born male, and thereby gain privileged entry to this holy place.

want to get a feel of the land.

Serres is best reached by the road branching off northeast of Salonika. Both Serres and Drama, further east, were important in Byzantine and Ottoman days, and continue to be prosperous provincial towns. Both offer pleasant resting spots in shady central plazas and give access to hiking and skiing in the mountains behind them. Serres was burnt down by the retreating Bulgarians in 1913 and was completely rebuilt, but two important Byzantine churches remain: the 11th-century **Church of the Holy Apostles** and the 14th-century **Church of St. Nikólaos**. A domed Ottoman building in the central square serves as the local museum.

The land and villages lying between this area and the sea are mainly agricultural. Some come alive at specific times of the year. The Sarakatsanides, a nomadic tribe of herdsmen, assemble every summer for their *panayiri* (fair) in the vicinity of Serres and Drama. **Langadas** is the site of an old Thracian ritual of hopping barefoot on red-hot coals, held on May 21 by the descendants of refugees from a Thracian village: the Anastenarides (from *anastenazo*, to groan) imitate the

groans of the icons rescued when their village church caught fire, and, like the icons then, their feet don't get burnt. In **Sohos**, a carnival tradition of dressing youths up in rows of heavy cow-bells is practiced every February.

The Chalcidice: The main road east of Salonika runs along the base of the Chalcidice Peninsula, skirting lakes Koronia and Volvi. The huge hand-like peninsula stretching three fingers out into the Aegean was sparsely populated until a recent tourist and development boom. Little is left to show its important role in classical times when the colonies of various southern Greek cities served as the battlefield for the Peloponnesian War between Athens and Sparta. **Potidea**, on the first finger, triggered off Sparta's declaration of war in 432 B.C., while the Battle of Amfipolis set an end to the conflict in this area ten years later. Armies clashed across the land, and fleets sailed and fought off the shores. A copy of Thucydides' *History of the Peloponnesian War* may help to evoke the life and military activity which once animated the site of today's sleepy villages. Finds from the area are kept in a museum at **Poliyiros**, the region's capital.

The aqueduct in Kavála.

The peninsula also bears marks of other times. At the **cave of Petralona**, fossils and a Neanderthal skull have revealed the existence of a prehistoric settlement. At **Stayira**, a modern marble statue overlooking the Ierissos Gulf marks Aristotle's birthplace. **Xerxes' Canal**, now filled up, was built around 482 B.C. to avoid the fate of the previous Persian campaign, when its fleet was wrecked sailing round Mount Athos. This and Xerxes' bridge over the Hellespont were considered by the Greeks as products of Persian megalomania: "marching over the sea and sailing ships through the land." The medieval **Potidea Canal** still separates the first finger from the mainland and serves as mooring ground for fishing boats.

Billowing hills and the beautiful forested slopes of Mount Holomon cover the peninsula's palm. You may drive around the first two fingers, **Kassandra** and **Sithonia**, always finding an idyllic spot: charming inland villages alternate with seaside fishing hamlets, luxury hotels with camping sites, protected coves with sandy beaches, pineclad slopes with bleak promontories. Sitting on the beach at **Sarti**, on the middle finger you can make out the form of Mount Athos rising like a pyramid from the haze across the gulf. Here, woman travelers should sign off for the Holy Mountain is a male preserve. (See pages 106–107.)

Back north: The main road leading east skirts the popular beaches at the head of the Strymonic Gulf on its way to **Amfipolis**. The city was founded by Athenian colonists in the fifth century B.C. on a Thracian site called "The Nine Ways" where, according to Herodotus, the passing Persians had seized nine boys and girls and buried them alive as a propitiatory sacrifice. Its new name, meaning "the surrounded city," was derived from its position in a loop of the River Strymon, strategically commanding the inland flatlands, the mouth of the river, and the coveted gold mines of Mount Pangeon. Here was fought the battle that decided the first phase of the Peloponnesian War. Today the table-top plateau is strewn with limbs of broken statues, Hellenistic mosaics and the foundations of early Christian basilicas.

Crossing the Strymon over a bridge guarded by the **Lion of Amfipolis**, a colossal statue re-assembled from the fourth- and third-century B.C. fragments,

the road forks out to Kavála. The old road runs the length of the beautiful green valley between Mounts Pangeon and Simvolon, passing through slate-roofed villages with panoramic views. The new highway, faster but less scenic, follows the coastline.

Rising in the shape of an amphitheater from the harbor up to the pine hills, **Kavála's** magnificent location and manageable size make it one of the most pleasant towns in Greece. A colony of Thasos by the name of Neapolis in antiquity, it became an important port with access to Philippi during Roman and Christian times, while today it is the major export center for tobacco from the surrounding plains. The local museum houses finds from Neapolis and Amfípolis.

The harbor has two parts: the modern part, and the old fishing harbor with small fish restaurants and a market backed by the arches of a 16th-century aqueduct. The old town surrounded by Byzantine walls rises on a promontory to the east. Walking up the narrow winding streets, you will notice a set of golden half-moons, the Sultan's symbol, shining above an outer wall. This was the Imaret, a Turkish almshouse, also known as

tembelhane, the loungers' home, as the lazy had soon outnumbered the needy. You can push open the heavy wooden gate and ramble through its now desolate courtyards.

At the top of the hill, **Mehemet Ali's house** is a fine example of traditional Turkish architecture. Born in Kavála in 1769 of Albanian descent, Mehemet Ali became Pasha of Egypt and founder of the Egyptian royal dynasty which lasted up to this century. In the square, his statue looks out to the south, the direction of the country which he set out to rule. You may think it strange that both the founders of the modern Egyptian dynasty and the Turkish Republic were born in Greek cities, but one should always keep in mind that both Salonika and Kavála were then part of the Ottoman Empire.

Philippi, although named by Philip II of Macedon, contains little that is Macedonian. From the Acropolis, where three medieval towers rise on the ruins of Macedonian walls, you get an extensive view of the battlefield which made this site famous. It was here that in 42 B.C. one of the decisive Roman battles was fought between the republican forces led

Left, one of few Greek Jewish holocaust survivors. Right, Poma women in th Xánthi mark

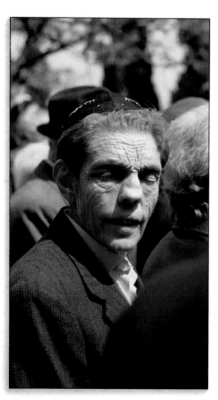

110

by Brutus and Cassius, who had taken part in the assassination of Julius Caesar in 44 B.C., and the latter's avengers, Antony and Octavius. In Julius Caesar, Shakespeare has the four men meet in this field for negotiations before battle:

Brutus: Words before blows? Is it so, countrymen?

Octavius: Not that we love words better, as you do.

Brutus: Good words are better than bad strokes, Octavius.

Antony: In your bad strokes, Brutus, you give good words;/Witness the hole you made in Caesar's heart,/Crying, "Long live, hail Caesar!"

Justice was meted out as both Cassius and Brutus committed suicide upon seeing their forces defeated. It was left to the Battle of Actium some eleven years later to decide the final struggle between the two victors of Philippi. The Roman ruins, mainly to the south of the highway, include the foundations of the **Forum** and the **Palaestra**, as well as the **Public Latrine** at the southwest corner of the grounds.

The beginning of Christianity: Philippi is reputed to be the first place in Europe where St. Paul preached the gospel nearly a century after the famous Roman battle. He arrived in A.D. 49, but was soon thrown into prison as the local religion was still a form of Thracian paganism. Six years later, however, he revisited the town to which he would later address his Epistle to the Philippians. By the sixth century, Christianity was thriving at Philippi, as the foundations of several early Christian churches of the bassilica type testify.

Ferries for the island of **Thasos** leave regularly from Kavála or, if you are traveling by car, from Keramoti further east. Thasos is endowed with great natural beauty. On the east, pine trees slope down to golden beaches, pine-scent mingling with the salty sea breeze. The western shore is flatter, serene and spectacular at sunset when the sun's rays catch the silver-green of olive groves. Between the two main seaside towns, **Limen**, the capital, and **Limenaría** on the other side of the island, small groups of houses along the shore alternate with large villages perched on the slopes. The slate roofs, running waters and shady plane trees of **Panayia** and **Potamia** could easily trick you into thinking you were deep in the mountains, were it not for

tourist kretches out n the ferry de to Thasos.

glimpses of sand and sea far below. **Theologos**, reached from the southwest, is the site where the medieval capital moved for protection from pirates. In antiquity, Thasos was a Parian colony and, later, a colony of the mainland shore opposite. In Limen, traces of the ancient naval and commercial harbors can still be seen. You can also make a long walking tour of the ancient walls enclosing the modern town. The theater has been informally restored with wooden benches placed amongst the pine trees. If you take the walk in late afternoon, be sure to carry a flashlight; it may be dark by the time you reach the crescent-shaped rock-hewn **Sanctuary of Pan** at the top of the hill and if you are not prepared you might experience the "panic" known to have been induced by this mysterious half-man half-goat god! A detailed guide of the grounds can be obtained at the museum.

Back on the mainland east of Kavála, the **Nestos River** flows through the **Yellow Plain** (known in Turkish as "Sari Saban"), a vast expanse of corn and tobacco fields. The Nestos marks the boundary between Eastern Macedonia and Thrace. Its estuary is surrounded by poplar plantations used as a hideout by birds. It can only be reached by dirt roads leading to the fine beaches facing Thasos. Some beautiful scenery along the Nestos Gorge can best be seen by train when you travel from Drama to Xánthi.

Muslim presence: Ancient Thrace used to stretch deep into present-day Bulgaria and the European side of Turkey. Greek colonization of the coast often led to conflict with the native Thracian tribes. The Roman Via Egnatia spanned the area, leaving scattered traces of Roman and, later, Byzantine fortifications. Thrace was overrun and settled by Slavs and Ottomans. It was eventually divided between Bulgaria, Turkey and Greece, as a result of 19th- and early 20th-century nationalist struggles. Although there was a population exchange between Turkey and Greece in 1923, the Turk inhabitants of the Greek part of Thrace were allowed to remain in return for protection granted to Greeks living in Istanbul. The Turkish minority is distributed between Xánthi, Komotini and the tobacco-growing plains south of the two cities. Gypsies who espoused the Muslim faith and the Turkish language are also settled here. Another Muslim minority, the Pomaks, **Pirated tapes**

live in the mountains of **Western** and **Eastern Rodopi**. They appear to be of Slavic descent as they tend to be fairer than Turks, and traditionally cultivate tobacco on the lush Rodopi terraces and valleys. This border area is a military zone and can only be visited with permission from the Ministry of Defense. Applications for permits can be made at the Xánthi police station, but the process can take a week.

The best place to see a motley crowd of Greek citizens belonging to different races is in the hubbub of **Xánthi's** Saturday **open air market**. The Muslim women look very graceful in long black satin overcoats and white *yashmaks* (scarves), which are gradually being replaced by gray or brown shorter coats and printed scarves. The gypsy women stand out in their colorful wide trousers and their scarves tied behind the ears, exposing their chin. Many of the men still wear burgundy-colored velvet or felt fezzes, or white praying caps. Greek priests, their cassocks blowing in the wind and tall black hats sticking out of the crowd, also do their week's shopping. This market mainly caters to local needs, so you may find little to purchase but it

is worth spending a Saturday morning here to see this aspect of Greece which you will not find in the rest of the country. In the evening, you can witness another aspect of Xánthi life; a street off the main square is closed off for the Saturday night *nifopázaro* or "brides' fair." Traditionally this was the time for young men and women to exchange glances. Today it is more an opportunity for the whole town to meet and promenade.

Xánthi became a prosperous commercial and administrative center in the 19th century. Renowned masons were brought from Epirus to build merchant homes, tobacco warehouses and *hans* (inns). The *hans*, large square buildings around a central courtyard, were resting-spots and trading-centers near the marketplace. South of the square, an intoxicating aroma of tobacco fills the air; this is the area of the tobacco warehouses, some still in use and featuring extraordinary facades. The whitewashed houses and slender minarets of the Turkish quarter rise up to north.

In **Komotini**, Muslims constitute more than 50 percent of the population. Two central mosques fill up with the faithful at prayer times. In the surrounding cobbled

photo store
window in
Xánthi.

streets, small shops spread a colorful array of everyday items. Old men wearing fezzes sit solemnly outside coffeehouses, playing with their worry-beads. The museum houses archaeological finds from all over Thrace, two of the most important sites being Abdera south of Xánthi, and Maronia south of Komotini.

Both sites have little to show apart from the foundations of layers and layers of civilization, but both are of historical significance. **Abdera**, especially affluent in the fifth century B.C., was the birthplace of two major philosophers in antiquity: Democritus, who expounded an atomic theory of the constitution of the world, and the sophist Protagoras who incapsulated his relativism in the phrase, "Man is the measure of all things." Further east, **Maronia** marks the site where Odysseus' ship is supposed to have strayed after leaving Troy for the return journey to Ithaca. Although the natives were unfriendly, it was their sweet-smelling red wine which later saved Odysseus and his companions from the terrifying cyclops Polyphemus. Trapped in his cave, they managed to get Polyphemus drunk on the delicious wine and then while he slept they poked his single eye out with a huge red-hot pole and escaped by hiding under the sheep's bellies. A cave to the north of Maronia retains the name of Polyphemus' Cave.

The Evros valley and Samothrace: The road from Komotini zigzags through barren limestone hills before coming down to the vast Evros plain and leading on to Alexandroupolis. Formerly a charming seaside town, **Alexandroupolis** has developed into an unruly urban conglomeration. Dirt roads lead to the western part of the Evros delta, an important wetland for migratory birds from northeast Europe, including flamingos. Ecological tourism will soon provide better access and facilities for observation. No access is permitted to the river itself, for it belongs to the border military zone. Ferries leave the harbor for the island of Samothrace, while the road continues east towards Turkey and north along the Evros valley.

Unlike the other island of the Thracian Sea, the green and golden Thasos, **Samothrace** raises its forbidding granite heights above stony beaches and murky waters. The landscape was not always so inhospitable. Homer has the mighty Poseidon watching from here the action in the plains of Troy: he "sat and marveled on the war and strife, high on the topmost crest of wooded Samothrace, for thence all Ida was plain to see, and plain to see was the city of Troy and the ships of the Achaians." With time the forest has receded, leaving the desolate lunar landscape of the aptly-named **Mount Fengari** (Mount Moon). Traces of the old luxuriant vegetation survive in the northeast, where a variety of butterflies mingle with the spray of small waterfalls formed by creeks gurgling down the mountainsides. The ancient native cult of the Great Gods was retained after Greek colonization of the island in the seventh century and flourished up to the third century. This site and the **museum of Paleopolis** display evidence of the cult, its grounds and its mysteries.

The road from Alexandroupolis leads northeast past the Roman staging-post of Trajanopolis to Ferai, where the 12th-century **Church of the Virgin** discloses fine but faded frescoes. Corn and sunflower fields, spectacular in midsummer, stretch as far as the eye can see.

Soufli was once famous for its silk production. The land sloping down to the Evros used to be planted with mulberry trees whose leaves nourished the silkworms. Today the trees have been replaced by corn fields and the single silk factory still in use imports cocoons from the East. A variety of silks are for sale at a shop near the central crossroads. **Didimotiho** has a Byzantine fortress with a commanding view of the Evros valley, and an abandoned pyramidal-roofed mosque. A folklore museum offers an interesting overview of the region's traditional culture and handicrafts.

Cross countries: There are two ways to cross from here into Turkey. One is by train from the small railway station of **Pithio**, a sleepy village below its once vigilant fortress. The other is from the border outpost of **Kastanies**. The passage cannot be made on foot, so you must either have a car, take the one-day bus trip leaving twice a week from **Orestiada**, or wait at the border for a lift. Just across the border, the four minarets of the 16th-century Selimiye Mosque, the architect Sinan's last masterpiece, rise above swaying poplar trees on the opposite bank of the Evros River. From the Turkish town of Edirne, built on the site of Roman Hadrianople, you can look back to the once Byzantine city of Salonika, and forward to the combined Byzantine and Ottoman grandeur of Istanbul.

Looking across the Turkish bord[e] at the Selim[iye] Mosque.

114

EPIRUS AND NW MACEDONIA

Epirus and the northwest corner of Macedonia are worlds apart from the azure, sun-bleached Greece of Zorba. Here instead, you will find jagged limestone peaks and deep sunless gorges, mountains manteled by forests and rimmed with snow, villages cut from the same stone mountains and timber. In a country like Greece whose history and people have been singularly shaped by the sea, this northern edge of the Hellenic peninsula is the often forgotten terra firma—indeed Epirus means the great dry place, the mainland, in Greek.

This tough, austere land sets the scene for a different way of life. You can feel the weight and sobriety of this existence when you walk down the stone streets of a village lined with stone houses or witness the slow, plodding steps of an Epirot dancing to the wailing clarinet. You can sense the social closure and restraint in the architecture of the Zagorahoria houses set off far from the street by large gates, or when, at a village festival, you are not asked to join in the dance, but rather expected to stand apart, forever the foreigner. Even the rain which falls here more abundantly than anywhere else in Greece reminds that you are not in Nauplia or Naxos. Still, the contrasts between this Mountain Greece and that of the Mediterranean are today beginning to blur in the increasing homogenization of the modern Greek nation.

, In their massive postwar migration to Athens, the Epirots have brought a bit of the mountains to the city, and, with each holiday vacation spent in their native villages, bring a bit of the city back to the mountains. Modern communications too have radically altered this area's isolation. Now electricity, telephones, radio and television link most villages and households with the rest of Greece, not to mention a fine network of roads and connections by air-plane. These days the Sarakatsani shepherd can finish milking his herd at noon in a highland pasture and, flying from Ioannina, still make a doctor's appointment in Athens at 5 p.m.

How it started: While Epirus becomes more and more integrated into and unified with the Greek nation, it is crucial to appreciate how distinct its past history has been from the rest of Greece. It

achieved Greek statehood less than 80 years ago, in 1913, some 80 years after most of the mainland had achieved sovereignty. At that time, moreover, it was hardly evident that this region was, in fact, Greece. For the population of this wide strip of land was a melange of ethnicities, languages, religions and customs: Greeks, Turks, Albanians and Macedonians, each language group having Christian or Muslim minorities, as well as the nomadic peoples—the Sarakatsanides, Vlachs and Kutsovlachs.

Following World War II and the Civil War, this region suffered a rapid loss of population to Greek and foreign cities. By the 1970s, many Epirot villages were in a state of rapid physical and social decline. Houses were left to decay, and the few ones still inhabited sheltered an ever-diminishing population of old, economically inactive men and women. The local economy was nearly at a standstill and ignored by national modernization schemes—after all, no immediate political benefit could be exacted from so sparsely populated a land.

But in the past decade, things have changed. The government has worked to integrate the region into the national economy, emigration trends have been reversed and attitudes towards village life modified, the "traditional" now viewed less as a stumbling block to economic prosperity and more as a cultural heritage to be preserved.

The associated benefits and tensions of this new era for Epirus are most visible in Zagori. Stiff government regulations of building permits and low interest loans and subsidies have led to the restoration of many buildings—both public and private—so much so that, whole villages have been preserved as traditional settlements in their pre-19th century architectural character. Simultaneously, new roads are being built, often right over old mule paths, giving access to the tiniest villages and most distant pasture lands. Finally, the ubiquitous "cultural club" in practically every village—a very recent phenomenon—now sponsors events ranging from traditional dance and music festivals during August to crosscountry races and dramatic productions of Bertolt Brecht's plays.

Conflicting interests: Behind all these manifestations of "modernization," the astute observer will see a microcosm of the Greek reality today—a stage for conflicting interests and world views. Conservationists who want to preserve the land as wilderness versus entrepreneurs who would like to develop skiing facilities on the slopes and aerial tramways in the gorges; farmers who rely on the constant flow of rivers versus the state-owned electric utility which has embarked on a series of low-head hydroelectric projects; mining versus land reclamation; and the ultimate question: what sort of tourism industry to develop?

The new concept that is emerging here is that of "low impact" tourism, or "eco-tourism." It is being promoted by conservation organizations and most agencies of the central government but resisted, predictably, by many local interest groups. Perhaps the "cultural clubs" composed of village youths who study in the major cities will contribute to the resolution of this urgent question. And so will travelers who take the trouble to study this land and to share their views with the local people who are always as eager to hear an outsider's opinion as they are to defend their own.

The territory covered here is vast by Greek standards, spanning some 233 miles (375 km) from Igumenitsa to Edessa, by the most direct route. A minimum of 10 days is suggested for this tour, but the more time you have the better. Note, too, that the coastal region of Párga, Efira, the Nakromantion of the Aheron, Kassopi, Préveza, Aktion and Arta (briefly treated in the Rúmeli section) forms an historically important part of Epirus and that the Igumenitsa-Árta-Ioannina loop is an appropriate addition to the route indicated here.

Igumenitsa: The modern port of **Igumenitsa** which welcomes a great share of the travelers entering Greece from the west is the major port of Epirus and indeed of northern Greece. It has the distinct atmosphere of a place which sees hundreds, in high season thousands, of tourists come and go, few remaining for more than the few required hours. You may not even notice you are in Epirus unless, walking by the man with his table of cassettes set up in the central square, you hear the plangent, bleating *klarino*— the Epirot clarinet. Realize it or not, you have set foot in the land of the *klarino*, whose sounds you will hear across the entire region—in summer at the local village festivals, in winter in the town *taverna*, and almost always on any bus you board. If you have the taste for it,

A priest in Kónitsa, Epirus.

pick up a cassette to accompany your travels and to remember it when you return home.

The road from Igumenitsa to Ioannina winds its way up through the valley of the **Kalamas River**, the ancient Thiamis, with every mile climbing further into the highlands of the **Pindos mountain range**. To the north lie the villages of the **Morgana**, one of which, **Lia**, was rendered infamous in recent years with the book (and movie) *Eleni*, which polemically recounts the tribulations suffered in this area during the Civil War. The Pindos is the largest Greek mountain formation and one of the largest in all of the Balkans, extending from Mount Morava in Albania to the Agrafa range in central Greece.

Ioannina: On entering the upland plain near the Konitsa road junction, the stark face of Mount Mitsikeli appears high above Lake Pambiotis and Ioannina which lines its shores. Over the last one thousand years, **Ioannina** has perennially been one of Greece's great cities, a center of Hellenic culture and education, an international crossroad of traders and, in its last glorious epoch, the citadel of Ali Pasha, the "Lion of Ioannina," the famed

maverick-tyrant who broke away from the Sultan to set up an autonomous Epirot kingdom. Today Ioannina remains one of Greece's most lively provincial centers and a home to one of Greece's six universities. Apart from its own interest and the beauty of its setting, Ioannina makes for a convenient base from which to explore the surrounding area: the Zagorahoria, Metsovo, Dodona.

Unlike most other large Greek cities, the history of Ioannina does not extend back to ancient times. It has distinctly medieval origins, supposedly taking its name from a local monastery of St. John the Baptist. In 1204 it burgeoned in size and importance as a result of the Latin conquest of Constantinople and subsequent establishment of the Despotate of Epirus. Refugees from "The City" swelled its population and in the late 13th century it achieved the status of an archbishopric. It fell, with the rest of Greece, to the Turks in the 15th century, and in the late 18th century Ali Pasha made this city of 35,000 inhabitants (large by standards then) his headquarters.

Ioannina today testifies ambivalently to Ali's legacy—for while he left behind the city's most distinctive monuments (its

annina is mous for its stry called *ugátsa*.

mosques and the redoubtable walls of the citadel), he also burned much of it to the ground during the siege by the Sultan's troops in 1820. This, along with the post-war penchant for building large apartment blocks, has left Ioannina with a decidedly modern face.

The people's square: The wide expanse of Ioannina's central square, lined by the regional army headquarters and various other public buildings, is the most obvious place to orient yourself for a tour of the city. This is where the people of Ioannina meet: the students at noon at the bright sidewalk cafes, the old men in the traditional cafes lining Averof Street playing *távli* and cards, families and old friends walking arm-in-arm for an evening *vólta*. Here too you can eat some of the *bougátsa* for which Ioannina is famed—the fine cream pastry in Greece. Try the **Olympio** on Odos Averof or follow your nose.

After a bit of nourishment, the **Archaeological Museum** at the north end of the square makes a good visit. It has a fine array of Epirot archaeological artifacts spanning from Paleolithic to modern times. Odos Averof descends finally to the **Kástro**, the fortress of numerous

Epirot despots and, lastly, of Ali Pasha himself. In this tangle of buildings and alleyways set on the promontory jutting out into the lake are the most salient reminders of Ioannina's past—the massive walls and its gateways, the **Aslan Pasha** and **Fetiye** mosques. The first mosque now houses the Municipal Museum with a diverse collection of Epirot costumes, jewelry and other relics.

The area around this mosque is the supposed scene of one of the famous stories linked to Ali Pasha in the popular imagination. Kýra Frosíni was the beautiful mistress of Ali's eldest son. In the most common variant of the story, the Pasha took a liking to her as well. But she resisted his advances and paid the price: a watery death. Ali had Kýra Frosíni and seventeen of her female companions tied up in weighted sacks and dropped in the lake. One thing Muslim and Orthodox men seem to have had in common was misogyny.

Further down the waterfront we reach the sealed-up Fetiye ("Victory") Mosque and the tomb of Ali Pasha in front of it. In these buildings, many of which now absent, the "Lion" roared and ruled over his pint-sized empire—taking his pleasure

Even in Gree
it rains
sometimes.

in his Seraglio, entertaining such guests as Lord Byron in grand style, and ordering the death of many an enemy. Before leaving the promontory's shore we may well reflect upon its name for a moment: Dionísiou Skilosófou, or Dionisios the Dog Sophist.

This peculiar fellow, who gave his name to the promontory, began his career as Bishop of Tríkala but soon got himself defrocked for dabbling in black magic and drunkenness. For his new occupation he chose that of rebel and rabble-rouser, which proved even more precarious. In 1611, after leading a violent uprising against the Turks, he was caught in the cave at the edge of the waterfront, flayed alive and stuffed with straw for display to the Sultan in Constantinople.

Monasteries, paths winding among fragrant flowers and trees, and a *taverna* serving local freshwater specialties all fit onto the islet of **Lake Pambiotis**, a brief boat ride from the city. The **Monastery of Áyos Nikólaos** near the fishing village houses vivid frescoes, one depicting unusually gruesome martyrdoms, another peopled by such ancient luminaries as Plato, Aristotle and Thucydides. At the **Monastery of Pantaleímon** is one last

piece of Ali Pasha memorabilia—the house into which he fled in 1822 when hunted by the Sultan's troops. Here his luck ran out, however. Stuck on the first floor, Ali was doomed when the soldiers fired through the ceiling from below. The bullet holes are still there today.

Zeus' sanctuary: South of Ioannina lies **Dodona**, Epirus' main archaeological attraction. The road winds up **Mount Tomaron** (with views of Ioannina, the lake and Mount Mitsikeli in the background) to a small valley whère the sanctuary is located. Homer calls it "wintry Dodona," emphasizing again Epirus' alpine otherness, its distance from Odysseus' "wine-dark sea." And it is a desolate site indeed. In antiquity the Dodona oracle was regarded as the oldest in Greece. Dodonian Zeus who was worshiped here was thought to reside in the trunk of the holy oak tree. Herodotus tells us that the tree (the second oldest in Greece after the willow in the sanctuary of Hera at Sámos) became holy when a dove flying from Thebes in Egypt landed on it, started talking in a human voice and ordered that an oracle of Zeus be set up there. Thereafter priests interpreted the rustlings of the holy oak

en chat at
bus stop in
etsovo.

tree in the wind. As at Delphi, their pronouncements were enigmatically worded. The importance of the sanctuary diminished by the fifth century B.C. as that of Delphi increased.

A guide to the site (sold at the entrance) will help identify the rather scant remains of the ancient buildings and temples, relating them to the Dodona exhibits in the Ioannina museum. The beautifully restored amphitheater which dates from the third century and the days of Pyrrhus, the great Epirot king who defeated the Romans in battle at the high price of most of his soldiers' lives, has a capacity of 18,000 spectators and hosts a festival of classical drama during the summer.

Worthwhile diversions: The road north out of Ioannina leads to the mountainous heart of Epirus—the Zagorahoria. If you are unable to take this extraordinary trip and are instead heading east into **Thessaly,** you can partially console yourself with a visit to **Metsovo,** 36 miles (58 km) from Ioannina. On this route you first pass **Perama,** one of Greece's most spectacular caves. Then, after a long circuitous ascent just before the **Katara Pass** ("the Damned"), the only motor-crossing of the central Pindos, Metsovo appears to

the southeast. It is a singular Greek village, justly famed for its stunning location, its popular architecture and handicrafts, and its inhabitants who still dress in their traditional clothes. Many of the Metsovites are Kutsovlachs—nomads who speak a Rumanian dialect. Some say they came from Walachia during the Middle Ages, and others that they were Greeks trained as mountain pass guards whose Latin language evolved into the present patois. As with the other minority languages of Greece (Macedonian, Albanian, Turk, Sarakatsani) the Vlach language and culture is a fading one. Metsovo is perhaps its last great bastion.

A fine display of the baronial side of this culture is at the **Tositsa Mansion,** an *archontiko,* or lord's manor, with much in common with the mansions of Siatista and Kastoría. Inside are fine examples of Metsovite woodcarving, weaving and carpets. Perhaps one other aspect of Metsovo will strike you—its fine state of preservation. This is thanks to the financing of the town's son, Evangelos Averof, patriarch of one of the richest and most powerful families in Greece, the same family which left its name on such august monuments as the Olympic Stadium in

Below, a bridge in Zagorahori and right, a close-up of stone-work. Far right, a Epirot wom accepts life it is.

122

Athens (built with his money) and the Battleship Averof. While pondering this mix of folk culture, fame and high finance you may also want to taste the local cheese. Greeks come on "cheese excursions" from as far as Préveza and Tríkala to buy the smoked yellow *metsovitiko* and the white, soft and saltless *mizithra*.

The Zagorahoria: The Zagoria District is a culturally and geographically distinct region of Epirus comprising 46 villages, the **Zagorahoria**. Its physical boundaries are the imposing mountains and deep gorges that define the Ioannina-Konitsa-Metsovo triangle. The region enjoyed relative autonomy during the Ottoman occupation, since wealth from trading allowed local leaders to pay off the Turkish overlords. It became a center of learning and the seat of affluent professional classes who emigrated to major commercial centers in the East and in Europe, subsequently returning to their homeland with even greater wealth. The West and East Zagori villages are themselves somewhat distinct from one another in history and present appearance.

The East is an area populated in large part by Vlachs, while the West bears the signs of more Slavic and Albanian influence. A more recent difference resulted from East Zagori's fierce resistance to the Germans during World War II. In retribution the Germans ravaged the area, so that today the West Zagori bears an architectural testimony to its past, while the eastern villages were almost entirely rebuilt following the devastations they suffered during the war.

The Zagoria landscape is dramatic and varied, embracing towering summits surrounded by sheer vertical rock faces, benign alpine meadows, deep forests, fertile plains and sinuous canyons. It is one of the few pockets of wilderness left in Greece and harbors the last remaining populations of wolves, bears, wild boars, lynx, the rare chamois and various types of eagles and hawks. Yet, even in the most remote corner the traveler will find signs of civilization: a Byzantine church; a graceful, slender arched bridge from the Ottoman period; a family of Sarakatsani or Vlach shepherds grazing their flocks in the high plains; a finely built roadside fountain; a half-deserted village whose central square and church have been incongruously renovated, presumably with donations of emigrants

who made it in America or Australia.

A Zagorahoria itinerary: Here are two suggested circuits in the central and west Zagoria region which can be done separately or linked together.

For the central route you leave the Ioannina-Konitsa road just past Karies and follow signs for the Vikos Gorge. The town of **Vitsa** hosts some fine traditional houses and one of the oldest churches in the region, **St. Nikólaos.** For entrance ask at the local police station. Just up the road, **Monodendri** has a fine central square with the huge plane tree and the **basilica of St. Athanasios,** not to mention delectable cheese pie at the cafe there. The short walk to the **monastery of St. Paraskevi** and beyond, along the ledge above the **Vikos Gorge** is literally breathtaking.

Next take the route to the villages of **Kipi, Negades,** and on foot to half-deserted **Vradeto.** An extraordinary three-arched Turkish bridge spans the torrent on the right just before entering Kipi, where, in the upper part of the city, there are well-preserved buildings, a church and school, in a *plateia* overlooking the town. Further up the road, Negades is known for its three-churches-in-one basilica dedicated to St. Demetrius, George and the Holy Trinity, containing good frescoes. For the excursion to Vradeto, take the road to Tsepelovo. A few hundred yards past the fork to Kepesovo a footpath marked by a sign veers to the left to Vradeto. This one-hour hike includes the crossing of a small gorge, a unique climb on a sinuous Turkish cobblestone path (which is one of the most notable pre-modern engineering feats in the region), and a taste of the eerie stillness of this remote village (population seven during the winter). With another thirty minutes of walking you arrive at **Beloi** from where you can see the entire Vikos Gorge. Finally, for somewhat uncharted adventure into the mountains continue up the road to Tsepelovo and to the remote villages beyond.

Western Zagorahoria: For the western Zagorahoria continue further north on the Ioannina-Konitsa road. **Kalpaki** marks one of the most glorified battle sites in modern Greek history. Here in the early winter of 1940 the Greeks met the invading Italian army which attacked from Albania. Mussolini had claimed the campaign would be a mere *passeggiata.* Instead the numerically inferior Greeks

A family eating together.

124

rolled them back into the snowy Albanian mountains for a winter of hell. It was not until the Germans came that Greece was vanquished. Various monuments commemorate the event.

Soon a sign indicates the road (on the right) to **Aristi** and **Pápingo**. This area, tucked among the high peaks of **Mount Gamila**, comprises some of the best-preserved traditional settlements in Epirus. In recent years the two villages of Pápingo (**Megalo** and **Mikró**) have gradually become known as idyllic mountain retreats. And with good reasons: the *Pirgi* (sheer limestone "Towers") rise 2000 feet (610 meters) at the villages' back door; some 20 traditional houses, beautifully restored by the National Tourism Organization, are readily available for rent; good cheese *pita* and fresh trout are served at the various local *tavernas*; and lastly, just off the road between the two villages there is an unusual swimming hole for a bit of alpine aquatics.

From here too you can set out on various hikes in the mountains around Mount Gamila. On the other side of the gorge, Vikos village commands a view of the whole valley of the Voidomatis, the Vikos Gorge, and Pápingo with the

"Towers" and Gamila peaks rising in the background. Seen from afar on a summer night, this village seems suspended among the stars.

Leave the valley of the ever ice-cold, spring-fed Voidomatis River and enter that of the temperate Aoos by way of the Ioannina-Konitsa road. Just before entering Konitsa, an old Turkish bridge, the longest in the region, spans the river alongside the new one. A three-hour walk up the river on the southern bank leads through the thick forest of the National Park to **Moni Stomiou**, magnificently perched on a cliff inside the gorge.

Konitsa is a regional center with a distinct military presence. It is a good place to take on provisions and have a meal either before or after your mountain perambulations. (Try Papakosta in the square.) It was severely battered during the winter of 1947–1948 when General Markos' communist forces mounted a major offensive to take it and make it their capital. Their failure to do so marks the beginning of the end for the communists.

Northwest Macedonia: The road from Konitsa to Neapolis (and Kastoría beyond) is the single connecting route

Epirot
lage.

HIKING IN THE PINDOS RANGE

Large tracks of unspoiled nature, a varied landscape with villages scattered at convenient intervals, and a vast network of trails make this region of Greece a hiker's paradise. A great number of walking trips are possible in the North Pindos, ranging from strenuous multi-day "*haute route*" traverses involving technical climbing, to a series of interconnected day hikes through wilderness and pasture lands between successive villages, to leisurely nature walks.

Travelers relying entirely on the automobile for the exploration of this region will be rewarded by taking short walks around the villages, monasteries, and churches mentioned in the itineraries suggested below. Hikers in good physical condition can opt for a series of day hikes, designing their trip according to time constraints, car availability, bus schedules, and special interests. Though the trail system is extensive, it is not always maintained and clearly marked, and may confuse the first-time traveler in the Greek backcountry. Thus, a good map and compass, a trail guide, a keen sense of direction, an ability to get and double-check trail information from villagers and shepherds, and a good sense of humor are necessary for the enjoyment of foot travelers in North Pindos.

Great caution is good advise for novices and seasoned hikers alike, as weather is known to change very rapidly with little warning. In recent years maps and excellent trail guides have become available (see Dubin, Salmon, Sfikas in bibliography). Here we will not attempt to duplicate in detail descriptions which can be found in these source books.

The hiking loop outlined here passes through a number of different ecosystems, and connects some of the most beautiful villages of the region. It begins and ends in the Pápingo villages where there are ample accommodation facilities (EOT houses, inns), and reliable *tavernas* and supply stores. It has the disadvantage of being the most popular route by far, though nowhere near as well-traveled as the footpaths of England and Central Europe. August is the peak month.

a. **Mikró Pápingo—Astrákas Hut:** (Mountain Refuge visible from Pápingo:

The moun refuge ab Pápingo.

126

get keys from Pápingo, or plan on bringing tent) on Mount Gamila col: 3–4 hours (water available at regular intervals), 3,000 feet (900 meters) ascent.

b. **Side trip to Drakólimni** (alpine lake at 6,900 feet [2,100 meters] altitude). An ideal site for views, meal, etc: 1–1½ hours each way. Overnight at the Refuge or camp on dry bed of Xeróloutsa pond (a 15-minute descent to the east of the refuge on the way to Drakólimni: spring water).

c. **Astrákas Hut/Xeróloutsa—Tsepelovo:** a day-long hike through alpine meadows, high plains, gorge (Mégas Lákkos) crossings, and, eventually, scree slopes, under the shadow of the sheer rock faces of Astrákas. Water is scarce, plan supplies accordingly: 5–7 hours depending on pace. Overnight at Tsepelovo (two inns — make reservations in advance during August).

d. **Tsepelovo—Vradeto—Kipi:** The first leg of the trip on foot (about 2 hours), then another hour down the Kalderimi ("Skala") of Vradeto onto the main asphalt road. Walk (2–3 hours), hitchhike, or take the bus to Kipi. Overnight in Kipi.

e. **Kipi—Vitsa—Monodendri—Vikos Gorge—Vikos (Vitsiko) Village:** From Monodendri follow signs to the Gorge: a well renovated *Kalderimi* (cobblestone path) takes you to the usually dry bed of Vikos (30–45 minutes). A strenuous path (red blazes) covers the length of the canyon, criss-crossing the river bed. Midway at the intersection of Vikos Gorge and the side canyon of Mégas Lákkos (2–3 hours), a series of freshwater ponds are formed by nearby spring water (potable). Stop for lunch and a swim, but do not leave any garbage. This is bear country, as evidenced by their huge droppings on and around the trail and scratch marks on trees. Continue through thick forest, and pass a small meadow before reaching the source of the Voidomatis River. Camp anywhere you want, but stay clear of the trail and hang food from tree branches out of bears' reach. Total hiking time: 5–7 hours depending on pace.

A variation is to take a left fork on the new cobblestone path to the village of Vikos (1 hour) and hitchhike or take a bus to Aristi and then to Pápingo, or cross Voidomatis and follow path to Mikró Pápingo (2–2½ hours).

between Epirus and northwest Macedonia. Out of Konitsa it climbs into the western foothills of **Mount Smolikas** (alt. 8650 feet [2640 meters]), the tallest in the Pindos range, and then descends into the valley of the **Sarandaporos River**. On this road just below Eptahorio is a 32-foot (10-meter) strip of bold blue letters emblazoned on the concrete embankment: FREEDOM FOR NORTHERN EPIRUS—a solemn reminder that, according to the reckoning of many Epirots, half of that region is out of reach in Albania.

On the other side of Mount Vion, having exited Epirus and entered Macedonia, you arrive in **Pentalofos**, which stands like a gateway between the two regions. Its fine gray stone houses, still very much in the Epirot style, drape across the hills which give the town its name—"Fivehills." During World War II some of these buildings formed the headquarters of the British Mission to the Greek Resistance. From Pentalofos the road continues eastward through remarkable limestone formations, waves of rock lying like so many layers of melted lead atop one another.

Siatista, a small town noted for its fine 18th-century mansions, is a brief detour from the road to Kastoría. These mansions, called *archontiká* because they were the residences of the archons, or town's "leading men," offer a glimpse into the feudal society that flourished there during the middle centuries of Turkish rule. It was a center of furring, tanning, winemaking and a stopping point for caravans on the trade route connecting the Balkans to Vienna, but fell from prosperity when, after Greek Independence, the commercial networks changed.

With some imagination, plus a bit of resourcefulness to gain entry into these houses, (ask at the cafe in the main street), you can learn a good deal about the lifestyle and world view of the people who inhabited these dwellings. The most interesting are the Manoussi, Poulikos and Nerantzopoulos houses. They are constructed in an architectural style which is widespread throughout northern Greece: a ground floor of solid stone wall whose few openings are often covered by iron gratings (as brigands abounded and security was uncertain), storage cellars and workshops; a second floor also of stone—the main winter residence; and a third floor of painted plaster board which

A furworker
Kastoría.

juts out over the rest of the building, supported by wooden brackets—a kind of summer parlor and reception room. The walls and ceilings of these are often finely painted. After Siatista you will be well-prepared to see the *archontiká* of Kastoría, another town which grew wealthy from the fur trade.

Returning north, the road follows the upper valley of the **Aliákmon**, the longest river in Greece, whose 185 miles (300 km) flow in a great arc from high in the Pindos to the Thermaic Gulf. Soon the road reaches **Kastoría Lake**, which the town, built on a peninsula, seems nearly to divide in half. Before entering town, on the left you pass a formidable military cemetery designed in latter-day fascist style. It commemorates the Greek soldiers of the government forces killed during the Civil War in this area, the so-called Grammos-Vitsi, where the last brutal stage of the Civil War was fought. The communist dead were left to rot in the hills. The whole scene is one of the most visible reminders of that era between 1946 and 1974 when citizens branded as "communists" were harassed, tortured and exiled. Only now, with the present government, are the communist fighters

being commemorated as well. And Kastoría, somehow, refuses to let you forget this legacy, for, entering the city proper, the central **General James Van Fleet Square** reminds you that American equipment and advisors helped to decide the Civil War in favor of the Nationalists.

A Byzantine center: Kastoría is one of northern Greece's most alluring cities. Its history as a Byzantine provincial center and as a hub of the fur industry is well-reflected by its fifty-four surviving churches, many of which were commissioned by rich furriers. Kastoría's churches embody the fine Byzantine art of a provincial center, far from the grand imperial mosaics of Constantinople and Thessaloníki. The work here often shows more folk and Slavic influence than that of the first and second cities of Byzantine. If you have a morning you can see at least a few of these winding through the city and ending up in **Kariadi**, the Old City, amidst Kastoría's fine *archontiká*.

Ayi Anargiri sits at the northeast edge of town, not far from the lake. It is the oldest church in Kastoría, built in 1018 by Emperor Basil II to celebrate his victory over the Bulgars. Note the fine exterior brick walls decorated with

below, the Pindos Mountains; and two Pirot women in traditional costumes.

various geometric forms, the arched windows above the apse divided by a colonnette, and the frescoes on the west facade of St. Peter and Paul flanked by Cosmas and Damian on either side. The dark interior contains frescoes including St. Basil and a scene of the Pentecost. This church is also known as the earliest example of groin-vaulting found in Greece.

To the south, **Panayia Kumbelidiki**, with its unusually tall drum-shaped dome contrasts strikingly with Ayi Anargiri. It too is from the 11th century, and has frescoes on the facade, not just in niches but covering the whole wall. Further south, it is the interior frescoes of **Ayios Nikólaos Kasnitzi** that stand out in this simple single-aisled basilica. Further south again, the **Taxiarchi** of the metropolis has both external and internal frescoes. It also contains the tomb of the Macedonian liberation fighter, Pavlos Mela, who was killed by the Turks in 1904 just north of Kastoría.

In the Old City above the city's south bank you find the many *archontiká* from the 17th and 18th centuries, with their characteristic painted upper floors which project over the windowless lower ones. Most of these are quite dilapidated, save that of Nazim and Emmanuel, the latter now turned into a folk museum.

Kastoría's fur industry: Strolling through these streets you'll also notice the most important aspect of Kastoría's present social and economic life: the hundreds of small workshops crowded with tailors, fur-cutters, rolls of sewn-together furs and patterns for coats-in-the-making, which form the network of Kastoría's famous fur trade. The history of this trade extends back at least five hundred years to when beavers made Kastoría Lake their home (Kastoría, in fact, roughly means the beaver-place in Greek.)

As these were hunted out of existence, however, Kastoría became the repository for the scraps of fur discarded by the fur industries of Europe and North America. Here in these workshops the scraps are cleaned and sewn together into one piece and then fashioned into a fur coat which is then re-exported to the same countries from which the scraps originated and is sold at relatively low prices. The Greeks, well-aware of their subordinate position in the production cycle, may discuss the economics of the business if you stop to chat with them in one of their shops.

Before leaving Kastoría take the time for a promenade along its shores. On the south side you can walk to the **Monastery of the Mavrotissa**.

To the Prespa Lakes and east: The road north out of Kastoría continues along one of the upper branches of the Aliákmon River. We are now heading towards an unusual corner of Greece, where Greece and all things Greek taper off into the cold blue waters of the **Prespa Lakes** and merge into Yugoslavia and Albania. These lakes are the nesting ground of two endangered species of pelicans (the Dalmatian pelican and wild pelican) as well as numerous other birds, and are today protected as a national bird sanctuary. Despite statutory protection, however, various construction projects have done much damage to this unique habitat in recent years.

The road to the east leads through Florina and Edessa and finally to Pella and Thessaloníki. We pass through **Florina**, badly battered during the Civil War, and join the **Via Egnatia**, which connected the Roman Empire from Durazzo to Constantinople. To the north is **Mount Voras**, the scene of numerous Balkan battles, and to the south, **Lake Vegoritis**. From Alexander the Great's campaigns to modern times, this has been a point where people converging from north, south, east and west have vied for turf. At the turn of the century this was the land of the "Macedonian Struggle," the guerrilla warfare conducted by Greeks against the Turks and Bulgarians. Indeed the area saw little peace in the first fifty years of this century—the Macedonian Struggle 1900–1908, the Balkan Wars 1912–1913, World War I and II, and the Civil War—a 20th century narrative of violence and contestation equaled by few corners of the globe.

Edessa is unlike any other town in Greece, thanks to the streams that wind through it and over its famous waterfall. Walking down its backstreets, or sitting in the square, the sound of rushing water is never far from your ears. A path takes you right down the cliffside and into the waterfall's mist. At the north end of town there is a Roman (or Byzantine) bridge which served the Via Egnatia. Edessa, perched on its high bluff, marks the edge of the Macedonian highlands, and from here you can gaze out to the well-cultured plains that spread towards Thessaloníki and the sea.

Ali Pasha, th famous desp of Ioannina, floating in hi lake.

RÚMELI AND THE IONIAN ISLANDS

The region of Greece commonly known as Rúmeli is too often visited just for the sake of the classical site at Delphi. Rúmeli is not, it is true, as rich in classical monuments as the Peloponnese. But a taste for Rúmeli, a part of the country which lets you travel largely in peace, is not hard to acquire and is difficult to lose.

Rúmeli's very name, not normally shown on maps, is an indication that there is much more of the past and present to explore than the classical past alone. "Rúmeli" is properly "Western Rúmeli," its name originating in the Ottoman term for the Greek nation within the Empire, *Rum Millet*. The word *Rum* is the one the Greeks themselves used: *romaio* or citizens of the eastern part of the Roman Empire. The notion of being, in today's Greek, a *romaios* is complex and persistent. *Romaiosini* (the noun) is everything in Greek life and the Greek identity that is *not* classical, *not* Hellenic; everything, in short, that a one-sided view of the Greeks is liable to reject as "un-Greek."

Hellenism and *Romaiosini* certainly do meet, merge and sometimes clash all over Rúmeli. At Delphi you will see shiny new shepherds' crooks being snapped up by pale Athenian schoolchildren. Or, in the smallest out-of-the-way place, you may ask to see *t'arhéa* ("the ancient remains") and then, following a shepherd up a winding path to the tinkle of sheep's bells, suddenly find yourself at a little ancient fort or acropolis. For Rúmeli is indeed rich in associations, and that the visible signs of these associations are a little harder to find than they are elsewhere adds to the fun of exploration.

It is probably Rúmeli's natural setting that leaves the deepest impression. The hiker has the chance to see everyday marvelous sights such as a herd of goats tumbling down a slope much greener close up than it seemed from the road below. By contrast, the visitor who goes in search of traditional architecture is likely to be disappointed. The main reason for this is that much of Rúmeli suffered a scorched-earth policy both in the War of Independence and later in 1940–1949.

And the inhabitants of the region have

long had a formidable reputation as guerrilla fighters. In the fifth century B.C. the Athenians found that with the "barbarian" Aetolians they had bitten off more than they could chew; in the middle of the last century the Athenian authorities were still having severe problems with banditry in Rúmeli. Some of the *klephts* who had indeed helped to dislodge the Turks in 1921 were reluctant to give up the lawless, free and profitable life of rustling, kidnapping and roast mutton. More recently, and more controversially, it was from Mount Velúhi (Tímfristos) in Rúmeli that the brilliant communist guerrilla Áris Veluhiótis took his *nom de guerre*.

Banditry, the visitor will be relieved to know, has disappeared, and good roads with buses that go everywhere have put Rúmeli's main towns and villages within easy reach of the capital; but the rural communities continue to live a pretty dour pastoral life. And the Rúmeliots' reputation in Greece is not for worldly sophistication. (One reason is their heavy accent: their speech is very short on vowels, which makes it laconic and often hard to understand.) There is a character in the traditional puppet show (*Karaghiozis*)

called Barbayiorgos (Uncle George), a good old boy who still wears a *foustanélla* (a pleated skirt), who hits out with his stick first and asks questions afterwards and who is a bit out of place in the modern world of pay phones and public toilets. Gruff but good-hearted, Barbayiorgos is still the popular image of the Rúmeliot.

Towards Parnassus: The **monastery of Ósios Lukás** (not Luke the Evangelist but an obscure Blessed Luke) is often visited in a hurry as a small Byzantine concession in the standard classical tour. But this 11th-century monastery with its two churches, an example of late Byzantine grandeur in scenic isolation, is well worth a longer visit. It is the nearest one will get to the experience of Mount Athos. There is, to be sure, something strange about descending in busloads on what was once a haven of unworldly peace; but if this is the price of a visit it is worth paying. The beautifully colored mosaics, some damaged and obscure, reveal themselves gradually to the eye as it accustoms itself to the darkness. They appeal, perhaps more than any others in Greece, to the visitor not yet attuned to the Byzantine aesthetic; and

Near Arta a stream is diverted to make a whirl pool for washing rugs

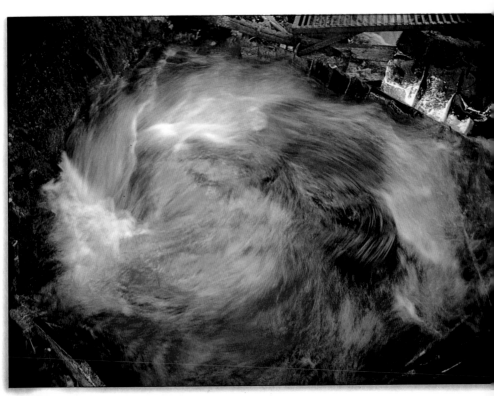

Ósios Lukás deserves a day to itself before passing on to Delphi.

Crossing the edge of the mass of **Mount Parnassus** does something to prepare one for the experience of Delphi. Parnassus dominates the center of Greece from whichever direction one approaches it, whether it be from Lamia north, Livadiá east, Návpaktos west or by ferry from the Peloponnese south. It is the mountain's breadth and shape rather than its sheer height—Giónas is taller—that render it so impressive. In fact the ascent can be performed—on a clear day from late spring on—by the fit as well as the fanatical. Ask for details at **Aráhova**, a fresh and invigorating village hung with expensive rural crafts. Aráhova's skiing facilities are its main attraction; some years back ski-racks became obligatory wear for the Athenian station-wagon. In the upper square by one of the village's many tumbling streams there is an excellent *taverna*. There is also a St. George's Day festival (23 April) on which the air is heavy with the scent of lambs, which the ancients offered to the gods above and which the moderns offer to their own senses, being roasted in the open air. Watch out for the old men's race; the old boys, some reputedly over eighty, run to the top of a steep slope and then unwind with a cigarette. Barbayiorgos is alive and well.

Delphi: From here, it is only a few curving miles down to **Delphi**. This is the place which, of all others in Greece, visitors have found most memorable—that is, since its excavation at the end of the last century. Mycenae and Olympia fascinate, Delphi awes. Abrupt crags rise above as vultures soar above them on winds that can suddenly turn to storms. The site involves steep climbs with, as their reward, the continual glimpsing of new angles and further treasures. So intriguing is the unfolding picture that it is easier here than on most sites to forget the throng around you.

Delphi's fascination is threefold: its stirring setting; the scale, beauty and diversity of its monuments; and, as a sub-text, its turbulent and often disreputable history. The site may be divided into three parts, each of which deserves a morning at least. (To appreciate Delphi to the full stay the night in one of the many hotels and get up at first light the next morning.)

At the upper site, dedicated to the

e Thólos at ·lphi; and a ·stival in ·meli.

Apollo of the oracle, follow the Sacred Way, past the treasuries given to the oracle by Greek states. The Treasury of the Athenians is of particular interest, covered as it is with inscriptions of Athens' glories and the city's thanks to Apollo. It is easy to forget that the whole building has been put back together like a jigsaw puzzle in modern times. From here the path winds up past the oracle itself (a little imagination is required at this point) and the theater to the stadium, the best preserved in Greece. The lower site, the preserve of Athina, contains the single most beautiful monument at Delphi, a columned rotunda. (From here one can walk down the valley into what is said to be the largest olive grove in the world, a sea of ancient trees threatened by a planned highway.) There's a bus back from Itéa. Finally the museum on the site contains numerous marvels, including the famous Charioteer. The large quantity of Roman statuary—including a bust of the Emperor Hadrian's lover Antínous—is a reminder that Delphi had an enduring attraction. We start to piece together— or fancy that we are piecing together— Delphi as it was.

Romanticism, of course. Like most great monuments, Delphi is a monument to folly, gloating and war. The oracle was always the object of corruption and ruthless power plays. Thrones rose and fell at its word—but by all-too-human, rather than divine, agency. And yet, even so, the place still inspires the piety that first founded it in the late Bronze Age. In the 1920s serious-looking young persons in various stages of undress performed ancient athletics and dramatics for a festival; today Delphi is the home of a Cultural Center which sees its task, improbably, as the bringing together of the world "in a spirit of amphictyony." (Yes, you'll need that dictionary—and so do they.)

Galaxídi and Návpaktos: A few miles below Delphi is the port of **Itéa**, from where we look across the bay to **Galaxídi**, a strange little enclave, in a rugged pastoral setting, of the Greek maritime past before the days of steam. Once the third port of Greece, Galaxídi looks as if it is a bit of Syros, perhaps, transferred to Rúmeli. The island atmosphere used to be heightened by the fact that before the construction of the main road, Galaxídi was most easily reached by ferry from Itéa.

View of Galaxídi.

It has a virtually unspoilt core of grand bourgeois houses (*archontiká*), some of which rest on sturdy lengths of ancient wall.

Galaxídi is now a well-preserved ghost-town; the ship-owners have long since left for Piraeus and rarely visit their old houses. But with charming details in the town—such as painted ceilings in some of the houses, if you can get a look inside—and impressive views outside it, Galaxídi has much to offer. Parnassus is magnificently prominent above the villages that scale its slopes; from the hills above Galaxídi, Corinth can be seen on a clear day; and at night the lights of Éyio in the Peloponnese twinkle across the water. Galaxídi was once spoken of as the future St. Tropez of Greece. It has escaped such a fate, but the rusting ships that lie offshore—victims of the Gulf War—and the scars from bauxite workings on the coast opposite—Greece's biggest source of foreign exchange—are a reminder that this region remains vulnerable to the pressures of a wider world.

The coast road continues with innumerable windings to **Návpaktos**. It was here that the Athenians defeated the Spartans in a naval battle in 429 B.C.

and dedicated a ship to Poseidon, god of the sea, at **Ríon** opposite. And in 1571 a famous battle took place (in fact fought just outside the Corinthian Gulf off the west coast of Greece) through which Návpaktos became famous as Lepanto. An Ottoman chronicler records, "The Imperial fleet encountered the fleet of the wretched infidels and the will of God turned another way." It is well worth the climb up from the toy-like Venetian harbor, past little gardens, to the almost impregnable castle above.

One can also take a trip into the hinterland; **Krávara** region had so little to offer its inhabitants in days gone by that they used to maim their own children and send them all over the Balkans to beg—a desperate variant of the Greek entrepreneurial spirit. After a day in these forbidding mountains where villages, still without water and electricity, perch on high crags, the return to the wide expanse of water comes as a relief.

From Návpaktos, one can return to Delphi by the old upland route, as beautiful as the coast road and more hazardous. On the way, the stone village of **Lidoríki** is near the birthplace of General Makriyánnis, a fighter in the War of

Independence whose *Memoirs* are the best insight into the mind of old Rúmeli. Here is a chance to breathe the air and stretch your legs before going on past the shining waters of the **Mórnos reservoir**, which supplies Athens with the water that the locals are denied. Stark rocks are intermittently set off by green valleys with cattle; mountain fauna such as eagles and rock thrushes are noticeable.

Finally the road reaches **Ámfissa**, an old town in a crater-like setting. The old tanneries (*ta tabákika*) give you a good idea of an old neighborhood without the old neighborhood smells. **Sálona**, the castle above is a reminder of Ámfissa heroic past; the reintroduction of classical place-names is a prime example of Hellenism versus *Romaiosini*.

Mesolóngion and Agrínio: Continuing from Návpaktos towards the west coast the landscape becomes flatter. **Mesolóngion** is the best known town here, one as rich in associations as Návpaktos but with a less attractive present face. The lagoon with its feluccas is an unusual sight in Greece, but after a night in the company of Mesolóngion's mosquitoes it is easy to see how it was that Byron came to die here and leave his name—as *Víron*—to a good many Greeks since.

Mesolóngion's role in the War of Independence continued with a grim siege and the slaughter of its inhabitants, events commemorated in an unfinished poem by the national poet Solomós. Unfortunately, the poem, however fragmentary, is more evocative than the visible reality. A forlorn little garden to the heroes is all that remains of the place that roused the conscience of the West. (A statue by the French sculptor David had to be removed after being used by the locals for target practice.)

From Mesolóngion there is a road up through the wild **Klisúra gorge**; further on, you will see tobacco leaves hanging outside almost every house. This is **Agrínio**, a prosperous commercial center. From here one can take a rough road into the upland district of **Karpenísi** and then skirt **Mount Tímfristos** and continue along the oppressive **Sperhiós valley** to **Lamia** (117 miles/188 km). Alternatively, we can deviate—and that's the word, for it's easy enough to get lost on the way—to the **monastery of Prusós**. Pilgrims on the last few miles of the journey cross themselves anxiously out of a well-grounded fear of rockfalls

The bridge of Árta.

from some of the most precipitous heights in Greece. The faint-hearted may prefer the shores of **Lake Trihonís**.

The west coast: At first sight **Árta** is unspectacular, but it is of great interest to the historically minded. The town saw its heyday in the 13th century as the seat of the Despot of Epirus, whose realm stretched all the way up the west coast of Greece to what is now Dürres in present-day southern Albania (Northern Epirus to Greek diehards). Árta's cultural flowering at this period is only now being properly pieced together as archaeologists excavate the many churches in the environs of the town. (Ask for the latest details at the Tourist Office.)

Árta is proverbial in Greece for its bridge, a fine Turkish construction clearly visible to the south of the town. A well-known folk song relates that the bridge's builder, despite his "forty masons and sixty apprentices" could not get it to stay up until he had immured a living thing in the foundations whose spirit would guard it. By ill luck—or so the tale has it—this turned out to be his own wife. For impressive and not much visited ancient monuments try the fortifications at **Strátos** to the south. The older residents of the rather forlorn village there speak not Greek but a sort of Latin, the Vlach dialect more common further north. Just north of Strátos one can turn left for **Astakós**, which has ferry connections with some of the Ionian Islands.

The main road continues to **Préveza**, a town which, like Árta, is known, if at all, through poetry—but in a rather unfortunate way. In 1928 a young civil servant who had received a posting there, Kóstas Kariotákis by name, tried to drown himself falling which, shot himself in the head. Before accomplishing this he had avenged himself on Préveza by writing a poem really entitled "Province" but which is universally known as "Préveza," in which the town is seen as the archetype of the boring, a place where hearing the band on Sunday is a major event. Even today teachers and civil servants quake at the thought of being sent to Préveza by central government; but the town's worthies revere the memory of their unwilling citizen.

A few miles away are the remains of **Nikópolis**, the city founded by the Roman emperor Augustus to celebrate his victory over Antony and Cleopatra

árga looking wards the nian islands.

off Actium in 31 B.C. Impressive walls and a theater survive as a reminder of the hated Roman domination. Foreign domination did bring tourism, however, and in the first two centuries, Nikópolis was a real tourist trap. Visitors arriving there from Rome would either show off their Greek and perhaps pay a call on the philosopher Epictetus or buy Greek trinkets and drink too much Greek wine. Some certainly visited the **Nakromantion** (the oracle of the dead) beyond Párga. Here, under the watchful eye of Hades, Lord of the Underworld, visitors would believe or half-believe that they were communicating with the souls of the dead, much as many Athenians today consult the small ads at the back of the newspaper for mediums. Archaeology has revealed what appears to be special effects equipment. A bit further up the coast we reach **Igumenitsa**, which is the port for Corfu or from there Italy. Rúmeli has been left behind.

The Ionian Islands: When people speak of "the Greek islands," it tends to be the Aegean that they have in mind. Very different in flavor, and largely free of the hubbub of the Aegean routes, are the Ionian Islands. (In Greek they are called *Eftánisa* after the number—seven—of the principal islands; one of them, **Kíthira**, no longer administered with the rest and geographically an extension of the Peloponnese, will not be dealt with here.) The visitor from any mainland country tends to relish the very insularity of the Aegean islands. The Ionian Islands by contrast are in two main respects far from insular.

In the first place, all of them are near the west coast of Greece, from Epirus north to Elis south of the Corinthian Gulf. From the island of Zante, birthplace of the national poet Solomós, one can see the turtle-shaped castle of **Hlemútsi** opposite; the poet himself describes the earth shaking from the cannon-fire at the siege of Mesolóngion some way to the northeast. Moreover, a formal and informal network of communications has always tied the main islands and numerous islets to small ports on the mainland (the meaning of "Epirus"), and such intercourse is the natural state of affairs. Cattle were taken across the straits in the world of Odysseus; today it is mainly smaller items—wine or those mysterious parcels that seem to fill every Greek mode of transportation. The Ottoman rulers of

An art deale in Corfu.

mainland Greece did not want to break this chain, and an important consequence in the present is that the population of the Ionian Islands has remained relatively stable by comparison with that of the Dodecanese, where the loss of the mainland coast to Turkey has deprived islanders of their livelihood and led to large-scale emigration. In the Ionian Islands a large rural population still exists and the twang of Chicago or Melbourne Greek is rarely to be heard.

The other way in which the Ionian Islands are far from insular is that they are, in the high culture at least, an amalgam of East and West. Under Venetian rule—which in Corfu, always the most important of the islands, lasted from 1386 till 1797—the rich were bilingual in Greek and Italian, often educated in Venice or Padua and in some cases honored with the noble titles of the *Libro d'Oro* in the manner of a European aristocracy. Many were Roman Catholics, and the religious paintings of the 17th and 18th centuries bear the mark of western developments, as does the architecture of the churches to which they belong. It was native traditions as much as any interference, kindly or otherwise,

by external powers, that made the Ionian Islands the first home, in the lands that now make up Greece, of a university and of a form of representative government.

But the islands' geographical position has been a source of more than a distinctive culture. It has also meant turbulent times for a region of great commercial and strategic importance, ever since Corinth's colonization of Kérkyra (now Corfu) in order to secure the Italian trade route. Between 1797 and 1864 the islands were ruled, under various constitutions, by Venice, France, the Ottoman Empire, France again, the United Kingdom and finally Greece. Today they are at peace threatened only by earthquakes, of which there are quite a few.

Corfu (Kérkyra) was famous in ancient times for a bloody civil war; more recently it came into vogue through the writings of the Durrell brothers. Much has changed since World War II, and the island is now Greece's single biggest tourist asset. At the same time, however, it remains an island of great agricultural wealth, especially in olives—a blessing of Venetian rule. Its population is still overwhelmingly rural, and in fact Greece's least literate. So it is still easy to escape

the "pubs" of the main tourist centers and find a quiet spot, especially to the northwest.

Despite its crowds and considerable war damage Corfu town remains a unique conglomeration of public and domestic buildings in which one can detect something of all the influences that have affected the island. Here and there the emblem of the lion of Venice; a French-style colonnade; houses with a Neapolitan flavor; and a clear legacy of British rule, cricket on the esplanade (fox-hunting never caught on). Opposite loom the forbidding mountains of Albania. Two members of the large Greek minority there recently braved the currents and swam across to Corfu.

Lefkáda is the least visited of the Ionian Islands; island lovers spurn it as being too similar to the mainland, from which it is separated only by a chain-ferry. Mainland affinities are indeed much more evident in Lefkáda, long subject to a tug-of-war between the Venetian and Ottoman empires. The influence of foreign rulers was but superficial. (Probably a majority of the inhabitants are descendants of refugees from the mainland.)

More often visited because of its name, but still very peaceful for most of the year, is **Itháki**. The reason of course is its fame as the home of Odysseus (though envious Lefkáda has disputed the claim). Homer correctly describes the island as rugged; it is also beautifully green. **Vathí** the capital, a deep port with white houses climbing steep slopes on either side, is the best place to stay (the north of the island is within easy reach). Go to the little museum; test your connoisseurship on the supposed El Greco in the Cathedral; walk out of town a way and even if you are not the romantic type you will see why Byron once wished he owned it.

Cephalonia, the largest and most rugged of the *Eftánisa*, is perhaps the island in which one most feels the loss of old ways and the passing of power and culture elsewhere. Lefkáda and Itháki were always humble, but **Argostóli** was a charming town before the disastrous earthquake of 1953, and plays from **Lixúri's** 18th-century days have recently been revived on the Athenian stage.

Zante (Zákinthos) appears from the boat (from Killíni in the Peloponnese) like a little model town. The churches and other buildings restored or rebuilt after the great earthquake of 1953 look just a little too bright and new. But while the atmosphere of the old streets has been largely lost, the public buildings and churches remain charmingly decorous. Less overrun by tourists than Corfu, Zante gives one some idea of what it was that the Ionian Islands brought to the Greece of today. One of the greatest contributions, especially valued by the Greeks, is poetry. After the fall of Crete in 1669 many of the aristocrats who had produced the literature of the Renaissance in Crete left for the Ionian Islands and Zante in particular. And the tradition was combined by the two great Romantic poets born in Zante, Count Dhionísios Solomós and Andréas Kálvos; a third poet, Ugo Foscolo, wrote in Italian, but the Greek government still claims him as Greek on his anniversary. Off the main square by the harbor there are in fact two fascinating museums, one devoted largely to Solomós and the other to the paintings of the distinctive Ionian School. These highbrow activities apart, it is only fair to mention that swimming in Zante is as good as anywhere in Greece, and that a subsequent evening meal will sometimes be accompanied by serenades after the Italian fashion.

Left, boatman from the Mesolóngion. Right, a woman from Corfu.

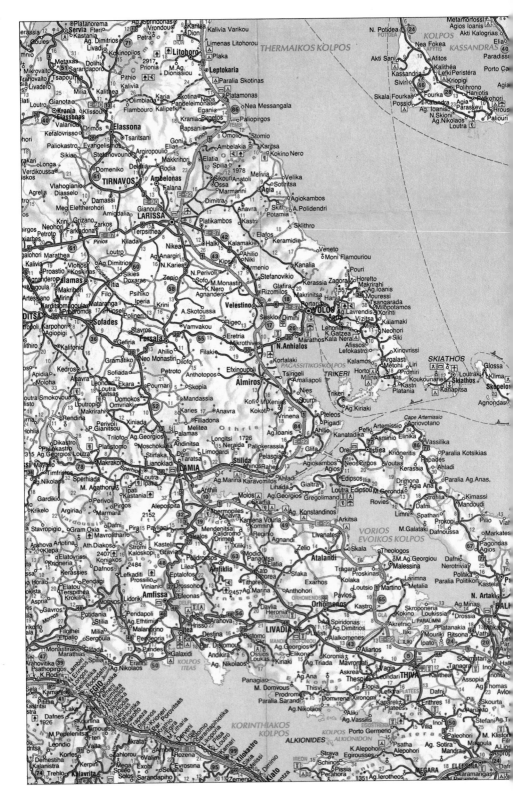

CENTRAL GREECE

What today we consider Central Greece was, until the end of the Balkan Wars in 1913, Northern Greece. At that point the northern boundary of Greece ran from Volos through Larissa, around the wide Thessalian plain, through the southern part of the great Pindos range to Árta on the west coast. Yet again territory in Greece proves to be temporary. But whatever the name of this middle part of the country, the area comprises the best that Greece has to offer: mountains, trees, fertile land, sandy beaches, islands, running rivers, and excellent harbors. Volos, situated about halfway between Thessaloníki and Athens, makes a convenient hub for our travels in Central Greece which can fan out in every direction—east to Pélion and the Sporades, south to Euboea, west to Metéora and north to Olympus.

One's first impression of **Volos** is that some giant took an accordion made of Athens, Piraeus, Thessaloníki, and all their outlying suburbs, and squished it together. The city has a little bit of everything found in a huge metropolis.

Once there, the visitor senses immediately the unique charm of the small busy town. There is a lovely promenade along the quay. The harbor reminds one of island harbors more than big city ports. Running down to the sea are numerous narrow streets in whose arcades are hidden some great little *ouzeri* places. To find one, wander up and down the little alleys till you hear the click of the *távli* (backgammon) dice, or see a couple of old men sitting on rickety chairs outside, sipping coffee. Inside there will be *oúzo* and *mezéthes* (little munchies to go with the *oúzo*).

Like most important port cities of Greece, Volos has an incredibly long history, dating back to neolithic times (about 4600 B.C.–2600 B.C.). The wonderful tale of the adventuresome Jason, who set out from Iolkos, portions of which have been excavated on the outskirts of Volos, in the famous ship *Argo* to find the Golden Fleece long before the Trojan War, seems to come alive as you gaze out at the gulf named after the ancient port of **Pagasae**. Mythology is everywhere in Volos.

The Sporades: Perhaps what makes

Volos such a fun town is the variety of places you can get to, setting off from the sea, the bus terminal, or of course by car. For those who choose the sea, Volos is the boarding point for the tiny, luscious group of islands known as the **Northern Sporades**. What a marvelous word! It means scattered, or sown, as the root of the word means seed. It is an accurate designation for these islands, strewn off the coast of Pélion.

Closest to Volos is **Skiáthos**, whose only rival in island tourism is Mykonos. This is partly due to its intensely lush greenery, but mostly to its sandy beaches. The most popular of these, Koukounariés, has a sandy stretch more than half a mile long, shaded by pines and shrubs. The place is so desirable that "villas" and houses and bungalows for rent are fully booked a year in advance. The international young crowd camps out wherever they can.

Skópelos, the next in the row of the Sporades as you sail eastward, has not been as yet devoured by tourism in spite of it being perhaps more picturesque. Its beaches are lovely. The one lying in the curve of the bay of the main town, **Skópelos**, is usually very crowded.

Others smaller and more intimate than those of Skiáthos, are accessible by car or bus. The most lovely are **Stáfylos Cove, Limonári**, near the main town, and **Miliá** and **Loutráki** nearer to **Glóssa**. Rent a "put-put" and chug to your own isolated beach, of which there are many.

You should not miss the opportunity to visit this beautifully green island. It has two ferry boat stops, Glóssa the "tongue," opposite Skiáthos, and past that the main harbor, which as you approach looks like a white-tiered wedding cake, decorated with brilliantly-colored flowers. The harbor is intensely busy, what with the four-times-daily ferry service and the many private yachts.

The interesting thing about Skópelos is that its central wooded spine once supported enough trees so that shipbuilding was a major source of income for its inhabitants for thousands of years. The trees are still there, but not in quantity or size for shipbuilding.

For those interested in chapels and fascinating convents (some of these produce handwoven goods), or remote monasteries, Skópelos, for all its tiny size, has about 360 such—white dots on a variegated green landscape of almond,

The island of Skiáthos.

plum, fig, and olive trees and thousands of grape arbors. Skópelos even boasts some antiquities, including the remains of a Cretan colony, and, as everywhere in Greece, a ruined *Kástro*.

Beyond Skópelos lies the oblong island of **Alónisos**, with its steep, rocky coastline on the northwest, and undulating hills. On the dock you will witness a phenomenon, not unique to Alónisos by any means, but surprisingly fervent here—that of soliciting rents for private-rooms. Some locals hold out discreet cards; others wave large signs. The practice is illegal, so the hopefuls keep one eye on the shore to watch out for the tourist police, and the other on the de-barking passengers. It is not such a bad idea, if you think about it. Most of the backpacking crowd, the majority of the Sporades tourism, have no place to stay and no money to afford the few nice hotels that exist. They have no way of knowing who has rooms or where these rooms might be. So pushy advertising can be helpful.

If, by renting a moped, or hiring a "put-put," you can get beyond the harbor town, you will find Alónisos one of the last bastions of unspoiled tourism in Greece. There ARE deserted beaches. There ARE green pine groves without discarded film boxes and plastic bottles. The only paved road which exists leads from the harbor to the old pre-1950 earthquake town of Alónisos. To get anywhere else you must go by dirt road or skiff. Renting a small boat is worth it because you can make a round-the-island and across-to-Peristéra trip at your own pace. **Peristéra** is the small island that hugs the shore of Alónisos on the eastern side. For other areas on the island, such as the beach at **Marpúnda** on the south, or **Kokinókastro** on the eastern peninsula, there are regular launches leaving from the main harbor during the summer. Before you go, make sure to order a lobster for your dinner from some seaside restaurant. It is not cheap but the fresh-from-the-sea flavor is worth a splurge.

Beyond Alónisos and its small companion, Peristéra, are scattered three or four more islands: **Pélagos** (also called Kyrá Panaghía), **Yiaoúra**, which has a cave worth investigating and **Pipéri**. These can only be reached by *caïque*, the Greek name for a fishing boat, or one's own yacht. It was off these rocky promontories that a Byzantine wreck was

discovered in the summer of 1968 and subsequently explored by a team of archaeologists, including the famous Throckmorton, under the auspices of the Greek Archaeological Service, supervised by Nikólaos Yialouris. The brilliantly-colored Byzantine plates, with their motifs of sailing vessels, fish and border designs, are now in the museum at Volos.

The fourth major island of the Northern Sporades, **Skyros**, has the most history and legend of the group. It was the island where the two-timer Theseus was put to death by the king of the island, Lycomedes. It was here that Thetis hid her son Achilles, disguised as a woman, with Lycomedes' daughters so he would not be drafted for the Trojan War. There were draft-dodgers even then!

The main town itself, also called **Skyros**, is built partly on a bluff overlooking the beach to the east, and then dips into lower ground where most of the shops are. A bust of Rupert Brooke, the British poet who died in Skyros while on his way to fight in the Dardanelles in 1915, dominates the tiny square of the uphill part of the town. From there the view to the sea is out of this world. Just beyond the square is a miniscule chapel,

tended with infinite care by a little old woman. This is the chapel so treasured by the Nobel prize-winning poet, Seferis. He loved the island, and often rented "The Mill," a refurbished old mill house close to the beach, sleeping four and having a lovely garden running down to the sea.

Clearly the wealth of legend surrounding the island is an indication of its commercial importance. It was a center of maritime commerce for thousands of years, and home to many of the Mediterranean pirates who defied law and order from the days of Pompey in 70 B.C. to the middle of the 19th century. All is calm there now, except during the hectic summer tourist season, when the few houses that have rooms are crammed. Go in October. With its variegated plant and forest growth melding into the sea and precious beaches, it is perhaps the most beautiful of all the Sporades.

Euboea (Évoia): From Skyros' harbor of **Linariá** a ferry boat leaves regularly for the east coast port on **Euboea** of **Kími**. Up from the noisy broil of the dock, the real village is charming. Stay there a night, if you can. Of course, Euboea, as you

must pronounce it or no one will know what you are talking about, is more usually reached via the road from Athens to the large sprawling city of **Chalkis**, the capital of Euboea. However, arriving on the island via the backway gives you a chance to get a taste of the landscape.

After Crete, Euboea (about 115 miles long) is the second largest island in Greece. A thorough exploration of the island is most rewarding. It is a microcosm of Greece. Museums, restaurants, beaches, factories, refineries, discos, glamorous hotels, pollution, ancient, Byzantine, Frankish, Venetian, 1821 relics—all are there. Chalkis (perhaps named for the Greek word for bronze, *halkós*) alone possesses all of these. The bustling city is located on the **Euripus channel** whose irregular currents change direction as many as 14 times a day. Its maritime significance was as important in the seventh century B.C. as it was in the period of Venetian dominance (A.D.1200–A.D.1400), when the island was known as Negropont. (No authority seems to know why the island was called Black Bridge—unless it was a reflection of the changeable waters of the Euripus strait and the difficulty of navigating it.)

All along the coast going north, and even further to the south, are the latest hotel development projects. Although the beaches are not very desirable for swimming, as they are mostly pebbly, and not very clean, the hotels are always full during the summer. This is true of the whole Miami-like coastline facing the continent, as well as the southern ferry port of **Karístos**, jutting up on its limestone hill.

The beautiful parts of Euboea are the central and northern portions. The road winds leisurely up and up, settles down in some valleys, and then goes up again. All are green and wooded. A 12-mile junket to the west from the main north-south road at **Strophyliá** leads you to the resort of **Límni**, very much the enclave of the British, who maintain summer homes or even stay the year round. It is also a great haven for yachtsmen. If you get that far, you should proceed along the narrow coastal road to the very attractive convent at **Galatáki** with its spotless refectory and peaceful rooms overlooking the sea between the island and the mainland. Its central fountain is surrounded by an ecstatic blaze of flowers. There is no beach to speak of but you can swim off

e monas-
ies of St.
:holas
it) and
usoúnou
low) in
itéora.

the rocks on which are perfect for reading and sunbathing as well.

In addition to the traces of Frankish and Venetian remains, sad relics of past glory, there are many ancient ruins. Most of these are in the northern part of the island near **Istiéa** and **Oreí**, and are rather disappointing to the non-expert. It is more rewarding to visit the **sanctuary of Artemis** near **Vathí** on the road to Chalkis from Athens. There, close by the immense cement works of Chalkis, you can visit famous **Avlis**, where Agamemnon's youngest daughter, Iphigénia, was sacrificed on the altar of Artemis, the virgin huntress goddess, so that the winds would be favorable for the Greek fleet to set sail for Troy. There are also some Mycenaean remains in Avlis which give credence to the importance of the spot during that early period. As a harbor, however, it seems hardly ideal for 1000 sailing vessels!

A final place to visit in Euboea is **Edipsós**, with its centuries-old renowned health springs. From there you can take off for the mainland. Sacred to the ancients for their healing powers, the springs were frequented by such famous Roman characters as Sulla, the con-queror of the east. Although the beach is hardly ideal, many large tourist hotels have been built around the small bay. Some of these nearest the springs boast mineral water piped directly into the rooms!

Thermopylae (Thermopile): The monument dedicated to the men who died at Thermopylae in July of 480 B.C., defending the Greeks against the hordes of Persians, is located on the National Road to Lamia, just beyond Kámena Vourla (a mineral spring center like Edipsós), mobbed in the summer in spite of mushy beaches and murky water. *Thermopylae* literally means "warm gates or pass" because of the area's innumerable hot sulfur springs which bubble up today as they did in 480 B.C.

The last part of Book VII of Herodotus has immortalized the romance of betrayal. How Leonídas and his 300 Spartan men were annihilated because of the treachery of a well-bribed local, Ephiáltes (the word means nightmare in modern Greek) is a well-known tale. Although Leonídas had known of the path over the heights of Mount Fríkion, the Persians slaughtered the thousand guarding it, and swooped down upon the

Along the coast of Pélion.

152

Spartan rear. And that was the end of the 300, Persians in front and Persians behind. Their immortal epitaph rings sacred: "O stranger, announce to the Spartans that we lie here, obedient to their words."

However, the monument is a let-down compared to the epitaph. It consists of a colossal Spartan in fighting stance, and a low structure with lots of names. You can easily get a picture by leaning out of your car or bus window.

Metéora: Suddenly, as you round a bend in the dull road that leads from Tríkala to Kalambáka, erectile, elemental rock formations piercing the sky confront you—the **Metéora**. Nothing you have ever seen in pictures can prepare you for this. On these projections are some of the most extraordinary monasteries in the world. The name is derived from the verb, *meteorízo*, which means to suspend in the air. That is certainly the impression you have when you get there, especially when the mist, creeping low on the plain, disengages the monasteries from the ground.

Few places in Greece are so intensely visual. The formations, which once supported 24 monasteries, defy description.

Most geologists hold to the theory that the strange outcroppings of rock were created by millions of years of erosion by the **Piniós River** as it split the Pindos range of the west on the Thessalian plain from that of Mount Olympus and Mount Ossa on the east.

Whoever was the first, Andrónikos or Athanásios, depending upon which of the various histories you may read, which aged monk gives you the *real* story, you can only marvel at how long it took to get stone by stone, brick by brick, board by board up to those heights with just a basket and a rope ladder. (Until recently that was still the only method of getting provisions or people to the summits.) The largest of the monasteries, the Grand Metéoron, also known as Metamórphosis (Transfiguration) took three centuries to complete, having been founded around 1356. Áyos Stéfanos (now run by nuns) was completed at the end of the 1300s. Of the twenty four monastic communities which flourished till the last part of the 17th century, their heyday being in the 14th and 15th centuries, seventeen are in ruins, and only five are open to visitors. Of these, only three are inhabited.

Clockwise, the visible monasteries are:

Áyos Nikólaos (uninhabited except by someone to collect a fee) built around 1388, with a small chapel containing frescoes by the monk Theophanes of the Cretan School (c. 1527); **Grand Metéoron**, looked after by a few monks of the St. Basil order, with a valuable collection of manuscripts dating to the ninth century and icons displayed in the old refectory; **Varlaám**, with 16th-century frescoes by Franco Catellano, restored in 1870; **Áyia Triátha** (Holy Trinity) which is approached by approximately 139 difficult steps chiseled out of the rock, and whose major claim to recent fame is being an on-sight location for the James Bond movie, "For Your Eyes Only"; **Áyos Stéfanos**, where although the nuns can often be less than friendly, the renovated chapel is easy of access, and whose small museum displays ecclesiastical robes, icons, manuscripts and similar treasures. All monasteries are open from 9 a.m. to 1 p.m., and 3:30 p.m to 6:30 p.m., *except* when they are closed! Grand Metéoron is closed Tuesday; Varlaám is closed Friday; Áyos Stéfanos is closed Monday. So if you want to "do" the grand circuit, choose your days with care, *and* bring a tiny flashlight! So much wax and oil has been burned in these rooms for centuries that you can see almost nothing of the icons or frescoes without one.

If you really want to understand the monasteries' beauty and awe, you should try to connect up with some local person from Kalambáka or Tríkala, who will know the entrances and exits and secret low doors out to the grassy meadow-like plots of green nestled in the secret hollows of the rocky pinnacles. While most tourists are shepherded back into their buses, you can explore, and after finding a secluded hedge, gaze out over the plain far below.

Olympus: Today, as you drive through the beautiful **Vale of Tempe** along the gorge of the Piniós River, you can hardly believe that until 1913, it was not even part of Greece. The Vale, however, oblivious of time and armies remains the same welcome lushness of cool and green as it has been for thousands of years. Even the encroachments of tourism have not changed the river, which forms the six-mile pass severing Mount Olympus from Mount Ossa. Along the way there are several touristy stops. One is the little church of **Áyia Paraskeví** across a

A Byzant monaster

narrow foot-bridge over the river. There you can light your candle and fill your canteen. Another is the **spring of Afrodíte** at the end of the pass. In spite of these tourist traps, no one should travel the "Vale," hymned by so many poets, without stopping somewhere—either to look down at the river and take a picture, or perhaps wander down a path to its edge.

Leaving the cool vale you head north, straight for the "home of the gods," Mount Olympus. There are several passages in Homer where he alludes to Zeus' habit of bringing down the clouds to cover the summit of Mount Olympus so that no one on earth could see what was going on. Well, that is just one way of stating an obvious fact. Very rarely can you get a good picture of the mountain from the narrow plain that lies between the mountain and the sea, the **Thermaic Gulf** (from the word *thermós*, meaning warm because of all the warm springs). Even more rarely can you get a good distant shot, so continuously is the summit girdled with clouds.

There are two major ways to ascend the mount of the gods—the slow and the fast. Basic details can be gotten from the offices of the Alpine Club in Athens, Volos or Thessaloníki (SEO). If you want to taste the nectar of the gods, the best plan is to go up the slow way, and down the fast. This requires some advance preparation. A direct contact through the Alpine Club or a travel agency is necessary so that the refuge camps and a guide to take you up the last rocky ascent will be available. The lower regions are easy to traverse, as the path from the Stavrós refuge camp is easy to follow. This first refuge camp on Olympus is accessible by bus from the village of **Litóchoron**, a 30-minute ride. You can also walk it.

Beyond Stavrós, a dirt road skirts the foothills, and then the real trail takes off along a gentle two hours of climbing through lovely wooded terrain. After some two hours of walking you will come to the "crossing" of the Enípeos stream which, further down, flows into the Piniós gorge. At the crossing, the rocks and fresh waterfalls with all the surrounding green are so enticing that you may feel like staying there all day. Beyond is the steep ascent, through pine, beech, oak and scrub, to the marvelous second refuge camp. This one has three large cabins which together can house as many

ΡΗΓΑΣ ΦΕΡΡΑΙΟΣ

„ Εἷς οἰωνὸς ἄριστος, ἀμύνασθαι περὶ Πάτρης."

Ἐκ τῆς Βασιλικῆς Λιθογραφίας ἐν Ἀθήναις.

as 70 people. You will need about five hours to reach this second refuge camp. If you are lucky, while you are panting up the steep trail, a donkey may pass, laden with bottles of orange drink. Its destination is the refuge camp, but the proprietor will sell you his wares on the way!

Most people end up staying at the second refuge camp, after nearly a seven-hour climb, and never make it to **Mítikas**, the top. This is because you really should have some experience as a rock-climber, unless you have the assistance of the guide. There is only one seam where steps have been cut in the rock face. Theoretically there is a guide who mans the refuge camp six months of the year. He is responsible for keeping tabs on climbers, and stocking the refuge with food and mountain tea (*tsaï tou vounóu*).

Having reached the top of Mítikas, however, you will find the descent via the fast route not too difficult, once you get down off the rocks. The trail is well marked, a direct plunge into the Thermaic Gulf. Via this trail, experts starting from the coastal village of **Platamónos** have made the ascent and return in one day. The major item to remember, whichever trail you take, is the water flask.

Pélion: Having navigated the austere heights of Mount Olympus, let us now return to the "hub" of Central Greece, Volos and **Mount Pélion**.

The mythological explanation for the mountains which circle the great Thessalian plain is wonderfully imaginative. Huge creatures called Titans or Giants (depending upon what version of the story you read—Homer, Hesiod, Ovid, Virgil) vied with each other to dominate the underlings, Zeus and Poseidon. What modern scientists call earthquakes, ice flows, seismic shifts of plates, or whatever, were simply credited to the Titans. It was they who tried to pile Pélion on Ossa, and both mountains on top of Olympus to reach the heavenly realm of the gods.

"And they were minded (the Titans) to pile Ossa on Pélion of the quivering leaves, in order to ascend to the sky."
—Odyssey XI.315

The legend is often laughed at as being a tall tale until you have been there. Then the close juxtaposition of the three mountain massifs and the precipital cleavage of the vale may make you wonder.

But let's leave such great endeavors to the gods and content ourselves with a trip around Mount Pélion, land of the centaurs. These famous beings had the legs and bodies of horses (indicating the importance of the horse in the development of civilization) and the arms and heads of men. These creatures were the teachers of many of the major heroes, Achilles being the most famous. The intriguing historical fact is that the entire Pélion region was *the* center of learning i.1 Greece throughout the 17th and 18th centuries. A whole slew of monasteries with research facilities grew up in the centaurs' habitat. Many of the important secretaries and governors of provinces in the Austro-Hungarian Empire, the Sultan's inner circle, the Russian court, not to mention many intelligentsia of Europe, were educated on Mount Pélion.

There are few remains of 'this grandeur, but **Zagorá**, the former center, still boasts an excellent library and **Makrinítsa**, about 12 miles from Volos, has preserved the 18th-century "Pélion-style" houses. Probably the original reason for becoming such a center of erudition was its lush water supply, and its inaccessibility to the Turks, which meant no revenues for the overlords.

The beaches, where Mount Pélion crashes into the sea, are beyond the power of words or pictures to describe. The sand is soft and creamy—real sand. The sea is more turquoise and filtered purple than any photograph. Sea-fashioned caves and hidden coves will lure you down the many steps at **Tsangaráda** or the twisty road that ends up at **Ayiá Yiánni**.

You will need a number of days to see all the villages nestled on Pélion's slopes: **Machriráchi, Miliés, Milopótamos, Makrinítsa**, one of Pélion's most beautiful villages with cobblestone streets and spectacular views to the north, or **Drakiá, Áyios Lavréndis**, dedicated to folk art, or **Argalásti** in the heel of Pélion's boot—to name a few.

However, it is worth the time. Indeed, time should be the password for the whole country. You cannot "do" Greece in two weeks. The ancients have left their relics, of which the museums are full. The Romans, Byzantines, Arabs, Slavs, Franks, Venetians, Turks have done the same. That encompasses about 6,000 years of high civilization. Nowhere in Greece has this heavy mass of history, triumph and tragedy made itself more evident than in so-called "Central Greece."

ATHENS

If there is one quality which Athens should be credited with unreservedly, it is elasticity. It might be compared to an indestructible old sweater which has shrunk and stretched and shrunk again through the centuries, changing its shape as circumstances required.

Athens is barely mentioned in Homer. It emerged as a growing power in the sixth century B.C. Then came the Periclean high noon, when Athens became a great center of art and literature, commerce and industry. With Macedonian expansion came the first shrinkage, though Athens remained a prestigious intellectual center with particular emphasis on philosophy and oratory. In the Hellenistic age, Athens was overshadowed by the great monarchies founded by Alexander's successors, but not obliterated; the rulers of Egypt, Syria, Pergamum courted the old city with gifts of buildings and works of art. Yet one can't help feeling it was perhaps already beginning to live on its past, to turn into a museum-city, a "cultural commodity" rather an active, living organism. Besieged and sacked by Sulla in 86 B.C., restored and pampered under two philathenian Roman emperors, Augustus and Hadrian, sacked again by the Herulians in A.D. 267 and Alaric the Goth in A.D. 395., Athens entered the Byzantine era shorn of all its glory—a small provincial town, a backwater. The edict of the Byzantine emperor Justinian forbidding the study of philosophy there (529) dealt the death-blow to the ancient city. Under Latin rule (1204–1456), invaded, occupied and fought over by the French, Catalans, Florentines and Venetians, Athens shrank even further. It was only after the Turkish conquest in the 15th century that it began to expand again, but still falling far short of its ancient limits. There were more setbacks, including a devastating Venetian incursion in 1687. Athens finally rose from its ruins after the War of Independence, an "exhausted city," as Christopher Wordsworth noted in 1832, and was suddenly raised, unprepared, to the status of capital of the new Greek state.

Growing up fast: Athens is thus a city that has grown haphazardly, and too fast. It never had a chance to mellow into venerable old age. Old and new have not blended too well; you can still sense the small pre-war city pushing through the huge messy sprawl of today's modern capital, like the proverbial thin man struggling to get out of every fat man. Expansion has also left its mark on the conformation of the population, which is extremely heterogeneous; few inhabitants can legitimately claim to be autochthonous Athenians.

An unmellow city, then; a city in transition, it is said apologetically. But then one might say it has always been in transition, not the natural kind, but violent and irregular, leaving visible marks, glaring contrasts, untidy seams. Not all that long ago, cows grazed in Patissia, and one of the busiest crossroads was probably a vineyard, judging from its name, Ambelokipi. You occasionally come across what must have been a country villa, ensconced between tall office buildings, its owner still fighting against the tide, its windows hermetically closed against dust, pollution, the roar of the traffic. For traffic in Athens has to be seen (and heard) to be believed. For one thing, Athens must have the highest number of motorcycles in Europe; cars are expensive and get stuck in the traffic, motorbikes wriggle through where everybody else fears to tread. They have become part of the Greek youth culture, a mystical status symbol spawning its own language, rituals, mythology.

But branching off from these frenzied central arteries are the minor veins of the city, relatively free from congestion: narrow streets where the architecture may be shrilly modern, yet life retains in part some of the old patterns. Most apartment blocks have balconies and verandahs, and there you can see the Athenians in summer emerging from their afternoon siesta in underpants and nighties, reading the paper, watching the neighbors, watering their plants, eating their evening meal. Across the street, a florid lady drinks coffee with a friend and then reads both their fortunes in the thick residue. (The squiggly patterns that form in the tilted cup lend themselves to such a variety of interpretations that this must surely be one of the most rewarding of soothsaying methods). Janitors bring out chairs on the sidewalk and converse with each other; the greengrocer brings out a folding table for a game of backgammon with the hardware shop man. The hot weather makes life in the open air a necessity; this in turn means gregariousness, a kind of social exhibitionism—it is no accident that there is no word for "privacy" in Greek—though nowadays the pale blue flicker of television draws more and more people indoors. Yet even television sometimes turns into an excuse for gregariousness; there are improvised World Cup parties, election-night parties; collective viewing while eating, drinking, talking, and playing cards.

Recently taxis have also turned into a sort of communal institution. Taxis are cheap in Athens and therefore in great demand. If you're lucky enough to get a taxi, you soon find you have to share it with others. But what began as a necessity has evolved into one more occasion for social exchange, whether heated argument or comfortable chatting. Are the Athenians then such sociable and fun-loving creatures? Not really; they are simply easily bored and immensely restless. Byron called the Greeks "an intriguing cunning unquiet generation." Another foreign traveler, the Frenchman Edmond About, observed in 1852 that the Greeks are vain, curious, furiously ambitious, set on a relentless quest for success and prosperity, as a result of the insecurity generated by decades of

poverty. (More than poverty, the sheer precariousness of life in Athens in those protracted dark ages). This is perhaps what gives the city its intent, bustling air, often mistaken—especially by disciplined northerners—for uninhibited Mediterranean exuberance. It's true that the incessant activity has nothing of the ant-like industriousness of the Protestant work ethos. Improvise, make do, contrive and combine, keep going, keep ahead, is more what it's all about. The feverishness is also due, no doubt, to the need for rapid adaptation to the modern world, to the crazy pace created by those abrupt, transitional pangs mentioned above.

It would be interesting to write a sociological study simply noting the kinds of shops that predominated in Athens with each successive transition: the sixties saw an extraordinary eruption of "Scandinavian" furniture shops; in the seventies it was fashion boutiques and art galleries; everybody became bathroom-conscious, and shop-windows displayed huge shell-shaped bathtubs, gold taps, an infinite variety of bathroom-tiles; then came the craze for Video Clubs — understandably, since Greek TV is not all that exciting, and there are only two channels, which

Until recently Floca was the place to be seen in Athens, as it had been since 1918.

seem to copy each other with amazing fidelity.

Yet for all its apparent openness, its ready appropriation of imported goods, fashions, techniques, this is in many aspects a closed society, turned in on itself, strangely self-absorbed; as if listening to distant deceptive voices magicking away the insecurity, insisting that this is still the omphalos of the world. Perhaps this is what makes the borrowings from abroad, though easily accepted, so hard to assimilate. There is a constant struggle to catch up with the West while clinging to the old traditional ways. *Tavernas*, competing with pizza and fast-food shops, try to keep up a semblance of *couleur locale* (which is fast turning into *couleur internationale*: you find better *taramosalata* in London supermarkets than in Athens). Arranged marriages are still going strong, but the matchmaker has been replaced by a computer service. Doughnuts and *koulóuri*, popcorn and *passatempo*; a priest, majestic in flowing black robes, licking an ice-cream cone or riding a motorbike—unthinkable ten or fifteen years ago. Co-existence—but the edges are still jagged.

City streets: One of the places where the meeting of old and new is most manifest is the commercial area between **Monastiraki** and **Omonoia Square**, at the heart of the city. It is a kind of huge chaotic bazaar, bringing to mind the market described in a comedy by Euboulos in the second century B.C., "Everything will be for sale together in the same place at Athens, figs, summoners, bunches of grapes, turnips, pears, apples, witnesses, roses, medlars, haggis, honeycombs, chickpeas, lawsuits, beestings-puddings, myrtle-berries, allotment machines, irises, lambs, water-clocks, laws, indictments."

Beestings-puddings and allotment machines sound mysterious enough, but the weird assortment of objects to be found in the market today is almost equally intriguing. Kitsch-collectors will find much to interest them; Greek kitsch is perhaps the most orgiastically hideous in the world. The modern age has brought mass production tourist trade on a grand scale. Even the shops around the **Mitropolis**, specializing in ecclesiastical articles, have turned touristy; the manufacturers have perhaps caught on to the fact that tourists often find bronze candle-stands just the thing for a garden-

passing priest caught against the backdrop of Greece's new consumerism.

party; a priest's heavily-embroidered robes can be turned into a stunning evening dress, while pectoral crosses outshine the flashiest *faux bijoux*. There's a whole religious no-man's-land where alabaster hands marked with the stigmata lie next to imitation ivory skulls and books on black magic and vampires. As for "historical" motifs, the most ingenious example, perhaps, is individual meat-skewers topped with the Byzantine double-headed eagle.

But if you move away from the robust vulgarity of **Pandrossou Street** to the narrow sidestreets off the **Flea Market**, you step into an almost pre-industrial era. This is the district of traditional crafts (crafts minus "arts"), wholesale shops selling refreshingly non-decorative, down-to-earth stuff like screws, all sizes and shapes, locks and keys, chains of varying thickness (for what? for whom? ships? dogs? people?), boxes and crates, brushes and brooms, mysterious implements like futurist sculptures, mouse-trap shops, herb-shops (the mountains of Greece are reputed to be a botanist's paradise), shops selling incense, rosin in big amber-colored chunks, contrasting bright blue chunks of sulfate of copper used for plants (and fishing octopus)—a whole serendipitous accumulation of things no longer to be found in our brave new ready-made world.

Head for the hills: There's a peaceful busyness in these narrow streets. Only a few steps beyond, you are back in the great melting-pot, the high-rise buildings, the fumes, the heat. You panic, but not for long. The saving grace of Athens is that there are easy ways out; better still, visible ways out. Just when you're feeling buried alive in the asphalt jungle, you see at the end of a street a fragment of mountain, a slice of open country, trees, breathing outlets. They seem startlingly near; in many cases this is an illusion, but not always. Athens is full of bumps, some big enough to deserve the name of hills, others mere excrescences. Streets go steeply uphill, downhill; driving a car, you may suddenly come up against a rocky cliff or a flight of steps leading up to one of the bumps. Eight of them have been counted, (one up on Rome!) but there may be more. **Mount Lycabettus** of course, you can't miss it; the equally conspicuous rock of the **Acropolis**, flanked by the **Pnyx** on one side, and the hill of **Philopappus** on the other where it

The best coffee in Athens.

is the custom to fly kites on the first day of Lent; the hill of **Ardittos**, next to the marble horseshoe **Stadium**, built by Herodes Atticus in A.D. 143 and totally reconstructed in 1896 (the first modern Olympic Games were held there); the hill of the **Nymphs**, capped by the gray dome of the **Observatory**; the barren, wind-blown **Tourkovounia range**; and the hill of **Strefi**, the poor man's Lycabettus, far less touristy, where the efforts of landscape-gardeners appear more strenuous than on the other hills. Sheer rock suddenly looms up through the straggling vegetation, reminding you that Attica is a land of stone: stone benches, fountains, footpaths, stone interspersed with white marble fragments; the opulence of marble amid this frugality; silver-green cactus and pink oleander, called "bitter laurel" in Greek, the hardy undemanding plants that are best able to survive the rigors of the Greek summer. There are small hidden cafes and a measure of coolness on some of these hills. Still, I don't suppose these small pockets of green deserve the name of oases—you have to go further afield for that, up one of the three mountains that encircle Athens. **Mount Hymettus**, beloved

of honey-bees, glowing violet at sunset, provides a real oasis. Driving up the winding road past the monastery of **Kaisariani** (15 minutes' drive) you reach a vantage-point of beauty and tranquility from which to contemplate the whole of Attica. (Also see page 171.) The city is panoramically visible, yet totally, eerily inaudible. On **Mount Parnes**, only two hours away, you can walk in a dark wilderness of fir-trees, play roulette at the casino, ski in winter. **Mount Pendeli** is crowded, lively, popular, with all the ensuing disadvantages: air thick with *souvlaki*-smoke and the screams of over-active children.

But if you're not much of a climber, if you're simply "*las des musées, cimetières des arts*," as Lamartine said, you can still escape to the **National Park**, within a stone's throw of the Byzantine, Benaki and War museums (see page 172). You walk down **Herodes Atticus Street**, watch—if you must—the changing of the Evzone Guard (whom Hemingway refers to as "those big tall babies in ballet skirts"), then turn right, into the park. Suddenly there is thick shade, tangled bowers, romantic arbors, and relative quiet. Do not expect anything lush, the

generous green expanses, the grassy carpets, the lakes and cascades of other European parks. Here are only modest fish-ponds, thin but constant trickles of water running along secret leafy troughs; a few forlorn deer, and a large population of surprisingly well-fed cats. Cicadas whirr away, peacocks cry, mournful for all their spotted blue-green glory. Here you can observe the Athenians at rest; here students come to study, lovers meet, old men meditate, mothers brood, weary hitchhikers sleep on a bench, under a roof of wisteria; even the busy briefcase-men use it sometimes as a bridge, an interlude in between two hurried appointments.

There is a solitary, unexpected stretch of green lawn on **Vass. Sofias Avenue**; beautifully designed, it serves as the setting for the giant bronze statue of the eminent statesman Venizelos (1864–1936), who seems on the point of plunging into the traffic, and then thinks better of it. If you climb over the green slope to the back of the site, you come upon the **Park of Freedom**. It is not a park, by no stretch of the imagination; as for the word freedom, it has here a propitiatory (expiatory?) function, for during the military dictatorship (1967–1974) this was the HQ of the dreaded military police, where dissidents were detained and tortured. There is a pleasant cafe, a lecture-hall, a tiny open-air theater. The torture-chambers have been turned into a museum; posing again that difficult moral problem: what does one do with places like this? Cover them up, preserve them, embellish them? Remember or forget? Remembrance may breed hatred, oblivion begets apathy. Here the effort seems to have been to preserve and transform at the same time; to commemorate the horror while creating around it an atmosphere in which the ghosts may be laid to rest. An optimistic, perhaps utopian message: life goes on, the present takes over without disowning the past. The Greeks are good at carrying the burden of the past, they've been doing it for ages; but like all burdens, it sometimes interferes with their sense of balance.

Not particularly green, but certainly an oasis, **Plaka**, the old quarter clustering at the foot of the Acropolis, has now been refurbished, restored to its former condition, or rather to a fairly good reproduction of it. The garish nightclubs and discos have been closed down, motor-vehicles prohibited, houses repainted,

Colossal lion at the foot of Hymettus.

streets tidied up. It has become a delightful, sheltered place to meander in; you almost think yourself in a remote village, miles from the urban monster below. You come upon small architectural beauties: Byzantine churches, the Tower of the Winds, the Old University, fragmented arches and walls.

Night moves: The night is sure to provide some respite from the heat, as most nocturnal activities take place in the open air: restaurants, cafes, theaters, cinemas. (Even the clattering garbage-collectors work at night). Do not mistake the open-air cinemas for drive-ins; they have rows of seats like ordinary cinemas, and the only customers on wheels are the midnight babies brought there in their pushchairs by their harassed mothers and silenced with ice-cream. As for theaters, apart from the **Herodes Atticus Theater** (also see page 170) which is the official venue of the Athens Festival, there is a large theater on Mount Lycabettus, used mostly for concerts of modern music, and several abandoned quarries (Attica, land of stone...) converted into theaters that put on some very good productions and provide a starkly dramatic setting.

The night is long in Athens; Athenians fiercely resist sleep, or make up for lost night-sleep with a long afternoon siesta (caution: *never* telephone an Athenian between 3 p.m. and 5 p.m.). Cafes and bars stay open till the small hours; bars and "pubs" here are unlike those of other European capital; they are larger, they have tables, provide music (usually loud) and serve food (usually expensive) as well as drinks.

Three o'clock in the morning, and the traffic still won't give up; groups of people linger at street-corners, goodnights take forever. The main streets are never entirely deserted; perhaps this is one of the reasons why Athens is a relatively safe city to walk in at night, except for the occasional petty bag-snatcher, but real violence is rare. The "unquiet generation" finally goes to bed; verandahs and balconies go dark, cats prowl, climbing jasmine smells stronger—and all the conflicting elements in the patchwork city seem momentarily resolved in the brief summer night.

Seeing the sites

Seen from the right angle—driving up the Ierá Odós (the Sacred Way) or

cool drink
fore seeing
e sights.

looking up at its rocky bulk from high in Plaka—the Acropolis still has a presence that makes the grimy concrete of modern Athens fade into insignificance. Climb up in early morning in summer or early afternoon in winter, when the crowds are thinnest and a strip of blue sea edged with gray hills marks the horizon. On a wet or windy day, walking across its uneven limestone surface feels like being on a ship's deck in a gale.

Until the year 2000 or so, the Acropolis will look like a stonemason's workshop, much as it must have done in the 440s B.C. when the Parthenon was under construction as the crowning glory of Pericles' giant public works program. Some of his contemporaries thought it much too extravagant: Pericles was accused of dressing his city up like a prostitute. In fact, the Parthenon celebrates Athina as a virgin goddess and the city's protector. Her statue, 39 feet (12 meters) high and made of ivory and gold plate to Pheidias' design, used to gleam in its dim interior. (It was carried off to Constantinople in late antiquity and disappeared.)

Conservators have installed a folding crane inside the Parthenon to lift down several hundred blocks of marble masonry and replace the rusting iron clamps inserted in the 1920s with non-corrosive titanium. Rust made the clamps expand, cracking the stone. Acid rain turned carved marble surfaces into soft plaster.

The restorers also succeeded in identifying and collecting about 1,600 chunks of Parthenon marble scattered over the hilltop—many blown off in a 1687 explosion of an Ottoman munitions dump inside the temple. When they are replaced, about 15 percent more building will be on view. New blocks cut from near the ancient quarries on Mount Penteli (nine miles north of Athens), which supplied the fifth century B.C. constructors, will fill the gaps.

The **Erechtheion**, an elegant architecturally complex repository of ancient cults going back to the Bronze Age, is already restored. The original Caryatids who supported a porch over the tomb of King Kekrops, a mythical founder of the ancient Athenian royal family, have been replaced with copies to prevent further damage from the *néfos*, the brown blanket of atmospheric pollution that hangs over Athens.

Completed in 395 B.C., a generation later than the Parthenon, the Erechtheion

Tourists "romancing the stone."

also housed an early wooden statue of Athina, along with the legendary olive tree that she conjured out of the rock to defeat Poseidon the sea god in their contest for sovereignty over Attica. In Ottoman times, the building was used by the Turkish military commander of Athens as a billet for his harem.

The **Propylaia**, the battered official entrance to the Acropolis built by Mnesikles in the 430s B.C., was cleverly designed with imposing outside columns to awe people coming up the hill. Parts of its coffered stone ceiling, once painted and gilded, are still visible as you walk through.

Roped off on what was once the citadel's southern bastion is the small, square temple of **Athina Nike**, finished in 421 B.C. It supposedly stands on the spot where Theseus' father, King Aegeus, threw himself to his death on seeing a black-sailed ship approaching harbor. Theseus had promised to hoist a white sail for the return voyage if he succeeded in killing the Minotaur on Crete but carelessly forgot.

The sculptures that Lord Elgin left behind are in the **Acropolis Museum**. Four Caryatids stare out from a nitrogen-filled case, scarred but still impressively female. The coquettish "korai" reveal a pre-classical ideal: looking closely, you can make out traces of make-up, earrings, and the patterns of their crinkled, close-fitting dresses (the spikes discouraged birds from sitting on their heads).

North of the Acropolis, the **Agorá**, the ancient city's political center, looks like a cluttered ruinfield. If archaeologists had their way, the whole of Plaka would have been leveled. But the reconstructed **Stoá** of Attalos, a second-century B.C. shopping mall, is a cool place to linger among scents of ancient herbs replanted by the meticulous American excavators. And a look at the stolid **Thisseion temple** opposite will make you appreciate that the Parthenon is truly a masterpiece.

Across from the Agorá, on the far side of the Piraeus metro line, one corner of the Painted Stoa has been exposed in Adrianou Street. This famous ancient building gave its name to Stoicism, the stiff-upper-lip brand of philosophy that Zeno the Cypriot taught there in the third-century B.C.

On the south side of the Acropolis lies the **Theater of Dionysos**. The marble seating tiers that survive date from

acelift for
Caryatids.

around 320 B.C. and later, but scholars are generally agreed that plays by Aeschylus, Sophocles, Euripides and Aristophanes were first staged here at fifth-century B.C. religious festivals. A state subsidy for theater-goers meant that every Athenian citizen could take time off to attend. Doves nest in niches in the Acropolis rock, which would have blocked the chill north winds at day-long performances during the Anthesteria celebrations early in the year.

Past Monastiraki, the **Kerameikos Cemetery** in the potters' district of the city was a burial place for prominent ancient Athenians. An extraordinary variety of sculptured monuments—tall stone urns, a prancing bull, winged sphinxes and melancholy scenes of farewell—overlooked the paved Sacred Way leading to the Dipylon Gate from Eleusis, where the mysteries were held.

Most of the original grave stelai are in the National Museum, but the replicas are still eloquent. It's the perfect place to recover from a hard day's sightseeing; turtles lumber through the undergrowth and frogs croak beside a slow-moving stream.

The Museum's collection of grave goods forms a magnificent guide to Greek vase-painting: from a squat geometric urn with a rusting iron sword twisted around its neck to the elegant white lekythoi of classical Athens and self-consciously sophisticated Hellenistic pottery.

Hadrian's Arch: A few Roman monuments recall a time when Athens was a city to be revered, but stripped of its movable artworks. The second-century Emperor Hadrian, a fervent admirer of classical Greece, erected an ornate arch marking the spot where the classical city ended and the provincial Roman university town began. He also finished off the **Temple of Olympian Zeus**, a vast building abandoned when its original constructors ran out of funds around 520 B.C., and dedicated it to himself.

Later in the century, Herodes Atticus, a wealthy Roman administrator, built the steeply-raked theater used now for Athens Festival performances, as a memorial to his wife.

And a first-century B.C. Syrian was responsible for the picturesque **Tower of the Winds**: a well-preserved marble octagon overlooking the scanty remains of the Roman Forum. It is decorated with

· eight relief figures, each depicting a different breeze, and once contained a water-clock.

Byzantine Athens is scantily represented: a dozen or so churches, many dating from the 11th century, can be tracked down in Plaka and others huddle below street level in the shadow of the city's tall, modern buildings. They are still in constant use: passers-by slip in to light a brown beeswax candle, cross themselves and kiss an icon in near-darkness before returning to the noise and jostling outside.

One of the handsomest is **Agii Theodori**, just off Klathmónos Square. It was built in the 11th century on the site of an earlier church in characteristic cruciform shape with a tiled dome. The masonry is picked out with slabs of brick and decorated with a terra-cotta frieze of animals and plants.

St. Nikodemos on Philhellinon Street dates from the same time but was bought by the Tsar of Russia in 1845 and redecorated inside. It now serves the city's small Russian Orthodox community and the singing there is renowned.

On Athens' eastern and western limits lie two famous monasteries: Kaisariani and Daphni.

Kaisariani on Mount Hymettus, surrounded by high stone walls, is named after a spring which fed an aqueduct constructed on Hadrian's orders. Its waters, once sacred to Aphrodite, the goddess of love, are still credited with healing powers (and encouraging child-bearing). The monastery church goes back to A.D. 1000 but the frescoed figures who gaze out of a blue-black ground date from the 17th century. Clustered around are stone-built cloisters, a kitchen and refectory and a former bath-house. The monks' wealth came from olive groves, beehives, vineyards and medicines made from mountain herbs.

Daphni, a curious architectural combination of Gothic and Byzantine decorated inside with magnificent 11th-century mosaics, occupies the site of an ancient sanctuary of Apollo. A fierce-looking Christ Pantocrator, set in gold and surrounded by Old Testament prophets, stares down from the vault of the dome. The present building dates from 1080 and the Gothic porch was added in the 13th century when Daphni belonged to Cistercian monks from Burgundy and was used as the burial place of the

Frankish Dukes of Athens.

Museum notes: Going back to 3000 B.C., the **Goulandris Museum** displays a unique collection of slim, schematic Cycladic idols in white marble, beautifully mounted and lit. They were scorned by 19th-century art critics as hopelessly primitive, but their smooth, simple lines attracted both Picasso and Modigliani. Mostly female and pregnant, the figures come from robbed graves in the Cyclades Islands and scholars are still uncertain of their purpose.

Crammed with badly-labeled treasures from every period of antiquity, the **National Archaeological Museum** should be visited early in the morning before the guided tours turn the echoing marble halls into a deafening Babel. Not to be missed are the Mycenaean collection, the Thíra frescoes and the major bronze sculptures, none of which is duplicated anywhere else.

The **Mycenaean Gallery**, containing Schliemann's finds from the shaft graves at Mycenae, is stuffed with treasures from the second millennium B.C. that repay close examination: miniaturism was prized on colored sealstones, daggers and signet rings. Gold gleams everywhere, barbaric and sometimes tawdry but a clear indicator of prehistoric Greek wealth.

Upstairs, the Thíra Fresco Room reveals a lighter side of Bronze Age life: small-sized rooms decorated with Aegean island scenes of dark-eyed boys boxing, blue monkeys swarming up a mountainside and statuesque, black-haired women with heavy makeup.

Few large-scale ancient bronzes have survived, but the statue of Zeus coolly poised to hurl a thunderbolt, which was netted by a fisherman off Cape Artemision in Central Greece, is one splendid exception. It dates from around 470 B.C. when classical naturalism in sculpture was just about to take off. By comparison, the bronze child jockey on his Hellenistic racehorse, cast two centuries later when heightened realism was the fashion, has a strained, almost frightened expression.

The bronzes in the **Piraeus Archaeological Museum** are more workmanlike but still fascinating. Both the heavy-limbed archaic Kouros, one of the earliest fullsized bronze statues, and the soulful, helmeted, Hellenistic Athina were found in a sewer excavation in 1959, and perhaps belonged to a cargo of Rome-bound loot awaiting shipment.

The **Byzantine Museum**, a mock-Florentine mansion built by an eccentric 19th-century American duchess, contains a brilliant array of icons and church relics from the 13th- to the 18th-century. Across the street, the **Benaki Museum** houses a wonderfully eclectic collection of treasures—including jewelry, costumes and two icons attributed to El Greco in the days when he was a young Cretan painter called Domenico Theotocopoulos.

The **Canellopoulos Museum**, a 19th-century mansion, is a similar treasure-trove of objects from every period of Greek art acquired by an erudite, obsessive collector. And the **City of Athens Museum**, an accumulation of 19th-century furnishings, pictures and fittings in a house where teenage King Otto lived while waiting for his palace to be completed, evokes the atmosphere of upperclass life in newly independent Greece.

Outside Athens, a 43-mile drive to **Cape Soúnion** on the windy tip of the Attica peninsula takes you to Poseidon's temple. Completed in 440 B.C. its slender, salt-white columns are still a landmark for ships headed toward Piraeus. Lord Byron carved his name on a column on the north side. The marble came from nearby Agríleza, where the Athenians also mined silver and lead. Following an impressive classical fortification wall down the hillside, you come to the remains of ancient shipsheds in the bay below: the Athenians once organized warship races off Soúnion and it later became a pirates' lair. Sunset here is often as dramatic as the tour organizers claim.

More out-of-the-way is the **Sanctuary of Artemis** at **Brauron**—now called Vravrona—on the east coast of Attica, 22 miles (35 km) from Athens through the wine-growing Mesolóngion district. A fifth-century B.C. colonnade visited by owls at twilight is flanked by a 16th-century Byzantine chapel, built on the site of an altar to Artemis. In classical times, wellborn girls aged from five to ten and known as "little bears" performed a ritual dance at a festival honoring Artemis as goddess of childbirth. Their statues are displayed in the site museum: plump with appealingly solemn expressions and dressed like miniature adults.

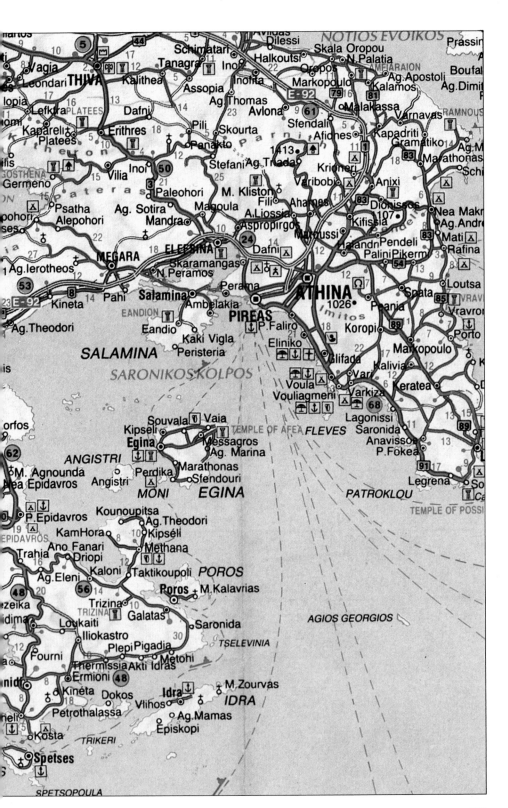

ISLANDS OF THE SARONIC GULF

Athens and the islands of the Saronic Gulf are often lumped together in guide books. There is sense to this since many Athenians frequent these islands on weekends, while during the summer these islands are veritable extensions of the more fashionable Athenian neighborhoods. Yet this view of the Argosaronic islands doesn't take into account their separate identities. They are islands, not suburbs. Each has its own character and deserves more than a page of our attention.

Aegina: Aegina is a privileged island, rich in natural beauty and prized for its healthy climate and clear air. About an hour and a half by ferry from Piraeus—or half an hour by the "flying dolphin" hydrofoil—Aegina has had little trouble attracting visitors. Although the island bears some of the scars inflicted by an expanding tourist industry it is large enough to allow refuge from the crowds. Long a favorite Athenian retreat it remains more popular among weekend smog evaders than among foreign tourists from elsewhere.

Shaped on the map like an upside-down triangle, Aegina's southern point is marked by the magnificent cone of **Mount Oros**, the highest peak in the Argosaronic islands, visible on a smog-free day from the Athens' Acropolis. The center and eastern side of the island is mountainous; a gently-sloping fertile plain runs down to the western extremity where Aegina town overlays in part the ancient capital of the island. Perhaps we should at this point take Aegina's history backwards for the comparatively unimportant town which now confronts us is not only connected with the great Aegina which strove with Athens for maritime supremacy but also with the first days of the new Greek state, formed after the successful revolution of 1821.

When the world was small and a city or an island could aspire to be a Great Power, Aegina, strategically situated between the Peloponnese and Attica, looking out upon the Aegean and all the Mediterranean beyond, became a wealthy trading state with shipyards, fleets and a sophisticated banking system. In the seventh century B.C. Aegina produced the first Greek coins—the silver 'tortoises'—and from these gained great financial leverage throughout the ancient world.

With the onset of the Persian Wars in 491 B.C. the Aeginetes first sided with the Persian army, to the chagrin of the besieged Athenians, but in 480 B.C. at Salamis, the greatest of all Greek sea battles, they returned to the Greek side and won the praise of the Delphic Oracle as the fleetest navy on the seas. But Aegina, the "eyesore of Piraeus" as Pericles called her, posed a threat to Athens' expanding maritime empire. In 457 B.C. and again during the Peloponnesian War the Athenians defeated the Aeginetes at sea, on the second occasion expelling the entire population and replacing it with Athenian colonialists. After the defeat of Athens in the Peloponnesian War, the spartan Lysander, in recognition of the help Aeginetes had given Sparta during the war, returned them to their home. After this Aegina played a less conspicuous role until the 1820s when she became the temporary capital of liberated Greece from 1826 to 1828.

The Aegina town one confronts today is typical of small Greek cities a century ago. A number of classical mansions stand at the edge of town. Several buildings constructed after the liberation of Greece in 1828, from the time of the island's first governor, Ioánnis Kapodístrias (1776–1831), are also preserved. The **Archaeological Museum** in the center of the town displays a number of interesting artifacts from the island's history. The modern harbor, oval in shape, and crowded with picturesque *caïques*, was the city's commercial wharf in antiquity; small additions were built in the Roman period and under Venetian rule. The **Military Harbor** lies near the village of **Karantína**, remnants of ancient moorings can still be seen there. To the left of the port as you enter is the hill of **Kolona** with the remains of the **Temple of Apollo** (formerly attributed to Aphrodite). All that is left from this famous temple is a single *kolóna* (column). The temple (Doric, six columns by 12, built in 520–500 B.C.) was superseded by a late Roman fortress, fragments of which survive on the seaward side. Although from the sea the position of the temple looks unimpressive, the view from the hill in late summer is breathtaking. Apart from the usual day trips to small resort towns (**Souvala, Perdika, Ayia Marína**) or to the two neighboring islands of **Angistri** and **Moni** you should, even if Greek ruins or

AEGINA: A PLACE OF RETURN

The well-loved poet Katerina Anghelaki-Rooke gives her impressions of Aegina...

Aegina is a place of return. It is a place that opens, receives, consoles and heals. Other islands are points of departure; you leave them behind and set off on expeditions, exploits, conquests. Dry, arid islands like Hydra, Ios, Mykonos and Santorin inspire action. Aegina, on the other hand, is a feminine island; as the boat turns the corner, the horse-shoe shaped harbor—the church of the little Virgin on the one side and the old yellow house on the other—provides the perfect enclosure for an aching heart. When I was small I thought the yellow house had become yellow from the passing of time, like an old photograph.

The harbor is alive. It is as alive in the winter as it is in the summer. Tourists barely alter this island. They make a brief appearance and then disappear mysteriously, like the summer sirocco the hot, humid wind that sweeps in from the south, the Sahara. In Sep-

tember the air smells of resin from the pistachio nuts that are harvested there and the freshly washed barrels ready for new wine. The light is soft and caressing, having lost the harshness of August. Across the water the mountain of Méthana turns a dusted blue. I sit at Skotadis' *oúzo* shop watching the *caïques* unload fruit and vegetables, while Babouas, the down syndrome idiot who owes his name to the only sound he can produce, paces up and down and smiles at the familiar faces. He is grateful for this place which forgives human and divine mistakes and accepts us all.

Inland, the landscape is reminiscent of Attica. Perhaps the island retains something from its motherland, across the water, in the same way we often keep the facial characteristics of our parents. The curves of the hills and the tops of the olive trees follow and at times interrupt the sky. The clouds add a touch of frivolous

A boy stop bike to g▶ the poet ▶ her dog, H▶

imagination in the midst of so much blue seriousness. These are the elements Aegina shares with Attica. But Aegina is distinctly an island; your nostrils quiver in the salty air which reaches you wherever you go. There's a sense of being cut-off, set apart; there's an atmosphere of independence, of autonomy, of solitude. A dual personality then is the key to this island's charm. Aegina is both the sweetness and the severeness of life, all in one slight stretch of land.

"Oh! to be in Aegina again!" wrote my godfather, the novelist, Kazantzákis when he was abroad, away from the island and his house by the sea. From his window on Aegina the adventures of Odysseus opened in front of his eyes like water-flowers of incredible intricacy and beauty. It is no surprise that in his famous sequel Kazantzákis took up where Homer left off, charting Odysseus' travels after he left Ithaca a second time. Both the author and his hero share a similar nostalgia for "islands of return."

Sometimes Kazantzákis for a bit of diversion would leave his rock promontory and go to town to buy sweets from Prokopis, the Greek from Asia Minor, a master when it came to Oriental pastry or

to chat with the village idiot—a different one then, at the end of the 30s. "Tell me, Thomas, have you ever gone to school? Couple of times, boss, I wasn't very good at it, but then I got sick, I became an idiot and now I don't have to worry about a thing!" Kazantzákis marveled at the wisdom of Thomas and never ceased repeating this story.

The deaf and dumb man cleaning fish in the market, the baker with his eternal grin and his apron covered with flour, the fishing boats nonchalantly bobbing in the little harbor, the dogs relentlessly sniffing the butcher's doorstep, the whole island stops as the sun sets across the sea...Ah! the sunsets of Aegina, the imperial gold and red glories that envelop us for a short instant filling us with nostalgia and anticipation.

I leave Skotadis' and the harbor and take the road up the hill back to my house. The trees and walls fence off my private history. What is here contains me and I contain it. Its presence is my continuity, the impersonal continuity of someone who has lived and loved a place: Aegina.

adis' oùzo

Byzantine churches are not your cup of tea, visit the **Temple of Afáia** and the **Monastery of Áyios Nektários**.

The Temple of Afáia stands at the top of a hill above the cape of Ayia Marína in a pine grove commanding a splendid view of the Aegean, superior to that of Soúnion or Lindos in Rhodes. Built in celebration of the victory at Salamis, it has been called "the most perfectly developed of the late Archaic temples in European Hellas." It is the only surviving Hellenic temple with a second row of small super-imposed columns in the interior of the sanctuary. The temple was explored in 1811 by Baron von Hellerstein and its sculptures were removed first to Zante and then to Italy. Ultimately they were auctioned and in 1813 they were acquired by the King of Bavaria Ludwig I, the father of Otto. At Ludwig's bequest the sculptures were returned to Rome and then placed in the Munich Glypthothek.

Áyios Nektários (Anastásios Kefalás: 1846–1920), Metropolitan of Pentapolis was the first saint to be canonized (1961) by the Orthodox church in modern times. The monastery named after him stands on a hill across from another which is covered with ruins of more than twenty churches and monasteries, survivors from the 13th century and later, some with remarkable stone iconostases (especially the **Monastery of Panayia Hrisoleóntissa**). These churches were once part of the old chora of the island (*Paleóhora*) where the islanders sought refuge from sudden attacks by pirates (the town was twice destroyed by the famous pirate Barbarossa and once by the Venetians). When the Turks were thrown off the island in the 1820s the Paleóhorites came down to the port leaving their churches behind.

A final word of advice: avoid the town of Ayia Marína (a dreadful package holiday center), though its beach is worth a visit. The beaches in the little islands of Angistri and Moni, admittedly not the most beautiful in the Aegean are still a good bet. Aegina town with its loud fish-market, its picturesque port where *caïques* unload their fruits and vegetables, its lively *ouzeris* and *tavernas* and its traditional pistachio sellers make up for a possibly uneventful swimming trip.

Hydra: The island of **Hydra**, once Idrea, "the well watered," is now ironically a long barren and waterless rock. The heart of the island is its harbor-town. All

Pistachios.

around the picturesque bay white houses climb the slope accented by massive gray *archontiká*, the houses of the gentry. Along the quay are the colorful shops of the marketplace, with the marble tower of the Holy Virgin Cloister in the center. The harbor, girded by a little thread of a breakwater, forms a soft and perfect crescent, its two ends flanked by 19th-century cannons. Crowded with island ferries, cruise ships, sleek sailboards and yachts and local fishing boats, it provides a colorful scene of maritime confusion. The town appeals to all kinds of visitors.

Since Mihalis Kakoyannis used Hydra as a location for his classic film *The Woman in Black* and the painter Gikas made his home on the island, Hydra has aspired to be a fashionable artists' colony and retreat for intellectuals, and has also attracted a less orthodox fringe of idlers. The combination of Hydra's raw natural beauty and the wonderful harbor town continues to be irresistible. Hydra is the Mediterranean island *par excellence*.

The foundation of Hydra's greatness was laid in the 18th century, when the reviving commerce of the Peloponnese coupled with the grain trade with South Russia provided the Hydriots with an outlet for their abilities. Hydra, once no more than a small port in the Venetian empire, gradually became the dominant maritime power in the Aegean. During the War of Independence the Hydriots threw themselves heart and soul into the fight with merchant families, notably that of Kunduriotis, converting at their own expense their trading vessels into warships. Among the many Hydriot naval commanders of the war were the Tombazis brothers (Yakomáki, the elder brother was responsible for sinking the first Turkish line-of-battle ship when the war broke out), Tsamádos, Vúlgaris, Saktúris (who probably gave his name to the *sakturia*, a small sailing ship invented by the Hydriots) and Andreas Miaulis, the commander-in-chief and one of the greatest of all the Greek heroes. Among their famous descendants are Admiral Pavlos Kunduriotis, hero of the war of 1912, later regent and president of Greece, and Dimítrios Vulgaris, Prime Minister in 1855.

The well-preserved and imposing houses of all these families are now little museums and open to visitors. In the huge **Mansion of Admiral Tombazis**, the Athens School of Fine Arts

has established a branch which hosts artists of international acclaim. A Merchant Navy Training School occupies the **House of Tsamados** and across the way are the Hydriot Archives.

The higher reaches of the town and the hills beyond remain surprisingly untouched, charming and full of Greek color. Narrow alleys and steep staircases lead from one quarter to the next. The uniformity of white walls is broken again and again by a century-old doorway, a bright blue window frame, scarlet steps, or a dark green garden fence.

With plenty of *tavernas,* cafes, bars and nightlife, Hydra should also appeal to the tourist who may have no interest in the island's glorious past and its various historical monuments. For many Hydra is just a point of departure, a base from which to organize a series of expeditions to the mainland and other islands. For others Hydra, this immaculate little town bathed in white and blue colors, is the Greece one is so eager to rediscover time and time again.

Poros: The island of **Poros** is separated from the Peloponnese by a small passage of water—the word *poros* in Greek means "strait." The island can be reached not only by ship and "flying dolphin" but also by driving along the Peloponnesian coast via the **Isthmus of Corinth** and **Epidauros** to the little town of **Galatás** which lies opposite the main harbor. As one sails in through the northern entrance, the harbor opens up. It is almost landlocked and one of the finest anchorages in the Aegean. Your first glimpse of the island will be of the white houses and bright orange rooftops of Poros town. Built on a hill with its highest point at the center, the town resembles an inverted amphitheater and the effect is disarming. On the mainland opposite, the village of Galatás with its white steps and dark alleys and its *Lemonodasos* where lemon groves grow amidst water-mills, makes a wonderful sight. It is easy to understand Henry Miller's enthusiasm (in his book '*The Colossus of Marousi*') as he sailed between Poros and Galatás. "I don't know which affected me more deeply—the story of the lemon groves just opposite us or the sight of Poros itself when suddenly I realized that we were sailing through the streets. If there is one dream which I like above all others it is that of sailing on land. Coming into Poros gives the illusion of the deep

Gypsy girl.

dream. Suddenly the land converges on all sides and the boat is squeezed into a narrow strait... To sail slowly through the streets of Poros is to recapture the joy of passing through the neck of the womb. It is a joy too deep almost to be remembered."

It is not an illusion that one is sailing between houses; friendly faces actually hang out of the windows just above your head while the scents of *retsina, oúzo,* lemon and grilled fish fill your nostrils.

Although a number of hotels have been built in Poros and prominent Athenians have owned vacation houses here for decades, the island has never been fashionable like Hydra or Spetses, but during summer it gets as crowded as Aegina.

On the southwestern coast are the remains of the old military harbor that the Russians laid out with the Sultan's blessing. In 1830 the first naval arsenal was established here which survived until 1877 when it was closed in favor of Salamis. The building now houses the **Boy's Naval Training School**. The famous Greek warship *Averof*, which played a major role during the Balkan Wars of 1912, is docked in front of the School. The anniversary of the battle

(December 6) is marked by a celebration (*panayiri*) and parades.

The main sight on Poros is the **Monastery of Panayis Zoodóhos Pigi** (Virgin of the Life-Giving Spring) beautifully situated in an overgrown glade. Only a few monks still live there today. Noteworthy is a wooden, gold painted iconostasis dating from the 18th century and adorned with late Byzantine illustrations from the New Testament. It was presumably brought to Poros from Asia Minor. In front of the monastery a new road encircling the heights to the east climbs through the pinewoods to the plateau of **Palatia**, where the ruins of the **Sanctuary of Poseidon** are situated in a saddle between the highest hills of the island. The temple was excavated at the turn of the century and little remains but its setting is rewarding.

The ancient town of **Kalávria** was situated nearby, and the sanctuary was the headquarters of the Kalavrian League, a religious association of several towns that included Athens as well. The sanctuary served as an asylum for shipwrecked sailors, pirates and political refugees. It was here that the famous Athenian orator Demosthenes in flight

achts docked
Hydra's
shionable
ort.

from Antipater's emissaries, took refuge, trusting that not even the Macedonians would dare to profane so ancient and famous a shrine. When they did, he poisoned himself.

The visitor to Poros must not leave without making a side trip to **Troezen** on the Peloponnese. To reach it you can take a boat from the harbor of Poros to the town of Galatás and then a bus to the ancient town. En route between Aegina and Poros, the boat stops at the town of **Méthana**. There is no need to stop in this tourist village. Poros is by far a more exciting choice.

Spetses: At the southern end of the Saronic Gulf, **Spetses**, the ancient *Pitiusa*, or pinetree island, offers the most picturesque beaches and the most sophisticated nightlife of the nearby islands. As a British commentator has rightly observed, "Spetses lacks only titular recognition as a possession of the United Kingdom." On any given weekend one finds as many British tourists in Spetses as Athenians in Aegina.

Although Spetses town is full of new hotels, noisy bars and cheap fast-food places, the eastern side of the island, the *Palio Limáni* (**Old Harbor**) still radiates a gentle grace, a particular magic that is apparent to even the short-term visitor. The 18th-century *archontiká* one sees in this part of the town are now the property of wealthy Athenian families who despite the summer invasion of tourists return to the island with the hope of finding their special *taverna*, their favorite boatman and their "old acquaintances" in the fish market. I am not sure if they find them but they do keep coming back.

Like Hydra, Spetses was one of the main centers of activity during the Greek War of Independence, having contributed a fleet of a hundred ships to the Greek cause. The island is distinguished for being the first in the archipelago to revolt against the Ottoman rule in 1821 and the fortified point, still bristling with cannons now forms the town's *Platia*, the **Dapia**. Bouboulína, Greece's national heroine, was a Spetsiot woman who took command of her husband's ship after he was murdered by the Turks. According to a story, the Turkish fleet arrived one day off the coast of Spetses when all of the men happened to be away, so Bouboulína and all the other women of the island, rather than hiding on the hills, collected all the fezzes they could find (all Turkish

subjects had to wear these hats) and placed them on the asphodel plants that grew in masses along the shore. From a distance the fezzes swaying in the wind looked like warlike hordes and the enemy fled at the sight. This "victory" and the more engaging one of Sept. 8, 1822, when Spetsiot brigs and fireships repelled a superior Ottoman force is celebrated annually by a *panayiri* in the name of *Panayia Armáta* (her little chapel stands on a hill close to the Old Harbor). A mock battle is staged, a Turkish flagship made out of cardboard is burned in the middle of the harbor and there follows a display of fireworks.

Although after the War of Independence Spetses' fleet declined with the emergence of Piraeus as the main seaport, the traditions of shipbuilding continues unabatedly. The small naval **museum** in the imposing 18th-century *archontiko* of Hadziyiannis Meksis, Spetses' first governor, contains coins, costumes, ship models, weapons and other memorabilia from the island's past including the bones of the famous Bouboulína. The house in which she lived is behind the **Dapia**. Outside the town near **Xenia beach** is the **Anargirios and Korgialénios College**. John Fowles taught here and memorialized both the institution and the island in his novel *The Magus*.

The town's beaches of **Ayios Mámas** and **Ayios Nikólaos** are polluted and quite unattractive in contrast to the beautiful beaches of **Zogeria, Vrélo, Ayia Paraskeví** and **Ayioi Anaryiri** which are appropriately situated in the pine-wooded part of the island. In addition one can go to the various beaches opposite Spetses on the Peloponnesian coast. The prettiest of these is probably **Hinitsa** and for those who enjoy water-skiing, **Porto Heli** with its protected bay provides the perfect setting.

Spetses can also be used as a useful communication link. From here one can get to Nauplia, Argos, Epidauros, Mycenae or to the southern town of Monemvasia where the Greek poet Ritsos was born. During the summer months when the Ancient Drama Festival is held in Epidauros a trip to one of the performances is a definite must.

An evening walk in the Old Harbor or in the woods of Ligoneri, a ride in a horse-drawn carriage to Ayia Marína, a taste of fish cooked *a la Spetsiota* are but a few of the pleasures that await the visitor in Spetses.

Bouboulína, Spétses' fiery heroine of the Greek War of Independence

183

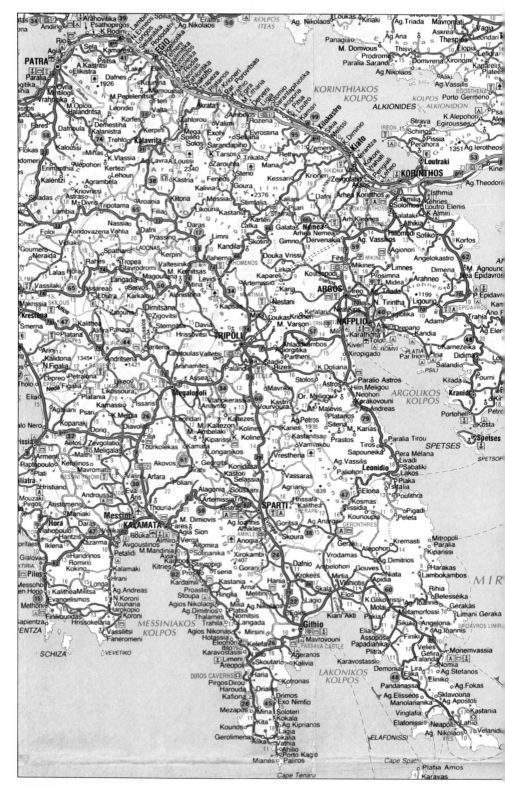

THE PELOPONNESE

The **Peloponnese** (Peloponnesos) takes its name from the fabled hero *Pelops*, and the word for island, *nisos*. But it is scarcely thought of as an island. Should you blink, however, in passing over from Attica you might miss the slight isthmus that joins the Peloponnese to the mainland.

The Peloponnese is divided into seven *nómoi* or provinces: Corinthia in the northeast; Argolis, the eastern peninsula, that juts towards the Aegean; Elis, pushing west towards the Ionian Sea; Achaea, to the north; Arcadia, in the central mountains with a brief shoreline along the Argolis Gulf; Laconia, the two southern prongs; and Messenia, the last promontory to the southwest.

The Peloponnese stands a world apart. Not only is its landscape unsurpassed in archaeological importance and variety, its history mirrors every major shift throughout the Greek peninsula, from the Mycenaean period to modern times. Even Athens has not been prone to so much upheaval. No other part of the Greek world has undergone so many changes, suffered so many invasions, or been subject to so much political strife. Little wonder, then, that a whole world of legends and myths have flourished here.

Of the many legends, the most fascinating is this: Tantalos butchered his son Pelops and served him at a banquet for the gods, to test their all-knowing powers. None of the gods touched the meat, of course. But Demeter, distracted and in grief over her stolen daughter Persephone, unwittingly ate a chunk of Pelops' shoulder. Luckily the other gods warned Demeter in time. Together they were able to bring the child Pelops back to life, replacing the ravaged shoulder with one of ivory.

However, the isle of Pelops smiles a bitter-sweet smile, taking her good-natured revenge on the traveler who is forever looking for the Peloponnese of his or her imagination. All is cut and tailored to scale, all excess becomes the debris of history, the half buried stones of the landscape.

Ancient ruins: The ruins of ancient **Corinth** convey a melancholy reality. The city was destroyed several times by earthquakes and what can be seen here,

particularly in the walkways with market-place stalls, are of Hellenistic-Roman vintage and comparatively late. The city was completely razed to the ground by the Romans in 146 B.C., and well into the next century, by order of Julius Caesar, Corinth was "founded" once again by the Roman Empire. It moved quickly into prosperity and influence. When St. Paul delivered his "Epistle to the Corinthians," the Apostle had God say to the city, "I will destroy the wisdom of the wise, make void the intelligence of the intellectuals..." Apparently Paul thought that this self-confident and affluent center of paganism needed instruction.

The ancient site is to the southeast of the modern town and built on rising plateaus with its acropolis at the top of the mount, the Acrocorinth. What stands of the Greek city today is the great temple of Apollo, or rather seven of its columns.

The rest is the Roman city with many homey touches along the walkways. But what makes the whole trip here worthwhile is the climb up to Acrocorinth. Here we find the most complete 17th-century Venetian fortresses. And the view from up here is spectacular: to the east, the expanse of the Saronic gulf; ahead, near the shore, lies Isthmia where the second most important games of the Hellenic world occurred every other spring. Next in the line of vision from this height lies the old part on the Saronic side where St. Paul had his head shaved; and nearby, the healing springs, called the Baths of Helen.

Nowadays a road runs along the shore which will get you to Epidauros in half the time you need by the inland route. The modern road is well engineered with spectacular views: you travel high up above the sea, looking down at the white-sand beaches; on a clear day you can see the islands of Salamis and Aegina. Looking in the other direction, to the west of the Acrocorinth, the Corinthian gulf with the mountains of Peloponnese is on your left. The road along the shore to the west is a modern highway that leads to Patras, the port city on Pelops' hump. The shore towns along the whole coast to Patras are very lovely as are the beaches; the landscape is tame and refined with a spattering of soft pine trees, particularly around Kyato and Aigion. It is only with a glance southward that you are brought up against a harsh contrast, the sheer cliffs of the Cyllene mountain range—wild nature close to the tame shore, a motif of the

Peloponnese terrain.

The renowned spring of Peirene, was one of the refreshing wonders of these parts. Pausanias, the first and greatest travel writer (second century) tells us: "They say the spring behind the temple was a gift to Sisyphus, given to him by old Aesopos. For Sisyphus, so runs the legend, had caught Zeus ravaging Aesopos' daughter Aegina, but he refused to be questioned about it by old Aesopos unless he was given a spring of running water on Acrocorinth. Such a spring was given to him; so he was compelled to tell on Zeus; and now deep down in Hades, if legends are to be believed, he pays a stiff price for his loose tongue." Sisyphus found his own Acrocorinth rolling that stone up the hill for all eternity.

Leaving Corinth: Let's leave Corinth, to take the road south to Argos, a bad road and treacherous for the newcomer. It crisscrosses several times the same rickety railroad line for no apparent reason.

The Argive valley is most spectacular when approached from the other end, the descent along the coiling road of the Arcadian mountains. In early morning, as you take the last turn for Mount Parthenion, you find yourself before a breathtaking panorama. The salt-air from the sea accents the smell of wild flowers that grow on the mountain; the deep shadows of the gorge to your left hang down into darkness; and the peak opposite the gorge is covered in early sun. The descent to the valley takes a short while. When you reach the straight road amid the citrus groves which are in bloom, you will be greeted by sweet perfumes of lemon and orange blossoms.

There is an amusing tale in Theophrastus about the people of **Tiryns**, a place in mid-valley between Argos and Nauplia, where Herakles was born. It seems the people here were incapable of any serious accomplishment because they laughed too much. So they sent an embassy to the oracle at Delphi to find out how they might cure themselves of this weakness. Delphi's answer: they must sacrifice a bull to Poseidon; throw the offering into the sea without laughing once; and the god would cure their affliction. So they prepared for the sacrifice, taking care to keep the children far away, for their laughter could not be easily controlled. After the sacred ceremony, as they were taking the offering to the sea, a little boy who had escaped from the **Preceding pages, a fie[ld] of poppies.**

others and followed the procession, asked some ingenuously funny question, and brought the entire population to their knees with fits of wild laughter.

Argos valley: Before you know it you find yourself in modern **Argos**. It is a bustling capital, the busy market center for the entire Argolis province. The people here live well by comparison with the rest of Peloponnese. Their valley produces fruit and olives. Their only complaint is they cannot find enough laborers at harvest-time. And it isn't rare these days to see German or English students working in these groves—probably to supplement their travel allowance. But modern Argos—apart from its exquisite climate—isn't a great deal of fun.

The true elegance of this valley is reserved for **Nauplia**, perhaps the most classy small city in the whole of Greece. It has a tradition and culture all its own. After the Greek revolution, between 1829 and 1834, Nauplia served as the first capital of Greece. Some of its neo-classical houses, its carefully planned streets along the sea, and the large official looking buildings date from this period. This small city seems to have retained its dignity: anybody who is anybody in

Peloponnese seems to live in Nauplia.

But this is less than half the story, of course. There are the poor farmers who cultivate small patches of olive groves and whose families were formerly migrant sheepherders. These herders would come every October from the Tziria (ancient Cyllene) and Parnon mountain ranges, leading their flocks to warmer climes, away from Arcadia's snow covered villages. In April they would leave again to escape the heat of the valley. You will recognize these migrants in the names of their small hamlets scattered across this fertile province, especially in the vicinity of Epidauros and Ligourio. Names such as: Gianouleika, Galaneika etc. are sur-names of old shepherd clans found deep in the Arcadian mountains.

The road to Nemea breaks off from the main pass at Dervenakia. At the southern end of the Nemean fields a decisive battle was fought in the 1820s, cutting off the Ottoman empire armies who came to squelch the revolution of the *Morea*. *Morea* was the alternate name at this time for Peloponnese; named so, they say, because of the abundance of mulberry trees (*moriés*) in the land. Others suggest

Now, an old lady sells souvenirs to travelers crossing the Corinth canal.

that its name came from the fact that its shape resembles the mulberry leaf. Nowadays that name is rarely used. At the great battle the "old man of the *Morea*," general Kolokotrónis himself, with his fierce revolutionaries, massacred the Pasha's superior armies in what surely was in fact a Herculean feat.

The Nemean games: The Nemean plain beyond this road was the roaming ground of the famous lion that Herakles defeated. Here, too, is the place where the Nemean games were held, which rivaled those of Isthmia and Olympia. Part of the stadium can still be seen. Legend has it that the games were started through a rather remarkable event: the Pythia at Delphi had told Opheltes, the Nemean king, that while being nursed his baby boy must never touch ground. One day as the fierce Seven were moving their spectacular armies toward Thebes, the young nurse holding the child placed him down, the better to see the Seven warriors. At once a monster serpent emerged from the Adrastea spring and ate up the boy. Opheltes started the games to commemorate the tragedy as well as the fact that the renowned Seven killed the Serpent. The judges at the Nemean games always wore black as if in mourning; and the main contest was always in full warrior dress.

The whole of the Argive plain: Nauplia, Tiryns, Mycenae, Nemea and the full distance of the fertile valley, can be seen from the castle on the top of Larissa hill that rises at the edge of Argos. The townscape below, undistinguished cement and brick buildings, dissolves into the primary shades of fields and groves in every direction.

On the other side of the Gulf lies Nauplia, while a little more than half way there the solitary Cyclopean walls of Tiryns rise up. To your left, and a bit northeast, stand the majestic ruins of Mycenae, and a little further, straight north, beyond Dervenakia pass lies Nemea. To the northwest and behind, you can always see Arcadian Cyllene and Artemision and their snow peaks, even in summer. You can even make out the white-stoned riverbed of Inachos, mostly streamless since ancient times and on a clear day, far down along the cape, a very deep blue sea.

The Tiryns ruins: The ruins of Tiryns, though not a fine spectacle, have their own majesty. The ruins here are older than those at Mycenae, and, as legend

Taking
provisions t●
the monaste●

would have it, this is where Perseus came to settle with Andromeda (though some say he was born here), bringing from Lydia the Cyclops who built the great walls. The blocks of the wall are a hundred cubic feet each making Pausanias marvel: "Why should we bother to visit the pyramids when we have something like it right here?" The tower and the several gates with a triangular gap, suggest a sophisticated knowledge of building long before architecture becomes a developed art.

Mycenae's buildings and walls are somewhat less impressive than those of Tiryns. The Cyclopean structures do not look as powerful or sturdy, but these are more tragic stones. Here Klytemnestra received her husband Agamemnon entering the Lion Gate, on his return from Troy. She decked the gate with blood-red carpets and insisted he step on them, along with his slave-paramour Casandra. Then, when he relaxed in a bath, she hacked him to death with an axe. Agamemnon's is one of the beehive tombs below the citadel. Here, in a shaft tomb, Schliemann excavated the famous golden death-masks and the other exquisite gold ornaments that excite the visitor upon

entering the Mycenaean room of the National Museum at Athens.

Away from Mycenae we pass again through Tiryns and Nauplia to reach the sanctuary of Epidauros to the east. Nauplia is more impressive when compared with Mycenae. Palamídi, its citadel, has one thousand steps to the top. Legend has it that the city was founded by Nauplius' son, Palamidis. On the promontory, there is a fortress which has a varied history. The dungeon was used during the late 1940s civil war as a prison for the whole Peloponnese.

The lower portion was built during the first years of the 18th century by the Venetians. The Senate of St. Mark at Venice decided to sacrifice the walls and temples of Aegina, and transferred the stone slabs here to build this fortress. The Greeks won their most decisive battle against the Ottoman armies on this hill in the 1820s. And while Nauplia served as the first capital of a newly independent Greece, in 1829 trouble was not far away. Here, outside the church of St. Spiridon, not far from Palamídi, the first president, Capodistria, was assassinated. You can still see the bullet that struck one of the pillars. Only a short distance from the

first step of Palamídi lies the port, and in the center of it the islet Bourtzí. This islet has a marvelous castle which covers nearly the whole of it. During the 19th century, after the revolution, it was the residence of the executioner. Now it is a pleasant inn and worth a short boat ride.

The theater at Epidauros: Epidauros lies just beyond the short Arachneon mountain range to the east along the Argolid peninsula. Epidauros comprises three towns: Ligourio, which is about a mile (two km) from the ancient sanctuary serves to receive the traveler; Old Epidauros, which is the port town as it was of old; and New Epidauros, above on the hillside, hidden behind the bend. Old Epidauros is now a resort town of exceptional charm; you are more likely to see a spattering of yachts coming and going than the arrival of pilgrims to the healing grounds. The beaches to the left of the town are memorable in early summer. New Epidauros, on the other hand, is virtually a mountain village; and in the old days most of its inhabitants were shepherds. Now they cultivate the small valley below which leads to a tiny gulf. The beach at the end of the fertile grove has gray-black sand and is clean,

warm and secluded.

Ligourio is an overcrowded village. Too small to accommodate the hordes who come during the theater festivals, it has become a place where every homeowner rents rooms in summer. So during the tourist season this village changes character altogether. During normal times the inhabitants cultivate a rich olive grove that extends all the way to the sanctuary. On the way to the ancient grounds, just before the left turn off the main road, you will see a *psistaría* with delicious lamb on the spit. This is the best place in Ligourio to eat roasted lamb after an Aristophanes comedy.

The sanctuary, less than a mile off the main road, is surrounded by pine trees. The ruins themselves present no special fascination, but the grounds have that sacred aura about them, a kind of mystical quality. This place exudes good health: the air, the trees, the aesthetics of it transmit a healing quality. You feel sure that Asklepios the physician, son of Apollo, still dwells here. When you reach the theater, the crowning glory of Epidauros even to this day, you feel sure this is a place of healing and of celebration.

The annual festival, begun in the early

Boúrtzi, 19th century island residence of the civic executioner.

1950s, has hosted some of the great performers of our time, from María Cállas to Katna Paxinoú. On any given summer you can see up to six or more tragedies, mostly by the National Theatre of Greece, though in more recent years other groups have been permitted to perform as well. Usually the performances are traditional in approach but, somehow, in this environment such an approach does not seem out of place as it would elsewhere. This has been proven recently with what seemed respectable experimentation (though staid enough in wider theatrical circles), which in this oddly sacred place appeared quite ludicrous. Of course, the performances are geared for the tourist, but it wasn't long ago when the shepherds and people from the surrounding villages came here on star-studded nights, and shed a tear or two over the plight of Agamemnon's daughter or Medea's children. This still happens on dress-rehearsal nights when the local townsfolk are admitted free of charge.

The theater at Epidauros faces west and is the finest extant example of its kind. Its design and acoustical engineering has never been matched. In our own day, it stands as the sacred monument—a kind of patron saint—of every theater artist the world over. It is every artist's dream to play at Epidauros. Most recently the National Theatre of Great Britain played at Epidauros, and each year requests to perform here abound.

The main road before the turn for the sanctuary continues in a southeast direction to end up at Galatas on the cape. The view of the *Lemonodassos* (forest of lemon trees) along the cape with the island of Poros in the distance, is an exquisite and refreshing experience. And some of the finest beaches are around Hermióni and Pórto Helí.

Tripolis: Back now to the road towards Arcadia and the central Peloponnese. We climb the face of Parthenion and leave behind the grand view of Argolis, ending up at **Tripolis** (the name denoting the three ancient cities, Tegea, Mantinia and Palladian). **Tegea** was the site of a remarkable temple of Athina whose pediment Pausanias claimed contained some of the greatest art of his time. Tegea is well-known for its annual fair. Here is the largest animal trading ground in all of Greece. Gypsies come from all over selling and trading horses, mules and

hepherd
d his flock
the Mani.

donkeys. **Mantinia** is now simply an elongated valley between two mountain ranges. Its ancient ruins contain a sanctuary. Of the three, **Palladian** is the only one with no ancient history. It was named by a fickle Roman emperor, who stopped there in the Antonine period. Tripolis was the capital of the Morea for the duration of the Ottoman occupation. It still retains some of its gruff, trading character.

The people of Tripolis are intensely political; you can observe them in the cafes, at the various squares, engaged in heated discussion. Aristotle's "man the political animal" (*zoon politikon*) is everywhere evident. Tripolis is too provincial to attract the traveler. But it has other charms: the best yoghurt anywhere can be found at *Kanatas*, on the sidestreet behind the Agios Vasilis church in the center of town. The town is sprawling, with the army at one end and the air force at the other. It serves as the "big city" of central Peloponnese, where many young laborers from surrounding villages end up for work. In contrast to the rowdiness of the marketplace during the day, the city's central square has a certain grace at night, when young couples take their stroll.

All roads that lead away from Tripolis take us along picturesque and important parts of Peloponnese. Our first direction will be towards the Olympia mountains. A short sidetrip northwest of Tripolis warrants attention. Here the traveler encounters a series of upland valleys which are narrowly linked from Tegea and Mantinia to Orchomenus, less than 15 miles (25 km) away. The irrigation of these valleys, lying as they do between mountain ranges, has always been a mystery and a contention. Pausanias, in A.D. 160, speaks of considerable controversy (and strife) when the Mantinians insisted on diverting the water from the Orchomenus valley to irrigate their own crops. By Pausanias' account this water came from subterranean springs, which is borne out by today's scientific accounts as well. It seems the entire Mainalon range converges its subterranean streams in this valley, forming in the winter season a virtual lake, just to the northwest of ancient Orchomenus. In 1986–87, the ancient controversy seems to have caught fire again, leading to major civil disobedience, with men and women from the surrounding villages lying flat on the

Nauplia seen from the Palamidi fortress.

ground before government bulldozers and heavy machinery. Evidently the Athens government has decided to lay down gigantic pipes and siphon the water through the Mantinian valley and into Tripolis for industrial use. Just as in ancient times, the controversy remains the same: what will become of the surrounding villages which depend on farming? Will they dry up and be turned into ghost towns? This was exactly the argument given to Pausanias during the first century.

Small villages: The road toward this valley away from Tripolis is an excellent one of travel. The mountain to the left is **Mainalon**. At its highest peak, Ayios Ilias, is a fine ski resort, limited in distances but very charming with a spectacular view of the valleys below. Along the main highway, at the foot of the mountain and just above ancient Orchomenus, is **Levidi**, a village of great beauty. It is built on the hillocks that lead to the lowlands, and provides the center for the villages which surround the valley. The people of Levidi, which is known for its excellent mountain climate, are the farmers of the Orchomenus valley, where the ancient water controversy has

been raging. This, too, is the birthplace of Alexandros Papanastasiou, who served as Prime Minister of the Republic in 1924, after the expulsion of the King. Orchomenus, on top of the hill that rises at mid-valley (and nearer to the Chelmos range on the opposite side), was, like Tegea and Mantinia, an ancient city; it had an acropolis overlooking the valley as its center. Three temples: to Apollo, to Aphrodite and to Artemis Mesopolitis, as well as a fairly well-preserved theater, stood here at one time. A certain loneliness and grace characterize this spot nowadays. Its water, has not yet been taken away, thanks to the clever arguments and civil disobedience of the populace.

Further along on this main highway are two noteworthy places. One is the village of **Vitina** which is a well-known mountain resort, frequented mainly by Athenian Greeks. It has a rather damp climate, since it is surrounded by a pine forest. Summer or winter, this little village is always bustling with visitors. Further on, you will find the spectacular town of **Lagadia**, built along a gorge. What makes this town remarkable is not only that it hangs on the edge of a

ustoms or
ustom's?

mountain, but that it is so sturdy. The houses are built by the stone masons of Lagadia, known throughout the whole of Greece for their skill. They have built most of the fine church walls across the country.

For the remainder of the road to Olympia, the land is tamer. This is the country where the Great Mother, Demeter herself, searched high and low for her daughter Persephone. She changed herself into a mare, the better to travel through the mountains. At Phigalia, a bit south of here, on Mount Eleos, she was raped by Poseidon who had taken the shape of a stallion for the sacrilege. For a long time after that she hid in a cave on the mountain until Panos, warm-hearted shepherd boy-god, found her and begged her to revive fertility for the earth that lay fallow since her absence. Nowadays the legend has been expanded to include the Christian mother with a small chapel at Demeter's sanctuary. Still, the old legend persists in local memory.

When the sacred flame burned: The Olympic games were the most renowned of all the festivals in Greece. They took place once every four years, at the time of the full moon in August or September.

The sacred flame burned long before the eloquent sanctuaries to Hera and Zeus and the Praxiteles statues were created. These can be seen at Olympia's excellent museum today. All enmity and war ceased during the games. A heavy fine was exacted on whoever disobeyed the Olympic committee. Hard-headed Sparta paid up more than once, so did many other cities. But, for the most part, everyone made a solemn effort to cease all hostilities. So sacred and serious were these games that the Hellenic world since 776 B.C. based its chronology on the four-year Olympiads, measuring its history accordingly.

Today the sight is peaceful and green, surrounded by pines, poplars and plane trees and bounded on two sides by the Alphios and Kladeos rivers. All the temples can be traced, so can the Stadium and the Gymnasium. The best preserved is the temple to Hera, inside whose sanctuary the masterful Hermes statue was found. Look for it in the museum. It's easy to spend a whole day here, to trace the pediments of the temples, each of the magnificent scenes depicting the chariot race between Pelops and the local king, Oenomaos, with Zeus presiding; or the great struggle between the Lapiths and

Climbing among Nauplia's ruins.

the Centaurs, with Apollo presiding.

The great athletes who came here for competition were not the only competitors, and the games were not the only feature. It seems that writers, historians and poets frequented the festivals, coming here to read their work. The historian Herodotus read part of his work at Olympia. And the ever-present poet-for-hire, Pindar himself, read his commissioned Odes.

Patras city: If you leave the Alphios valley, the road north will bring you to the lush and fertile province of Achaea and the city of Patras. If you turn south along the coast, you will enter the province of Messenia and will come to some of the loveliest beaches along the Ionian coast. **Patras** is Greece's third largest city, after Athens-Piraeus and Thessaloníki. Its patron saint is St. Andreas, and many people keep his namesake in the family. Greece's current Prime Minister, Andreas Papandreou, comes from here. Patras is a sprawling city, both a bustling port and a University town. Being the center of traffic for the Ionian sea, Patras is the first place travelers from Italy see. There is also a ferryboat service for the Ionian islands, Zante, Cephalonia and

Ithaca. Although the various occupations by the Venetians have given the city a certain finesse, one's first impression is still of an unappealing port city.

Backtracking from the Alphios valley, once again through Arcadia, we reach Bassai, where one of the most complete and isolated temples to Apollo is located. We then continue to Megalopolis, and finally down the Aegean coast of Arcadia through Leonidion to Monemvasia.

The oak trees of Megalopolis look as if they are dying from the pollution of the hydroelectric plant. Megalopolis was always an artificial city. It was built in haste in the 300s B.C. as the new capital. People were brought here from all over central Peloponnese in an ancient experiment in migrant labor and political relations. Today, the electric plant has also drawn workers from other regions. But if the ancient experiment did not work, the modern one is doing no better. Political historians insist, however, that the original experiment was one of the noblest of all in representative democracy, and that had it succeeded, it would have far outpassed the Athenian model.

The shore drive from Astros to Leonidion has a special charm, with a towering

The renowned theater of Epidauros.

mountain range on the right, and brilliant blue sea on the left. After Leonidion, however, the road must veer inland up the mountain, for only eagles can travel near the water as the mountain itself falls suddenly into the sea. The monastery of Elonis perches atop these cliffs. Terracotta red buildings hang from the highest rock. Then, within a short distance past the monastery the world changes again, as we are greeted by soft green almond trees and oaks at the border of Laconia.

Gibraltar of Greece: Monemvasia is the most extraordinary, and perhaps most beautiful place in all of Peloponnese. Certainly it is the most unique spot in Laconia. It boasts the other history of the Morea, the Medieval one, and it throws light on all the minor fortresses we have been encountering along the way. Monemvasia is often called the "Gibraltar of Greece." An impregnable fortress, it had the reputation of being self-governed from the sixth century though later it did come under the Byzantine empire. Monemvasia is a great rock in the sea, connected to the mainland by a man-made causeway, hence its name *moni embasis* (only one way in). Its fame across western Europe was for the excellent wine

that went by the name of Malmsey or Malvoisie, the Western variations of its name. The dark, fruity wine was at first a product of Laconia, but later it came from Crete and other islands. Monemvasia served as the broker and merchant port for its transfer west.

As you walk on the causeway from the mainland town you see nothing ahead of you but a bulky squarish hill of solid stone. The fortress town is well hidden from view. But from inside the gate, though the street is initially dark and narrow, you will suddenly catch sight of the blue Aegean. Along this main street is the home of one of Greece's greatest living poets, Yannis Ritsos. When you reach the small courtyard of *Elkomenos Christos* (Christ in chains), stop and take in the vista. Above you is the old town, and further up the great castle. The architecture is of Byzantine origin, but with the many invasions, the rebuilding and remodeling it would be difficult to date any of the structures.

This strategic place, which commanded the Aegean from the west, lies on the east side of the Malea promontory and only about 18 miles (30 km) north of its cape. Until 1246 when it fell into the

A photographer in Sparta.

hands of Guillaume de Villehardouin, only the Byzantine Eagle flew here. But even under Villehardouin its inhabitants insisted on self-rule and self-taxation with feudal service to the conqueror. Since that time it passed again to Constantinople, then later to the Turks, again to the Venetians (and even to the Pope for a brief period), and once more to the Greeks during their War of Independence. Whether under the Byzantine Eagle, the Venetian Lion or the Turkish Crescent, Monemvasia remained a strangely independent and virtually impregnable community. Its two soft ports far below its retaining wall made it a great trading center, like a giant battleship setting up business in the middle of the sea.

Mistra: While Monemvasia was mainly secular, **Mistra**, the other great center of the Byzantine Greeks, was purely a holy place. Only three miles (five km) outside of Sparta toward the sea, it is an imposing promontory, almost like a toy hill in the vicinity of the great Taïgetos range. Mistra is the most romantic chapter of eastern Christendom, with its churches still standing, many of its icons recovered, and only the perishable frescoes and adornments lost to conquerors and to centuries of disuse.

Among the most notable architectural structures stand the Pantanassa monasteries, Ayi Dimitrios (the Metropolis), Evangelistria and the monastic area of Vrontokion with its cultural center and the burial place of Byzantine prelates. Aghii Theodori, built at this spot in the late 1200s, is one of the last of its kind, with a central octagon as a tholos.

Mistra enjoyed a cultural and intellectual life for much of its existence before 1460, when it went into decline and disuse with the Turkish occupation. In 1400 Mistra produced the last of the Greek philosophers, Gemistos Plethon, a Platonist, who lectured extensively on the works of Plato. Some of his students taught subsequently at Oxford. But his views were not in accord with those of the church, so he was often criticized in Greece.

Sparta: **Sparta**, the ancient ruins and the modern town, are best approached from the north, from the Tripolis road. From the top of the pass, flanked as we are by the Parnon range, the view is splendid. Once again the landscape has shifted radically. The Eurotas valley, lush and fertile, extends as far as the eye can

low, steps
Persian
ntain in
cenae.
ght, prickly
ars in the
ni.

see. Alongside the valley, as if leading it by the hand all the way to the sea, Taïgetos rises with such grace that you are only intermittently aware of the optical illusions it is about to play on you. When the light falls at a certain angle the mountain stands right next to you; at other times, crowned by mist, it lurks at a distance. Today's Spartans seem to play similar tricks. Sometimes their calm appearance veils a wild temperament.

Sparta's ruins are not well preserved. You can make out a sanctuary and a theater on the gentle rise, but no acropolis, no grand hillsides with citadels, and no walls to enclose it. The kinds of warriors that they were, they did not need walls to protect them. Besides the Spartans never put much stock in the aesthetic look of things. These monuments were never spectacular, only functional. This is a fact which prompted Thucydides to write: "If the city of the Lacedaemonians were destroyed, and only its temples and the foundations of its buildings left, remote posterity would greatly doubt whether their power were ever equal to their renown." Thucydides lamented the fact that the city didn't have a unified civil and sacred policy which would produce the right kinds of monuments.

The Spartans embarked on the disastrous Peloponnesian War with some reluctance, goaded by their allies; but once in the war, their very nature was not to relent. As late as the second century Pausanias told of how the people of the mountains of Mani would call themselves Lacedaemonians and look upon themselves as the direct descendants of the ancient Spartans. In fact, these same Lacedaemonians, were still not converted to Christianity as late as the 12th century. They remained self-governed in willful isolation, and no conqueror, friend or foe, would traverse the terrain, fearing the wild Spartans. Their terrible disillusionment and decision to abandon the social world must have come after the Romans destroyed their city at the end of the Hellenistic era. Neither Augustus later nor the Turks in our own era dared to invade them. They all acknowledged Mani's independence.

Gythion: Traveling south from Sparta toward Gythion, it's difficult to imagine this dark history. The fertile valley with its olive and citrus trees is peaceful. The road towards Gythion is excellent. We leave Mistra behind to one side

A cemetery (below) and the ruins of Venetian house (right Monemvasia

ΓΕΩΡΓΙΟΣ Κ. ΚΥΡΙΑΚΟΓΚΩΝΑΣ
ΑΠ. 19-7-1986 ΕΤΩΝ 54

and travel with the mountain always to our right. Along the way signs point to villages deep in the mountain. One such village is **Arna**. This is the place which boasts that all its children make it to the university. This is quite a claim considering how competitive entrance examinations are. The village is the schoolteacher's dream. You can see a certain austerity in the eyes of the children, an intensity and gentleness—boys and girls alike—and your thoughts return to the ancient youth and their austere training for success in the world.

Gythion is a port town, and the astounding fact about it is that it hasn't undergone what the tourist-minded businessmen call "development." It is still, on any weekday, a populous bazaar. It doesn't put on airs or fancy clothes for the evening promenade, as opulent Sparta does nowadays. The sea, they say, makes people different, more refined—it blunts the edges. If that is true, the people of Gythion have much of the sea in them. In ancient times this served as Sparta's port. It was from here that Helen sailed to Troy with Paris. The place they were supposed to have sailed from is marked on the long causeway connecting the islet of Marathonisi with the mainland.

The road that heads for the mountain, towards Cape Matapan (or Cape Tenaron, as it is often called) leads first to Areopolis, across Taïgetos and almost to the other side on the Messenian Gulf. It is best to travel down the cape on the west side and return by climbing the face of the mountain on the east. **Areopolis** is already the deep Mani, and here you begin to discern a wild nature in the people. Deep isolation, as a way of. life, has brought all manner of contradiction to the surface. The church of Areopolis has a telling militant nature. It is the church of the martial saints, *ton Taksiarchon*, and is adorned by primitive reliefs of these warring figures. The war-god Ares would certainly approve of his modern Areopolis.

Here the people of Mani cultivate olive trees; but the trees are so puny, growing on such tiny patches of red earth that you wonder how they manage to survive, both the trees and their tenders. The view down the coast is spectacular. After the stalagmite and stalactite Caves of Diros, the road to Cape Matapan becomes more and more forlorn. In the distance you can see the architecturally distinctive cylin-

drical towers breaking the bareness of the landscape (see Vendettas in the Cultural Dictionary).

The windy vistas and the aura of the sea far below end as we ease down to the fishing village of **Gerolymin**. The few boats of the fishermen lie aslant along the jetty. You can read the surprise in the faces of the villagers whenever they see that anyone has arrived by land.

The remainder of the drive to Matapan is treacherous along unpaved road, but well worth the spectacular view at the cape. You can see the island of Kíthira to your left off the coast of Cape Malea, south of Monemvasia; and you can see, too, Cape Akritas to your right south of Koroni. And here a shiver runs down your spine as you turn your head 180 degrees and take in these three prongs of southern Peloponnese and remember the time-worn stories of the old seawolves who have sailed along these capes. Since ancient times this has been the most dreaded sea for all Greek sailors. Here, at Matapan, the free Lacedaemonians had their headquarters; and, where the temple to Poseidon used to be, the small church of Asomaton has taken its place.

From Sparta, embarking on the last leg of the journey, you leave Laconia behind and enter the province of Messenia. The drive is the most spectacular of all, for you scale the highest peak of Taïgetos and begin your descent from the western side high above Kalamata. Still, one final detail of their "gymnopaideia" should detain you. The *Keadas*, just before the village of Trypi, is the dark and bottomless pit, marked now by a wire mesh in front of an opening between two rocks, where military-minded Spartans threw their "unformed" children, those unfit for battle. The hole is unmarked; from its depth rises a cold air, a true chill several degrees cooler than the warm atmosphere. The mountain beckons, yet it's hard to get that eerie hole out of your mind.

Messenia province: Leaving Laconia the road travels up the great Lagada gorge over Taïgetos, and already we are in Messenia. The people in this province are famous for always trying to sell you something. They are the butt of many jokes across Peloponnese. The inn on the descent here is too opulent-looking to belong to any but Messenians, as are the trinkets that are sold along the road. Those are fine handcrafts and make good mementos of a visit.

Kalamata down the valley produces olives, the best export olives from all of Greece. You also see the cigarette factory at a distance. It is a city with inexcusable amount of pollution and dull buildings, saved only by a fair stretch along its shoreline and port, which displays some old-fashioned charm: a tumble of docks, jetties and riggings looking in the direction of the sea, the port thumbing its nose at the tawny central plain and sprawling city of Messenia. Kalamata recently suffered a tragic earthquake that showed the sham of its building contractors who profitted from not making the buildings earthquake-proof with extensive foundations and steel girders as the law requires. The best way to cope with Kalamata is to leave it and head directly for the Ionian coast. After a brief detour to the Methoni and Koroni promontories, where splendid Venetian castles will remind you once more of medieval Greece you can head for Pylos the city of old Nestor from Homer's *Odyssey*.

You should stay at **Pylos** as many days as you can for this is a quiet, restful place by the sea. The fish is inexpensive and plentiful. The walk along the beach, beyond the gymnasium, under the pine trees, comes as a healing and celebratory experience, after one had braved all these many centuries of Peloponnese. And you can contemplate, if you wish, the terrible battle that took place just at the islet across the way, Sphacteria, between the Spartans and the Athenians, described in masterful detail by Thucydides. Or, you might prefer to contemplate the later battle at Navarino Bay, the one you're looking at, for in the 1820s the Bay at Sphacteria was called Navarino. Here, the three fleets, French, Russian, and English decided to help the Greek revolution by engaging the navy of Ibrahim Pasha, and destroying all his ships. The people of Pylos have erected bronze busts of three admirals in their town square to commemorate the event. Another battle to contemplate is more recent: against a Japanese company who wanted to build giant oil refineries in the Bay. The people of Pylos and the ecologists won. For the more romantic there is Telemachos of Ithaca to remember. Odysseus' young son was sent here by his mother Penelope to ask old Nestor for news of his father. Maybe he did find out something about his father's wanderlust from Nestor. In any case, Pylos is a fine place to conclude a visit to Peloponnese.

An Olympia finish at Olympia's stadium.

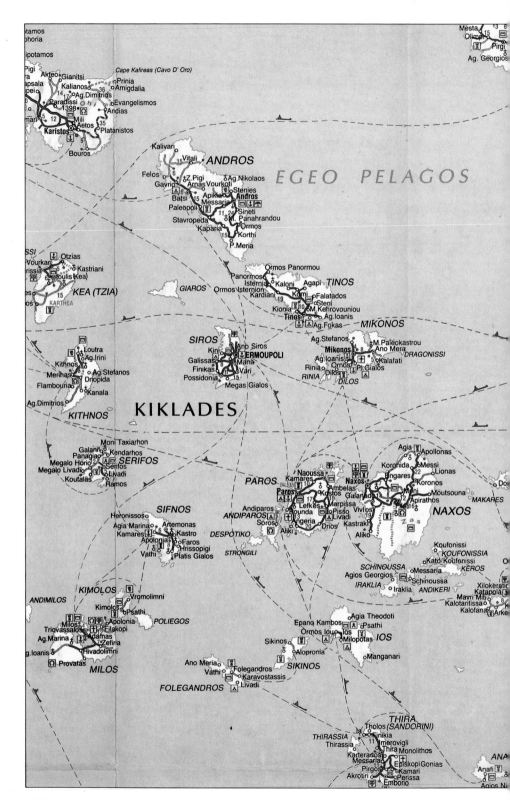

THE CYCLADES ISLANDS

The Cyclades are quintessential Greek islands. They are what people think of when they think of Greece. Images of white and blue: whitewashed houses and domed churches surrounded in all directions by a shocking blue—the sea, the sky, even doors and window frames are painted an electric blue.

Mykonos, Santorin, Folégandros ... they are as magical as their names sound. But should you go in search of an unspoiled haven, beware; the Cyclades have been the site of mass tourism of late. It's best to avoid peak summer months, and visit instead in June or September.

The Cyclades islands—39 in all, 24 inhabited—offer diversity, something for everyone. Mykonos and Santorin have more "action" than most large cities. In fact, single folk visiting any Cyclades island can expect not to remain single for long; here are better meeting places than any pub or club at home. Greek men look forward to the tourist season for *kamáki*, (see pages 283–284 of cultural dictionary) which translates roughly into "picking up" women. They've got it down to a science, staking out the discos in twos and threes, and using the few English words they know and think women want to hear.

Couples wanting a romantic holiday will find it in the narrow winding lanes of each island's *chora* (main town), in the turquoise-green sea you dip into to escape the blaze of the Aegean sun, and at *tavernas* where dining is alfresco and wine abounds. If money is no object, fine yachts can be chartered for personally-designed "island hopping" tours, or villas rented for lengthy and decidedly non-touristy stays.

There is another version of island hopping: strap on a backpack and use the inexpensive network of Greek ferries to rough it out at island campgrounds. It's a way of traveling much favored by Europeans and young Americans, though islanders disdain it as it leaves little monetary profit. To their credit, backpackers discovered Greece's lesser-known islands. Greeks themselves followed the backpackers' example and started touring their own islands; Athenian youths can now be seen sleeping bag in hand, wearing jeans and writing postcards from tiny villages they would never have thought to explore ten years ago. The bad news about the backpacking phenomenon is that it crowds the islands with no monetary profits for the islanders.

No matter what mass tourism has done or will do to the Cyclades, they simply must be seen. Visually, they compare with nothing else in this world. Cycladic architecture is so unique and impressive, it has influenced the work of many famous modern architects, including Le Corbusier.

Some say the "Cyclades" are named after nymphs who were transformed into rocks when they refused to offer sacrifices to Poseidon. The truth is, the inner ring of the archipelago forms a circle, or *cyclos*, around the holy island Dilos.

The Cyclades were inhabited as early as 6000 B.C. The heyday of Cycladic civilization came during the Bronze Age (2800 B.C.–1100 B.C.) and paralleled the rise of Cretan and Helladic civilizations. The Cyclades islanders traded with Crete, mainland Greece, Cyprus, even Asia Minor and Africa. They enjoyed a high standard of living, judging from jewelry and household wares found by archaeologists. Toward 2000 B.C., Cycladic maritime activity declined because of competition from Crete, and by 1500 B.C.–1000 B.C., the Cyclades fell under the domination of Mycenaean civilization. Later, in 487 B.C., the islands came under the rule of Athens, but when Athens' power waned, a succession of foreign conquerors ensued: the Romans (second century), the Venetians (13th century), and finally the Turks (16th century). It wasn't until after the Greek War of Independence (1825) that the islands became Greek again. All this history—approximately 5000 years—isn't readily apparent as you sip a *frappé* (iced coffee) in Paros harbor. But a little digging through island museums and souvenir books brings the past to the surface and enriches your stay. (Note: The world's first museum devoted to Cycladic art, the Goulandris Museum, opened in 1986 in Athens.)

Geographically, the Cyclades are flung like boulders in the Aegean Sea, south of the mainland between the Peloponnese and the Dodecanese islands. As you approach they look like huge, sterile rocks, grayish-brown in color, jutting ungracefully from the sea; their only inviting quality is a cove here and there, with turquoise water lapping onto a tiny bit of shore. Still, their aridness takes on a charm of its own and of course there is the bustling harbor, and all the white-washed houses you've read about.

When traveling to the Cyclades, the only unpleasant task is deciding which island to stop at. Asking the advice of friends or even Greeks won't help much. Each island has a distinct appearance and personality; a beauty to some is a bore to others and so on. It becomes apparent you will have to risk it all and just choose. Where to begin? Chances are you won't want to miss Mykonos and Santorin, the most trumpeted of all Greek isles.

Mykonos' tourism trade began 30 years ago, unlike other Cyclades islands which only recently have drawn tourists' attention. In the 1950s, Mykonos must have been surreal, otherworldly. Even today, under the trappings of souvenir shops, glitzy watering holes, Mykonos' natural beauty is astounding—and evident at first sight of its semicircle harbor, sugarcube houses, and white-washed windmills.

Every year from May to October, Mykonos comes alive. Owners of bars, boutiques and hotels flock back to the island from their winter homes in Athens or Europe, to open for "the season." The hordes descend; frenetic holidaying has begun. Though local inhabitants may frown at the intrusion of tourism in their lives, most natives admit they prefer the new standard of living to their pre-tourism poverty. Land that was in their families for generations suddenly became an unimagined source of income. Fortunately, through zoning laws which dictate that buildings in Mykonos can be only two stories high, their island has managed to maintain its human scale and original charm.

Mykonos has two scenes: beach and bar. At the beach you take off your clothes, at bars you put them on—your expensive, most fashionable clothes. It's a chic island where people come to see and be seen: Scandinavian models, Austrian doctors, Hollywood actors, Greek ship-ping types and the international yachting set. You may have heard Mykonos is a gay haven. True, true. Mykonos' first bar, Pierro—opened in 1955 and still operating—offers nightly all-male floor shows.

A typical day in Mykonos goes like this: you wake up late and go out for a

Preceding pages, **Mykonos.** Left, sunset and windmills Below, shipowner's daughter wearing a **Cyclades T-shirt.**

large breakfast around 11 or 12 o'clock (not a Greek custom at all but probably imported from America to ease hangovers). You swim and sun-worship at your choice of beach: Paradise, Super Paradise, Elia (all nude), or Áyos Stéfanos, Plates Ialos, Psaras and Ornos (at least topless). In the evening, showered and carefully dressed, you stroll down streets lined with designer boutiques and galleries. You can shop or drop into an outdoor cafe for people-watching, a favorite pastime. Dinner is late, around 10 or 11 o'clock, at the waterfronts of Little Venice or the harbor, where you dine on grilled octopus and crab, fried calamari, french fries, salad—all washed down with smooth retsina or cold frosty beer. Mykonos has elegant restaurants as well, serving continental cuisine; it's best to take advantage of them here as this type of establishment is a rarity on the islands. At midnight, the nightlife that never stops begins. Take your pick: Remezzo (celebrity-studded disco), Couccos Nest (new wave), Kouneni (pop Greek), Argo (a mix), Kastro (classical), Yachting Club et al (after-hours).

With all this club-hopping, it's good to know there isn't much archaeological importance on Mykonos. But nearby **Dilos**, an uninhabited isle should be seen. It's the holy island of the ancients where, as mythology holds, the twin gods Apollo and Artemis were born. The entire island is an archaeological site where you see floor mosaics, three marble temples to Apollo, sites of sacrifices, and the most impressive Street of the Lions—all bathed in a light and mystery that can't have changed much in 5000 years.

Greece's modern-day holy land, the island of **Tínos**, is just an hour from Mykonos. Tínos is the site of a spectacular religious pilgrimage every August 15, a date commemorating the Ascension of the Virgin Mary. Thousands of faithful miracle-seekers flock to Tínos' shrine dedicated to the Virgin, **Panagia Evangelistra**, and pray to a sacred icon said to have healing powers. Tínos is more than this famous church; notable are its pretty interior villages and over 1000 whitewashed dovecots—master-pieces of folk architecture.

If Mykonos is cozy and like a storybook town, **Santorin** is shocking, its topography an impossible triumph of nature and man. The island, also known

A HARD NIGHT ON MYKONOS

"Follow me to Paradise," says the inscription on a van waiting by the waterfront. The bold lettering leads up to the figure of a female Pied Piper, a brown lithe girl dancing under a huge yellow sun. Below, in small letters: *Paradise Camping, Mykonos.*

Even after discovering this is simply an advertisement, the invitation retains its potency. During these brilliant summer months, the small brown-and-white island seems to reiterate the promise: follow me to Paradise. And the crowds raptly obey the summons.

The search begins the moment you set foot on the swarming landing stage, where the knapsack tribe with their huge Quasimodo humps mix with returning islanders (the jet-set tribe prefer to fly), gleaming motorbikes collide with primitive wheelbarrows, beach-buggies with heavily loaded lorries. First, the search for accommodation. A frantic question rings in the air: "Room? Room?" In August, the cruellest month of tourism, a note of despair creeps in; the question changes to "Roof? Roof?" Even a roof will do (the white, cube-shaped houses all have flat roofs), a verandah, a balcony, anything. If you walk around late at night, you will see them: dark shapes, like Egyptian mummies, lying side by side in some sheltered corner, or on the beach. With the first rays of the sun, stray dogs will nudge them awake, or the steady slap of a fisherman beating an octopus on a nearby rock.

The provident or fortunate ones who have secured a roof over, rather than under their heads, sleep on till mid-morning. Most shops, geared to the needs of the late sleepers, don't open before 10:30. Serving breakfast is a thriving business; some places are famous for their Gargantuan breakfasts, which are really brunches. Then there is the exodus to the beaches. Public transport is surprisingly good. Some people prefer to walk: brown leathery health-fiends in sensible shoes and straw hats. At Platy-Yialo the man who runs the boat-shuttle lures undecided bathers with the familiar summons: "Paradise!" he shouts. "This way to Paradise!" And if you think Paradise isn't good enough, there's Super-Paradise (Super for short) further along the coast.

The choice of a beach requires subtle consideration. I've heard it said that there are 200 beaches on Mykonos. Let us play safe and say there are at least a dozen easily accessible ones, with fine yellow sand, blue-green waters like great sea-chambers of flawless glass, tawny rocks all around, as smooth as giant pebbles. Nudism varies; choice ranges from fully-clothed "family-beaches" (rare) to those exhibiting pure, Edenic nakedness. But the nuances are finer than that. Innumerable small cliques subsist on mysterious distinctions: there are those who only bathe at Super and those who will consider no other beach than Elià; both look down on those who go to Rolex beach, so designated by the initiates to indicate it is frequented by the nouveaux riches. The same goes for bars and discos at night: in Mykonos you *are* where you *go*.

In the late afternoon, after the return of the bathers, Mykonos hoists its pennants, flies the banners of summer: huge mauve beach towels; flimsy, elementary swimsuits; *pareos; sarongs; loongies*; are hung up to dry in the wind, while their owners sink into a late, late siesta.

Around 11 o'clock, the pleasure-seekers emerge, spangled, draped, tasseled, painted, scented, ready for the festivities of the night. They squeeze through the narrow meandering streets— conflicting currents, this way, that way, wherever the call of pleasure sounds stronger. Here and there small knots of people form, instantly attracting more people; the knot becomes a group, a crowd, what's going on, who is it, what are they doing, let us in. Sometimes there is a real center of attraction: a film star; a man impersonating a robot; a drag queen; a woman sporting a live snake like a long undulating scarf. Actors and spectators, insiders and outsiders. Some people look exhilarated, almost surprised at themselves, at the ease with which they have slipped out of their city-bodies. Others are simply drunk, comfortably or miserably so. There are the over-eager, or the timid and the lonely, and those who look sullen, restless, having searched but not found. Pleasure is a hard and capricious taskmaster, and is it not a commonplace that the only paradise is paradise lost? Here is a large blonde woman with burnt thighs tapering into extremely tight white cowboy-boots, blowing thoughtfully into a pink balloon. Here is a hybrid figure in striped bermudas, top-hat, high-heeled lame sandals, stranded with a loadful of wasted efforts, allurements unused and useless. And all through the night, you hear the steady beat of music, picked in relays by one disco after another.

The old lovers of Mykonos, who "discovered" it in the '50s, keep lamenting the desecration. The place has become another St. Tropez, they sneer; or worse, Capri, or worse still, Blackpool; yet they still come back every summer, carrying around their bile and their scorn, putting on proprietary airs, betrayed but persistent lovers. Perhaps it is the invincible beauty of the place, the purity of the light, the linear perfection. Perhaps they are dimly aware that this island can never be totally "spoilt." Is it the wind, the unpredictable north-northwesterly *meltemi*, endemic to the Cyclades, that

sweeps and brushes it clean, dispels the fumes, burns away with briny breath the sediment of over-consumption, over-manipulation?

Long before the "beautiful" people wake up, the Mykoniots go about their business as if the invasion hadn't taken place. They gossip, discuss the coming municipal elections, cluster round the fishing-boats that have just come in with the night-catch. The sleepy idyllic island of the '50s? Not quite. Many of the boats' names have changed, fewer *Aghia Marinas* and *Thomadakis*, more fancy names like *Troubadour, Romantica, Super*. The ubiquitous whitewash that makes Mykonos look like a snow-city in the middle of summer is often defaced by advertisements and graffiti, stained with the brown blood of melted chocolate ice-cream. There are still donkeys carrying large baskets of melons, figs, tomatoes, bunches of flowers interspersed with fresh basil and verbena; but you can't help suspecting it's a deliberate touch of *couleur locale*; most other peddlers have switched to three Wheelers long ago. You are never sure what is genuine and what is there for show. A local boy rides bareback on a white horse along the beach, a romantic image if ever there was one. He gets off the horse, picks two white sea-lilies in the sand, sticks them behind the horse's ears. Two ladies in flowing djellabahs come up and talk to him; he offers them the lilies. Was it all stage-managed?

No matter how crowded, there is a peculiar sense of lebensraum on Mykonos—dare one call it a capacity for freedom? A quality that can easily topple into destructive excess at one end, indifference at the other; yet somehow, most of the time, a delicate balance is maintained. Consider this scene: a little withered old woman, bundled in black clothes from top to toe, trudges every morning along one of the more dedicated nudist beaches selling fresh figs. She picks her way carefully through the tangle of naked bodies; looking neither right nor left, she hands out figs, pockets money. When she reaches the far end of the beach, she sits down on a rock and puts away her basket. Very cautiously, she lifts the hem of her black skirt and dips one foot, then the other, in the shallow waters—untouched, in her small pool of privacy.

as Thíra, has the misfortune of being located where two of the earth's plates meet. Brutal volcanic activity has destroyed the island again and again, yet people continue to live on the precipice, cultivating whatever is left of the land and building new homes.

It is eerie, religious, exhilarating, to look from your white terrace at a volcano's crater floating in the sea. This dark, amoeba-like mass of land is surrounded by an ominous haze; though dormant, the volcano emits gas and steam at 80°C even today. Again from the terrace you look down at the sheer drop of cliffs, actually walls of the caldera. Chunks of land have been blown away, exposing colored layers of pumice and lavas—gray, brick, black—each stripe the trace of a different volcanic eruption. Once more from your terrace, you look right and left at the band of white cylindrical cottages surrounding yours, carved into the cliffside and fitting together like a jigsaw puzzle: your terrace is some else's roof and so on.

This land is a ghost of what it once was, a crescent remnant of what used to be a perfectly round "Strongyle" island. The volcanic eruption circa 1500 B.C. which shattered Strongyle is said to have taken Crete's Minoan civilization with it. Santorin's geological history is much too complex to do justice to there. Suffice it to say that what you see and learn supports the most spine-chilling theories: Could Santorin be Plato's lost Atlantis?

Today, approaching the island by boat, you see what seems to be a snow-capped mountain. Getting closer, you realize the snow is actually whitewashed houses perched atop cliffs. Six hundred spiral stairs lead up from the harbor to **Fira**, the island capital, but you can hire a mule for what proves to be a rollicking adventure, or ride the modern funicular recently donated by one of Greece's shipping families. Fira is a disappointment though, drowned in a commercialism of "B" class *tavernas* and pushy jewelry store salesmen who live for American cruise passengers, the proverbial "big spenders." Santorin's population swells from 9000 to 70,000 in summer, and most of its visitors congregate in the capital. You should stop in at **Franco's Bar** one night, a landmark on the island, and eat seafood at **Zorba's**, but it's best to stay elsewhere on the island.

From Fira, a 10-minute walk along the

Religious knick-knacks.

cliff path brings you to **Firostefani**, the ideal spot to unpack your bags. Firostefani offers the best view of the volcano on the island, and the most dramatic streaks of red and violet during sunset. It's almost exclusively residential, with fabulous villas tucked inconspicuously away, plus it affords easy access to the hub of Fira.

Oia, the village on Santorin's northern tip, is billed as the most picturesque on the island. It is the old commercial center where elegant mansions (damaged by a 1956 earthquake) testify to the wealth of the seafolk who lived here. You may remember Oia as the setting for "Summer Lovers," a Hollywood movie; in fact, the house featured in this film is owned by the Greek government and is still rented as a guesthouse today. Life is quieter here, with fewer bars and *tavernas* and earlier closing hours. Evening begins with a local ritual, watching the sunset, followed by a drink at **Oasis Bar** where a balcony overlooks the twinkling lights of Fira. Dinner is an occasion at **Karra's Taverna**. The food is simple and inexpensive, and Saturday night features a bouzouki band playing local folk songs while Karra's daughters dance with the

crowd. The owner serves wine from his own barrels as well as Santorin's bottled favorites, with namebrands such as "Lava" and "Volcano."

Renting a jeep is a good way to see the island. In the morning, set out for Akrotiri, one of the greatest archaeological finds in recent decades. Here, under a roof built to protect the excavation, is the 3500-year-old city found buried under pumice and volcanic ash from the explosion which destroyed it around 1500 B.C. A civilization of great wealth thrived here, as revealed by paved streets (which you actually walk on), two- and three-story homes complete with toilets, wood furniture, elaborate pottery and wall paintings. No bones were found, which means the inhabitants were warned of the coming eruption. The wall frescoes, similar to those of Minoan Crete, were found in surprisingly good condition and are on display in Athens' National Archaeological Museum. They depict monkeys, antelopes, and papyrus that never lived or grew on Santorin, thus suggesting commercial ties with Egypt and Africa. Today, the dig is carried on by Athens University students during summer months, under the direction of

Pilgrims sleeping outside the Church of the Virgin Mary in Tinos.

Professor Christos Doumas; he estimates that, working at the present rate, it will take 100 years to complete the Akrotiri excavation!

By midday on Santorin, it's always time to swim. **Perissa Beach** is a favorite. Though the bay is packed with travelers who've arrived by bus from Fira, the stretch of black sand is five miles (eight km) long and there are plenty of isolated spots. The sand resembles mounds of caviar, and its unusual color reminds you that this *is* an explosive island you're swimming on. **Kamari Beach** is also popular but crowded, often you won't find a place to lay your towel. It is separated from Perissa by a mountain which houses the site of ancient Thíra, a steep climb but well worth the hike. **Monolithos Beach** is far from the madding crowd and features three of the island's best *tavernas*.

More than any other Cyclades isle, Santorin must be seen, and preferably before tourism alters it further. To be perfectly fair, tourism has had positive side-effects. Previously, the whitewashed cylindrical houses so characteristic of the island were deserted, crumbled caves. When the island was "discovered,"

natives moved back and rebuilt Santorin. The architects who came were committed to maintaining the traditional style in restorations and new constructions and they succeeded. Today, Greeks and even foreigners will pay 2 to 7 million drachmas (U$13,000 to U$46,000) for a cottage, and almost twice the buying price for restoration. It's hard to imagine paying hard-earned cash for so primitive and dilapidated a dwelling, but easier to fathom once you step into a would-be bedroom and witness the view.

This is Santorin: the spectacle, the view. There is a bizarre irony in spending holidays here, in this grim, freak-of-nature setting. But above all there is awe, the wonder of what you see, and see and see.

If you can't find accommodations on Mykonos, **Paros** is a good second choice; it has begun of late to rival Mykonos in its vibrant nightlife and cosmopolitan atmosphere. Although underneath, Paros is an uncomplicated, indistinctive fisherman's island with excellent beaches and whitewashed villages.

Parikia, the harbor town, and tiny **Antiparos**, a nearby island known for its stalactite caves, are backpackers'

Santorini.

meccas. For more "class" and fewer crowds, a Greek magazine recommends **Naoussa**, the snow-white fishing village on the northern coast. The truth is, it's too late: Naoussa is overun by "Rooms for Rent" signs and droves of trendy youths dressed up for drinks at **Labyrinth Bar** on the waterfront. Still, tourism is fairly new here and the villagers unjaded enough to stare wide-eyed at the night's happenings from their balconies and to whisper to each other: "I read something terrible in the paper today. There's Hashish in Naoussa."

Forty years ago, the Greek poet George Seferis called Paros the loveliest of all the Cyclades. From Naoussa, rent a jeep and head west to **Kolibithres**, a swimming beach with giant rock formations reminiscent of Greece's Metéora. A five-minute drive east from Naoussa, in the direction of Santa Maria, reveals splendid beaches which—for unknown reasons—are empty. The water is shallow here and deliciously transparent. But the best beach on Paros is on the east coast, just past Molos where a small handwritten sign indicates "Kalogiros." This small bay is framed by cliffs that jut in and out, creating semi-private spaces for nude

bathers. A swim here affords a fine view of Naxos. Continuing south, you arrive at the coastal towns of Pisso Livadi, Logaras and Drios, all commercial but with pleasant, sandy beaches.

Lefkes, an inland mountain village and the old capital of Paros, is off the beaten track and too often missed by travelers. Have a snack at **Paradise Cafe** overlooking the sea, then visit Virginia Kidonea's workshop/home (villagers will point the way).

Mrs. Kidonea is an elderly woman whose life is ceramics. Her works were previously sold in Mykonos, Athens and Thessaloníki, but since the death of her husband, her partner on the potter's wheel, Mrs. Kidonea has limited herself to Lefkes. "We put all the money we ever earned back into materials," she tells visitors, "all we wanted to do was work. My husband was a simple man, we asked only for two chairs and a place to sit." Mr. Kidonea is pictured on a postcard still sold in Paros, and his wife proudly shows visitors a copy she keeps in their scrapbook. It's evident that when you purchase a vase or mural from Mrs. Kidonea, you are taking home more than just another souvenir.

man in axos carries s shopping me.

If there is time, visit **Marpissa village** and the ancient quarry at **Marathi**, where the coveted Parian marble was mined. To round out your stay, keep your eyes open for Paros' famous son, superstar, singer Giannis Parios. He was spotted wearing a painter's cap and sunglasses one morning at a cafe along Parikia's harbor. Parios Paries is a master of love songs and has been Greece's darling for over 15 years.

Paros' central location in the Cyclades makes it a hub for boat connections to almost anyplace in the Aegean. The standard sea route brings you to **Naxos** next, the Cyclades' largest and most fertile isle, where in mythology Theseus abandoned Ariadne after she'd helped him kill the Minotaur. Naxos is still a fairly well-kept secret and offers a fine complement to Paros with its orchards and vineyards, medieval fortresses, and giant archaic stone *kouroj*. From Naxos, boats leave two or three times weekly for Koufonissia, a group of microscopic Robinson Crusoe islands (only six of 23 are inhabited) with names like Donoussa and Skinoussa, virgin beaches, and only a few rooms to let. **Ios**, next on the ferry route from Naxos, has an idyllic Cycladic harbor and spotless white town. But Ios—allegedly where Homer died—has been claimed by "partyers" and counter-culture types, as you can see by the nudists sunning on cliffs as your ferry passes by.

Folégandros, the next stop, is worth getting excited about. Don't be fooled by what could be the blandest harbor in the Cyclades, save for neighboring Sikinos'. Folégandros gives you a sense that you are unearthing it, you are partaking in island life rarely glimpsed by tourists.

Visually, it's astonishing: rough, mean terrain, arrogant and forgotten. Its bald gray hills look like lunar landscape, while here and there efforts by the inhabitants to build terraces have succeeded, giving rise to olives and vineyards, though preciously few.

Folégandros, named for a son of King Minos, has a population of 800. Since there is only one road and very few cars the islanders get around on foot and donkey. Public transportation consists of two minibuses, one running from Karavostasi harbor up the steep mountain to **Chóra**, and one from Chóra to Folégandros' only other village, tiny **Ano Meria**.

Foléngandros terraced landscape.

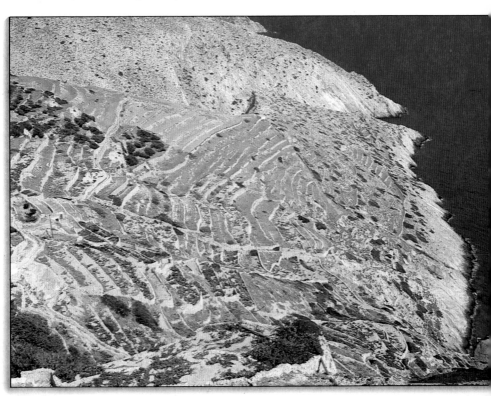

216

There are inexpensive rooms to let and at least one second-class hotel in Chóra, a whitewashed village typical of the Cyclades but perhaps less self-consciously so. **Kástro**, the old quarter, is built on a huge cliff and has an entrance and exit which used to be sealed off each evening to protect against pirate invasions; pots of scalding oil, too, lay in wait for the plundering intruders. The isolation and topography of Kástro are such that when you look out across the unchanged sea, you can imagine pirates still attacking today as they did until the 19th century.

You wake up early on Folégandros to a breathtaking view of whitewashed **Panagia Church** towering over Chóra on a hillside. As you go in search of morning coffee, you soon discover island life revolves around three squares, situated back-to-back and framed by white churches. Breakfast, lunch and dinner are served here, and tourists can be seen at all hours of the day reading and underscoring book passages, writing postcards, holding hands, staring into space. You easily adapt to the lazy island pace, and as you walk through Chóra to get ready for the beach, you take in the smells of onions and olive oil cooking.

Villagers still stare curiously when they see *Xéni* (foreigners), and watch as they collect a day's water supply from the fountain.

Folégandros' **Angali Beach** is also memorable. Yes, for its crystal-clear bay, two good *tavernas*, and a funny sign saying "Please, no nude bathing here, you have Fira and St. Nicholas Beaches for that." But mostly for how one gets to and from Angali. The minibus lets you off on the paved road, high above sea level, and you climb down a steep mountain path for some 20 minutes, using whatever leg muscles you own for brakes. The return? Either you are wise enough to take the six o'clock *caïque* to Karavostasi, or you hike back up the mountain. There are donkeys to aid your trip, but there's something to be said for beating this forbidding terrain.

A Folégandros evening begins with coffee and the sunset, both readily available at **Rainbow Pizzeria**, where you are served on a terrace overhanging the cliffs. Next, you'll want to compare dinner menus at **Kritikos'** and **Niko's**, Chóra's two main *tavernas*. Don't expect to eat fresh fish on the island; your choice usually includes Greek salad with *souroto*

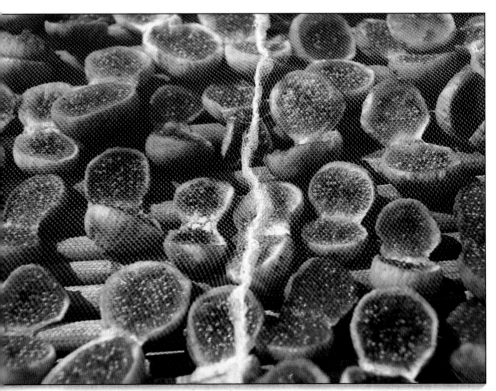

gs drying in
e sun.

cheese instead of feta, stuffed tomatoes, meatballs, *souvlaki, tzatziki,* french fries, and delicious local bread. After a leisurely dinner, it's time to move on to one or another square for coffee, or better yet to Chóra's only pub, **Laoumi**. Finally, just before bed, stop back into Rainbow Pizzeria for homemade *baklava* that is out of this world.

You may get stuck in Folégandros, not wanting to leave. It's a harmonious existence where tourism for once hasn't upset the traditional balance (save for a few large hotel constructions now underway). A waiter says visitor traffic has been on the rise since 1980. When asked the secret of keeping tourism controlled, he relates a story about the time the islanders chased out 50 undesirables, literally ran them off Folégandros.

Another island which maintains its natural flavor is **Syros**, capital of the Cyclades. This is a thriving metropolis, not a fisherman's town, with an economy based on Greece's first boat yards and textile factories, not summer tourism. Don't misunderstand; Syros is pleasant for vacationing. Actress Catherine DeNeuve spent her first-ever trip to Greece here in 1986. But Syros has an opulent, independent past and is proud to live in it. The island capital, **Ermoúpolis**, was Greece's greatest trading center, its most important port until the rise of Piraeus at the turn of the century.

Ermoúpolis (named for Hermes, god of trade and commerce) is built on two lofts, one topped by a Catholic church and the other by an Orthodox. It is full of Italian-designed neoclassical mansions, many open to the public today. Skylights, sweeping spiral staircases, painted ceilings and chandeliers are testimony to the fortunes made here, many in black market racketeering. **Ta Vaporia** (The Boats) is the city's most aristocratic corner, a line of neoclassical homes along a cliff over the sea, where waves crack against rocks in the style of Gothic thrillers. One of these mansions has been luxuriously transformed into the **Hotel Vourlis**, which in 1985 won an award as one of the seven best renovated buildings in Europe.

High above Ermoúpolis, on the Catholic peak, you can walk through 13th-century **Ano Syros**, the typical Cycladic old town built up high for protection against pirates. **Lili's Taverna** offers a terrace view of the city and harbor below; on a clear night, you can make out the lights of Mykonos.

Syros has lovely seaside towns, including Vari, Achladi, Megas Ialos and Galyssas, the latter featuring a popular campground. But the most impressive resorts are Delagrazia (or Posidonia), with its enormous Italian villas and castles, Agathopes and Finikia. All are within a five-minute drive of each other and offer a good alternative to staying in Ermoúpolis.

While most Cyclades islands can be reached by ferry from Piraeus, there are several which require leaving from Rafina and Lavrion—Andros and Kea, for example. Being slightly out of the way has kept their beauties unsung, to the point of being omitted from guidebooks on the area, though certainly not for long.

Andros, the northernmost of the Cyclades and home of many Greek shipowners, has two ports, **Gavrion** and **Batsi**, plus all-white villages with red-tile roofs. The island has much green, good beaches, and a noteworthy museum of modern art which opened in 1986.

Kea, also known as Tzia, heads the westernmost chain of Cyclades. It's just south of the mainland and has been popular for years with weekending Athenians who have summer homes there. What the island lacks in sandy beaches it more than makes up for in rocky coves and red-tile roof homes like Andros'. Neighboring **Serifos** and **Sifnos** are particularly attractive islands and often pictured on Greek postcards. Today there are no traces of the gold mines for which Sifnos was celebrated in antiquity, but over the past few years it has become a favorite with tourists seeking the "out of the way." There are ferry connections direct from Paros and other well-known islands.

Also part of this westernmost chain, **Kinolos'** chalk-white cliffs add to the already dazzling brilliance of its towns. Finally, you arrive at **Milos**, where the famous *Venus de Milo*, now in the Louvre, was found. The island's 5000-year-old civilization was on a par with Crete's, thus there are plenty of cultural attractions to enjoy in addition to good swimming and eating.

To be sure, one could spend a lifetime getting to know each and every island in this group. It is overwhelming to think there is no becoming an expert on the Cyclades, yet heartwarming too, that there will always be one more Ámorgos or Kithnos or Heraklia to fill up the summer.

Amorgos' celebrated Kozoviótissa the convent of the Presentation of the Virgin founded by Aléxis Comnénus.

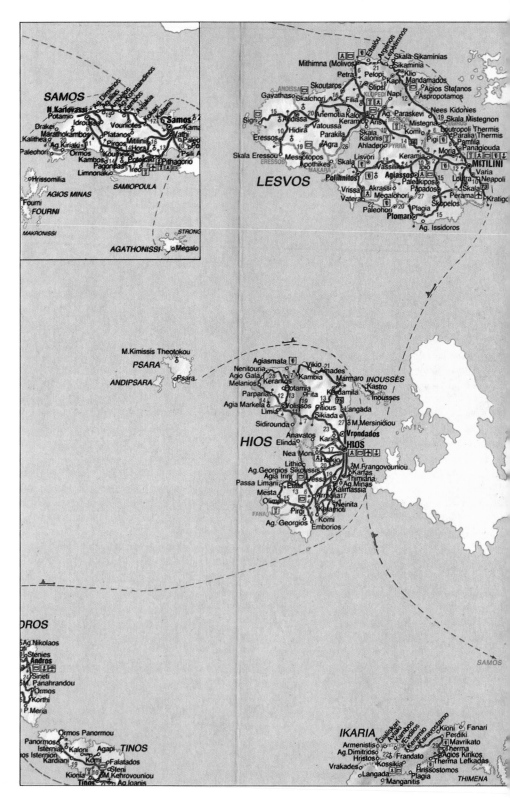

SAMOS

N.Karlovassi
Potamio
Drakei
Marathokambos
Kalithea
Ag. Kiriaki
Paleohori
Ormos
Kambos
Pagondas
Limnonaki

Ag. Dimitrios
Ag. Konstandinos

Idroussa
Vourliotes
Pirgos
Koumeika
Pandrossos
Mitilini

Vathi
Samos
Kama

Psili A.
Pithagorio
Ireo
Potokaki

SAMIOPOULA

AGIOS MINAS
Fourni
FOURNI

Hrissomilia

MAKRONISSI

AGATHONISSI   Megalo

STRONG

LESVOS

Mithimna (Molivos)
Argenos
Lepetimnos
Enallou
Skala Sikaminias
Petra   Pelopi   Sikaminia
Klio
Skoutaros   Stipsi   Kaph   Mandamados
ANDISSA   Napi   Agios Stefanos
Gavathaso   Skalchori   Filia   KLIOPEDI   Aspropotamos
Sigri   Andissa   Ariemotia Kalonis   Nees Kidonies
Hidira   Vatoussa   Keramio Arisvi   Skala Mistegnon
Eressos   Parakila   Skala   Komi   Loutropoli Thermis
Agra   Kalonis   PYRRA   Pigi   Paralia Thermis
Skala Eressou   Messotopos   Lisvori   Keramia   Pamfila
Apothikes   Skala   Panagiouda
MAKARA   Vassilika   Ipio   MITILINI
ERESSOS   Polihnitos   Agiasso   Moria
Vrissa   Akrassi   Paleokipos   Varia
Vatera   Megalohori   Papados   Skala   Neapoli
Paleohori   Plagia   Skopelos   Perama   Kratigo
Plomarii   Ag. Issidoros

PSARA
M.Kimissis Theotokou
ANDIPSARA   Psara

HIOS

Agiasmata
Nenitouria   Vikio   Amades
Agio Gala   Kambia   Marmaro   INOUSSES
Melanios   Keramos   Kastro
Parpanias   Potamia   Inousses
Agia Markela   Fita   Kardamila
Volissos   Pitious
Limia   Sikiada
Sidirounda   Langada
M.Mersinidiou
Anavatos   Karies   Vrondados
HIOS   Elinda   HIOS
Nea Moni   Halkio
Lithio   M.Frangovouniou
Ag.Georgios Sikoussis   Karfas
Agia Irini   Vessa   Thimiana
Passa Limani   Elata   Ag. Minas
Mesta   Kalimassia
Olimpi   Armolia   Neinita
Pirgi   Kalapoti
FANA   Ag. Georgios   Komi
Emborios

DROS
Ag.Nikolaos
Stenies
Andros
Sineti
M. Panahrandou
Ormos
Korthi
P.Meria

Ormos Panormou
Panormos   Isternia   Kaloni   Agapi   TINOS
os Isternion   Kardiani   Komi   Falatados
Kionia   Steni
Tinos   M.Kehrovouniou   Ag.Ioanis

IKARIA

Glaikari   Kioni   Fanari
Armenistis   Avlaki   Kambos   Perdiki
Ag. Dimitrios   Evdilos   Keramio   Mavrikato
Hristos   Frandato   Karavostamo   Therma
Vrakades   Kossikia   Agios Kirikos
Langada   Plagia   Therma Lefkadas
Manganitis   Hrissostomos
THIMENA

THE NORTHEASTERN AEGEAN ISLANDS

Lésvos, Chios and Samos form an extraordinary, if slightly arbitrary, trio. They are grand by Aegean standards and, marking the extreme eastern edge of Greek territory, are far from mainland Greece. They lie, moreover, at considerable distances from each other; geographically they are not a chain of islands but extensions of the Asia Minor mainland, to which they have been bound for millennia. Clearly they have distinct personalities, proud and resistant to being grouped together. They do, however, share a common East Aegean history, which merits a moment's reflection.

On Lésvos, Chios and Samos, Turkey is a constant presence. It manifests itself in everyday life in many ways: as a threat to the Greek soldier who mans the pillboxes and camps that spot the coasts and hills, and who peers out across those narrowest straits that separate him from the Turk; as the lure of another world, "Asia," for the tourist who wants to venture beyond; as a lost homeland to the elderly Greek refugee who, seeing it from her window, remembers what she left some 70 years before. For it was here, along this coast around Smyrna that the Greeks were driven into the sea in 1922 by Mustafa Kemal's troops. With this the dream of taking back their city, the "Megalí Idéa," vanished in flames and smoke and a millennial cohabitation was cut in two. Hundreds of thousands of Turkish speaking Greek Orthodox poured across these islands (those that were not slaughtered in the melee), and the door to Asia was closed for good.

In the formidable depths of these islands' histories an interplay of shared and divergent fates can be traced. The early (third and fourth millennium B.C.) inhabitants of these islands appear to have been closely linked to the East—both "Chios" and "Samos" are said to derive from Phoenician words. But it is in the West, in the dusk of the Bronze Age, that these islands' early destiny was forged. In c.1100 shock waves of the Dorian Invasion of the Greek mainland rippled across the Aegean to the coast of Asia Minor—whole peoples, Ionians mostly, transferring their homes to safer shores. Here too the first seed of difference between the three islands was sown—Ionian Greeks, apparently from Attica, settled on Chios and Samos; on Lésvos it was the Aetolians from Thessaly who differed in culture, language and customs from the Ionians.

Separate ways: These differences soon became clear in the civilizations that evolved on these islands between 900 and 500 B.C. Lésvos developed as an independent island-state, achieving great economic and cultural prosperity in the sixth century under Pittacus, one of the Seven Sages. This was an era of innovation in music and poetry, the age of Alcaeus and Sappho. Meanwhile Chios and Samos were prospering as well, but as a part of a great economic and cultural network—the Ionic Confederacy, a league of 12 Ionian cities. Out of this matrix came Pythagoras of Samos, Thales of Miletus and, it is said, Homer of Chios.

This efflorescent moment in the East Aegean was soon shaken, however, by the new political force in the east Aegean—the Persians. Just as the islands' history had been shaped by the shock waves of the Dorian Invasian moving east, they were the first to be hit by westward moving Persian tsunami which shortly struck, and, in so doing, galvanized the mainland Greek world. From c.550 to 480 the three islands were overrun by the Persians. Clearly their loyalties were somewhat divided in the Greco-Persian conflict—Samos, for example, fought *against* the Greeks at Salamis, with the Greeks at Mycale only to revolt against and be crushed by Pericles' forces decades later. The middle of the fifth century belonged, of course, to Athens and consequently during this time the three islands "belonged" to the Athenian sphere of power. But by the turn of the century they began to sway this way and that with the arrival and departure of Spartans, Macedonians and Ptolemies, finally finding some stability and favor under the Romans.

Little is known about life on the islands in the centuries following Roman decline. With the growing force of Christianity the Byzantines gained control of them, though not without devastating setbacks at the hands of Saracen pirates in the eighth and ninth centuries. The year twelve hundred and four roughly marks the rise of Latin power—first the Venetians and then for two centuries the Genoese (1350–1550) who established important centers of trade and commerce on Lésvos and Chios. The Turks then arrived to rule for three and a half centuries—Greek independence was declared in 1821, and the Turks were defeated at Samos, yet the islands did not join the Greek state until 1913.

In the Middle Ages and the Modern Period it is the differences as much as the similiarities which strike us. Samos, for example, was nearly deserted for much of this time, while Lésvos and Chios were dynamos of the Genoan trade machine. Their participation in the Greek Independence struggle varied too. Chios was the favored island of the Sultan and its wealthy traders, shippers and landowners enjoyed semi-independence. They were not eager to rock the boat that kept them afloat. The Samians, with less to lose, were fiercely opposed to the Sultan and dealt him numerous defeats—"to go to Samos" was a Turkish periphrasis for certain death.

Today too the islands are an admixture of the common and unique. Since independence Lésvos has been a somewhat "cosmopolitan" island with developed olive and spirit industries and a tradition of artists and poets. Its tourism is varied—from Lesbians to meditators to beachcombers. Chios, on the other hand, was drastically depopulated in the 19th century by its two catastrophes (see below) only to become the home of Greece's wealthiest shipowners. It is a rich island and does relatively little to solicit tourists who, at least until recently, have not visited there in great numbers. Tourism has probably changed Samos the most. It has given a great boost to the formerly exiguous economy of wine-producing, olive growing and lumbering.

Samos: This island of dense forests and vineyard-clad hills, wild mountains and Byron-praised wines can, in its rich diversity, accommodate nearly every type of traveler. The antiquities buff, mountain-climber, monastery-hopper, aficionado of popular Greek architecture or sun-worshiper will all find something here to satisfy their desires. Here, at Pythagoreio especially, are the brazen blond crowds freshly arrived from northern Europe by direct charter with cheeks still ruddy. Yet here too are sleepy mountain villages that rarely see tourists. This tour proceeds in a circle around the island, beginning from Pythagoreio (though you may arrive at Samos town or even Karlovassi). One word of caution, though—

A beach near Kokári, Samos.

Pythagoreio is just the beginning and is the noisiest part of the island. When you've had enough of it, the hills and coasts await you.

Pythagoreio is on the site of the ancient city of Samos whose three surviving monuments are the town's main attractions—the Temple of Hera, the Tunnel of Euplinius and the harbor mole. They are all worth a visit, but perhaps the last of the trio is the most pleasant. Strolling down that immense arm originally constructed by Lesbian slaves you can watch the majesty of Cape Mykale, Turkey, fading into the golden evening. Then perhaps you'll duck around the raucous waterfront into the tree-lined cobblestone streets where *yia yias* (grandmothers) pass the cool evening hours on their doorsteps and families dine on their verandahs. By day these neighborhoods are alive with children playing hopscotch, vegetable vendors selling their wares from their pick-up trucks and an occasional baby gurgling under the shade of a cypress tree. These are the endlessly repeating rituals that go on just a block in from the blond clamor of the waterfront. This is the "frying-pan" (*Tigani*) as the town

used to be called for the harbor's shape, a name in keeping with the sound of motorcycles, the smell of sun-lotion and the sizzling disco-beat that prevails here. Disco-cocktail bars lit with candles rim the frying-pan, booming out an aural smorgasbord. Walk briskly down the esplanade and you may well feel like a human tuner zipping down the dial of an unrelenting sensurround radio: Falco's disco "Amadeus"/synthesized "Erik Satie"/the Doors/Greek musaak, ad infinitum.

A change of names: The name "frying-pan" was perhaps too prophetic of what the town actually turned into. And so in 1955 the town fathers changed it to Pythagoreio, harking back to its most famous "son"—Pythagoras. But this breeds a second irony—for it seems that Pythagoras exiled himself from Samos (for southern Italy) in disgust over King Polycrates' policies. Nevertheless, under Polycrates, Samos achieved its moment of glory between 550–500, earning Herodotus' highest praise: "I have spoken at greater length of the Samians because of all the Greeks they have achieved the three greatest projects."

The ruins of the **Temple of Hera** lie

outside of town past the airport. One unusual column and the temple foundations are all that remain to suggest the immensity of what was once one of the largest Greek temples ever built. The **Tunnel of Euplinius** is perhaps even more notable (certainly better preserved) as it presents an underemphasized aspect of the Greek civilization—their technological expertise. The tunnel was built as an aqueduct to carry water through the mountain to the city and in later Byzantine times served as a refuge from pirate raids. Today you can walk through a good part of it. You may want to visit two other pleasant corners of Pythagoreio before leaving. The minute **Archaeological Museum** has a number of beautiful *anthemia* (flower tops) from grave steles and some fine Roman busts. On the other side of town the **Logothétis Castle** and the **Church of the Transfiguration** with its graveyard is an interesting complex of buildings strewn with architectural fragments. On this site overlooking the sea the Samians under the command of General Logothétis defeated the Persians in 1824.

Vathí, the capital: Samos town or Vathí lies facing a large bay on the north coast. It is the island's capital and, in contrast to Pythagoreio, its civic life is not dominated by tourism. In both size and population (8,000) it is a large town and has a bustling social and economic activity of its own. Its most striking area is **Ano Vathy**, the "old city" a few miles up the hill from the town center, the red-tile roofs of its old Turkish houses visible from afar. An hour's walk will take you through the winding streets (built for donkey and cart, but now used by cars), of a traditional Greek community which carries on a rather separate life from the rest of Samos town. The style of these wooden houses with the over-hanging second floor is architecturally linked with that of the Turkish houses of Macedonia but worlds apart from the whitewashed stone Cycladic houses.

In the town center there are some fine shop-lined streets, and a colorful garden across from the post office and Archaeological Museum. The Museum has a fine collection of finds from the island, but, as it is closed for repairs, you may want to console yourself with a coffee or *oúzo-meze* at the nice *kaffaneio* in the park.

The road to the western part of the

Painting boats in Pythagorián harbor.

island takes you along the harbor, winding through lush stands of pines and along the north coast to **Kokkari**. With its long, pebbly beach it is one of the island's favorite resort spots. A small fishing village built on a spit of land forms the original center of this town which now sprawls down the entire beach, and there at the edge of all the bars and *tavernas*, the barechested fishermen string out their nets for mending. Kokkari lies in the craggy shadow of Mount Karvounis. The road continues west from Kokkari and traverses the mountain's vineyard-clad foothills. **Tsamadou** and **Avlakia** beaches come at intervals. Just after Avlakia a road on the left leads towards **Moni Vrondiani** founded in 1566, the oldest on the island. It is a pleasant two-mile (three-km) walk from Vourliotes to get there. The road continues to Karlovassi and for one fine stretch passes right along the sea's edge.

Karlovassi: Karlovassi is a strange town. It may fascinate you, or disenchant you—but it probably won't bore you. First of all it is difficult to get your bearings here, for it is divided into at least four parts—**Old Karlovassi** at the far western edge perched on the moun-tain next to the Agia Triada church; the **waterfront**, a kind of no man's land; **Middle Karlovassi**, full of old mansions from the turn of the century when the town was set up as a tanning center (which collapsed after the war when that industry was centralized in Athens); and, perhaps the most interesting, **New Karlovassi**, which, like most towns in Greece prefaced with "neo," was settled in 1922 as a community for refugees from Asia Minor. Like the old city of Samos, it is filled with fine old houses, lovely winding lanes and, best, the voices of *yia yias* yapping in their little gardens, of children arguing over who won the game, and, even an occasional man's voice, a carpenter squaring a wall. Most of the men, though, are off in town, working in the stores, sitting in the *kaffeneia*. Just beyond Karlovassi on the coast lies an immense and usually deserted pebble beach called **Potami**. The sea here is clean and outrageously blue. This too is the end of the line—to get to the rugged west end of the island you will either have to walk (a fine walk at that), to take a boat or come around from the south side.

Karlovassi roughly marks the halfway point in this circle around Samos. From

here all roads lead into the island's mountainous interior, dotted with small villages, few of which have any special "sites" to be seen, all of which have the simple attraction of being what they are: quiet, old settlements where the men drink coffee in plane-shaded squares; where the well in the square bubbles cool spring water for the mothers washing their families' clothes, the greengrocer and the laden donkey; where wooden Turkish houses line the streets with the typical Samian churches of golden sandstone and a blue-and-white-striped cupola standing in the center of town. These are villages for quiet exploring, for sipping a coffee in the *kaffaneio* and for mustering all the Greek you've learned so far, to talk with the villagers.

There are basically three possible routes through this territory: one takes you most directly back to Pythagoreio, by-passing the island's west side, through Koudeika, Platanos and eventually Pyrgos before reaching Pythagoreio. (**Pyrgos** is a fine old town worth visiting, and, **Spatherei**, just down the road, has one of the finest views on the entire island.) The second takes you on the best road to the Aghi Theodori junction

where you can head for Marathokampos or back to Pythagoreio. And the third leads you up and around the slopes of **Mount Kerkis** which rises to the west 4725 majestic feet (1440 meters). This is a rough road at spots.

Mount Kerkis: Mount Kerkis covers the west of Samos and dominates the horizon of the eastern Aegean. From the summit you can take in Patmos and other Dodecanese islands, Chios and Turkey. Climbing it is a worthwhile challenge, requiring most of a day for both the ascent and descent. Start from Kosmadei, from Drakei or even from Votasakia Beach, the trickiest route. In the days of pirate raids, Samians left their villages and took refuge on Mount Kerkis. More recently Greek guerrilla fighters in World War II and during the Civil War made it their hideout. Some 400 guerrillas are said to have held out here during the Resistance.

The Resistance links Mount Kerkis to the destiny of the village of Kastanea, where 27 villagers were shot by an Italian firing squad in 1943. Near the simple monument in the ravine just outside the village where they were shot I met an old man returning from his field. When asked

Left, groves of mastic trees on the slopes of Chios. Below scraping res off the masti trees.

what had happened there, he pointed to the names listed in marble: "That one was my brother, my fiancee, my uncle, my cousin....." As there were only 400 residents in the village, each was in a similar position and had lost as many relations as this man. The man, Costas, told me the story: the guerrillas had detained a squadron of Italians on Mount Kerkis, then let them go. But the incensed Italian Commander demanded retaliation. As they had seen his brother and his fiancee leading a donkey up the mountain the day before, they interrogated these two about the incident. They wouldn't confess and were taken, along with twenty-five villagers chosen at random, to be executed. The Italian soldiers wept as they led them to the ravine. Every year on August 30th the villagers in the area walk to the site to commemorate the event.

A rough road leads from Kastanea south crossing the bizarre, burn-out landscape of a more recent local tragedy. In mid-summer 1986 a man-made fire ravaged much of this area, destroying not only precious forests but century-old olive groves as well. And for some residents of Marathokampos this has meant economic ruin. The same sunny dry weather that attracts tourists also makes Greece extremely prone to forest fires in summer. By being cautious with matches, cigarettes, etc., travelers can do their part in preventing such disasters.

From Marathokampos you descend to Ormos Marathokampos which has a long beach extending to the west. The beautiful, untouristed west coast will reward you for the troubles of traveling its unpaved road with the forested hillsides of Mount Kerkis, deserted coves only to be reached by foot, and the few quiet villages that lie between here and Karlovassi.

Chios: "The history of Chios is too voluminous to be brought into the compass of a letter" the French traveler Tournefort wrote in 1701. Since then three history-filled centuries have gone by rendering a survey of this island's past all the more formidable. Chios, in contrast to Samos, thrived during much of the Middle Ages and the modern era. The foundation of Nea Moni, Chios' renowned Byzantine monastery, in 1049 marks the beginning of a millennium in which Chios would play an important commercial and cultural role in the East Aegean. During the centuries of Genoan

and Turkish rule (1333–1556 and 1556–1912) Chios became wealthy trading in silk, wines and, most importantly, mastic, the milky resin of the lentisk tree. Today Chios prospers in the shipping trade, home to some of Greece's wealthiest shipping dynasties.

Between Chios' former glory as Genoan and Turkish trade center and its present modern shipping wealth stands Chios' catastrophic 19th century. In the span of sixty years most of its people were either killed or driven away, its social and economic order decimated, and its cities destroyed. Chios had enjoyed great privileges and favor from the Sultan. In 1821 as movements for independence were stirring on the mainland and on neighboring Psara and Samos, the Chiots were disinclined to disturb the order that brought them such prosperity. On the night of March 22–23 of 1822 General Logothétis and 1500 men arrived from Samos to instigate an uprising on Chios. Word reached Istanbul immediately and the Sultan allegedly ordered: "Every Chiot must die." Within a week the Turkish troops landed and began a massacre which would last some two months. Some 30,000 Chiots were killed and another 45,000 enslaved. Life on Chios as it had been known was over. Sixty years later, in 1881, the worst earthquake in modern Greek history destroyed what was left, killing 4,000 people.

Starting from scratch: It should be no surprise then that Chios greets you upon arrival with a waterfront of concrete and steel buildings, not the quaint old houses of a fishing village. It almost seems from the look of Chóra that, building on nothing, the Chiots have been so much the more enterprising. Chios today is a bustling shipping center of some 25,000 inhabitants and so preoccupied with that trade which provides over three quarters of the island's annual revenues that it pays little attention to tourism. To many this is a relief. Nonetheless, Chóra is not all shiny modern businesses. In at least three places it preserves a strong link with its past: in the "old city" inside the Kastro; in the Archaeological Museum and Korais Library; and in Kampos, the southern suburb of old aristocratic gardens and mansions.

The **Kastro** with its towers and massive walls was the fortress built and modified by the Byzantines, Genoans and Turks. It formed the protected civic

... then machines flatten and press the mastic loaves into "chickle" shapes, left. Below, a Jewish cemetery.

228

center for the town—here were the state, offices and churches and aristocrats homes. Under the Turks it was the Turkish quarter, the Greeks living in the settlement outside the wall. Today you can still walk through its alleys and by the old Turkish houses, visit the rather sumptuous church of **Agios Giorgos**, the "dark dungeon" where the Chiot nobles were imprisoned in 1822 and the **tomb of Kara Aly** in the Turkish cemetery—the Turkish admiral who supervised the massacres and was blown up by one of Admiral Kanaris' fireboats the same year.

The more archaeological and archival side of Chios' past is preserved in the **Archaeological Museum** (housed in the mosque on the far side of Platea Vounakia, presently closed) and in the **Korais Library**, which with 95,000 volumes is the fourth largest library in Greece. In the same building you will find the **Argenti Ethnographic and Folklore Museum**. Also, before leaving the center of town walk through the "bazaar" of old shops on **Aploteria Street**.

On the way out of Chóra heading south you pass through **Kampos**, a "suburban" area of old mansions and country gardens and former residence of the Chiot aristocracy. Only a few remain from its former glory of 200 when European travelers described this place as a kind of paradise. Today you can see the high stone walls that enclosed these luxuriant abodes; the arched gateways, some etched with fine Turkish calligraphy and; peeking inside here and there, buildings in varying states of disrepair. One house has been restored, that of the historian Phillip Argenti. Inquire at the tourist office at the port about seeing it.

Beach, villages and the coast: The road leads out of Kampos towards the fascinating southern end of Chios. First comes the turn-off for **Emporio**, a fine, black pebble beach set on the side of some cliffs of unusually textured brown rock. This was the site of different settlements starting in the early Bronze Age and ending in the early Middle Ages. Returning to the interior we enter the mastic region around the villages of Pyrgi and Mesta.

Chios is the unique source of mastic whose name is derived from *mastazo*, meaning "to chew" in Greek (like *masticate* in English). Once used as chewing gum it was extremely popular in Istanbul and allegedly freshened the breaths of the Sultan's concubines. The

suary taining skulls of istians ed by the ks in the ssacre of os.

Romans had their toothpicks made from mastic because it kept their teeth white and prevented tooth decay. Even the "father of medicine," Hippocrates, praised its therapeutic value for coughs and colds. Today the pharmaceutics and chewing gum industries have found more "modern" substances for our oral needs; now it is mostly used in producing certain liquors, industrial paints and glues. Many Greeks still chew it, however, and if you want to try it, ask at most any periptera (see Cultural Dictionary pages 295–296).

The first stages of the mastic production process are basically the same today as in ancient times. The villagers set off in the morning for the mastic groves, some on donkey, some in a pick-up. They carefully scrape the resin "tears" from the bark of the lentisk tree and then bring them home to be separated from the leaves and twigs. In the last stage the material is sent to a central processing plant where the "tears" are washed, baked and formed into "chiclets." Some 150 tons of mastic are produced annually, most of it exported to France, Bulgaria and Saudi Arabia for up to 35 dollars a kilo.

Pyrgi, the first of the two fine mastic villages visited here, still showily displays the wealth it accumulated over the years in the mastic trade. The facades of many of its houses are designed with black and white geometric shapes. In its fine square you'll also find the **Church of Agio Apostoli** colorfully frescoed and with an imposing "pantokrator" in the dome. A walk through the alleyways of Pyrgi will take you under the stone arches built to protect buildings from earthquakes, by cellars where a donkey eats hay next to the woman making coffee on a gas stove and, on certain midsummer days, around corners where the breeze blows thick with oregano, the men sifting truckloads of it to send to New York.

Mesta, to the west is a graver, more somber village which lacks the colors of Pyrgi. Here one is left with the brute sensation of stone—of deep arched alleyways, walls, streets and homes. The NTOG has set up some guesthouses there and tourism has begun to stir things up somewhat. For those with adventuresome spirits (and motorbikes or a sturdy car) the beautiful and quite deserted western coast awaits. Between **Limnos Meston** and **Siderounta** are some very fine coves and pebble beaches set among

A woman stringing tomatoes, below, and right, men playing backgamm0 in Pirgi, Ch▪

scenic promontories. The freshly cut gravel road (quite rough in places) eventually takes you to **Volissos** in the north. Otherwise you will pass through Chóra again in order to explore the island's middle region: Nea Moni and, if you want to push further, the "ghost towns" of Avgonima and Anavatos.

Nea Moni is one of the finest surviving examples of mid-Byzantine architecture, founded in 1049 during the Patriarchate of Constantine Monomachus IX. It suffered along with the rest of Chios the double disasters of 1822 and 1881, its monks being killed and relics and manuscripts pillaged, in the former and cupola cracked, in the latter. Its mosaics, cracked as they are, are outstanding. The refectory and ruins of monks' cells evoke the days when a religious life thrived there. Ask the caretaker to see the charnel house where the skulls of deceased monks are kept. Those bones, stacked as they are, mark how differently they conceived of an individual life—not that of one man but of legions of men passing their existence on earth under the knowing gaze of the "pantokrator" depicted in the dome. It is said that many of these bones date from the massacre of 1822.

The deserted villages of **Avgonima** and **Anavatos** are further along the gravel road. Perhaps Anavatos gives the best idea of Chios' 19th-century fall from prosperity. The village set up on the hill for defense was inhabited through the last century. Today it crumbles away, its houses and churches losing their human forms, slowly merging into the dry brown hillside. Meanwhile an old man runs a makeshift *kaffaneio* at the bottom of the hill, and a woman tries to eke out a living selling figs, honey and spices to the few tourists who pass by.

The north of the island is a sparsely populated area of ruined towers and fortresses, semi-deserted villages and a few good beaches. Certain parts were severely scarred in the forest fires of 1981. Perhaps in compensation for its relative poverty, the richest shipping families come from the north of Chios, the town of **Vrontados** in particular. Just north of Vrontados is the so-called **Stone of Homer**, where local tradition says that Homer sung his rhapsodies and taught his pupils. There are also some fine little Byzantine churches in the north, such as **Panayia Ayiogalousenas** in Ayios Galas.

The island of **Psara** can be taken in as a side-trip, either by scheduled boat from Chóra or by leasing a fishing boat from Volissos. It is a quiet island with a small fishing village. It became famous as one of the most active islands in the Greek Revolution and the home of Admiral Kanaris. For continuously harrying Turkish troops it paid dearly—in 1824 14,000 Janissaries landed in the north. Three thousand islanders escaped. The other 17,000 died.

Lésvos: Lésvos has always been "an island with a touch of class" as the Ionian poet Anacreon enviously put it in the sixth century B.C. A lot has changed since then—and yet today Lésvos stands for roughly the same things it stood for in antiquity: poetry, culture, education and a democratic spirit. In those days one thought of the poetess Sappho, the Philosophical Academy where Aristotle and Epicurus taught, and the democritizing rule of Pittacus, one of the Seven Sages. Today the Nobel prize poet Odysseus Elytis; the folk painter Theophilos; the educated, cosmopolitan Lesbian upper class and a tradition of progressive leftist government come to mind.

There may be few real continuities between the Lésvos of then and today, but something about its vast size, its fertile olive-green expanses and its position on the margins of the Greek world seems to have favored a Lesbian identity not wholly bound to the present. Lésvos is the opposite of the *nissaki*, the quaint little island; it is in fact Greece's third largest, measuring 44 by 24 miles (70 by 39 km) at its extremities, with a population of 90,000 inhabitants. Throughout its history it has set itself apart, culturally and politically, from mainland Greece. Its earliest inhabitants probably formed a part of the Trojan race. At the time of the Trojan War both Achilles and Odysseus came with Achaean forces to punish and plunder Lésvos for siding with Troy. In the wake of the Dorian Invasion Lésvos was settled, not by Ionian Greeks who occupied the whole Asia Minor coast to the south, but by the Aetolians of Thessaly, a different ethnic group.

Through centuries of struggle between the island's five cities Lésvos as a whole developed into a cultural dynamo, exporting to mainland Greece such poet-musicians as Terpander and Arion whose particular Aetolian styles and innovations helped to shape the new cultural move-

Lésvos harbor.

ment from the Homeric epics and Hesiodic narratives to the lyric and later to classical tragedy. With Alcaeus and Sappho the lyric reaches unparalleled heights of refined thought and sentiment. At the same time the ruler Pittacus (who was no friend of the aristocrats Alcaeus and Sappho) was busy initiating democratic reforms. But the Lesbian heyday soon ended as the Persians gained control of the East, Aegean. Lésvos sided with Athens for some years, only to rebel against her in the early years of the Peloponnesian Wars, an incident made famous by Thucydides. Lésvos generally then shared the vicissitudes of Chios and Samos, dominated by Macedonians, Romans (who made it a favorite holiday spot), Byzantines, Venetians, Genoese and Turks.

During the early modern era a landowning aristocracy developed on Lésvos along with a large population of laboring peasants. Peasant and working class movements took hold here and to the present day it has been a center of progressive left government, earning the title of "the red island" among fellow Greeks. Accompanying such economic and political activity, the arts and education have flourished since independence, producing numerous writers, thinkers and painters as well as an upper class noted for its high level of education. Since the last world war Lésvos' social and economic fabric has shrunk considerably with steady emigration to Athens, Australia and America. And yet the foundation of the University of the Northeast Aegean this year is a hopeful sign for the continuation of Lésvos' cultural autonomy and strength.

Sightseeing: Mitilini is a bustling port town of c.25,000 inhabitants facing the Asia Minor coast. The Mitilini waterfront is lined with some fine old *kaffaneia* behind which runs the main thoroughfare of the market. On the pier-arm which extends out into the harbor, opposite the ferry landing, there are a number of fine *tavernas* which the Mitilineans frequent, dining late into the evening. Look for the *taverna* with the ancient juke box playing *rembetika* classics. Over behind the ferry landing you find the small, delightful **Archaeological Museum** housed in a villa, containing Roman mosaics depicting scenes from Menander's comedies, a rare Aetolian capital and some other nice sculptural knick-knacks. Just around the

oftops of
Mássos,
svos.

wooded hill stands the Genoan castle, a remnant from the hundred-odd years of Gattelusi rule (1354–1462). If you have the inclination for folk culture you can visit the **Popular Art Museum** behind the bus stand on the harbor. But even more noteworthy is the **Theophilos Museum** in Varia, $2\frac{1}{2}$ miles (four km) south of town. This has paintings by Theophilos, one of Greece's most noted "primitive" painters. The road to Varia passes through the part of town where Lésvos' aristocracy built their mansions, living there until after the last war when most left for Athens and abroad.

The road running north from Mitilini skirts the coast facing Turkey. To the west of Moria a few arches still stand from the Roman aqueduct that supplied water to Mitilini. **Madamados** is the site of the **Taxiarchon Church**, famed for its black icon of the archangel Michael. Here too a strong ceramics tradition survives. South of Madamados, in the village of **Aghia Paraskevi**, an unusual festival takes place in the period after Easter. In this "festival of the bull" a procession of costumed men and women and cavaliers parade to the village chapel. After the church service a bull is sacrificed, a banquet held and horses raced. At **Kari** the road divides in two, the north fork descending to the little seaside village of **Sikaminia**, the west fork skirting around the edge of **Mount Lepetimnos** and eventually reaching the sea at **Petra**. Petra has a long pebble beach which spreads out below the **Church of Panayia Glikofiloussa** (Virgin of the Sweet Kiss) perched on a cliff. Petra is also the home of the Women's Agricultural-Tourist Collective.

Molyvos, a hillside town of old stone and mortar houses with red tile roofs surmounted by a Genoan castle is Lésvos' favorite tourist retreat. In Molyvos' *tavernas* you may sit next to a group of transcendental meditators, members of a health food conference or a group of Lesbians on pilgrimage.

In pursuit of beaches: The west of Lésvos lies at an imposing distance from Mitilini and, if you are pressed for time, you will probably want to limit your travels to the east of Kalloni. If you do have the time you'll find the west more barren and rugged than the east, consisting in large part of lunar volcanic terrain. Many of those who do venture west do so in pursuit of some of Lésvos' finest beaches. **Skala Eressos** probably wins the prize,

and is turning into quite a little tourist resort. **Sigri**, to the north, is a quieter, less touristed village with a good beach.

The southeast of Lésvos is striking in its diversity. On the south coast **Plomari** combines a moderate orientation towards tourism with its indigenous industry—the production of *oúzo*. The **Varvaryianni distillery** is just east of town and produces a "deluxe" *oúzo* which is arguably the best in the world. Stop in to see the process and try a free sample. There are some decent beaches along the coast here, the best being at **Agios Isodoros** just to the east of Plomari.

Perhaps the most remarkable place on Lésvos is the village of **Aghiassos**. Tucked away from the thoroughfares of tourism on the shaded hillsides below Mount Olympos, Aghiassos seems, indeed, to live by rhythms remote from the modern world. Its traditions of weaving and pottery still continue, and the dialect spoken here is quite distinct from standard modern Greek. The Church has a renowned miracle-working icon and on Assumption Day (August 15) it is the site of pilgrimage for men and women from all over the island. Carnival is celebrated with gusto here as well.

Below, men playing cards in a cafe in Vathí old town, Samos. Right, pony bedecked with flowers for local festival in Lésvos.

THEODOR ELIADI
FRANKFURT A/M

PLAKAT-FABRIK
WUSTEN & KÖRNSAND FRANKFURT A/M.

Die Sch-

1. Ein Schwamm-Taucher, welcher von einem Haifisch verschlungen wird.
2. Ertrunkener Taucher, weil er Tau und Ballaststein verloren.
3. Schwämme-Sammler.
4. Taucher, das Zeichen zum Aufziehen gebend.
5. Taucher, die Wurzeln eines grossen Schwammes ausziehend.
6. Taucher, der die Besinnung verloren hat und ertrinken muss.
7. Zu Hilfe eilender Taucher.
8. Taucher, welcher sein Tau verloren hat und nach oben zu schwimmen versucht.
9. Zu Hilfe eilender Taucher mit Tau und Stein.
10. Taucher, im Moment des Aufziehens.
11. Taucher, welcher Tau und Stein verloren, mit Hilfe der Ankerkette heraufgezogen wird.
12. Tau... Ober...
13. und
15. Tau... griff
16. Tau.

SCHWAMM-GROSSHANDLUNG
EIGENE SCHWAMM-FISCHEREI auf der SPORADE-INSEL KALYMNOS.

Fischerei.

anoth an die

de Männer.
sin, im Bo-

Tauchen.

17. Taucher, den Befehl zum Tauchen gebend.
18. Zwei Männer, den Taucher aufziehend.
19. Matrose, das Hinablassen eines Tauchers vorbereitend.
20. Taucher, welcher sich vor dem Ankleiden abtrocknet.

21. Matrosen, das Taucherschiff leitend.
22. Matrose, den Sack mit Schwämmen in Empfang nehmend.
23. Luft-Pumpe für den Taucher mit Taucher-Apparat.
24. Fundort der Schwämme, 25—30 Meter tief.

25. Schwamm, genannt Zimocca-Schwamm.
26. Felsen auf dem Meeresboden, mit Schwämmen bewachsen.
27. Netz zum Abreissen der Schwämme vom Meeresboden.
28. Taucher mit Taucheranzug, Schwämme ins Sammelnetz werfend.

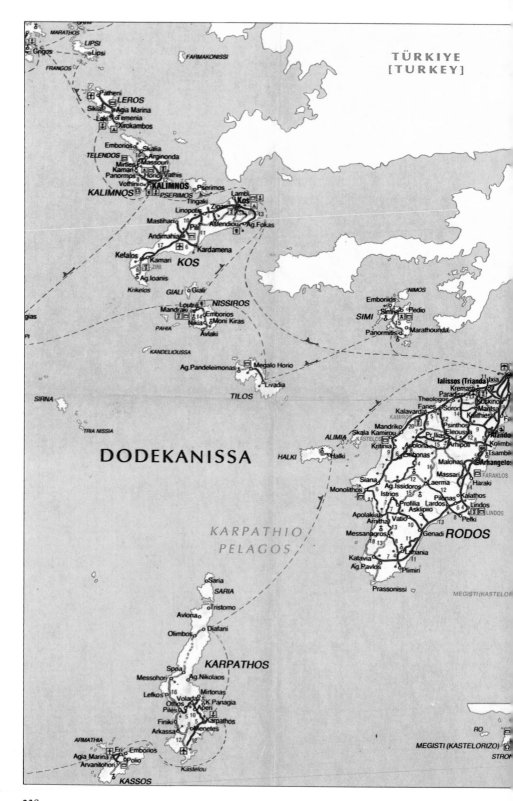

TÜRKIYE
[TURKEY]

MARATHOS
LIPSI
Grigos
Lipsi
FRANIGOS
FARMAKONISSI

Patheni
LEROS
Sikia
Agia Marina
Laki
Temenia
Xirokambos

Emborios
Skalia
Arginonda
TELENDOS
Massouri
Mirties
Kamari
Panormos
Horios Vathis
Vothini
KALIMNOS
KALIMNOS
PSERIMOS
Pserimos
Tingaki
Lambi
Kos
Linopots
Ziga
Mastihario
Astendiou
Ag.Fokas
Pili
Andimahia
Kardamena
Kefalos
Kamari
KOS
ZINI
Ag.Ioanis
Knikelos
GIALI
Giali
NISSIROS
Loutra
Mandraki
Emborios
Nikia
Moni Kiras
PAHIA
Avlaki
KANDELIOUSSA

Emborios
Pedio
NIMOS
SIMI
Simi
Marathounda
Panormitis

Ag.Pandeleimonas
Megalo Horio
Livadia
TILOS

SIRINA

Ialissos (Trianda)
Ixia
Kremasti
Paradisi
Theologos
TRIA NISSIA
Soron
Fanes
Kalavarda
KAMIROS
Mandriko
Psinthos
Eleoussa
Skala Kamirou
Pr.Ilias
ALIMIA
Kritinia
Afandou
Kolimbi
KASTELOS
Asclonia
Arhipoli
DODEKANISSA
HALKI
Halki
Cribonas
Tsambik
Malonas
Arhangelos
Massari
FARAKLOS
Siana
Ag.Issidoros
Laerma
Haraki
Monolithos
Istrios
Pilonas
Kalathos
Profilia
Lardos
Lindos
Apolakia
Arnitha
Vatio
Asklipiio
Pefki
LINDOS
Messanagros
Genadi
RODOS
Katavia
Lahania
Ag.Pavlos
Plimiri
Prassonissi
MEGISTI (KASTELO

KARPATHIO
PELAGOS

Saria
SARIA
Aviona
Tristomo
Olimbos
Diafani

ARMATHIA
KARPATHOS
Spoa
Messohori
Ag.Nikolaos
Lefkos
Mirtonas
Volada
K.Panagia
Othos
Aperi
Piles
Finiki
Karpathos
Arkassa
Menetes
Agia Marina
Fri
Emborios
Arvanitohori
Polio
Kastelou
KASSOS

RO

MEGISTI (KASTELORIZO)
STRON

THE DODECANESE ISLANDS

The names of places in Greece often tell much about their past history, and the **Dodecanese Islands** are no exception. Dodecanese is a new name by Greek standards. For the 450 years of Turkish rule they were called, instead, the Southern Sporades. In this period the Turks granted these islands considerable privileges and tax-breaks by, generally, treating them with benign neglect. Thus, for the most part, these islands administered their own government, schools and medical care. But when the Ottomans hit on harder times they annulled the privileges, and in 1908 twelve islands (*dódeka nísia* in Greek) banded together in protest. Though the protest failed, the new name stuck—Dodecanese. This, despite the fact that today these islands number twelve, not fourteen, but who's counting?

Today the Dodecanese form Greece's southeastern-most territory. Indeed, they were Greece's last territorial acquisition, making the Greek map we know today. In 1912 the islands passed from the Turks to the Italians, who promptly re-named them the "Italian Islands of the Aegean." The Italians were busy colonialists in their brief 20-year stay, building numerous odd edifices from Patmos to Rhodes and imposing their language and culture in the schools. Today many middle-aged islanders can still utter bits of their scholastic Italian. In 1943 the Italians surrendered the islands to the Germans who in turn surrendered the islands to the British two years later. Finally in 1947 these islands spread in an arc across the Turkish coast, were united with Greece to be ruled by Greeks.

Today the people of Dodecanese live in large part as they always have—off the sea. In recent years the sea has brought them a novel catch and one of vital importance to the local economy—tourists.

Let's look at a few of these islands more closely—Rhodes (Ródhos), Kos, Patmos, Kárpathos and Sími and the sponge diving capital of the world, Kalymnos.

Rhodes: Rhodes, the best known of the Dodecanese islands, is rich with natural beauty, architectural variety and bears the signs of a colorful history. Hillsides greet the visitor with extravagant displays of rock roses—it is known as "The Island of Roses." Another name, "Butterfly Island," does not take much imagination to appreciate—butterflies are everywhere. And of course there is the sun and the exquisitely clean sea whose currents, combined with summer winds, keep the air and water pure. Endless sandy beaches only a few miles from the hotels are so pristine that it is easy to imagine being the first to set foot there.

The City of Rhodes is one of the most architecturally varied cities in all of Europe. Within a few steps one can pass from the ancient splendors of Apollo's Temple, through the little Odeon Theatre, probably used for rhetoric lessons in Hellenistic times, to Byzantine churches some of which were turned into mosques by the Turks. A beautifully decorated Turkish bath is here, too. And still working. The best way to enjoy it? Go and take a bath! Greek neoclassical examples are contrasted with heavy state buildings, an ugly legacy of fascism, in this case the World War II Italian variety. Amidst this architectural variety travelers talk with animated gestures, catch each other's attention, and flirt in a babel of languages as they wander past ancient monuments, improvised record and souvenir stores and small *tavernas*.

Far across the Aegean from the Greek mainland, separated from Asia Minor by only seven miles, Rhodes in ancient times was renowned for its wealth and aggressive navy and was Athen's most feared enemy. At the beginning of the fifth century B.C., Athens attacked and pillaged what were then three independent villages, Líndos, Kámiros and Iálysos. The elders consulted the Olympian gods and decided it was time to join forces and become one, the City of Rhodes. Secretly and with great speed, fortifications and a city wall were completed in 408 B.C. Well-defended, the city prospered. Because its strong economy was built on trade, Rhodes tried to stay on good terms with her neighbors. But twists of history brought trouble. Allied to Persia at the time when Alexander the Great (Macedonian) laid siege to Tyre, Rhodes had to endure a Macedonian garrison. As soon as Alexander died, the garrison was thrown out and it was back to business. Wars followed, but Rhodes sided with Rome and prospered. Ptolemy I came to their aid when the city was besieged by Demetrios Poliorketes in 305. Demetrios was defeated but was so impressed by the defenders' valor that he left them his artillery when he and his armies were forced to leave. The citizens sold this unneeded military hardware and used the proceeds to build a monument that became one of the Seven Wonders of the World, the Colossus.

The Colossus: The work of a local sculptor named Cháris of Líndos, the Colossus, by most accounts stood 70 forearms high, about 102 feet (31 meters), and was a representation of Apollo. Impressive by any standards, rumor made it even more so by describing the figure standing with one foot on either side of the harbor entrance so that ships passed between its legs! But to do so it would have had to have been 1,650 feet (500 meters) high, an impossible architectural feat. Nonetheless this beacon to passing ships and monument to peaceful prosperity stood for over a century before it fell to the ground during an earthquake in 226 B.C.

Rhodes remained at peace and at the height of prosperity until, ironically, she tried to reconcile the warring Romans and Macedonians only to have Rome take revenge in 168 B.C. by declaring Dilos an open port and ceding it to Athens. Rhodes lost 15 percent of its trade. This punishment and the threat of more forced Rhodes to give up much

of its independence and become subservient to Rome, which was not an easy course to take because the Romans were forever engaging in civil wars. Rhodes' trading partners took a dim view of her alliance with the trouble-making Romans. In one chapter of Roman intrigue, Rhodes sided with Julius Caesar only to have Cassius, after Caesar's murder, destroy her fleet, plunder the city and fill up Rome with her treasures. Two years later in 42 B.C., Octavius triumphed over Cassius who committed suicide and Rhodes regained much of its autonomy. However, its fleet was gone as was much of its wealth. But Rhodes did regain its cultural influence and for three centuries was the place where many statesmen and literary leaders of the age received their education.

Changing tides swept Rhodes into obscurity after the second century. It moved in and out of anarchy on the fringes of a waning Roman Empire, the Byzantine Empire and the Crusades. In the 14th century, the Knights of St. John took control, ruling the island for two centuries until 1522. During this period the walls and fortresses that stand today were built around the medieval

Preceding pages, a 19th century advertisement for Kalymnian sponges. Below, antelopes at the entrance to the Mandráki harbor in Rhodes.

city. Even Suleiman the Great and his Turkish armies could not invade the city. A chain stretched across the harbor and the fortress Castle of St. Nicholas at the end of the breakwater kept his ships at bay; the walls were impregnable. Finally, hunger, disease and spent ammunition forced defeat. The wall was breached and the Turks marched in as the 180 surviving brethren of the Knights of St. John capitulated on honorable terms and were given safe passage. Churches were turned into mosques.

A Christian order, the Fathers of the Mission, were admitted to care for Christian slaves in 1660; French Franciscan Sisters came and built schools in 1873; the Brothers of Christian Doctrine founded the College of St. John in 1889. The 20th century brought other visitors— once again armies. In 1912, the Turks, then the Italians and, during World War II, the Germans. British and Greek commandos liberated Rhodes in 1945 and with the other Dodecanese it became united with Greece in 1947. The **Castle of St. Nicholas**, once an armed fortress, is now a lighthouse that welcomes today's visitors.

Island resorts and the rest of Rhodes: Rhodes is a big island, and it has more to offer than this marvelous city. Summer resorts are scattered across the northern part of the island; **Líndos**, a very old city, dating back to the Bronze age, continues to thrive. It's the only natural harbor in Rhodes, except for the small **Mandráki**, the ancient defense harbor, now full of yachts. Its medieval city is extremely well preserved, an ancient acropolis also remains with two re-erected classical temples and later Byzantine and Frankish elements. Near the main square there is one of the most beautiful Byzantine churches on the island, with well-preserved frescoes. The water in the fountain there still runs through the ancient water pipes. Líndos' large harbor with long sandy beaches adds the finishing touch. However it's the light that has made Líndos so famous. The jagged barren mountains which surround Líndos reflect the light so that it almost blinds you. The Italian and German painters were the first to rediscover Líndos; some moved there for good. Only later did the tourists catch on. The small city can't hold too many people so most come on day trips by bus or in small boats.

Ancient **Kámiros** is well worth a visit. There's no new Kámiros so that what has been uncovered of the acropolis has been beautifully laid out and gives the visitor an unadulterated picture of ancient life. This is partially true for **Filárimo** as well. At the top of the low hill the ancient acropolis of Iálysos is preserved. Over to the south we find the most beautiful doric fountain with its water system amazingly still intact. The **Butterfly Valley** is also a must. Here a small stream meanders through the plane trees and creates little lakes. On the shore the vegetation grows thick as in a jungle. The plane trees are a particularly wonderful kind; the scent of their resin draws red winged butterflies by the thousands. One abrupt movement or a cry and the butterflies rise up around you.

Rhodes' size means that tourists will never succeed in taking over. Many towns keep their traditional, untainted character, especially the inland towns. The archaeological sites are plentiful and remind visitors of a time when Rhodes was even more densely populated. But all that said, it's the exquisite clean sea full of shells with its endless sandy beaches which is the greatest attraction, and of course the sun.

Kos: Kos is the second largest island in terms of population (20,000), and third largest in terms of size, after Rhodes and Kárpathos. It is a flat island with only one high mountain, **Mount Díktaio**, almost exactly in the middle. **Mandráki** is its only protected port. In 1933 a horrible earthquake destroyed the city but the damage was restricted to a very small area. So, although it flattened the city, it hardly touched the nearby towns. Italian archaeologists took advantage of this and excavated the area which they knew overlaid the ancient city. For this reason Kos' archaeological site offers more to the visitor than any other in the Dodecanese islands. It is in the middle of the new city and constitutes a functional part of this new city which was rebuilt after the earthquake. The castle is the only part left from the medieval city. And since it was only used for defense it doesn't offer much information about the culture at that time.

In **Áspri Pétra** (literally White Rock) in the western part of the island the finds from excavations go back even further, and it is obvious that there once existed a neolithic settlement there. Quite a few

Hellenistic fish (left) and real fish (right).

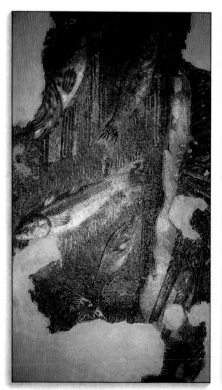

archaeological finds from the Mycenean period have been found in the city of Kos. Astypalaia, the second most important city of this period is also referred to but it still hasn't been located. Other cities have gotten lost; for example it is written that Alkibíades in the fifth century B.C. defended Meropída, but again no one is sure where it was.

Clinging on at the top of Díktaio is **Gía**, the most beautiful town of the island. The houses are built way up on the rocks and look like the monasteries of Metéora. Water rushes down in small streams and large walnut trees grow alongside.

Kos follows exactly the same course of fate as Rhodes. It reached its heights and declines during the same epochs; it suffered the same invasions and adventures. Its most famous ruin is the **Asklepíon**, built in the fourth century B.C. where Hippocrates, the father of medicine, conducted classes and cured the sick. The island from the time of the Romans has been used as a place of rest and hospitality; it has a long tourist tradition. But in tourist developments and economic achievements too it follows Rhodes. Hotels spring up like huge

mushrooms on the sandy beaches that surround the island.

Kárpathos: The most dramatic way to arrive at **Kárpathos** is on the *Panormítis* from Rhodes. This old but sturdy ship serves all of the Dodecanese islands, stopping at various obscure ports while its crew—who are as old and as strange-looking as the ship itself—frantically unload provisions (everything from watermelons to pampers) to cover local needs. After seven hours of traveling on seas which are often rough in this part of the Mediterranean, Kárpathos comes into view with its imposing cloud-capped mountains.

The first port-of-call is **Diapháni**, a fishing village in the northeast, where passengers are ferried to shore on a small boat, as there is no pier for large ships to dock at. The few passengers who continue have the opportunity to enjoy another hour and a half of the *Panormítis* and its bizarre crew (the one-eyed deck-hand, the foul-mouthed captain, and the tattooed navigator to name but a few), as well as to get acquainted with Kárpathos itself. All down the 40-mile (25-km) coastline the slopes rise steeply, and the pine-forests which cover much of the

island dip right into the sea. The massive forest fire which swept over much of the island in 1983 has left behind a charcoal scar on much of northern Kárpathos but even this somehow seems to lend an added mystery to the unworldly landscape. Occasionally, the slopes give way to large, white, empty beaches—proof that the island was a good choice.

After these magical first impressions, the main port of **Pigádia** is inevitably a disappointment, with little to recommend it beyond the fact that it is well situated to tour most of the island.

If you like warm seas, deep clear water with interesting underwater rock formations splashed with color, and large beaches with white pebbles, then the southeast coast has some of the best (and least crowded) specimens in Greece. Try for example **Áppella, Aháta** and **Kyrapanagiá**. You can visit them by boat, but the land route will give you the chance to see some of the villages, as well as enjoy the breathtaking view of the beaches from the road above. If you hire a moped, though, be warned—the roads are very bumpy, the cliffs are high, and in places the wind is strong enough to blow you across the road.

The villages are mostly grafted high on the mountain slopes, primarily for historical reasons of security. Piracy was rampant in this region. The wealthiest villages are in the south (**Apéri, Óthon** and **Ménetes**), as is evident from the number of traditional and contemporary villas. What is less evident is the source of wealth, for there is hardly any flat farmland, industry is non-existent, and there is no mass tourism. In fact, most wealth is created outside the island, by Kárpathian seamen and emigrants (mostly in the United States), who send remittances to family members left behind, or to their native village in order to build churches and other public buildings, and who also boost the local economy when they return on vacation to see their homeland (and show off their fortune).

This economic structure has profound effects on local culture and attitudes, from their attitude towards tourists (which ranges from indifferent to negative—you won't find cultivated smiles or servile behavior in Kárpathos) to the position of women (which are both more dominant and more traditional than the men due to the fact that they used to stay

Olympus, Kárpathos.

behind while their menfolk sought their fortune abroad). One of the "cultural imports" has been the establishment of a football tournament every summer, through which the traditional rivalries between villages can be played out on the field rather than by the more violent means of former times. Another area where modernization and emigration have left their mark is on the architecture and decoration of houses.

You can trace these changes easily as nearly all houses have the date of construction (as well as the initials of the owner and very often a decorative emblem—such as a mermaid or an eagle) painted or sculpted above the entrance.

The traditional Kárpathian houses consist of one room which is split into two parts. In one corner is the "dórva" which is a wooden platform, bordered by an intricate railing, which is at a higher level than the rest of the room, which generally has a mud floor. This platform houses the trunks where clothes and linen from the woman's dowry are kept, as well as straw mattresses which are rolled out every night for the family to sleep; in the day they are rolled up to leave more living space, and they are covered with em-broidered cloths for decoration. In the center of the room stands a wooden pole which reaches to the ceiling, and is also covered with embroidered cloths and beads. This is the "pillar of the house," and to complete the symbolism a painting or photograph of the couple is pinned to the pole under their wedding wreaths ("stefána")—perhaps this custom developed in order to acquaint children with their fathers, who were mostly absent. The walls are decked with rows of shelves with hundreds of decorative plates and other ornaments. Local handicraft products perhaps? Mostly not—they are plates from Hong Kong and France, dolls from Spain and Japan, and a myriad other seamen's trinkets from ports all over the world. The overall impression is a wonderful splurge of silver, gold and bright colors which miraculously avoids being kitsch.

In modern villas needless to say the house is not limited to one room. However, although the external neighborhood wood oven has been replaced by electric stoves, and although bathrooms and washing machines have become a necessity, Kárpathians still model their living-room on the traditional style. And

o women are a joke.

here Kárpathian women still display their embroideries and the presents they have received from abroad with the same pride as their foremothers.

In fact the most fascinating aspect of Kárpathos—beyond its natural beauty—is the way that foreign influences have been adopted and adapted to fit local needs and tastes. For example, in many villages, women still wear traditional clothes daily, .whereas the well-traveled men have worn western clothes for as long as anyone can remember. The women's pantaloons, tunic and boots are all traditional local handicrafts, but the costume is completed by a woolen scarf which is imported from Ireland and modified to satisfy local tastes by adding a trimming of sequins and tassles.

At festivals, the tunic is replaced by magnificent dresses, in shades of silver and gold as well as flourescent pinks and lime-greens on which families spend a small fortune and the ultimate decoration is a collar of gold coins, the number of which indicates a girl's economic position. It is well worth attending one of the major festivals in order to see the young girls decked in all their finery, on display for prospective suitors, patiently dancing to the monotonous long-winded "*mantinádes*." They steal glances to see who is interested in them when their fathers aren't looking.

One of the main annual festivals takes place in **Olýmpoi**, a village in the north. Perched on a mountain ridge, windswept and literally in the clouds, it is close to how one pictures the abode of the ancient gods at Olympus. The mountainside is cut into with endless terraces, giving the impression of a roughly chiseled sculpture. It is difficult to imagine that these terraces were cultivated as recently as World War II. Olýmpoi is very isolated and its inhabitants seem almost unaware of the 20th century. They marry among themselves and speak a dialect which retains many ancient Greek constructions. The women, dressed traditionally, bake their bread in neighborhood ovens and even get their flour from a windmill which still functions. You are left with a bittersweet taste: on the one hand feeling privileged to have seen the windmill's sails still turning, and on the other sensing that your very presence there, as a tourist, is speeding up the process by which they will inevitably grind to a halt.

Skála port and the bay of Patmos.

246

It is this same taste that you carry with you as you leave Kárpathos, an *ex ante* nostalgia for a less frenzied way of life which you fear will not be there the next time you return.

Sími is the closest island to Rhodes, 24 miles from one port to the other. Completely barren, it doesn't even have enough water for drinking, so the inhabitants gather rainwater in cisterns.

This island was at its height at the end of the last century, mainly thanks to the sponge divers and merchants. The **Panochorió** (literally upper city) was an important city, both for its large population, over 20,000, and for its wealth and even more for its extremely well-organized local government.

Interestingly enough, the provinces of this local government didn't go under with the Italian occupation; sponge fishing developed even more, even when the Italians occupied the Lybian coasts so rich in sponges. Somehow the Greeks managed to hold the monopoly on the trade in which they had always excelled.

It's worth a digression to talk about the way the local government organized itself at the time of the island's prosperity. The local elections happened every year on January 25. The brief term of office implies that the voters were informed of common problems—otherwise their voting power made no sense. Voters had to be under eighty, literate, energetic, impartial, capable of bearing witness, and to have no penal sentence hanging over their head. The number of voters was unlimited. They called the local ruler a *Demogérontas*, and his council was voted in for life by general assembly until 1902, and later by secret ballots. All male youths over the age of twenty one, who had paid their taxes had the right to vote. The reason for the election of a first and second *Demogérontas* is straightforward enough. The first presided over the council and commanded the executive and judicial matters of the community, as well as relations with the High Gate and Turkish generals. The second took care of the community's revenues.

In the middle of this time of prosperity World War II broke out. The sponge fishing stopped, sea trade was destroyed, even the ferrying of food to the island became problematic and the islanders deserted their island. The end of the war didn't bring back many of the inhabitants, who were scattered all over

VIEWS OF PATMOS

Perhaps we were not snobbish, really, but a trifle ambitious: we hoped that if we learned some Greek we might be able to get beyond the tourist world of knick-knack shops and *tavernas* and the hoards of tourists on the beaches. But it soon began to seem that even if we did, my wife and I would have quite different perceptions of Greek society and culture. Her modern Greek primer, recently published, taught her to say things like "Where can I buy a kilo of tomatoes?" From mine, an earlier work, I learned "His uncle was very rich, but lost all his money." By the time that she had persuaded a chemist to sell her aspirins and some ointment, I would be assuring a Greek friend that "Russell was a great philosopher." While she was booking a room in a hotel—a small room, with shower, but no bath—I would be arranging to rent a spacious flat. True, by the time we each reached the last lesson she would be comparing horoscopes with her new friends Viky and Yiorgos; but I would be quoting Ca-vafy on the Alexandrians.

We seemed destined for different worlds. Her conversations were to be overwhelmingly practical. Mine were not only of an intellectual nature, but they often dealt with delicate family relationships, and sometimes carried quite sinister undertones: "Do you know my brother? Yes, but he is no friend of mine." Or: "He had approached noiselessly, and was watching them, smiling." Finally, I was to be led into adventurous grammatical constructions like the passive voice: I would actually be able to say "I shall be put." "*I shall be put*"?!!! Why yes, of course: "I shall be put in an impossible position."

The question then was: how would these different attitudes affect our views of Patmos, for it was to that most lovely and numinous of Greek islands that we were going. The divergence turned out less serious than I had feared: Greek society, at least in Patmos, proved to be quite deft at reconciling the elevated with the everyday. We met a girl called Thia, and learned that her full name was not Thisbe, or Theodora, or Theone, or Thetis, but Theologiya; and our landlady employed a builder called Theologos.

Deserted street in Patmos.

St. John the Divine, or the Theologian, as he is known in the Orthodox Church, is a very powerful presence in and out of church in Patmos.

One of our first days in Patmos, we took a small motorboat from Skála, the port, to the bay of Diakofti, where the little church of Stavros—the Holy Cross—was celebrating its annual feast day. In the boat with us were four or five Greek ladies, dressed in their best, and looking as if all their uncles had been, if not very rich, at least comfortably well off. Polka-dot dresses were favored —a fashion older than Princess Di, I think—and there was one tremendous coiffure, jet black, lacquered and *bouffante*, like an expanded ball of shiny plastic threads.

At the church, the congregation was made up of seafarers and farmers, and their wives and children, from the island. No rich uncles there, if there were, they were not obvious; but the Abbot's sister was among us, a prosperous Greek-American lady, 36 years in the United States, and very elegant in green linen. When I began to flag from long standing —and slipped away outside the east end of the church where it cast its shadow from the setting sun, I found a gentlemen's club, old and young in shirt-sleeves, sitting against the church wall and gossiping. I approached noiselessly and watched them, smiling...

After the service we all moved to a nearby field, where a talented taxi-driver played the violin and his son the electronic organ, and bouzouki music and French songs, vastly amplified, were hurled across the landscape and the shining sea beyond. The man who keeps the cafe by the bus stop at Chóra was caterer for the evening, and my wife duly ordered us a plate of *taramasalata* and other delicacies. The lady with the black coiffure ate no less eagerly. For that evening, under the influence of music, food and drink—and the Holy Cross and St. John—the contrasting perceptions were in harmony. Is this characteristic just of Patmos, a sort of *Patiniosýne*; the essence of being a Patmiot? or is it just a part of *Romaios*, the essence of being a modern Greek?

Well, these are big questions, and if I launch into them, I shall overrun my limit, and my editor will not be pleased: indeed, "I shall be put in an impossible position."

courtyard and arches of the monastery of St. John.

Rhodes, Athens and abroad, and the island never grew back to a population larger than 3,000. In the last three years the island has become more lively because of the tourists who come by day boats from Rhodes, to see the distinctive city, and the famous **monastery of Panormítis**.

Patmos: In the morning at sunrise the sea in the closed bay looks like a mirror. Beyond the bay stretch the archipelagos where a handful of islands seems to have been flung. And **Patmos**, the last of the Dodecanese islands in this direction, must have landed farthest north.

Legend has it that St. John wrote *Revelations* in the cave which later was walled in and made into a church. You can still see the rock where the evangelist sat inside the **Monastery of Revelations** halfway up the hill to Chóra.

The island's port, **Skála**, is touristy with many hotels. However, **Chóra**, 40 minutes by foot uphill is one of the most beautiful traditional towns. Bulky and well built, the town huddles around a medieval castle.

Inside the castle is the famous monastery of St. John the Divine and the large and beautiful church bearing his name with its great wealth of icons, consecrated vessels and votive offerings. The monastery was the object of the Byzantine emperors' devotions and countless private contributors and was certainly the richest in the Dodecanese. Its great wealth helped it to establish a theological school of Patmos which to this day attracts students. It is situated just below the Monastery of Revelations.

Kalymnos is even more famous than Sími for its sponge-diving. Although the island on first acquaintance looks austere and dry, it is well worth further investigation. There are many lovely swimming coves and small out-of-the-way villages which offer simple pleasures—a plane tree for shade or a *kaffaneio* for a "cafe" or "Sprite." But these you can easily discover on your own. The history of sponge diving is more difficult to come by. Signs of this dying trade are everywhere: Kalymnian mantlepieces laden with huge sponges and shell encrusted amphoras, old men crippled from the bends, women in black, mourning the divers that never came back, but the visitor is often left with more questions than explanations.

Sponge story: Here is some background information. The sponge is a living

The colorful houses of Kalymnos, below and right.

organism, a colony of sea animals. Its size increases by a third each year. For this reason it is necessary to farm sponges selectively. Unfortunately this rule is rarely obeyed, with the result that the sponges of the Aegean are rapidly disappearing. The coasts of Lybia and Cyrenaica have also been exploited although to a lesser degree since these countries impose prohibitive taxes.

The "*imero*" (cultivated) sponge is different from most of the common black sponges you see at the bottom of the sea. But only a well-trained eye can tell which is which. The "*imero*" is softer and can be cleaned and shaped with clippers while the wilder version is less pliable. There are various grades of "*imero*" sponges. The heavier ones are for industry and the finer ones for cosmetic use. The preparation of sponges for the market has two stages. First the divers beat them hard on the *caïque* deck "to get the milk out of them." Then they string them together and drop them back into the sea for two-to-three days of cleaning. The soft fleshlike part dissolves and only the golden brown sponge skeleton remains. Then they compress them so that they fit in sacks for export.

Although artificial sponges have taken over the market there are still some people who will pay for the more resilient natural sponge. Be careful, though, that the natural sponge you buy has not been bleached; bleaching may make the sponge look more inviting to the uninformed tourist, but it weakens the fibers of the sponge.

Over the years fishermen have developed various methods of gathering sponges: spearing the sponges in shallow water, dragging a heavy razor and net behind the *caïque* along the bottom of the sea, so that everything—stones, seaweed as well as the odd sponge—gets pulled up together, and finally, diving. In the olden days the divers used to sink themselves by tying heavy stones to their waists. Holding their breath they scraped the sponges off the rocks which they had spotted from the surface; they could usually get two or three before they had to return to the surface for air. There were divers who could dive 40 fathoms deep long before the "machine" was introduced.

The "machine" is what islanders still call the diving apparatus. This consists of a rubber suit with a bronze helmet

which connects to a long rubberhose and a handpowered airpump. The diver is let out on a long wire and given enough rubber hose for the distance he is diving. He can stay down as long as he wants because he has a constant air supply.

The sponge industry aided by the "machine" gained renown while the sponge divers were less lucky: they got the bends. The air hose allowed the divers to go farther, but the human organism couldn't withstand the new depths; many were paralysed and many died.

Although this "machine" now appears quite outdated you can imagine what an innovation it was when it was first introduced. It made both the captains and the sponge merchants rich but ironically the increased consumption of sponges also brought upon the downfall of the sponge industry. The seabed was stripped bare to provide for commercial demands. *Caïques* had to go farther and farther to find sponges. Today sponge fishing is a dying art but there are many Greeks fishing sponges in Tampa Springs, Florida and a fleet of *caïques* can still be seen setting out from the Kalymnian harbor for six months of sponge fishing on Saint Geórgos' day.

To complete the picture, here is a short passage from my own novella on sponge diving:

"Captain Andónis had four *maggíore* suits for deep water. First he sent down two old-timers, then came the turn of a new man. The youth hung back, white as a sheet. The captain cajoled him—wasn't his father a brave man?—but to no avail. He put up a struggle when they began to dress him in the suit, and fought to break free, but they enclosed him in it and forced him to go down.

"Thodorís felt a great emptiness in the pit of his stomach. He tried to swallow but his throat had gone dry. He would have asked for water, but was ashamed to. They gave him no time to think. Without fully realizing what was happening, he found himself enclosed in the heavy rubber clothing, and the helmet was screwed down over his head. He could hardly move. They helped him down the short ladder that hung over the side of the boat and he began slowly to descend.

"Once in the water his hands and feet felt light and easy, and he no longer felt scared. He remembered his father's advice and all that the old-timers had told him—not to go right to the bottom, but to keep two or three fathoms above

it until he sighted sponge; not to move against the current, to move in zig-zags, so as not to get the bends; to keep still if he saw a shark and if necessary to frighten it away with a cloud of bubble from his air valve. All this he knew, but he had no experience. Sometimes he rose to eight or ten fathoms and had a hard job getting within reach of the sponge, other times he went straight to the bottom—the tricks of the water fooled him. He didn't know how to distinguish currents and when he sighted a shark he lost his nerve entirely and made an ass of himself, tugging on the line for them to bring him up. Luckily, the fish was quite small.

"As most of the divers were new, Captain Andónis had taken them to a shallow spot. It was no more than twenty fathoms, without difficult currents, and although a poor place for sponge it gave them time to find their feet. The sea here was thick with divers, using shallow-water suits. You'd have said they had only to take a stroll to pick up sponge.

"They didn't stay long. The old-timers complained that their dividends wouldn't even pay for mastic (see Chios [page 230] for how it is made), and the captain decided he was wasting his time. What was the good of having *maggíore* suits if they only used them in the shallows?

"They moved into other waters—thirty to forty fathoms deep and rich in sponge. Before allowing them to go down the captain told them, "No fooling now. The water's deep. There are currents. We'll soon see who's best among you."

"It wasn't in Captain Andónis' interest to lose divers. His suits were of good quality and much sought after. Now the fishing would begin in earnest."

Whether in Kalymnos for its folklore or its beaches and secluded villages the visitor can't help but feel how this barren island offers a different kind of holiday than the more lush islands of the Dodecanese, the Kalymnians will tell you why this is. With an uncle in Tampa or a cousin in Astoria most have learned some English and are quite willing to tell you their story. Usually, it's worth listening.

Kalymnian sponges for export.

CRETE

The soul of Crete lies in its mountains: the Díkti peaks to the east, Psilorítis in the center, and the White Mountains to the west, including Pachnes (8,020 feet/ 2,450 meters), the island's highest point. Dramatic, savage, awesome, they have for centuries provided the metaphors for the embattled *palikári*, the warriors of Crete. As a quotation from a Cretan *mantináda* has it:

I will cut daphne and myrtle
From Mount Psilorítis
To crown the dead
That glorified Crete.

As the light changes, the mountains recede or come closer, sometimes a translucent shimmering white, other times, a burnt umber. But they are omnipresent, and dominate, exemplify the history and psychology of the ferociously proud and independent people of this "Great Island." If you want to know the "real" Crete, head for the mountain villages you see from the main coastal road, nestling in the foothills of the mountains and looking almost as if they grew there.

Access to Crete is easy from April until early October, and not difficult outside these periods. Domestic flights within Greece are both plentiful and cheap; in the summer months, there are six flights a day from Athens to Iráklion, and four from Athens to Chanía. But without a doubt the most romantic way to arrive in Crete is on one of the many overnight ferries from Piraeus, the port of Athens. If you arise early, you will experience the never-to-be-forgotten spectacle of the dawning sun gilding the mountain peaks pink way above the skyline, long before the coastline is visible. Friends say I exaggerate, but if the wind is right, you can actually *smell* Crete before you see it —that unique blend of mountain thyme, oregano, sage, rosemary and wild flowers that assails your nostrils as you walk along mountain trails.

One can visit Crete at any time of the year as the winter is mild by British and American standards, and the south coast is always warm—it is only 200 miles (320 km) from the coast of north Africa. But the best seasons for many are spring and autumn. From the end of March until the end of June, Crete is breath-

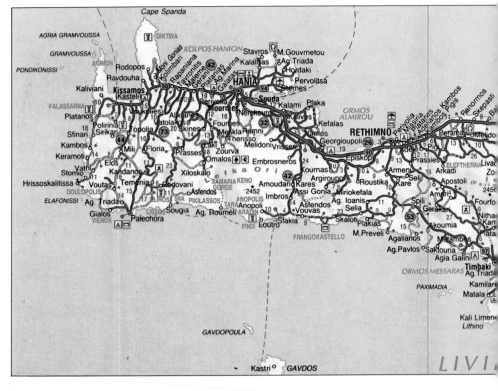

taking. It is pleasantly warm without the relentless heat which can characterize July and August. September and October are also temperate months, although a sudden downpour is not unusual in October. But these autumnal harbingers of winter blow themselves out in a day or two, and the sun soon returns.

Background: Crete has always been divided into mountain, plain and coast. In previous centuries invaders remained within the walls of their strategic coastal forts whilst the peasants in the outlying villages acknowledged a change of master. Less than 100 years ago, there were only five miles of paved road in the entire island. Tourism has changed many of the coastal villages throughout the island and encouraged people to move from remoter parts into the towns. Between a quarter and a third of the island's inhabitants now live in towns. But behind the statistics the old ties with the land linger on. In winter and summer people who live in towns increases. Many people winter in the towns, and return to their upland villages in the spring. Some are attracted to the towns to work in the tourist industry during summer. During spring and autumn, however, people return to

their villages for planting and harvesting, for few Cretans are without some land, and all Cretans are emotionally close to the soil. Every family owns something.

The "real" Crete is very much alive and well in its villages, although this is perhaps not immediately discernible. But the polite and intelligent tourist is likely to receive a warm welcome there of a kind that is difficult to find in the coast resorts. It helps if you can speak a little Greek, even if only a few phrases.

Once on Crete the few major towns on the north coast, each the capital of their respective provinces, make good bases for exploring the island. Excellent networks of local bus routes fan out from each of these towns.

Iráklion is the largest town in Crete, and is noisy, bustling and dusty in the July heat. Until this century it was known as Candia, the Venetian corruption of the Arabic El Khandak, "The Ditch," which was the name given to it. It was given this name by the Saracen marauders who seized it in 827. Its history is one of long and violent sieges. Byzantine admirals made repeated efforts to wrest it back from the Arabs before Nikephoros Fokas succeeded in 961, perhaps helped

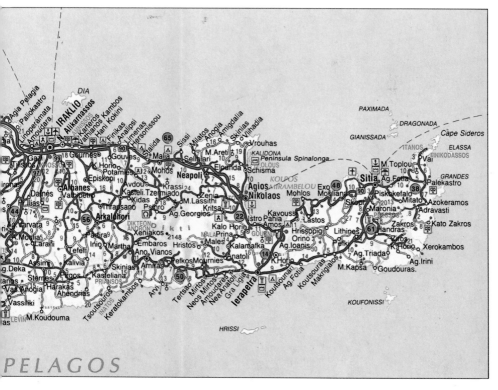

PELAGOS

by his habit of catapulting the heads of Muslim prisoners over the city walls to break morale. The Venetians had less trouble in capturing the town in the 13th century, but their rule was ended by one of the longest sieges in history. For twenty-one years the Turks besieged the town, kept out by the massive fortifications which had been erected the previous century, before finally gaining control in 1669. Today only isolated traces of their past remain. But there are two excellent museums: the **Archaeological Museum**, whose vast collection from Unosios and elsewhere is the best introduction to Minoan Crete, and the **Historical and Folklore Museum**, filled with mementoes of the island's more recent past, as well as a well-displayed collection of textiles.

Just south of Iráklion (there are frequent buses) lies **Knossos**, the extensive late Minoan palace complex excavated and partially reconstructed by Sir Arthur Evans earlier this century. The site is well-known and usually crowded. For those who prefer their ruins untouched and more peaceful, there are several other Minoan settlements in this part of the island: **Féstos** and **Gortyn**, to the south,

and **Malía**, to the east are all an hour's drive from Iráklion. Also in the vicinity is the **church of Asómatos**, near Acharnés, with Byzantine frescoes, and the Byzantine church complex at Ardon.

Áyos Nikólaos is the most popular resort in Crete. It is a clean well-organized tourist town, though bathing is surprisingly limited. Although it has become an international playground for the tour operators, it remains a good base for the adventurous visitor. The foothills of Mount Díkti are sprinkled with fine painted churches, including perhaps the best on the island—the **church of Panayía Véra**, with its superb Byzantine frescoes, at Kristsa. Nearby lie the deserted ruins of the Doric city of Lato, just several hours' walk from Áyos Nikólaos. A little further afield to the west is the windmill-studded Lassíthi plain, one of the most fertile areas of the island and worth visiting as an antidote to the tourist culture of the coastal towns. For a good day's swimming, leave Áyos Nikólaos and head south to the old port of Ierápetra from where you can catch a boat to one of the small coves that dot the south coast.

Réthimnon: From Iráklion there are

Preceding pages, an oliv grove. Below rocky coast of southern Crete. Right, shepherd in Ayia Galíni.

two routes westwards to Réthimnon. You can follow the main road along the coast and through the foothills of **Mount Ida**. The bus does this regularly in just over two hours. Alternatively, if you have more time you can head south on the Dafni road. This brings you much closer to the overwhelming massif of Ida itself. Following the road which skirts the mountain, you come to the town of **Záros**, and just beyond that, two monasteries, **Vrondísi and Valsa-monerá**, which contain some of the most beautiful Byzantine frescoes in Crete. The road north to Réthimnon gives some idea of the rarity of the Cretan landscape. Below lie the lush orange groves of the Mersara plain and high above on your right tower flanks of the mountain itself which remains capped with snow till well into May. From Plátanos the road winds through unspoilt country to emerge at Filákio at the head of a valley fifteen miles north of Réthimnon.

Réthimnon itself is an attractive, small port with an Oriental feel. When the Venetians took it over as a stopping-point for ships on the run between Chanía and Iráklion its inhabitants were largely Greek Orthodox. Under Ottoman rule many people converted to Islam, as they did throughout Crete. These converts continued to speak Greek and failed to follow their new religion with any fervor, drinking wine, for example, and marrying Christians. By the 19th century the population was largely Muslim and even today the old town behind the Venetian harbor, with its narrow lanes, and painted wooden houses with their over-hanging upper stories, retains Turkish air. In 1923 most of Réthimnon's Muslim inhabitants were uprooted in the compulsory exchange between Greece and Turkey: their melancholy departure is described in the Cretan novelist Prevelákis' work *Chronicle of a City*. But the slender minarets which punctuate the Réthimnon skyline are a reminder of their presence. Climb the spiral steps to the top of the minaret in Odos Man. Bernárdo and you will see the rooftops of Réthimnon spread beneath you. The Venetian harbor with its attractive waterfront restaurants, is a good place to eat at but it is worth exploring the back streets below the fortress where several less pretentious *tavernas* are hidden away.

Chanía is by far the most attractive of the provincial capitals. A bustling and

Beach in Iráklion.

vigorous town, Chanía has a superb waterfront dominated by the "Old Harbour," comprising a Venetian mole, shipbuilding slip, light-house and fortifications. The town has an excellent range of hotels, pensions, *tavernas*, and restaurants—and not all of them cluster round the Old Habour, which tends to be more expensive. The **Kavouriá restaurant**, at the east end of the waterfront under the Hotel Plaza, is a good place to while away an evening, watching the lights reflected in the water, the local Greeks leisurely pursuing their evening *vólta*, or promenade, along with the technicolored tourists. The large and genial owner, Dimítris Vréttos, is an expert chef in both Greek and European cuisines, and knows how to be patient in several European languages!

Chanía has a superb market with small but seductive *tavernas* where you can see the stall-owners and market-porters having an early lunch of fish soup or a roasted sheep's head. Chanía is a town which infinitely repays a slow investigation on foot. The Kastéli quarter behind the Kavouría is a maze of narrow, mysterious alleys, of starkly contrasted light and shade, of tiny artisan shops and *ouzeris*. Outside the houses, caged finches and linnets sing in the sun, while high above your head, housewives exchange gossip from their geranium-bedecked balconies only a few feet from each other.

Slightly further out, in the **Halépa** neighborhood, there are many fine houses dating from the occupation of Crete by the Great Powers at the turn of the century. Here you can still find neoclassical villas which look for all the world as if they have been magically transplanted from Paris. Chanía has—compared with Iráklion—a small but interesting archaeological museum, several art galleries, a surprisingly good public library, a municipal swimming pool and a beach. But an easy bus ride from the center brings you to the more attractive beaches of **Kalamáta**, a few miles to the west of Chanía, or to **Stavró**, to the east, on the Akrotíri Peninsula. The town also contains the central bus-station from Nómos Xaníon, the province of west Crete.

Mountain excursions: If you want to explore the mountain villages of this scenic province from Chanía, you must first of all acquire a map, and secondly, a bus timetable. Here you encounter your

he fashionable port Áyos ikólaos.

first problem. The rural buses are quite properly scheduled to suit villagers, not tourists. Hence they tend to leave the outlying areas for Chaniá at about 6 a.m. or 7 a.m, and return in the late afternoon. This is a nuisance. But remember that in Crete, taxis are plentiful and cheap, and cars can readily be hired. Take a taxi out early one morning to one of the villages—let us say, **Thérisso**, about 11 miles (18 km) south of Chaniá. If you return the locals' greetings you may be asked to sit down for a glass of *tsichoudiá*, the local *ráki*. (*Ráki*, or *tsipouro*, is the main Greek spirit. It is distilled from the skins of grapes after pressing.) This is always offered with a dish of walnuts, or olives, or cheese, for Greeks do not drink without eating. A word of advice: Cretans, even in the mountain villages, are inured to the sartorial eccentricities of tourists. But though they are used to women walking about in bikinis, or men in shorts, they do not approve, and at the very least, regard such people with amusement. Mountain villages are not the places for trendy and revealing beach-wear. Dressing with modesty will certainly make it easier to pass among the morally conservative people of the mountains.

From Thérisso, a dirt road climbs up and contours along the mountains, heading initially south, then west. It passes through the tiny but impressively situated village of Zourvá, and drops down to the attractive village of Mesklá. Wear light sports shoes and always carry a sun hat, water and a picnic basket. This walk would take you no less than three or four hours at a slow pace but the views are splendid: the ramparts of the White Mountains tower above you to the south, split by dizzy ravines and small gorges as they tumble down precipitously to the foothills. To the north, there is extensive agricultural development among these hills, which are patterned like a patchwork quilt with small fields of wheat, olive- and orange-groves, vineyards and pasture.

On the outskirts of the villages, you are likely to come across a curious bald circular patch, perhaps four to five yards in diameter, and rimmed by stones stuck vertically into the ground. This is an *alóni*, or threshing-ground, still used to this day in many of the villages. If you are about in the right season, you may be lucky enough to see a donkey being

Goat cheese and fresh vegetables in the Iráklion market.

262

driven round and round the *alóni*, towing a heavy wooden sled over the wheat or whatever cereal it is. A couple of women sit on the sled with a pan and brush; their function is not immediately clear. Suddenly, however, amidst much laughing they dart forward to catch the donkey's droppings before they get mixed up with the wheat!

Again, you may see a small group of women and children peering up into a tree and shouting encouragement and directions. As you approach, you will see the head of the household perched up the tree in his bare feet, knocking down walnuts with a long pole. The women below husk the green fruit with a knife, and their hands are stained a dark brown with the natural dye of the husk which is also favored by some women as the local substitute for henna. Inevitably, you will be offered an armful of walnuts.

In spring, Crete is garlanded with a seemingly limitless array of wild flowers, and the roadside meadows are ablaze with color you should easily be able to identify—by smell, if nothing else!—the wild herbs such as mountain thyme, oregano and rosemary, which grow in clumps along the roadside. Birdlife, too,

is rich; you will certainly see swooping flights of gold-finch, many kinds of warbler and bunting, and high up, planning on the thermals, you may see griffon vultures, or lammargeyer.

There are two areas which perhaps particularly repay exploration in west Crete. The first is the tangle of villages southeast of Chanía and west of Vámos, west of the main road to Réthimnon: Frés, Tzitzífes, Kiriakosélia, Mahéri. Secondly, there is the grouping south of Kastéli in northwest Crete: Vúlgaro, Kalathénes, Sfakopigádi, Horitianá. This area contains two interesting sites at **Poliriniá** and **Falasárna**. The sleepy small town of **Kastéli**, with its lovely beach, makes an ideal base for exploring this area. The monastery at Kolimbarión, with its impressive frescoes, and Turkish cannonball embedded in its outer, seaward-facing wall, is easily accessible, and there is pleasant walking on both the Rodópou and Grambúsa peninsulas. A boat-trip to **Grambúsa island** for swimming and a picnic makes an exciting and unusual excursion, and weather permitting, can be easily arranged in Kastéli. A longer trip, perhaps necessitating car hire for the day, is to the spectacular coral beach at

Lafonisos on the southwest tip of Crete. This is a truly beautiful spot, totally undeveloped, although there is a proposal to build a large hotel there. In the meantime, if going there, take a picnic and adequate water—there is no water supply in the neighborhood.

No visit to west Crete would be complete without a visit to Ómalos, and the Gorge of Samaría. The **Ómalos** is an upland plateau characteristic of the limestone of the Cretan mountains. It is rimmed by mountains, and is perhaps two-and-a-half miles (four km) across, with the **Gorge of Samaría** starting from its southeast corner. This area was the very epicenter of resistance against the Turks, celebrated in a famous Cretan ballad, roared out when mountain men are eating and drinking together:

When will the sun break out,
And when will February come,
That I can take my rifle,
My beautiful Patróna,
And go down to the Ómalos…

Today, it is a tranquil place where potatoes are grown, and where the shepherds of villages like Lákki and Ayía Iríni bring their flocks for the summer grazing. Alas, a plethora of white concrete *taver-*

nas is beginning to appear at the entrance to the plateau. The two or three modest *tavernas* already in existence are more than capable of handling the current tourist traffic.

Most people hardly see the Ómalos. They take their tourist or public bus up from Chanía about 6 a.m. to do the Gorge. Thus they miss the spectacular nature of the drive itself, which is undertaken in the dark. A better way is to take the day's last public service bus up to the Ómalos, where you can spend the night and enjoy its still beauty in the evening. The **Ómalos Taverna** is recommended—simple, clean rooms and good food; tel. 0821–93269. It is delightfully tranquil to sit outside the *taverna* in the last hour of sunlight, looking south out over the Ómalos, watching the face of the mountains glow in the evening sun, and being slowly mesmerized by the sound of sheeps' and goats' bells.

The "Wooden Steps": In the morning, you can be up early to catch the first bus to Ksyloskalo—the "wooden steps" —the abrupt start of the Gorge of Samaría. A word of warning: while there is a well-made path all the way down the Gorge, and while there is plenty of water,

Chanía port.

and while first aid facilities are available at the deserted village of Samaría in the park ranger's house, wear something sensible on your feet! At the very least, sneakers are necessary. Strapless slip-on sandals and stiletto-heels are definitely not recommended.

The view from the top of the "wooden steps" is truly spectacular. Directly opposite you is the massive crenellated face of **Gíngilos** (6,834 feet [2,083 meters]), a fine, imposing mountain. Although it is hardly credible from this position, the summit is fairly easily accessible along a well-marked path ... to the experienced *and* properly-equipped mountain-walker only. (For information on this and other mountain-walking routes, contact the Greek Alpine Club hut at Kallérghi, above the Ómalos, or the author of this piece via the travel agency given in guide in brief). The Gorge is a National Park; the route through it is 11 miles (18 km) long, and the park authorities have done an efficient job of fencing the path, providing water- and rest-stops, and information boards. It is impossible to get lost. The best advice is start early, take your time and gape! The Gorge is without a doubt one of Europe's great wonders.

Coastal visits: When you finally leave the Gorge on the south coast, you may well be surprised at the intensity of the heat. As you head into the sea for that well-deserved swim, beware! The stony beach is red-hot! The village where you end up, **Áyia Rúmeli**, is an unlovely place designed only to hoover money from as many tourists as possible. But one can sympathize with the villagers' need to make money while the sun shines —Áyia Rúmeli is a desolate and deserted spot in winter. Take the first ferry-boat out, and go to the idyllic coastal village of **Loutró**, along the coast to the east. Loutró, the ancient port of Phoenix, surrounded by interesting and picturesque ruins, used to be a fishing village; now it subsists totally on tourism. However, as it is very small, there is an absolute threshold to the number of tourists it can absorb. But it is still a lovely spot, ideal for lotus-eating, swimming and idle contemplating. The water around Loutró is crystal-clear, this is because there is a layer of freshwater over the seawater. A short hour's walk to the west brings you to an attractive deserted pebble beach. A small *taverna* not far away supplies cold drinks and basic food. You can leave

low, a man
th his
rry-beads.
ght,
woman
uning her
e.

Loutró by boat, or preferably, walk east along the coast on a clearly marked path until you come to Hóra Sfákion.

Hóra Sfákion serves principally as the boat/coach interchange point for tourists coming down the Gorge. But there is an attractive walk from there, along the coast road to **Frankocástelo**, about seven miles (12 km) away. Here, there is superb swimming in a lagoon under the ruined but still impressive ramparts of a Venetian castle. This road passes through several east Sfákiot villages which although not particularly impressive in themselves, *are* working villages where many traditional agricultural and pastoral activities persist. From Frankocástelo, it is easy to return to Chanía by bus via Hóra Sfákion, while for the more adventurous, a walking trip can be made inland on clearly marked paths, either to the village of **Kalikratés**, or up the **Gorge of Imbrós**, on a smaller scale than that at Samaría, and much less known, but equally spectacular. A little elementary map-reading is necessary for either of these expeditions, plus some help from the locals. Exit from both places is possible by public bus.

While on the south coast, those who like boat-trips have the option of hopping between Hóra Sfákion, Loutró, Áyia Rúmeli, Suyía and Paleohóra. Indeed, this route is strongly recommended for those who are not into walking. These trips afford unbeatable views of the southwest coast of Crete, where the mountains drop dramatically into the sea. It is a stunning, and at times—particularly in the evening—a slightly sinister coastscape; the sense of profound depth in the sea is inescapable.

Every now and then, you will see a small white church nestling close to the sea, or perched upon a high promontory. It is a feature of rural Greek Orthodox churches that they are frequently constructed on a site with good views—and often, water. If you are in one of these coastal villages, and you see a church high above, it is well worth the effort to find the way there—there is bound to be a path. There is a chapel above the long beach at Paleohóra, for example, which gives a complete panorama out over the peninsula. Some of these chapels, for example at Anídri, an hour on foot northeast of Paleohóra, have fine Byzantine frescoes dating from the 14th or 15th centuries. Resist the temptation to **Rugs drying.**

266

take flash photographs; this inevitably exacerbates the process of deterioration.

"The Cretan Bus": While talking of travel, mention must be made of "The Cretan Bus"—not the big, efficient coaches which make the regular runs east-west along the main road in the north of the island, or to the popular tourist destinations such as Hóra Sfákion, Ksilóskalo, or Paleohóra. Instead these are the much smaller, sturdier, and more battered village buses which make the run into Chanía in the early morning and out again in the afternoon. The driver and conductor are usually regulars, often residents of the village in question. The bus takes passengers, of course; but it also takes an amazing range of parcels and boxes, the mail, and carries messages and gossips up and down the district.

Although there is a timetable, there are infinite minor variations in its operation, and the bus is more likely to go when full rather than exactly on the appointed hour. So the way to outwit the driver is to check the departure time on the big destination board in the main bus-station; then ask for the *number* of the bus at the information desk (displayed on a round sticker on the windscreen—never mind what is said on the bus's destination-indicator!); then find that bus, and watch it like a hawk! These rural buses, however, are a safe and reliable way to travel, and afford a unique opportunity to meet locals.

Food: A word now about food. The food in restaurants is by-and-large very good. But one must distinguish between "tourist-Greek-food," and food which the Cretans eat in the villages. In the former case, dishes such as moussaká, stuffed tomatoes and aubergines, *stifádo*, *taramsaláta* and so on are common and excellent. But these are not daily foods in the villages. Villagers eat what is in season, so their food, while wholesome, often lacks variety. In winter and spring, snails and *hórta* are common; the latter is a wild grass, not unlike spinach in taste, and equally full of iron. Cretan snails are widely favored outside Greece as well as by locals, and many are exported to France. They—and dishes like chicken and braised meat—are often served with a *piláfi* of rice cooked in the fat and juices of the meat. It is delicious. All meat, of course, is cooked in olive oil. Roasted sheeps' heads are common, and are eaten

decorated
nshade;
etan bus
ivers are
mous for
eir dare-devil
iving.

down to the bone: flesh, brains, tongue, and eyes. Another popular dish is *ko korétzi*, a very tasty sausage-shaped dish made of offal roasted inside the intestine.

All kinds of sheep's meat is eaten: boiled, roasted, stewed; including the liver, of course. A common proverb in the mountains of Crete says that the best tasting mutton is that which is stolen! It is all cooked in plenty of oil, and always, always served with bread. Similarly, wine is drunk with all meals, but never on its own. Cretans, like all Greeks, regard people who drink without eating as mildly barbaric. Bottled wine is distrusted intensely; locals drink their own draught red wine, which is of good quality, having a slight "afterburn" like sherry, and is highly recommended. Bottled Greek wine is ridiculously expensive, with the exception of retsina. So, ask for *krasí mávro*, dark wine, or *húna*, wine on draught; it comes by the kilo, or multiples thereof. Fresh fish, although available, is comparatively rare and very expensive. In waterfront restaurants, fish is charged by the weight. Off the south coast of Crete, many fisherman can only make ends meet by using dynamite. The sea is terribly overfished. Fishing with

dynamite, although prohibited, continues with predictably tragic consequences. Last year, a man fishing from his boat in this manner blew himself to bits in front of one of his children.

Traveling through a village in Crete you will sooner or later be invited to sit and have some food with the locals. This reflects the Cretan code of *philoksenia*, literally, "love of strangers," or, a most generous hospitality. If asked to sit, it is best to do so. A refusal offends the local rules of hospitality, which are very powerful in Cretan culture. The generosity with which villagers press food and drink upon you would betoken a very close friendship in Anglo-Saxon culture. But do remember that you are in a different culture, where hospitality reflects honor upon the donor family. Do not offer money—this would be a terrible insult! This *philoksenia* is one of the most attractive of local customs, and if you make an effort to keep up your end of the conversation, and praise the local food and wine, you will have amply repaid the villagers' hospitality. The mountain people of Crete love "*kali paréa*," good company, good conversation, and, a good joke! And of course just as important as the spoken Greek language is the unspoken one. *Kali paréa* is possible without exchanging a word; just use your hands and smile a lot. (See *Hospitality* and *Friends/Paréa* in the Cultural Dictionary, pages 276–278 and 280.)

"Greekspeak": A final word about the Greek language, which is dealt with at length elsewhere in this book (*Language* in the Cultural Dictionary). Cretans are ferociously proud of their language, believe it to be fiendishly difficult (not without reason!), and believe that no foreigner can ever speak it properly. In the more popular tourist areas of Crete— Chanía, Paleohóra, Hóra Sfákion etc.— English and German are widely spoken, and to a lesser extent French and Swedish; most travelers should manage. In the villages, of course, this is very much less common, especially off the tourist routes, so it is a good idea to learn a little Greek. Mastering the alphabet is useful, because not only can you then read what is on the front of buses, but it is helpful to realize that "øΑPMΑΚΕΙΟΝ" means pharmacy. By the same token, knowing the standard daily greetings is most useful.

Now, it is up to you. *Sto Kalo na pate!*

Left, snowy mountains at the head of Omalos gorge and right, the Samaria gorge.

A	(letterforms)
B	(letterforms)
Γ	(letterforms)
Δ	(letterforms)
E	(letterforms)
Z	(letterforms)
H	(letterforms)
Θ	(letterforms)
I	(letterforms)
K	(letterforms)
Λ	(letterforms)
M	(letterforms)
N	(letterforms)
Ξ	(letterforms)
O	(letterforms)
Π	(letterforms)
P	(letterforms)
Σ	(letterforms)
T	(letterforms)
Υ	(letterforms)
Φ	(letterforms)
X	(letterforms)
Ψ	(letterforms)
Ω	(letterforms)

CULTURAL ABCS

Newcomers to Greece are often baffled by the Greek alphabet. Even if they have trouble understanding other European languages they can at least read road signs and figure out which is the ladies and the gents. In Greece even international catch words like EXPRESS have a bizarre appearance: ΕΞΠΡΕΣ. Perhaps as much as anything else it is the strange alphabet that makes foreigners throw up their hands and say, "It's all Greek to me!"

The cultural ABCs that follows won't help anyone overcome their fear of ξs, φs, or ψs, but it may provide a key to another set of symbols that are equally strange. Greece is full of untranslatable concepts. What follows is an alphabet's worth of these indigenous phenomena. From E for Evil Eye to K for Kamáki to Z for Zorba these entries introduce the newcomer to aspects of contemporary Greek culture which are not immediately obvious. Here readers will find out why no one bothers about birthdays (see Namedays), why kiosks dot every corner (see Periptera), why old women dress in black (see Women), why Greeks are at odds over tourism (see Xenophobia/Xenomania).

Of course this kaleidoscope of incongruous items is only one of many possible collections. The various writers who have contributed to this alphabet are not set on fixing Greece's cultural topography, on the contrary, each—whether linguist, anthropologist or journalist—is interested in tapping the shifting assumptions that go into making myths and shaping cultural identity. Sometimes humorous, sometimes serious, these entries map out another Greece, as important as the Greece already represented by geographical region in the previous section. As a dictionary or as a set of social commentaries, use these pages as you please.

ACRONYMS

Even classicists, who can bumble their way through the more conservative newspapers with their many archaisms and purist forms (see Language), would have a difficult time deciphering the strings of acronyms that appear in most articles today. Always used for the names of political parties (KKE, ΠΑΣΟΚ, ΝΔ, ΚΟΔΗΣΟ, ΕΠΕΝ, ΔΗΑΝΑ), acronyms now stand in for everything from social services (IKA, EES, ANAT, IKY, ΔΕΗ, ΟΨΔ) to soccer clubs (ΠΑΟΚ, AEK).

A contemporary Greek painter, commenting on the recent proliferation of acronyms, chided that soon the Greek novel would consist solely of abbreviations. It could be he was merely denigrating language as a lesser medium—we all know that according to painters, a picture speaks a thousand words—but even so he had a point: acronyms are the fast-food of modern Greek discourse. Just as Americans have begun to wonder what McDonald's really means, so Greeks are beginning to wonder what acronyms are all about. Why, ironically enough, have public announcements and newspaper articles started to resemble their ancient stone predecessors with their long lines of unpunctuated capitals?

This may be an exaggeration, but the abundance of acronyms is still a notable cultural phenomenon. Especially since acronyms, like fast-food hamburgers, have an uncanny ability to camouflage what they contain. One soon forgets what an acronym really stands for. It suddenly has an association all its own, completely separate from its components. The prime minister Andreas Papandreou recently took advantage of this slippage and decided to use the same acronym for the Greek police force as the left-wing resistance fighters had used during Greece's civil war. ΕΛΑΣ now stands for both. In this case an acronym proved a subtle way of legitimizing a particular moment of leftist history.

But subtleties aside, even if it would take a lifetime to decipher the politics of acronyms it doesn't take long to learn those that are most frequently used. And although Greek phrase books rarely mention them you would be hard pressed to phone overseas if you didn't know that the public phones in every Greek town or city were housed in a building called OTE (pronounced "oteh"). You might save yourself quite a bit of time if you knew that the Greek tourist organization is called EOT (pronounced "ehot"), and some embarrassment if you knew that the great hordes shouting ΠΑΟΚ (pronounced "paok") in the streets of Salonika on Sunday were not political activists but soccer fans.

BYZANTINE CHURCH MUSIC

Q: In most parts of Greece on Sundays and Namedays (see Namedays) radios are turned on full blast and towns resound with the nasal half, and less than half, tone dips of the Athens' Mitropóleos cantors. Can you briefly explain why this chanting sounds "eastern" to a westerner's ear?

A: Traditional modern Greek music has many oriental features, as indeed had the music of the ancient Greeks: not only tones and semitones, but other smaller and larger intervals, oriental chromatic scales, a nasal quality in the voice and characteristic motifs decorated with grace-notes such as are particularly common in the East.

Q: How did Byzantium give birth to two such different church musics as the Roman Catholic and the Greek Orthodox?

A: Were these two kinds of music really so different 1000 years ago? Plenty of scholars doubt this. For example, this is what Igor Reznikoff believes: "At the end of the 19th century French Benedictines wanted to revive the "Gregorian chant" and created melodies based upon notes with identical time-value, often indeed beautiful, but which have no connection with the genuine ancient chant as we know it from manuscript sources on the one hand and from the tradition of model music on the other."

Q: What does Orthodoxy have to say about music? Has it always been an integral part of the Greek church service? Has there ever been any instrumental accompaniment?

A: Music has been used in the Christian Church since Apostolic times, and is regarded by the Orthodox Church as an integral part of the liturgy, to be preserved by each generation as a holy relic and to be performed contritely, humbly and with due decorum. Ancient ecclesiastical tradition, which is still maintained, holds that musical instruments are alien to the spirit of Orthodox worship, because their sounds are associated with worldly festivity.

That is why Orthodox church music is purely vocal.

Q: It seems to me that the history of western music is closely connected with the evolution of church music. Leonard Bernstein's rock mass is a far cry from a Bach Fugue. Has there ever been any attempt in the Greek church to compose new masses in any way like in the Protestant and Catholic traditions?

A: A number of pieces of Greek church music have been written in a more modern style. Theodorakis, for example, has composed a polyphonic Requiem for choir "a capella." These works could be performed in certain churches, but neither the congregations nor the clergy would ever wish to replace the traditional chant.

Q: How has this music survived? Are cantors trained or are they just expected to pick it up from their elders?

A: The church music of the Byzantines, and of the Greeks in general, began to be written down around A.D. 950, and for that purpose a special system of notation was worked out. Thus, up to A.D. 950, religious music was handed down by oral transmission. From then onwards, however, it has been transmitted with the help of manuscripts, and later, since 1820, in books. But the pupil has to overcome a very considerable obstacle before he can be considered a good psaltis or cantor. He must learn to chant in the appropriate style, and in this no written music can help him, only his teacher.

Q: Are there any women cantors? Do women play an active role in church music?

A: If a woman becomes a nun, and has a good voice, then she may chant in her nunnery. Otherwise it is not usual for her to chant. Nevertheless, a number of women in Byzantine times did occupy themselves in writing hymns and setting them to music. An interesting recent study on this subject was written by Diane Touliatos-Banker, under the title of *Medieval Women Composers in Byzantium and the West*.

Q: If visitors want to hear chanting at its best where should they go? In Athens?

A: There are churches with good cantors and choirs in every Greek city, and also in Constantinople. In Athens, where I live, I recommend my friends to attend the liturgy in Ayia Iríni (St. Irene's), where Lycurgos Angelópoulos and his choir may be heard.

COFFEE

"Would you like a cup of coffee?" It's the classic come-on from Syntagma to Sámos. Fair enough, women tourists should not be fooled by the sobriety of the homely brew, for coffee has long been the drink of erotic encounters. Among Greeks themselves, offering coffee to a stranger is a gesture of hospitality and an excuse for light conversation. A chance invitation for coffee with an acquaintance and his or her *paréa* isn't easily refused. It's the perfect drink for "exploratory" sociability, for jokes and mild flirtation,

and many a romance has begun with shy glances over the cups.

Its place in more mundane social intercourse is just as prevalent. Greek men drink it in the ubiquitous *kaffaneia*, housewives drink it in the houses with their neighbors during breaks from their chores. Working people drink it, too, but you won't find a coffee machine at their workplace. They "order out" from the local *kaffaneia*, and on downtown streets, ducking in and out of office buildings, you can often see the white-aproned proprietor carrying an ingenuous deep-dished tray crowded with coffee cups, the dish suspended —lantern-like—by bowed metal supports.

In name, as in quality, it's much closer to the Arabic original, *gahwah*, than our own watery brew. Ground into a fine powder and boiled with water and varying amounts of sugar, *kafé* is served in tiny cups. You can order it sweet (*glikó*), very sweet and boiled (*varí glikó*), medium (*métrio*) and plain (*skéto*) —and if those few teaspoonfuls don't satisfy your caffeine addiction, double (*dhipló*). Connoisseurs know that what distinguishes the exquisite cup from the mediocre is a thick topping of froth (*kaïmáki*). Greeks used to call it "Turkish coffee" (*turkikó kafé*), until the 1974 war in Cyprus, when it was angrily crossed off menus across the land. Cyprus is still a sore point, so unless you want to risk an irate waiter, ask for Greek coffee (*ellinikó kafé*).

Even the dregs have their uses. If you leave a trace of liquid so that the dregs can be swished around the cup, you can turn it over and let the wet residue run down the sides into the saucer. It leaves swirling patterns, and many a Greek woman can decipher symbols embedded in them to "predict" the future. Most men wouldn't be caught dead "saying the cup," and since the church frowns on it, many women hesitate to admit to it. But in their houses, women trade cups and interpretations "for a laugh." Wedding rings and tall, dark, handsome men seem to populate the cup. But one wonders now that Nescafé has become fashionable, what will become of the next generation's fortunes?

DELECTABLES

"And, I, hungry once more, gaze at the sweet biscuits." This heartfelt yearning, expressed more than 2000 years ago by a female character in one of Sophocles' lost plays, is still experienced in today's Greece, where sweets supply an important national need. The *zacharoplastio* (sweet-shop), with its mounds of crescent- and cone-shaped biscuits decorated with chocolate, almonds, sesame, apricots or coconut; with its giant baking-tins—*tapsia*—crammed with diamond wedges of *baklavas* glossy with syrup and bulging with nuts; with its extravagant European-style *pastés* too; is indeed a mouthwatering sight. Not less tempting are the smells of rose- or orange-flower water, roasted almonds and cinnamon which drift from the kitchens often

open to the street, where the curious may peer at the skills of the chef.

The *zacharoplastio* is more than a shop. One can often sit for some time, as in a cafe, eating a *kadaïfi* (finely shredded pastry stuffed with almonds and soaked in honey) or a *profiterol* (not the light French *choux* pastry but sponge softened with syrup and liqueur, covered with chocolate custard and cream), always served with a glass of iced water. In the northern cities—where the abundance of almonds and fruit and the presence of a large population from Asia Minor have fostered a sweet tooth among the inhabitants—sweet-shops are plentiful and often very smart. The city-dweller will eat a *baklavas*—or the even sweeter zeppelin-shaped *tulumba*—in the early evening, after a siesta and before dinner. Surrounded by glass cases packed with all variety of cakes (which present a constant temptation), one is usually not enough.

At home, deliciously fragrant sweet rusks, *koulourakia*, are dipped into tea or coffee at any time. On entering a home you are likely to be offered—refuse at your peril—a piece of

preserved fruit in syrup, *tou koutaliou* (off the spoon), a cross between jam and crystallized fruit. All sorts of fruit and vegetables are preserved in this way; especially delicious are the green walnuts and little damsons of Thasos. The more adventurous will sample a jar of baby aubergines or marrows such as cram the stalls in Salonika's street market. The humblest variety of the "spoon" family is the "submarine," a spoonful of vanilla (a vanilla-flavored mastic cream) served in a glass of iced water which then makes a delicately perfumed drink.

The range of Greek confectionery is greater than the disgruntled visitor supposes. Foreigners rarely meet with more than the ubiquitous stale *baklavas* or the oily *halva* packaged in foil. The best *baklavas* is to be found in Thasos, made unusually with walnuts and heavily spiced. Two variants of this oriental pastry found less often in shops are *galaktobourreko*, milk pie (*fillo* pastry filled with a thick egg custard flavored with orange flower and cinnamon) and *revani*, a Madeira-type sponge made with semolina and soused with a cognac and orange syrup. (Try them when visiting Aegina.)

Halva comes in many types. *Smyrnan halva*, now alas hard to find in shops, is made in huge flat circles and is of a coarse, grainy texture and rich amber color. *Pharsalian halva*, to be found in Thessaly, is more gelatinous, closer to Turkish delight (be sure to call it *loukoumi*!). Both are excellent when sprinkled with lemon and cinnamon. *Halva* should be bought in the street market, sliced from huge loaves, spotted with pistachios and almonds or marbled with chocolate. Even more sybaritic is *karidoplastos*, a rich "paté" made from chocolate and walnuts.

One final word. When surrounded by the

proliferation of unknown delicacies don't be overwhelmed. Ask for a bag of *amigdalota*—almond macaroons of numerous shapes and flavors—and you can't go wrong.

The sweet addict may like to sample this recipe for *revani*:

Mix 2 teacups flour with $3\frac{1}{2}$ tsps baking soda. Beat 6 eggwhites with a pinch of salt to a stiff meringue and gradually add $\frac{1}{2}$ teacup sugar. Beat the yolks with $\frac{1}{2}$ teacup sugar and $1\frac{1}{2}$ teacups butter until frothy. Add the grated rind of an orange, the flour, the juice of an orange, 1 teacup semolina, and finally the eggwhites. Decorate with chopped almonds. Bake in a tin 25 × 35 cm in a medium oven

for 40 mins or until springy to touch.

Make a syrup by boiling 3 parts sugar with 2 parts water, and 2 tbsps cognac and pour over *revani*. Cut in squares when cold. Serves 10–12.

EVIL EYE

Greeks seldom call it the "evil eye"—just "the eye" (*to máti*). Perhaps the malevolence of "the eye" goes without saying. Belief in the existence of "the eye" is not confined to those from remote or provincial places. The jet set, the middle-class as well as the proletariat, and not a few university-educated, swear that it exists. They insist that even doctors acknowledge its reality, just as the Church accepts the existence of demonic possession. Undoubtedly, the experience of "being eyed" is real and widespread, however much one might quarrel with the diagnosis.

Concepts of "the evil eye" abound in Mediterranean societies. Whether these different concepts are about the "same" thing is hotly contested by scholars of this region. But the debate itself underlines just how much "the evil eye" is a social affliction rather than anything particularly metaphysical. Probably, the "evil eye" is about envy. It tends to appear in communities relatively undifferentiated by social class or wealth—"egalitarian," in a sense—but where resources are scarce and competition over them keen. In such places, the increments of "superiority" of one family over another are tiny, yet all-important. Prestige or honor, variously, requires one to "stand out" from one's neighbors. But not too much, for that invites jealousy and bad will. Out of this paradox—the need to be better, the need to be the same—comes "the eye." "The eye" is a consequence of envy, but it is envy expressed surreptitiously, even unconsciously.

This qualification is important. A Greek will rarely give "the eye" to someone intentionally. What we'd call "sorcery"—saying special words or doing special actions in order to make something happen to someone—falls into a rather different category, that of "magic" (*mayiá*). "The eye," by contrast, is cast by accident. The kind of person who casts "the eye" on you or yours is probably a neighbor or an acquaintance, someone with whom relations are—if not warm—at least cordial. It can happen inadvertently when something is praised, or even silently admired. This is why people take precautions by spitting delicately ("Phthew! phthew! phthew!") on an infant they cuddle or admire, to forestall any ill effects.

The sorts of living beings and inanimate objects most vulnerable to "the eye" are those of unusual beauty, rarity or value. Tiny babies, appealing toddlers, pretty girls and twins are all at risk. Horses and cattle can be afflicted as well. When automobiles "die" for no apparent reason, people blame it on "the eye," and in certain parts of Macedonia you can find one tractor after another with an apotropaic string of blue beads hung from its front fender. On a parched islet in the Dodecanese, the water supply for one household is stored in white-washed barrels on its rooftop; on each barrel has been painted, with unabashed simplicity, a large blue eyeball.

Certain people are said to be prone to casting the eye. Often, an individual so labeled (sometimes called a *grousoúzis*) is quarrelsome, odd, or marginal in some way to the community. Blue-eyed persons (a trait Greeks associate with Turks!) are also especially hazardous. Wearing blue—blue beads or the little blue pupil encased in plastic—repels that danger. Many adults place one of these blue plastic eyes next to the cross they wear on a chain around their neck. And until recently all children had some sort of charm—a cross, an eye, an image of the Virgin and Child—pinned to their under-clothes to protect them.

There is no way to know precisely who has cast "the eye." First, the effects are noticed, and only afterwards is a culprit surmised. All concerned anxiously pool their memories to reconstruct the recent past, straining to identify possible suspects with possible motivations. This response of suspicion reinforces belief in "the eye." It also reinforces its precipitating conditions: those of superficial cordiality and subterranean mistrust among unrelated families. Oddly enough, then, identifying the culprit is usually quite irrelevant to the cure's effectiveness.

Symptoms of affliction are fairly well-defined: in humans, they include sudden dizziness, headaches, a "weight" on the head or a tightening in the chest, a feeling of paralysis. Significantly, the head and chest are the sites of "breath" and "spirit." Animals show their affliction by bizarre behaviors or suddenly falling sick, while vehicles break down. When it happens, people know who to go to. It's often an old woman who is trusted and respected and who "knows about these things." The cure has many variations, but this one is typical: the curer takes a glass of water and makes the sign of the cross over it three times. Then, she repeats three times silently to herself a special, secret set of holy words, usually a short passage from the Bible, and simultaneously drops from her finger three droplets of olive oil into the glass. If the oil remains in globules, the person is not afflicted with "the eye." If it dissolves, this is both the proof and its cure. The curer may yawn and her eyes may tear, while the afflicted person may feel a dramatic "lifting." This blessed water is then dabbed on the forehead, belly, and two points on the chest—that is, at the points of the crucifix—of the afflicted.

Often enough, it works. Why it works isn't clear, but the moral is. Illness isn't about germs alone. It's also about social relations. If that fact has eluded the Western medical establishment, Greeks know it all too well.

FRIENDS OR PARÉA

Individualistic Americans hardly have a name for it. "My gang" or "my buddies" sound embarassingly corny. "My crowd"? Maybe, but most opt for the delicately vague "my friends." Yet these are seldom more than conglomerations of individuals, drifting together and then apart in a madly mobile society. It's only in team sports, campus "Greek" societies (wouldn't you know?) and fringy cults that Americans experience that sense of a small tight-knit group that most of the world takes for granted. Across the Atlantic, Europeans seem more sociable. The English working classes have their "mates" from cradle to grave, but the French, with their *companie*, perhaps come closest to the Greek notion of *paréa*. For *paréa* combines both senses of the French word: of companionship, and of the group of friends itself.

"Do you have *paréa*?" means "Do you have company?" In Greece, without *paréa*, things aren't worth doing. Living alone, going off by yourself for a vacation, taking a lone stroll, these are not signs of independence but of desperation. This is a society whose language has no word for "privacy." The closest translation is *monaxia*—"isolation," connoting deprivation, loneliness and loss. Who would choose such a state? Young women on their own are especially suspect: surely they're "looking" for something. Before the days of mass tourism, big-hearted Greeks felt obliged to "adopt" lone tourists wandering their countryside, to "protect" the woman and befriend the fellow. Even today, "do you have *paréa*?" is less a question than an offer: "I'll come along."

The "naturalness" of *paréa* for Greeks is fostered in their family experience where a myriad of what we'd call "incompatible" activities happen all in one place so that nobody is left alone. Traditional peasant houses had one main room for cooking, eating, working and sleeping, and even in new village houses and Athenian apartments, everything seems to happen in the living room-kitchen. With television droning in the background, the teenage girl pores over her school books while her father passionately argues politics with his brother-in-law, her brother shouts into the phone and her mother clangs pots and scolds the grandchildren. People often say that the primary unit of Greek society is the family, not the individual, and this is manifested in a different sense of

captains."

Paréa partakes of both fixity and flux. "My *paréa*" can mean a fairly fixed group. For young Greeks, it's usually school friends. For those still childless, or far from home at university, the *paréa* becomes an alternate "family." Such a *paréa* can last for years. Its members are always together, and think and talk about each other obsessively. They create a shared history. For their parents, especially if they've lived most of their lives in one town or one neighborhood, the *paréa* combines long-time friends with relatives and new in-laws with their spouses, people with common interests and common responsibilities.

For the young and unattached, the *paréa* can be all-consuming. Its members meet for coffee before lunch, coffee after, a brandy at

personal boundaries. Greek families are not a place for "respecting the other person's space." They are interactive—indeed, interfering. How else can they show they care? This is where "Greek individualism" differs from the American variety. Americans believe they have the right to "do their own thing" and should allow others the same. Greek individualism is rooted in the family and the *paréa*, with their intense loyalties and equally intense conflicts. Greeks advise, criticize, make sacrifices for and demand them from those they consider "their own." No laissez-faire here! If American individualism is about the lone cowboy, the Greek version is about the leader of the pack. "Twelve Greeks," they remark in wry self-recognition, "thirteen

four, and a meal in a *taverna* at ten. Their political convictions probably don't diverge much (only kinship—sometimes—bridges political quarrels), yet over these little cups of coffee, they debate the fine points of their differences incessantly. They also joke and tell stories, and in their fragmented state of twos and threes, take up their other favorite subject: relationships. Friendships, family relationships, the continuing saga of lovers—all are minutely examined and deep emotional intimacies are thus forged. Friends measure their closeness by the pain they've shared.

Like a family, such a *paréa* sometimes has a kind of incest taboo. Jokey flirtations are part of the *paréa*'s spice but for serious affairs, members of the opposite sex are quite literally so "familiar" that they seem more like siblings. Lovers are brought to the *paréa* more than found within it. Except perhaps at marriage, people don't leave the *paréa* to form a "couple." "Dating" itself is alien to Greek experience.

The *paréa* nurtures vehement loyalties, especially in the face of outsiders' criticisms. But such relentless intimacy can also be suffocating and breed a kind of bitchiness. *Paréa* life can verge on melodrama: imagined slights take on huge proportions. Sooner or later, there's a fight, or a cooling, and the membership changes.

Parées fluctuate over time, but flux is also built in to the notion itself. The *paréa* is always expandable—a Greek doesn't fuss about bringing along a new friend uninvited. He expects the implicit response, "your friend is our friend," from the rest. They, in turn, don't fuss over this new person's "unique individuality"—the point is to make him part of the group. At the *taverna*, where the *paréa* typically gathers for long hours of jokes and singing over food and wine, chairs are always being added for friends who happen to come by. They cram chairs in until no more fit. Then everybody squeezes in, two broad bottoms sharing each lumpy, hard-backed chair. Comfort succumbs to sociability, but nobody complains.

For *paréa* life has its own etiquette. "Being together" is its object, not eating or drinking. In the *taverna*, the *paréa* members submit these creaturely needs to a grander, collective ideal. Endless plates of food come to rest not at each individual's place but haphazardly on the table. Each wields his fork to spear a morsel, then rests it. Meals like this can last for hours. That is the point. The table must be brimming—stinginess Greeks find contemptible, but greediness in *paréa* is almost as bad. So, for all their exhortations to others to "Eat!" they can be surprisingly reticent themselves. The same goes for drinking. Greeks drink only with food, and never alone. The point is not to get drunk. Drinking is only a means to "opening up," to entering a pleasant and sociable state that Greeks call *kéfi*. For all they drink (and that's usually less than it first seems) there are fewer alcoholics here than anywhere else in Europe. They regard with distaste tourists who drink to stupefaction. Especially tourist women; Greeks may grudgingly respect a woman who can hold her liquor, but they are unforgiving when she can't. It's seen as another proof of the immorality they already take for granted. So the double standard operates here with a vengeance, and in more puritanical locales, females ostentatiously spike their retsina with

soda water or coca-cola.

As they've eaten—collectively—so do they pay. It used to be that men always paid for women, splitting the bill equally among themselves. Things are more in flux these days. Men will pay for wives and girlfriends, but in university *parées* everyone is equally impoverished, regardless of sex, so all contribute. Guests—especially if they are foreigners—are a stickier matter. Greeks are proud of their reputation for hospitality. And they would never let a foreigner pay his—and especially her—way without a fight. But they are sensitive about being taken advantage of. The best policy is always to plunk your money down with the rest—indeed, to show your willingness to pay with as much drama and determination as you can muster—and if you find yourself overruled, to accept graciously.

GRAFFITI AND POLITICS

In Procopius' day, Constantinople was brought to a standstill as fans of rival chariot teams, the Reds, Blues and Greens, rampaged through the streets. Nowadays the chariot-racing is gone, but its place in Greek life is filled by politics.

Come election-time, the Athens streets are jammed solid with thousands of banners, flags and posters as supporters flood into Syntagma Square for the big rallies. Walls, bridges, the bare sides of apartment blocks become so many mottled configurations of slogans. Hit squads from the political parties' youth groups head out at night to whitewash op-

ponents' slogans and paint up their own. Outside the towns it's the same story. Way up in the deserted foothills of Mount Parnassus the lurid green sun of PASOK is daubed across the face of remote cowsheds.

Graffiti are essential to political success in Greece and they impose requirements of their own. Above all, color. If you think about it, the choice is limited: white is out since it won't show up against whitewash, yellow likewise. Black is confined to the extreme Right. The conservative New Democracy has bagged blue, a light turquoise which conveniently echoes the national flag. The KKE, the communist party (now split into two) of course uses red.

One of the keys to the success of the ruling socialist party, PASOK, had been their appropriation of the color green: highly visible, obviously suggesting close ties with the natural world, which helped to offset their radical reputation in the eyes of conservative farmers.

The other essential behind effective graffiti is the snappy slogan. Here's where the difference emerges between parties who know what they want and those who can't make up their mind. One word won the 1981 election for Andreas Papandreou—*allaghi* (change). This simple formula had already worked wonders four years earlier against a feeble array of alternatives such as New Democracy's own "It found Chaos: it created a State" which might arguably have been true but certainly fell flat, failing even to rhyme properly. The center party's own motto *allaghi me sigouria* (change with security) was a laughable imitation of PASOK, a virtual admission of defeat.

PASOK's rise to power has taken place under the painted rays of a bright green sun, a symbol which has not had the disturbing effects that one might have expected. Defying the laws of nature seemed only to underline the party's potency.

This idea of a political rebirth, the dawning of a new era, has been helped by the charisma of Andreas Papandreou himself. Charismatic political leaders recur in Greek affairs, but usually in the guise of elderly father figures, such as the Cretan Venizelos. The sons of such men tend to remain in their father's shadow. But the case of the Papandreou dynasty is different; Andreas' father George achieved charismatic status late in life and was popularly known as "The Old Man." His son, referred to universally as "Andreas," has managed to retain his charismatic mantle whilst keeping his youthful image—an unprecedented feat in recent history and one which keeps his opponents on the defensive.

Recently, with the entry of one of his own sons into Parliament, "Andreas" has begun gingerly to make the transition to charismatic "father." PASOK posters in the last election talked of creating a "better future for our children" as the public relations men shepherded an array of preoccupied little girls across the country's platforms and television screens.

Once again, PASOK's opponents were caught on the hop. The mainstream Communist Party remained cooped up in its proletarian ghetto, whilst New Democracy, with a new leader at the helm, talked unconvincingly of *zodani ananeosi* (real renewal)—*allaghi* by another name.

As in Procopius' Constantinople, modern Greek politics is dominated by Reds, Blues and Greens. There are endless factions, personal groupings which come and go, but for the time being the walls are full, the brightest colors bagged, and any change in the political spectrum will require an imaginative palette.

HOSPITALITY

Almost every travel guide to Greece opens its entry on "hospitality" with the story of Zeus, the disguised stranger-guest. And who are we to break tradition? In its ancient form —and still so, today—the word usually translated as "hospitality" was a bit of an oxymoron. *Philoksenia* is a compound word, combining *philo*, "to love," and *Xénos*, a word meaning—oddly—both "stranger" and "guest." Now, those were pretty rough times back then, and folks tended to be a little suspicious of strangers turning up on their

is somehow always more hospitable than the one down the road. In some ways, the "truth" is in the declamation. But certain places achieve a national reputation. Cretans—never a folk for middling gestures—are thought to be as extreme in hospitality as they are in temper. Predictably, the label becomes self-fulfilling. Other locales (Chios? The Máni?) fare less well in the eyes of their compatriots—but being an issue of local patriotism, well, it's all rather subjective, isn't it?

Hospitality isn't measured merely by its lavishness. It helps, of course. At weddings or namedays when guests are being fed, Greeks orchestrate an atmosphere of plenty—of copious quantities of meat, wine glasses constantly refilled, of a table choked with platters and bottles—so that all can enjoy

doorstep. But Zeus, it appears, liked to travel incognito, the better to seduce the lovely mortals he fancied. So Zeus—a trifle opportunistically, perhaps—decreed *philoksenia* not just an exalted virtue, but an obligation. The *Xénos*, he said, should be treated in a princely fashion, because—who knows?—that stranger might really be a god in disguise, even Zeus himself!

Though the onslaught of mass tourism has jaded it a bit, hospitality remains a virtue. Indeed, it is the very quality Greeks believe most distinguishes them from other peoples, especially the cooler hearts of cooler climes. They're positively competitive about it: every house insists its own hospitality is more genuine than the neighbor's, and "our" village

themselves, and also, so that none can call them "cheap." Yet poverty is not an insurmountable barrier. Greeks quote little homilies about the poor having little but giving of it freely, and the old woman who brings a glass of fresh water, bread and a few olives to feed unexpected guests, since it's all she has, is thought almost saintly. What counts, ideally, is purity of motive, a selfless generosity which compels one to give whatever one has—however great or humble —without thought of reward.

The reality is more complex. Hospitality creates a relationship, but it is not of equals. The host brings the guest into his own domain, then increases his prestige by giving. The guest, receiving, becomes "obliged" to the host. Once you know this, the common power struggle over food suddenly makes sense. The guest is obliged, ultimately, to receive but is at the same time "ashamed" to seem too eager. Proverbially, the guest was supposed to refuse an offer of food or drink twice, and only—after much coaxing—to relent the third time. It's quite a delicate game, really. It can be disastrous for the unsuspecting traveler. The Greek host thinks your refusals are just politeness, that saying "no" you really mean "yes." There aren't any magic solutions. You can try to argue "diabetes" or "bad teeth" if you can't bear the sight of another dish of jellied fruit, but be prepared to accept something in the end, so as not to insult your hosts. And if you're invited to dinner, it wouldn't hurt to skip a meal or two before.

Most travelers will have more superficial contacts with Greeks, but few will leave without being invited—at least once—into the house for coffee. Fortunately, rituals of hospitality have a fairly standardized form (though this varies regionally). Their formality doesn't compromise their sincerity. And that very predictability can be a boon to the traveler. A few phrases, carefully memorized and strategically deployed, can put you on surer footing, and your host will be tickled that you bothered to learn their ways. If you are invited for coffee, you will probably be led to the *salóni*, the formal living room, and left to wait while your hostess retires to the kitchen. She will return in a few minutes with a tray covered in a doilie, with a tiny cup of coffee, a saucer of cookies and a glass of water. Take the coffee first: raise it up slightly, and say *Stin iyiá sas*! ("To your health!"), then take a sip. You can then eat the cookies with the coffee (dunking is usually respectable). When you've finished, raise the glass slightly, toasting your hostess, and drink the water. When you leave, you can say *sas ef haristó*! ("I thank you") or even better, *hárika poli*. The latter is something you say when you've just been introduced ("I'm very pleased [to meet you]") but here, it can also mean "I've enjoyed myself." Hospitality, after all, is about both.

ICONS
AND ORTHODOXY

To be Greek is, in the case of 97 percent of the population, to be Greek Orthodox. True, many people demonstrate no interest in Orthodoxy. When I asked one young man what faith he belonged to he pulled out his state identity card and said, "This I.D. card says I'm Orthodox. Personally, I don't really know."

Traditionally Greek identity has always been strongly bound up with Orthodoxy. This includes the period of the Byzantine Empire when the populace viewed itself as dwelling in a world which had reached its perfect state and was a refraction of the Kingdom of Heaven. Later, after the Ottoman conquest (1453), the Greeks were administered as followers of the Orthodox faith, not as members of a particular national group. The Church was thus the main representative of Greek national identity until independence in 1832.

To those brought up in the largely Protestant if not wholly secular surroundings of northern Europe or North America the

religion of Greece appears threateningly mystical and obsessed by ritual. Any casual visitor to Greece could potentially pass the same verdict as the great Protestant theologian Harnack who wrote: "I do not expect to be contradicted if I answer that this official ecclesiasticism with its priests and its cult, with all its vessels, saints, vestments, pictures and amulets, with its ordinances of fasting and its festivals, has nothing to do with the religion of Christ."

Such a view is uncharitable in the extreme. The use of icons, for example, is one of the most frequently misunderstood aspects of Orthodoxy. These beautiful and highly stylized pictures are not objects of idolatrous worship. This was precisely the indictment of the so-called iconoclasts in the seventh and eighth centuries. In an effort to purify the religion of this idolatry they proceeded to literally deface thousands of icons throughout Byzantium. Intact pre-ninth century icons are consequently very rare.

The use of icons was ultimately upheld by the Church with the understanding that icons only symbolize the holy person depicted upon them. They are an instrument by means of which this holy person may be venerated. In no instance are they themselves an object of worship. This accounts for why there is no tradition of naturalistic realism in their execution. On the contrary the depiction of each personage is governed by strict conventions and approaches an ideal type. Through the material icon we are directed beyond to a transcendental glory. As John of Damascus wrote, "I do not worship matter but I worship the Creator of matter, who for my sake became material and deigned to dwell in matter, who through matter effected my salvation. I will not cease from worshipping

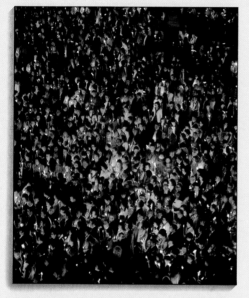

the matter through which my salvation has been effected."

The icons painted on the walls of churches throughout Greece are an early form of animation. They are a book explaining the Orthodox faith for those unable to read—a writing in images.

Icons are not only revered in Church; virtually every house contains an icon stand (*iconostásis*) containing various icons deemed to have a particular importance for the family. They may represent certain saints for whom family members are named. Almost all personal names in Greece are shared in common with a saint and instead of birthdays, saints' days are celebrated (see Namedays). In times of need a person may beseech these saints for help.

Perhaps the single most widely revered icon

in Greece is that of the Virgin Mary on the island of Tínos. It is said to have been painted by St. Luke and to have special wonder-working power. Every year on the 15th of August, the celebration of the Assumption of the Virgin, thousands of pilgrims flock to the island to make requests of the Virgin or to leave devotions as repayment for miracles that were performed (see pictures on pages 212–213). In one corner of the monastery which houses the icon a pile of crutches left behind by those healed on the spot can be seen.

In Orthodoxy the miraculous and wondrous seem to be closer at hand than in other Christian traditions. When a miracle happens the people are not particularly surprised. In fact they expect them to happen. Stories abound regarding people who have been "illuminated" by one of the saints and are able to tell the future. Other traditions concern those who imprudently decided to work on the day of St. Spyridon, or some other saint, and were smitten for not resting.

In conclusion, Orthodoxy is more than a religion, it is a way of life. Orthodox feasts mark public holidays and so touch everyone. Greeks may not all believe in it, but none can deny that it has exerted an influence over them and marked them in a distinctive fashion.

JUNTA

At 2 a.m. on the morning of Apr. 21, 1967, the people of Greece discovered that during the night the army, in a swift, well-planned coup, had overthrown the government and in its place established a military regime. Using a NATO contingency plan developed for use in the event of a communist invasion from Greece's northern neighbors, and code-named "Prometheus," the conspirators justified their putsch on the grounds that they "were saving Greece from the precipice of communism."

Later in the morning of April 21 a decree was issued proclaiming martial law. Various articles in the constitution guaranteeing human rights were suspended, special military courts were established in Athens and Salonika, political parties were dissolved and the right to strike abolished. Newspapers were submitted to strict censorship and required to publish exactly what was supplied by the government, and all gatherings, indoors or outdoors were forbidden. Many thousands of people with a record of left-wing political views or activity were arrested and sent into exile in bleak camps on remote islands. A large number of parliamentary leaders were taken into custody.

The new government ran true to form. Like other military dictatorships, its measures were alternately savage and ludicrous. Its leaders, the Colonels, were fanatical, if unintelligent, anticommunist salvationists who, no less than Hitler, saw politics in black and white terms, a simple and fierce contest between good and evil. Like the pre-war dictator General Metaxas, they placed much emphasis on the need to discipline and reform the Greek character. They condemned long-hair on men and mini-skirts on women and ordered both to go to church. Even foreign tourists were subjected to some of these regulations, though the government was anxious not to frighten them away altogether. But like other "moralists," they did not escape making themselves ridiculous. For example, through the official propaganda machine they tried to humiliate the Nobel prize-peot George Seferis for handing out a memorable statement of protest against the dictatorship; they deprived the celebrated film-star Melina Mercouri of her citizenship for criticizing them; they banned the songs of Mikis Theodorakis, a leading composer because he had been a left-wing deputy; and they censored the tragedies and comedies of the classical theater.

After the coup, little was heard of the communist threat which was supposed to justify it, and the seizure of the papers of the left-wing party failed to produce any evidence in support. The coup was a simple seizure of power by a handful of military bigots. The regime resorted to torture and brutality on a big scale as a deliberate instrument of policy to maintain its grip on power. Torture by the police was not unknown to Greece but the extent to which it was practiced and approved by the dictators appalled the outside world when the facts became known.

The Nixon administration, however, viewed these developments with no more than embarrassment and after a brief period of indecision gave the regime its accolade in the shape of arm supplies. Greece as a *place d'armes* for NATO seemed more important than Greece as a conforming member of the society of free and democratic nations which NATO was proclaimed to be.

The first blow in the downfall of the junta was initiated by students. In November 1973 a large number of them occupied the Athens Polytechnic and university buildings in Salonika and Patra. When it became clear that they were attracting widespread sympathy, and when the Athens Polytechnic students began broadcasting appeals on a clandestine radio for a worker-student alliance to overthrow the dictatorship, Papadopoulous, the regime's strong-man, sent in troops and tanks to crush them. The eviction of the students from the Polytechnic was carried out with extreme brutality, and at least 40 students and other sympathizers were killed, several hundreds wounded and thousands arrested. This ruthless demonstration of force in the center of Athens turned the stomachs of most Greeks. The days of the dictatorship were numbered.

The regime collapsed eight months later, in July 1974, under the weight of its bungling in Cyprus which led to a confrontation with Turkey and a military call-up for which the military rulers of the country had prepared with a farcical incompetence reminiscent of the equally empty militarism of an earlier Mediterranean dictator, Mussolini. The conservative leader Karamanlis, who had been living in exile in Paris, returned to Greece in the early hours of July 24 to oversee the dismantling of the dictatorship and the return to democratic rule. Seven years of a brutal, corrupt and unpopular dictatorship had ended as abruptly as it had began.

KAMAKI

Kamáki literally means a fishing trident, but now the word also refers to picking up or "hunting" foreign tourist women, and to the "hunter" himself. While picking up women is nothing new, the Greek *kamáki* knows that he is playing a well defined game with its own rules, techniques and vocabulary. Another less romantic mythology has built up around this seasonal activity, fueled by press coverage, television, and above all, the exaggerated "fishing stories" of the perpetrators.

The development of *kamáki* has paralleled the increase in tourism in Greece over the last 25 years. In the 1960s young Greek women were extremely restricted in their movements, and were kept closely tied to the family. There was therefore little prospect for romance, sex, or even an evening out with a young woman for the comparatively independent young man. The arrival of women tourists, who were not only sexually liberated, but were sometimes in search of "the four Ss" (sun, sand, sea and sex), was an opportunity not to be missed. *Kamáki* started to be practiced wherever foreign women were present, and not only by organized connoisseurs such as the members of the former "Octopus" club in Nauplia, but by any man who cared to try his luck. The "professionals," who roam certain highly touristic areas such as Syntagma Square in Athens, are said to make a living from their occupation, and they are certainly offensive to many tourist women. It could also be that their widely-publicized philosophy influences the potentially more genuine attentions of other Greek men.

The aim of the pursuit is to have sex, and according to the *kamáki* rules, as soon as possible after meeting a tourist woman, and with as many women as possible. Competitive friends compare "scores" at the end of the summer season, and winter-time *kamáki* conversation dwells on the glory of summer-time conquests. It is obviously the chase and not the "kill" that provides the entertainment. Inexperienced men may get no further than asking dozens of foreign women for coffee, and being rejected. Alternatively, the more sophisticated hunter realizes that the initial approach is crucial, and that he has to survey the hunting-ground, lay traps, and be ready to approach, or lay off until the time is ripe.

The intention is to make contact with the tourist woman without her realizing that she is being picked up by a *kamáki*. One *kamáki* ploy is to ask the woman the way to the Post Office, and if she does not know, explain the directions to her. The newer the arrival to Greece, the better, because she will not have become wise to the ways of Greek men. Women of different nationalities are said to require different techniques, and among the first questions a tourist woman is asked is "where are you from?". There are various theories as to which nationalities are easy, awkward, arrogant or beautiful, but all agree that if the respondent is Greek or Italian, there is little hope for success, and one should try elsewhere: Mediterranean women know the old tricks of their men too well to be duped.

If the tourist woman agrees to go for coffee or whatever, she is unlikely to be seen as independent, but rather as naive. Here lies the contradiction of the game: a *kamáki* will not view himself as the prey of a foreign female *kamáki*. A tourist woman who is evidently out to "catch" men in numbers will probably be labeled a prostitute, as a Greek woman would be. The classic *kamáki* wants at least to appear to be in control; the kudos comes from persuading unwilling or unknowing women into going to bed.

In general among Greeks, *kamáki* has a bad reputation. Most foreign women scoff at these men, and even former protagonists claim that it has lost its pioneering glamour, and become crude and vulgar. However, some see the *kamáki* as continuing the long tradition of hospitality in Greece. He can introduce or add to the delights of being abroad with sparkling sun and sea, exotic music and food, romance, and other elements of the ideal holiday. The foreign woman who understands the rules of *kamáki* can choose whether or not to play the game.

LANGUAGE

Imagine a language which has two sets of unrelated words for basic concepts, such as "nose," "cheek," "shoe," "house," "door," "street," "moon," "red" and "white." Suppose, also, that—together with its own distinct grammar—is used in everyday life, while the other is obligatory in official parlance, in education, and even in most newspapers.

That language is Modern Greek, or at least it was until 1974. For the first century and a half after Greece gained its independence from the Ottoman Empire in 1821 there were two versions of Greek, used in different situations, which overlapped in pronunciation and in many areas of vocabulary and grammar, but differed radically in others. This situation is not unique to Greece. The Arabs, for instance, also use different versions of Arabic in different circumstances. The Greeks have traditionally revered the language of ancient Greek literature and the New Testament—almost as much as the Arabs have valued the language of the Koran. For centuries the Greeks have felt that their own writings should depart as little as possible from the language of their illustrious ancestors and the language of their Holy Book.

Some acquaintance with the Greek language question is essential to an understanding of Greek culture as a whole over the last two hundred years, since the controversies over the language sum up the conflicting attitudes of the modern Greeks to their ancient compatriots. It has never been doubted in Greece that the present-day inhabitants of the country are the direct descendants of the ancient Greeks, who laid the foundations of European civilization.

This assumption presented the Greeks who were preparing the way for independence in the 1820s with the problem of what national ideology to adopt in order both to unite the nation from within and to present a national image to the outside world. Within Greece itself—and among adherents of the Greek Orthodox faith in general—a bewildering variety of different languages was spoken, and the Greek language itself was split into various dialects, some of them mutually incomprehensible. Nevertheless, Greek was the most widespread language spoken in the area, and Greek (albeit Greek of more than one and a half millennia before) was the language of the Church. So Greek intellectuals of the early 19th century agreed that the best way to cement national unity and to secure assistance from the West in their national liberation struggle was to promote as much as possible their links with Ancient Greece, to which Europeans and Americans at the time had a strong romantic attachment. Their case was

Greeks should call themselves. From the early centuries of the Christian era until the beginning of the 19th century almost all Greeks had called themselves "Romans" and their spoken language "Romaic," since they were conscious of belonging to the traditions of the Byzantine Empire, which was historically the continuation of the Roman Empire. They tended to reserve the words "Hellene" and "Hellenic" (i.e. Greek) for the pagan ancient Greeks and their language. By insisting on calling themselves and their compatriots "Hellenes" some intellectuals were able to envisage the resurrection of the ancient Greek language along with its name; yet at the same time, whereas everyone knows the difference between the Italians and the Romans, the word "Greek" is used indiscriminately and

supported by the undoubtedly close connection between the ancient and modern Greek languages.

From here on, however, there was profound disagreement. Some Greek intellectuals believed that the modern language was crude and barbaric (this they attributed to centuries of Turkish rule) and that the only way for the Greeks to prosper was a return to the pristine beauties of Ancient Greek, which they saw as a peak of perfection from which any later developments represented a decline. This return would ensure the rebirth of ancient Greek culture, their belief being that anyone who learned to speak like Plato would automatically begin to think like Plato. Connected with this was the problem of what the modern

confusingly to refer to the people and language of both ancient and modern Greece.

Others, realizing the impracticality of persuading the Greeks to renounce their mother tongue, preferred to look at the example of European nations such as the French, who had reached cultural eminence after abandoning Latin and cultivating their own language. These intellectuals argued that only through the use of the spoken language could the Greeks become sufficiently educated and enlightened to drag their country out of the economic and cultural morass into which centuries of subjection had sunk them. They urged their compatriots to follow the example of the ancient Greeks, who had used their mother tongue to reach the heights of civilization.

Among those who opposed the imposition of a fully resurrected Ancient Greek was Adamándios Koraís (1748–1833), a former merchant and physician living in Paris who became the leader of the intellectual movement preparing for Greece's independence. But although he constantly attacked the archaists, he was equally scathing about those who insisted on using the modern language as it was spoken by the common people. Instead he proposed a "corrected" version of Modern Greek, corrected, that is, according to the rules of Ancient Greek grammar. This language would have the advantage of being not too far removed either from any of the modern Greek dialects (and thus avoiding giving an unfair advantage to the speakers of any one dialect) or from Ancient Greek. It would display both the underlying unity among the speakers of Greek in the present day and the profound identity (despite superficial differences) between the Ancient and the Modern Greeks. Koraís' compromise language, which was neither fully ancient nor fully modern (and had never been spoken by anyone), was adopted by the fathers of the nation as the basis of the official language, later known as *katharévousa* (literally 'the purifying language').

It is difficult for non-Greeks to imagine the almost magic power invested in the ancient written word in Greece. Throughout the 19th century Greek intellectuals, frustrated and disillusioned by the problems facing the Greek state (poverty, disunity, economic and political subjection to the West), seemed convinced that every aspect of modern Greece represented an inferior and tarnished version of some glorious ancient counterpart. The ancient language was looked upon, quite irrationally, as an instrument of absolute perfection; and—precisely because it was no longer spoken, but only written—it appeared to be timeless and eternal, exempt from the change and decay that affect all living bodies (including, of course, spoken language, which is constantly in a state of flux).

It is notoriously difficult to create a standardized language—look at the differences between the varieties of English spoken within any one English-speaking country, let alone in different English-speaking countries. The Greek intellectual leaders created an added difficulty of trying to forge a standard that would contain material from two separate, albeit related, languages (Ancient and Modern Greek), each of which had never been standardized in itself but was split into widely diverging dialects. So any user of *katharévousa* had to walk an unsteady tightrope and avoid falling into either incomprehensibility or vulgarity. Those without laborious training in such verbal acrobatics (which meant the vast majority of the Greek population) could choose to ignore the official language altogether and thus exclude themselves from direct access to the law and the state apparatus. Otherwise, they could parrot-learn set formulas which they might not fully comprehend but which would in any case enable them to muddle through.

While the academics were busy deriding the popular language, the poets were writing in it and exhorting people to abandon their prejudices against it. By the end of the 19th century almost all creative writers were using the "demotic" (spoken) language in their works, so that *katharévousa* became solely the language of official parlance and no longer that of cultural life. Nevertheless the struggle continued: people were killed in riots involving adherents of the two opposing linguistic varieties in 1901 and again in 1903, and the article of the Greek Constitution specifying *katharévousa* as the official language (inserted in 1911, in response to this violent polarization) was not abolished until after the Colonels' dictatorship fell in 1974. During this century the language controversy has often tended to be identified with political divisions, *katharévousa* being promoted by the Right and demotic by the Left. It was partly because *katharévousa* had become tainted by its identification with the Colonels' regime that the more liberal (though still conservative) government of Karamanlis that immediately followed it was able to begin replacing *katharévousa* by demotic in all areas of public life.

But the Greeks haven't stopped arguing about their language; indeed, it is still a frequent topic of discussion among intellectuals and non-intellectuals alike. Since 1981 Papandreou's socialist government has continued the process of dismantling *katharévousa*, and the more laid-back style of its speeches and pronouncements has offended many who have found it hard to accustom themselves to a casual use of language for official purposes. The government's abolition of many of the actually functionless diacritics used in writing Greek for two thousand years (but not in the Classical period), which caused so much misery and embarrassment both to schoolchildren and to adults, has been widely criticized. More justified is the criticism of the official policy on the teaching of Ancient Greek, which used to be a compulsory high-school subject but now cannot be studied at school before the age of 16. These moves are often seen as ploys to cut modern Greece off from her roots, depriving the nation of its firm basis in the past and making it easy prey for Americans, Russians, or any other foreign power that might wish to exert its cultural dominance.

The Greeks' desire to bridge the gap between their language and culture and those of the ancients has enormously enriched modern Greek life. However, the Greeks need not be ashamed (as generations of schoolteachers tried to make them) of the language and culture that had developed over the last millennium. Pride in their ancestors often gave the Greeks either an excessive sense of self-satisfaction or, conversely, a feeling of inferiority in relation to their glorious ancestors and their unsatisfactory contemporary condition. Others held the more constructive view that the Greeks should be proud of having kept the Greek language alive through successive periods of foreign domination. Having had their native language wrenched from their mouths in the first grades of school, the Greeks have now been given back their mother tongue. The Greeks were probably the first people to carry out a successful war of national liberation against an alien imperial power; but the poet Dhionísios Solomós warned in 1824 while this war was being waged, that the Greeks would not be free until they had rid themselves not only of their Turkish occupiers but of the pedants who tried to teach them that they were something other than they were. This second liberation did not come until 1974, a century and a half after the first.

Nevertheless, one positive consequence of the language controversy is a fondness shared by all Greeks—whether peasants, poets, neither, or both—for playing with the different varieties of their language. For the Greeks, language isn't simply a means of expression, but an arena in which they can practice their creativity, display their wits, and generally have fun.

MOVIES

On sultry summer nights in Greece, most of the evening entertainment occurs outdoors, and movies are no exception. Few indoor cinemas are air-conditioned. Some are equipped with a rare innovation; the convertible roof remains closed during the screenings before sundown, then movable panels creakily slide apart to expose the

audience to cool breezes and an occasional starry sky.

The rest of the indoor cinemas move to empty gravel-covered lots, alleys or rooftops where people are usually seated on sagging lawn chairs. According to the union of outdoor cinema owners, a survey of tourists named the open-air cinemas as the number two tourist attraction in Athens after the Acropolis.

The atmosphere is appropriately relaxed. Whole families attend and snack bars serve soft drinks, beer, crackers and crisps, but no fresh popcorn. A few operate as cinematic *ouzeries* where one can sit at little tables and nibble on *mezedes* (hors d'oevvres) while sipping an *oúzo*. At drive-in movies, porno movies are usually featured and carhops deliver orders of sandwiches, mini-pizzas and chilled bottles of wine to those adult viewers who are reticent to emerge from their vehicles.

Since many theaters are located in the center of the city, the volume is decreased during the late showing out of consideration for the neighbors. One has a choice of viewing a rather dim picture with adequate sound at the first screening which starts before dark or a clearly defined image with a faint soundtrack during the late showings. Fortunately for foreign viewers, Greeks, in contrast to the

French or Italians, prefer subtitles to dubbing, so only original language versions are shown.

In any case, open-air cinemas are a relaxing, quaint form of entertainment. No new releases are opened during the summer. But there is a veritable feast of films to choose from including popular re-releases of the previous season and weeklong festivals of older classics by notable directors such as Hitchcock, Bergman or Fellini plus the inevitable Kung-Fu movies and slapstick comedies.

Although cinema attendance has dropped in the past couple of years, the 150 or so indoor cinemas remaining in the greater Athens area are still doing respectable business. The admission price is incredibly low, set at an average of 200 drachmas (US$1.50) or less. Much of the decrease in attendance must be attributed to the increased popularity of video players with an estimated $1\frac{1}{2}$ million in use in this nation of 9 million and with sales remaining steady.

Traditionally, domestic fare topped the popularity list but this has been reversed in recent years when foreign action adventures and romances sold the most tickets. The heavy European influence in Greek cinema made many of the quality films too "arty" and slow-moving for general audiences who have grown used to a diet of fast-paced imports, or the crudely-made buffoonery of some Greek comedies. Technically speaking, Greek films show high standards in cinematography and sound.

Greeks often wander into a film in the middle and eat and talk throughout it. Yet, lest one think there is no serious audience, a few art houses in central Athens are doing a solid business by booking earnest European imports and a smattering of American independents. Meanwhile, the after-midnight movie trend has reemerged in Athens in a few central cinemas which show "B" grade thrillers, science fiction and horror flicks. They inspire the spirited and vociferous young audiences to shout humorous commentaries and to create innovative sound effects.

Only a few Greek low-budget farcical comedies and a handful of quality films sold more than 100,000 tickets in recent seasons. The gulf between commercial movies and artistic ones has been great. However, the most popular domestic films of recent years managed to combine "Greekness" with well-developed scripts that have international appeal. Poor scenarios have long been the Achilles' heel in Greek cinema. Some successful recent releases which overcame this weakness are George Katakouzinos' "Angelos," a tragic homosexual love story; Kostas Ferris'

"Rembetiko," a dramatic musical based on the life of a "rembetika" (see Rembetika) singer; Nikos Perakis' "Goldbrick and Camouflage," a clever spoof of the shennanigans of the recruits of a military television station during the Junta period; Nikos Vergitsis' "Revanche," which imparts the flair of youthful Athenian society in a tale of a ménage à trois; and Tonia Markatakis' "Price of Love," about a young woman who defies society in turn-of-the-century Corfu.

The Civil War, following World War II, had been a forbidden topic in Greek cinema until the election of a socialist government in 1981. Pandelis Voulgaris' "Stone Years" based on a true story, focuses on the romance of a couple who were arrested for their Communist affiliations and were only reunited after 20 years imprisonment. This film, along with the others mentioned previously, has been on the foreign festival circuit and was included in the second series of the "Seven from Greece program" which toured the major U.S. cities.

It is painfully obvious that Greek films cannot even recoup their initial investment with domestic distribution alone. The Greek Film Centre, now state run, contributes up to 50 percent of the films' budgets. In order to promote international distribution of Greek films, it has stepped up its festival participation to 35 and 40, including the prestigious Cannes and Berlin Festivals.

The Salonika Film Festival, held each year in October in the National Theatre, screens all of the 20 or so quality films made each year. The notorious third balcony "peanut gallery" is jammed with restless students who are prone to clap and stamp their feet while shouting synchronized slogans if a movie is not appreciated. It can be a grueling experience for a director. However, those who have not fled down the back stairs might be surprised by an enthusiastic ovation at the finish of the film. If you are in Salonika in October, it is worth a visit.

NAMEDAYS

"What's in a name?" asked Romeo. He should have asked a Greek! For here, all sorts of stories piggyback onto names, if you know how to read them. Place of origin, for instance: *Theodorakis* is clearly Cretan, for a name ending with *akis* (meaning "little") bears the slyly ironic tag of this ferocious people. Any *Yannoglou* is sure to have ties to "the City"

(Constantinople), and the common suffix *poulos* (meaning "bird," or "child of") points back to the Peloponnese, as in the case of one clownish ex-dictator, Papadopoulos, "son of the priest."

Since 1983, women are obliged to keep their "maiden" name for life. For legal matters, that is. But before the revision of Family Law, a woman seldom imagined—unless she were rich or Melina Mercouri—keeping her father's surname. Rendered in the possessive case, female surnames (single and married alike) are grammatically telling: Mrs. Papadopoulos really reads "Papadopoulos' Mrs." In mainland Greece, a woman traditionally lost even her first name at marriage, and was known by the feminized form of her husband's: Yorgos' wife became "Yorgina." The symbolism persists. At weddings, girlfriends of the bride jokingly write their names on the sole of her shoe, and explain that she whose name is "rubbed out" first will marry first.

Names are not matters of fashion (how many Yuppies do you know named Mildred or Virgil? how many grandes dames named Tracey?). You find the odd "Tzimmi"— that Greek-American who made good in Tuscarawa and came home to retire—and "Babbi," and (as if "Maria" were not perfectly respectable) "Mary," it's true. And in eras when neo-classical romanticism rages, hordes of mischievous middle-class toddlers are saddled with ponderous names like Kleanthis, Andromachi, Aristotelis, Periklis. Even Lord Byron, the English poet who—though he never saw a battlefield—died

a hero of the Greek Revolution, is regularly reincarnated. But never imagine that naming is a trivial matter.

A Greek baby is not fully a person when it is born, but only when it is baptized, and given a name. Baptism, a ritual more solemn than marriage, which initiates the child into the Orthodox community, is celebrated between forty days and a year after birth. Until then, the child is called simply "Baby," and if—as was more common in past years of high infant mortality—it died before someone —anyone—could baptize it "in the air" by "making the cross" over it three times and uttering a name, it would not be buried in the church graveyard, and its soul was thought to linger in a shadowy netherworld between hell and paradise.

Greeks are amazed how Westerners name their children guided by little more than fashion and personal whim. They themselves follow fairly strict rules: the first boy is named after the father's father, and the first girl after the father's mother (in mainland Greece) or the mother's mother (in most of the Aegean islands). Naming the son after the father, as Americans do, is thought extremely unlucky, even vaguely incestuous: a premature usurping of the father's name. But between grandparents and grandchildren, the inheritance is not fraught. The grandmother greets with delight the baptism of a child with her name. While it ritually acknowledges her individual mortality, it nonetheless assures family continuity: "the name will be heard." Property, too, may be linked to names. On

many islands, first-born Kalliope inherits the house from her mother, Marina, who inherited it from her mother, Kalliope, and so on in an infinite alternation of Kalliopes and Marinas. Likewise, the boy "with the name" will inherit his grandfather's fields, and he (and his wife) will be obliged to mourn for him when he dies.

Certain events can distort this ideal pattern. A man with many nephews bearing his father's name will yield to his father-in-law's desire for a namesake, or a woman trying to conceive may visit a miraculous icon of a particular saint and entreat its help by promising to give the child its name. These do not alter the Greeks' sense that names connect one to a long line of ancestors, perpetually reproducing itself.

If you are Greek, your name links you not just to your own blood ancestors but to the entire Greek (or more accurately, Orthodox) community. Most Greek names refer to a saint or some holy quality, hence, "Sofia," the sacred wisdom. Birthday parties are for kids; the adult Greek has instead a "nameday," the day when the saint for whom he or she was named was "born into" the life hereafter, usually through a rather unpleasant martyrdom. This day is now "celebrated" by the Orthodox faithful. It's an ingenious system; everybody knows your nameday, sparing you the embarrassment of dropping hints to your friends when you want somebody to celebrate with. But there are a few new twists.

The one who celebrates "treats" the guests. The guest may bring sweets or flowers or a bottle of whiskey, but the host provides the feast. On St. Demetrius Day, everyone with a friend or relative named Dimitrises or Dimitra must "remember" him or her (and people often know many Dimitrises and Dimitras) by phoning or stopping by, and at the houses of all these Dimitrises and Dimitras, the evening is a jolly chaos of doorbells buzzing, phones ringing and a constant flow of guests slightly green with the evening's fifth peppermint liqueur, proferring formal good wishes, and absently munching roasted chickpeas.

Mortal namedays blend the formal and the festive, but for the saint it's a more lavish affair. Every community has a saint (sometimes several) which specially protects it, and on that patron saint's feastday, the Orthodox community celebrates with a *panayiri*. The word derives from ancient Greek, referring to a public assembly (all—*pan*—those gathered in the marketplace—*agora*). *Paniyiria* of pagan Greece honored gods and goddesses in a manner combining worship and pleasure, spiritual obligation and commercial interest.

From the fourth century onwards, however, celebrations of the Christian martyrs absorbed the form and many practices of the pagans, and the *panayiri* with its vast bazaar became a distinctively Byzantine institution. Church fathers then—as now—reviled the more worldly preoccupations of buyers and sellers. A Christian writer of the fourth century warned, "A believer must not go to a *panayiri* except to buy a slave, to take care of life and to buy certain other things fitting for existence."

Today's *panayiri* involves the entire community. The saints are honored with prayer and processions, followed by feasting and dance into the wee hours. Like its Byzantine predecessor, many a *panayiri* resembles a Balkan country fair. Crammed and haphazard on a dusty stretch of ground, often a good mile or two from the village, are parked a wild assortment of carts and caravans. At its edges, wizened old ladies and amputees sit cross-legged on shabby rags, beseeching believers, palms cupped for alms. Next to the van selling Sprite and cloying ice-cream bars is a horsecart spread with roasted chickpeas, peanuts, raisins and sunflower seeds. Wedged in between are tables covered with crocheted doilies and embroidered towels for sale to the girl preparing her trousseau, and next to that a table with religious trinkets. Amidst the crucifixes and "Lives of the Saints" pamphlets you can find tiny blue pupils cased in plastic, dangling alongside a silver cross, amulets against the "evil eye." (See "Evil Eye" on pages 275–276).

Baptismal names are public and fixed, but *paratsoúklia* celebrate the idiosyncracies of individual lives. Nicknames of a sort, *paratsoúklia* are an insiders' code. Strangers and tax collectors aren't supposed to know them. Rude and ironic, they commemorate quirks of body and character: Manolis' brawny virility is wryly recalled in the feminized "Manola," Yiorgos' philanderings in "Pouli" ("Birdie"), Theofanis' melancholy in "Katsoufis" ("long-faced"). Men get *paratsoúklia* from their comrades, women hardly ever, except by way of men. The man who worked twenty years in America and returned to marry is dubbed "Amerikanos," and his wife, "Amerikana," though she's never left Macedonia. Badges of individual peculiarity, they sometimes stick, and get passed on to sons and grandsons, until (with the "real" surname slowly erased from memory) the shaggy, secret *paratsoúkli* slips quietly into the bland respectability of an "official" surname.

ORAL TRADITION AND POETRY

Poetry matters in Greece, and this is due, in part, to the fact that for centuries it was sung, not read. Poetry has always been a kind of performance in Greece, a social event. Even today contemporary poets can fill soccer stadiums with fans. Until the late 19th century Greek poetry had little in common with the solitary quill pen traditions of other Western European cultures. This may be because oral poetry was a much more successful way of preserving Greek national identity during the many centuries that Greece was under foreign rule; writing could be censored but no despot could confiscate songs. Even in this century oral transmission, because of its resistance to censorship, has been necessary. **Yannis Ritsos** (1909–), one of Greece's best known poets, was sent to prison along with many other suspected communists during the civil war. There he continued to write his poems. He would bury them in bottles to keep them from the guards but the only way he could get them to his readers was with the help of freed prisoners who, before leaving, learned his poems by heart and smuggled them out.

The fall of Constantinople (or "the City" as Greeks commonly call it) paradoxically enough marks both the beginning of Turkish domination and of Modern Greek poetry. It is at this point that versions of folk songs still sung today were first recorded or referred to in literary texts. The stock formula "I come from the City," although obviously about the fall is also found in modern folk songs, and the well-loved 16th-century Cretan romance *Erotókritos* incorporated many verses from folk songs, verses that are still familiar to Greeks today. Since oral transmission is an inherently creative process, phrases are not expected to resemble their antecedents word for word; the old phrases serve merely as a structure on which to base new variations. While not all critics believe in a continuous poetic tradition dating back to Homer, most agree that a certain continuity can be traced from the 15th century.

Until the War of Independence in 1821 and the founding of the Greek State, song and poetry were inseparably linked, whether composed on paper or passed down orally from generation to generation. In fact writing and singing were often equated:

I don't know how to read or write
but so I wouldn't forget her

I made a song about her, to guard
her well.

But with the emancipation from the Turks national identity was no longer a clandestine matter. Oral transmission formerly the *only* transmission possible now was seen as unreliable. Writing—more fixed and more permanent—became the preferred means for spreading nationalist ideology. The folk song was a stepping stone for poets but not an adequate means of expression in itself. It wasn't reliable enough. The following couplet

recorded more than a hundred years after the passage above, suggests a different relation to writing. The bard is now aware of how writing's permanence makes it the more enviable skill:

I'd like to be a poet and to know
how to write—
then on paper, heroes, I'd fix your
deathly plight.

One of the first proponents of a National Greek Literature was the poet **Dhionísios**

Solomós (1798–1857) from the Ionian Islands. In a letter to a friend he expressed his interest in klephtic folk songs but also stressed that the poet's task was different:

Klephtic poetry is fine and interesting as an ingenuous manifestation by the Klephts of their lives, thoughts and feelings. It does not have the same interest on our lips; the nation requires from us the treasure of our individual intelligence clothed in national forms.

As a matter of fact Solomós' "Hymn to Freedom" has become the Greek national anthem. Nationalist poets such as Solomós may have criticized the ingenuousness of the oral tradition but their poems always aspired to song. Perhaps a similar tendency in British poetry explains Rudyard Kipling's choice to translate Solomós' hymn:

We know thee of old,
  Oh, divinely restored,
 By the light of thine eyes
  And the light of thy Sword.

From the graves of our lain
  Shall thy valour prevail
As we greet thee again—
  Hail, Liberty! Hail!

Along with educators who struggled over which Greek to teach, the *demotic* or the purist hybrid of ancient and modern called *katharévousa* (see Language), poets were also fervently debating language. Their indebtedness to the oral tradition and their romantic organicism made them favor demotic Greek over the more synthetic *katharévousa*. Written poetry was not viewed as particularly different from sung poetry; it was just one step further in the natural development of a Greek National Literature. **Kostis Palamas** (1859–1943) sets up the homeless gypsy as the modern Greek hero who blasphemes tyranny in all forms, not only the Turk but also the supremacy of Ancient Hellas and those who wanted to reinstate her using *katharévousa*. He wrote:

I fear no Turk.
Slavery cannot strike me down
Nor can your Hellas dazzle me.
No outworn creed or cult
Can drug me with its incense.
If I discover a papyrus, I burn it
  to make heat or light.
Unconcerned I watch it kindle
In whatever mouldering ruin it may be,
Palace, abbey, school or temple ...

It would be too simple even in as brief an overview as this to suggest that Greek poetry in the 19th and 20th centuries was all lyricism and nationalism. Over in Alexandria Greece's greatest modern poet, **Constantine Cavafy,** (1863–1933) was doing something totally different. His poetry emphasized writing over song. His poetry seemed to suggest that the human intimacy associated with the oral tradition was no longer possible. His historical frame was neither the glories of classical Greece nor the emancipation from the Turks but rather the slow decay of the pre-Christian and Christian eras. He invoked the pathos of deterioration, and repeatedly poetry was the only solace. Written language had the power to construct something material out of what was being lost. Writing for Cavafy was not just a more durable substitute for singing as it was for Solomós and Palamas but a radically different means of expression. The poem took the place of what was missing. It could even fill the geographical space left by the destruction of a city. This preoccupation is illustrated in his poem "The God abandons Antony":

When suddenly at midnight you hear
an invisible procession going by
with exquisite music, voices,
don't mourn your luck that's
  failing you now,
work gone wrong, your plans
all proving deceptive—don't
  mourn them uselessly:
as one long prepared, and full of courage,
say goodbye to her, the
  Alexandria that is leaving,
Above all, don't fool yourself, don't say
it was a dream, your ears deceived you
don't degrade yourself with empty hopes
  like these.
As one long prepared, and full of courage,
as is right for you who were given this kind
  of city,
go firmly to the window
and listen with deep emotion;
but not with the whining, the pleas of
  a coward;
listen—your final pleasure—to the voices,
to the exquisite music of that
  strange procession;
and say goodbye to her, to the
  Alexandria you are losing.

Even in his love poems there is the sense that by writing the poem becomes a physical replacement for the absent loved ones.

Try to keep them poet,
  those erotic visions of yours,

however few of them there are that can
be stilled.
Put them, half-hidden, in your lines.
Try to hold them, poet,
when they come alive in your mind
at night or in the noonday brightness.

In Cavafy's poetry memory and experience
merge in a distinctly written formulation.

Although the literary establishment to this
day promotes poetry that is more indebted to
the oral tradition, to the supremacy and intimacy of the voice, an alternative canon
might be traced back to Cavafy's more textual
verse. This alternative canon would be more
concerned with writing as the recognition of a
loss, than writing as the preserver of a glorious
past. Outside of Greece Cavafy is certainly
Greece's only well-known exponent of this less
lyrical style. But inside Greece there are many
poets whose poetry problematizes language
and prioritizes writing over singing (for example the poetry of Kostas Karyotakis and

The delphic priestess with her wild, windswept words is the inspiration for the incanta-
tory verse of this modern poet who lived in
Delphi. In his poem "First Rain" he writes:

I became a lyre caressed
by the breath's profusion.
Sweetness filled my palate;
and as our eyes met again
all my blood sang out.

Women poets at the turn of the century
were also very active defining their particular
subjectivity, a doubly difficult task since
society and their fellow poets constantly set
them up as the object, not the subject, of desire
or admiration. **Maria Polidoúri** (1902–1930)
in her poem "To a Bouquet of Roses" expresses
this tension:

If I am the butterfly
you are lacking, open between my lips
the passage, the half-closed heart

some of the surrealist poets like Andreas
Embirikos and Nikos Engonopoulos). Yet
since the lyrical half of Greek poetry is more
readily available in translation I will concentrate on that and only intermittently
refer to the less well-known poetry.

Continuing in the wake of Solomós and
Palamas comes another nationalist poet,
Angelos Sikelianós (1884–1951). But in
Sikelianos' poetry "being Greek" has become
less of the collective project it was in Palamas'
poetry and more a matter of personal identity.

that belongs to you.
Or if you wish, I'll rape
your blossoming secret,
with a passion unknown to your generation
the admiration which keeps you young ...
My breath, your inspiration,
I do not know which wilted your petals ...
which extinguished the light in my eyes ...

She cannot speak for the new emerging nation.
As the female persona she is the butterfly, the
image of emancipation which the male poets

have already appropriated. Instead she takes her positionlessness as the topic and substance of her poem. Like Cavafy and other poets of the alternative canon I suggested above, Polidoúri is interested in how the written text differs from a song. The grammatical confusion between the I and the You in this poem is only possible in writing.

Very much a part of the established canon and probably best known of all the modern Greek poets are the two nobel prize winners **George Seferis** (1900–1971) and **Odysseus Elytis** (1911–). Although their poetry is certainly not devoid of questions about writing both these poets of the generation of the thirties draw heavily on the oral tradition. Rather than comprising a Greek avant garde themselves these poets were just extremely adept at incorporating the techniques of other European modernisms. Seferis introduced Greece to the modernism of T.S. Eliot with its reliance on myth while Elytis imported the other extreme of modernism, French surrealism. And perhaps it is telling that their poetry gained popularity by the oldest trick in the book, oral transmission, through the ingenious scores of the composer Mikis Theodorakis (see Theodorakis etc.). Often in the most out of-the-way places you will hear people singing Seferis' "On the secret seashore/white like a dove/we grew thirsty at noon: /but the water was brackish ..." or Elytis' "A solitary swallow and a costly spring,/For the sun to turn it takes a job of work ..." Some of the poets' phrases may not be as familiar as the old and oral formulas from laments and wedding songs, but in the context of modernization their words are somehow necessary; they provide a choral response to experiences that are outside the vocabulary of traditional folk songs. As part of his Mythhistorema (both a history through myth and a myth through history) Seferis constructs a modern mythology where nature is no longer authentic. In his catalog of the Greek landscape nature is mechanically reproduced like everything else:

Three rocks, a few burnt pines, a
   solitary chapel
and farther above
the same landscape repeated starts again:
three rocks in the shape of a
   gate-way, rusted,
a few burnt pines, black and yellow,
and a square hut buried in whitewash;
and still farther above, many times over,
the same landscape recurs level after level
to the horizon, to the twilight sky.

Here we moored the ship to splice the
   broken oars,

to drink water and to sleep.
The sea that embittered us is deep
   and unexplored
and unfolds a boundless calm.
Here among the pebbles we found a coin
and threw dice for it.
The youngest won it and disappeared.
We set out again with our broken oars.

For Seferis' argonauts myth and history have a message but for Elytis' speaker myth and history have turned into something more like dream:

In petticoats of April first and cicadas of
   the feast of mid-August
Tell me, that which plays, that which rages,
   that which can entice
Shaking out of threats their evil
   black darkness
Spilling in the sun's embrace
   intoxicating birds
Tell me, that which opens its wings on the
   breast of things
On the breast of our deepest dreams, is
   that the mad pomegranate tree?

As it was with the folk song the bard in Seferis' and Elytis' poetry speaks for the community. Their poetry is meant to be read in the context of this longer oral tradition.

The various fragments of poems in this introduction, whether read as parts of a continuous tradition or as disruptive alternatives, are all here to entice the reader to read further. By framing Greek poetry in the context of the oral tradition I have not meant to trap it there; a strong oral tradition has certainly contributed to poetry's popularity in Greece but exclusive emphasis upon it has also helped to draw attention away from the more textual tradition in Greek poetry. If there were more space the contemporary poetry scene would also be worthy of attention, and would certainly present another angle on these issues of orality and literacy. The generation of the seventies in particular are indebted to Cavafy's alternative poetics. In conclusion let us return to Yannis Ritsos whose poetry over the past fifty years has perhaps most dramatically registered this tension between the sung and written text. On the eve of his emergence from the concentration camp on Levros in 1968, Ritsos tried to imagine a new kind of poetry, a regenerative poetry, which would be less concerned with recapturing the past and more concerned with constructing a future. His poem "Return" anticipates the fall of the Dictatorship and without being prescriptive, the ensuing poetic activity of the Seventies and Eighties:

The statues left first. A little later
the trees, people animals. The land became
    entirely desert. The wind blew.
Newspapers and thorns circled in
    the streets.
At dusk the lights went on by themselves.
A man came back alone, looked
    around him,
took out his key, stuck it in the ground
as though entrusting it to an
    underground hand
or as though planting a tree. Then
    he climbed
the marble stairs and gazed down at
    the city.
Cautiously, one by one, the
    statues returned.

[The author is indebted to Rodrick Beaton's
Folk Poetry of Modern Greece, *to Margaret*
Alexiou's The Ritual Lament in Greek Tradi-
tion *and to the translations of George Thomson,*
Edmund Keeley and Philip Sherrard.]

PERIPTERA

Although they may appear limited by their
diminutive structures kiosks are really multi-
purpose powerhouses. Besides filling the
obvious function of newsagent/candystore
they may double as mini amusement parks

(with kiddie rides), sporting goods stores
(including sleeping bags on occasion), iron-
mongers, locksmiths, and for customers with
problems the proprietor may dispense psy-
chiatric or medical advice. Running a kiosk is
like directing an orchestra—one eye on the
telephone meter, one hand giving change and
one ear tuned to the voice of a friend who has
stopped around the back for a chat. How do
kiosk owners cope?

The view from inside a kiosk, or *periptera* as
it is called in Greek, is tight, complex and most
resembles the cockpit of a DC-9. Down low
are a series of tiny drawers in which are
sequestered various sewing needles, thread,
zippers, anti-biotics and usually a supply of
condoms; shelved up higher are sweets and the
rainbow array of cigarettes, while still higher
are assorted shampoos, washing powder and
worrybeads. Items of value, pocket calcu-
lators, watches, gold cigarette lighters and the
like are displayed in little show windows. In
the center sits the *peripteras*, the proprietor,
jammed into two square feet of space yet
firmly in control of the till responding to the
images as they appear on the screen—that
small opening to the front where customers
pronounce their orders.

It is not unusual for a *periptera* to work
shifts of twelve hours in conditions which vary
from furnace-like in summer to chill and damp
in winter (when most cramp their already tiny
space with electric fires or some form of heating). Yet they remain a generally good-
humored lot eager to oblige the lost foreigner
with directions or even the recommendation of

a good local *taverna.*

The kiosks started as gifts from the government to wounded veterans of the Balkan and First World Wars. Many will remark the similarity between the architecture of kiosks and that of military guardposts such as those used by the honor guard in front of the Parliament on Syntagma Square. In a symbolic way the *periptera* are also guard houses where old soldiers prolong their duty, emerging from the military into the commercial sector, watching over and serving the community. Happily they are no longer under attack although thieves do occasionally jimmy their locks in the night.

In Greece everyone wants to run their own business and the more than three thousand *periptera* in Athens alone obviously make this a possibility. Kiosks are almost all family-run and one cannot help noticing the children or grandchildren of the proprietors stopping by for a sweet on the way home from school, or in summer the whole family sitting around a seafront *periptera* eating watermelon which they may offer to share with customers. Kiosks have a personality, and a charm which is part of Greek commerce generally; everything is personal. If a kiosk owner finds that you know a few words of Greek it may take a bit longer to conclude your purchase. They will want to know where you are from.

With only a quarter of the population of England, Greece has nearly the same number of retail shops. Partly this is the reflection of a society which subdivides itself sharply into family and kindred groups, each of which seeks to own a shop, a *magazi.* The idea of working for a stranger is odious; in fact, the word for "employee" in Greek literally means "someone beneath another." Consequently, instead of expanding and enlarging, businesses tend to remain relatively small in size while new businesses are opened to accommodate an expanding market. This swollen number of retail shops cause Greece to have the highest mark-up price in the Common Market. Thus the profusion of kiosks throughout Greece is more than just a peculiarity or a coincidence; it is a part of a whole economic mentality—the *periptera* mentality—the basis of which may be summed up in the slogan, "One family, one business."

QUEUEING

Americans call it "standing in line." Born of American "straight" dealing, it falls positively flat next to the elegant British verb, "to queue," from the Latin *cauda*, for "tail." American "lines" exude a democratic egalitarianism, British "queues" fair play mixed with social distance. But both reveal a belief in rationality and order in the ways of the world.

The Greek version is something else altogether. Can you really call it a "queue?" Waiting at a bus stop in Academias in central Athens, you can just make out a semblance of linearity among the bodies, if only because the metal rails installed for this purpose nudge them into orderliness. Once the bus appears, however, the pretense collapses, and a chaos of anxiously pressing bodies pushes relentlessly through the doorway. Some Athenians say it's just life in a city bursting its seams—too many passengers squeezing into too few buses. That's indisputable. But you see the same anxious crowding on airport runways where—clutching a boarding pass with a guaranteed seat number—passengers trip all over each other to board the plane.

A different body language is no doubt part of the explanation. Greeks are comfortable with their bodies, and they touch each other constantly—in handshakes and kisses of greeting, in the loving pinch to a baby, in the slap on the arm to a comrade—in ways the "colder" northerners touch only their intimates. So, you may discern no hostility in the face of that old lady whose sharp finger jabs into your back and propels you forward onto the bus. But its blankness can be just as annoying. Because when you're a foreigner, with a different sense of your personal space, it's easy to feel you're being treated like just a bulky obstacle in the path of somebody else's seat.

This impersonality has a logic though. It's the inverse of the much-vaunted "personalism" of the Greeks, but not its opposite. Unlike ourselves, Greeks don't imagine they live in a rational universe where all things come to those who wait. There's no place here for the Anglo-Saxon concept of "fairness." For Greeks, the universe is arbitrary and unpredictable—and that goes for God, the Turks and the Greek bureaucracy. Life is a struggle. The goodies are few and the claimants many. You've got to push forward or you're lost. For centuries, the little guys have survived through personal ties to the landowner, the grocer, the banker, and by making friends with more powerful men who had "means" (*mésa*) enough to "help," or who, in turn, had even more powerful "friends." Perhaps these chains of influence linking the peasant farmer to the highest ranks in the centers of power are the nearest thing to an indigenous queue!

REMBETIKA

Q: What is *rembetika*? Maybe when the old *rembetika* composer Rovertákis said, "Rembétika songs were written *for* people who sing rembétika *by* people who sing rembétika .... The *rembetis* is a man who had sorrow and threw it out," he was suggesting that these were private songs that belonged to a particular group of people at a particular historical moment? Could you tell us something about the political/historical environment that originally brought about *rembétika*? How is its early history linked to the 1922 Asia Minor

illegalities on the margins of society, or among the deprived and impoverished urban dwellers? The destruction of Smyrna in 1922 certainly increased the production of *rembétika* and speeded up the processes that led to the development of their singular quality.

Q: Do you think that in contrast to the rural folk song which is often a communal expression of a common sorrow or joy, these urban folk songs are an expression of a more alienated individual?

A: The words of the *rembétika* certainly express more specialized and individualized feelings than do the demotic or rural folk songs. They also differ to some extent from the demotic songs in their vocabulary and metri-

disaster?

A: The *rembétika* is the most original kind of song to have appeared in Greece over the last hundred years. A few examples of the type were already known throughout Greece by as early as 1930, and in the next 15 years these songs became more and more popular, without, however, managing to secure a following among the more well-to-do classes. They received their first recognition from respectable criticism in the '50s. Unfortunately we do not know either when or where or amongst whom they originated. Was it in 1850, in 1880, or in 1910? In Smyrna, in Sýros, or in Piraeus? Among underworld characters living from hand to mouth by various petty

cal structure, borrowing new elements from the lyrics of the light songs popular in the period between the wars, but using the phraseology in a different way, transforming it from the sugary and insipid into something serious and often tragic.

Q: When and why did *rembétika* come back into fashion? What made it possible for a larger audience to appreciate this music?

A: *Rembétika* never completely lost its public. It is simply that in the '60s this public was not to be found so much in the working-class districts of the towns, where most of the population had succumbed to the craze for "light-popular" songs and "smooth" *rembe-*

tika, but among the students and intellectuals.

It was these intellectuals who initiated the rest of the middle class into the world of *rembétika*, which it had previously despised. Thus *rembetika* finally addressed itself to everyone, because it brought back a nostalgic and picturesque past, poverty-stricken perhaps, but in a way more carefree and certainly more genuine than the alienated present.

Q: Do you think there's any use in comparing *rembétika* with the American Blues?

A: The conditions that gave birth respectively to the *rembétika* and the blues are completely different, and the vast geographical distance separating Greece from the United States rules out any mutual influence. The occasional similarities one meets in the verses are entirely accidental.

Q: What was the role of the *rembétissa*, the woman who sang with these underworld characters?

A: Woman, as mother, daughter, lover, is the central figure in the verses of the *rembetika*. But the title of *rembétissa* is appropriate only to the woman who follows the shiftless life of the *rembetis*. And she follows him because she has a good voice and wants to *be* someone, to make a name for herself. She in her turn inspires the men who surround her and, above all liberates herself, becoming the original of the independent woman in Greek society.

Q: Could you tell us something about the two most important *rembetika* instruments, the bouzouki and the baglama?

A: They are very ancient instruments, used by the Assyrians, the Egyptians and the ancient Greeks. The Greeks never ceased to use them, but from time to time simply modified them and changed their names. Thus the ancient *pandoúra* or *pandouris*, the Byzantine *thamboúra* and the post-Byzantine *tamboúras* do not correspond exactly to the modern bouzouki, but they certainly belong to the same family. It is not known when the word "bouzouki" came into Greece from the Lebanon, but it is to be found in certain demotic songs.

Q: For the newcomer baffled by all the available cassettes and records of *rembétika* what do you recommend as a first purchase?

A: Some good records for a first taste of *rembétika* are:

(i) Authentic Songs Recorded in Smyrna and Constantinople before 1922. ACBA 1402 (1982)
(ii) Greek Oriental Smyrnaic-Rebetic Songs and Dances. Folklyric Records 9033 (c.1983)
(iii) Greek Popular Songs in America. Falirea Bros. 22–23 (1984)
(iv) Grèce. Hommage à Tsitsánis. Bouzóuki Ocora. 558.632 (1984)
(v) Grèce. La tradition du ·Rebétiko. Ocora 558648 (1984)

(For good places to listen to live *rembétika* see the Guide-in-Brief).

SHADOW PUPPET THEATER

Shadow puppet theater, whose protagonist in the Greek version is Karaghiozis, was first recorded in Java, China and India from where it spread to Turkey and then to Greece. Karaghiozis takes his name from his prominent black pupil or "karagöz" (black eye in Turkish). He is a short balding hunchback with an enormous arm that he uses to club others over the head. He is a poverty-stricken, uneducated Everyman dressed in ragged clothing and usually barefoot.

Yet Karaghiozis is comical rather than pathetic. He is insatiably hungry, constantly preoccupied with finding food for himself and his family. He survives by his cunning and as need arises, impersonates prominent characters and professionals. These ruses provide only temporary solutions to his problems and eventually he is caught and often beaten and thrown in jail. Although he frequently moans "Ach manoula mou, ti epatha?" ("Oh Mom, what happened?"), he always reappears undaunted in the next episode.

The Karaghiozis stage has a screen of any fine white material stretched across a frame. The figures which are designed by the player, are made of painted leather and synthetic material. They are flat, clean-cut silhouettes held against the screen by the operator and manipulated by horizontal rods with a hinge to facilitate change of direction. A light source from behind, originally oil lamps but now usually electric bulbs, shines through the transparent material of the figures to make them look like stained glass.

The most popular legend about the origin of Karaghiozis identifies him as a blacksmith in Turkey during the reign of Sultan Orhan

(1326–1359). While working on a mosque in Bursa, he and his friend, the mason Hadjiavat, had such humorous exchanges that all construction ceased as their co-workers listened. The enraged Sultan had them hanged but later was remorseful and missed them. To console him, one of his subjects manipulated likenesses of the two dead men on a screen and Karaghiozis theater was born.

The early plays were passed along orally and the puppeteers memorized them but added their own improvisations or created new scripts. Many players adapt classical plots to include comments on politics and to satirize local personalities and events.

Although the Karaghiozis player has assistants, he is still a one-man wonder with an endless array of intonations to suit all roles of the air. More subtly, repetition is used in gesture, movement and speech to parody character types such as the pompous dandy Morfonios from the Ionian Islands. Disguise and concealment are common; Karaghiozis masquerades as a bride which shocks the hapless bridegroom as he lifts the veil. Oddity of physical appearance and behavior is exaggerated.

A typical story is "Days and Tricks of Karaghiozis" written and performed by Frixos Gazepides, a spry septuagenarian who became infatuated with the shadow theater as a young boy. Popular figures of Karaghiozis who are included in this vignette are Aghlaia, Karaghiozis' nagging wife; Hadjiavatis, a well-educated, restrained philosopher who is Karaghiozis' best friend; Barbayiorgos (Uncle

both sexes. He is judged by his mastery of mimicry of regional dialects and speech defects such as stuttering. Energy and skill are needed to coordinate the actions of the figures with the speech. Besides all this, in many performances the player recites poetry, sings and plays an instrument such as the guitar for the musical themes often associated with particular characters.

Above all, Karaghiozis is a theater of laughter. At the most basic level, this is achieved through crude jokes and slapstick; Karaghiozis and his three mischievous children are chased by a foe which results in furniture and bodies being catapulted through George), a tall rough-mannered shepherd from the mountains of Rúmeli. Mr. Skordalias (Mr. Garlic Dip), a wealthy merchant from Nauplia who is an uncle of Aghlaia, is a creation of Gazepides.

"Days and Tricks of Karaghiozis" involves Karaghiozis in a usual money-making scheme that backfires. Mr. Skordalias is preparing to leave for Switzerland for treatment of his extreme near-sightedness. Hadjiavatis meets him and tells him that Karaghiozis died that morning and left without a drachma. Aghlaia is naturally distraught; Skordalias believes him and goes to the house to pay his last respects.

He stoops to kiss the prone body but due to his myopia, kisses the backside rather than the face. The odor emanating convinces him that Karaghiozis is dead and he rushes to the bank to withdraw a large sum of money. He encounters Barbayiorgos on the way who has often been the victim of Karaghiozis' pranks and is skeptical about the news. They both go to Karaghiozis' house to investigate. Instead of finding the dead body and grieving widow, they witness the whole family prematurely celebrating their new wealth by eating, drinking and dancing. The play ends with Karaghiozis getting his inevitable thrashing from the angry Barbayorgios. As he lies bruised on the floor he proclaims, "I couldn't die before because I was hungry; but I would die happily now, because for once, I am full."

Before World War II, Mollas, a famous puppet-master commented, "A monster has come to us from America." He was referring to the cinema which had a technical sophistication that captured the general audience which had been attending the shadow theater performances (see Movies). With the emergence of television in Greece in the 1960s, the shadow plays which were once the entertainment highlight of many a neighborhood, seemed to many oldfashioned and naive.

Less than ten older Karaghiozis players perform now in Greece with no young apprentices being recruited. Just one summer theater and a weekly television program are regularly devoted to shadow theater. Yet, it was apparent while watching an enthusiastic audience of all ages and nationalities during a recent request performance of Gazepides, that this folk art has not lost its universal appeal. The cast of characters reflects the divergence of influences still evident in Greece today. Karaghiozis himself is the embodiment of the innate spirit of the Greek nation. He survives all adversity and starts every new adventure with renewed optimism and energy.

Karaghiozis Players in Athens

Yiorgos Haridimos
Shadow Theatre Haridimos, Lysikratos Square, Plaka, Athens. Tel: 322–4845.
Open from end of May through October.
Performance 9 p.m. Closed on Monday.

Frixos Gazepides
Kyparissias 9, Aegaleo, Athens, Greece.
Tel: 590–5257

Thanassis Spyropoulos Tel: 262–9046

Vangos Tel: 490–0109

THEODORAKIS ETC.

Q: Can you describe what was happening in music during the 1967–1974 military junta?

A: Certain songs which in the ordinary way would have circulated freely went underground, while there was a general increase in the number of songs with hinted messages against the dictators; in fact, a kind of resistance activity and democratic communication went on through the medium of songs.

Q: Why do you think Theodorakis and the ballad writers of the Néo Kýma had enough success during the '60s to ensure Greece a popular music unchallenged by disco and other Anglo-American imports?

A: The '60s was a time of political unrest and saw the suppression of democratic institutions. Since the words 'Greece' and 'Democracy' are inseparably linked, a tyrannical regime must always be foreign to Greece. In times of slavery all peoples go back to their roots, from which they derive the strength to survive as peoples. Nevertheless, this does not mean that the Greeks turned their backs on music from abroad during this period.

Q: Could you describe some of the differences between the calculated compositions of Theodorakis, Hadjidakis and the other Greek composers who have studied abroad and the more spontaneous rembetika and folk musics. Do they appeal to the same audiences?

A: In certain of their songs (especially those written for the cinema) Theodorakis and Hadjidakis faithfully follow the spirit of the rembetika. But in their genuinely important songs they express themselves more personally, and in these one seldom finds striking similarities with the rembetika, even when these songs have a bouzouki accompaniment. The public, of course, has its preferences, but it is not uncommon for the admirers of modern Greek 'composer' songs to like rembetika too.

Q: Even if Greek popular music is not at all like classical, rock, disco or punk, could you still say that it is more influenced by the West than by the East?

A: What is noteworthy in Theodorakis and

Hadjidakis, as in quite a number of their successors, is how well they blend the frequently contradictory western and eastern (Greco-Byzantine) compositional processes. However, I am not prepared to say which source influences them most. In this matter I think that each composer chooses his own path.

Q: Can you talk a little about the collaboration that goes on between Greece's contemporary composers and poets?

A: I don't think we can talk about "collaboration" between composers and poets. The composers usually open anthologies of poetry and set those poems which they like, as they like; in fact they often choose to set the work of poets who are no longer alive, such as Solomós, Kálvos, Sikelianós and Kavadías.

Q: Where do you think Greek music is going?

A: In the days before 1945, when the Greeks were writing waltzes and tangoes, could anyone have foreseen that in a few years Theodorakis and Hadjidakis would open a new epoch in the history of Greek song? I think not. Therefore I prefer to leave this question unanswered.

Unfinished Buildings

There are many jokes about Greek bureaucracy and endless red tape. It's a well known fact that in the Greek civil service there are five people to every one job. Although this diminishes unemployment it has its side effects as well: it often takes five times longer to do anything whether it's going through customs, paying road tax, changing money or registering for school.

For many outsiders it is unfathomable that such simple tasks could take so long. But you have only to take into consideration such practices as *hartósima* (the tax stamps) to realize that efficiency is not one of the main objectives. By law you are required to affix these tax stamps to most official documents but, for some reason, state offices rarely have their own stock. So, in the middle of filing an application you must run down to the nearest kiosk (see *Periptera*) to buy some. Then after climbing four flights of stairs or surviving the ancient elevator crammed with people and coffee trays (see Coffee) you arrive only to find

that the coffee you so charitably balanced on your shoulder in the elevator on the way up was meant for the very civil servant who had been serving you and would therefore hold you up another half an hour. After his coffee break you find out that you also need three copies of one page and a photograph of yourself taken by a particular photographer on the other side of town and so the story goes.

One of the main symptoms of this bureaucracy, or *graphiokratia* as the Greeks call it, is the multitude of unfinished buildings that dot the Greek cityscape. If paying road tax takes a day just think how long a building project could take. It is impossible to forsee the many setbacks. Not only do the zoning laws change with every new government but cultural expectations shift as well. Ten years ago most parents felt it was their obligation to build their daughters houses as part of their dowry even if it was beyond their means. Now, though a young woman may receive an education rather than a house as "dowry," many of these building projects persist, gaining a wall or floor every summer, and, if the house is being built in a strictly zoned area, only at night. This is due to the peculiar law that zoning orders can only be enforced if the offender is caught in the act. Whole floors and extensions and fences go up in the dark. But in all this shady business one law holds: covering over the iron supporting rods and putting on the roof come last, if ever. As long as a few iron supports stick out no tax is levied. This, of course, is the main reason there are so many unfinished buildings in Greece.

Vendetta

Unlike brigandage, which was common throughout Greece, the vendetta tradition was found in only a few regions, where large families, a passionate sensitivity to personal honor and a love for fighting farmed an unholy trinity. Epirus was one such feud-ridden region, but the heartland of the Greek vendetta was the Mani.

William Leake, visiting the Mani village of Vathia in 1805, decided not to spend the night there after learning that a feud had been raging for the past forty years, "in which time they reckon that about a hundred men have been killed."

Some observers, debunking the vendetta "myth" claimed that reports of casualties had been much exaggerated and that there was more shooting than bloodshed. But the 18th-century casebooks of Dr. Papadakis, a Maniot surgeon with a flourishing practice, present a different picture—of heads crushed by rocks, bullet-ridden limbs, stiletto and sword wounds commonplace. "... And one hunts another, and another yet someone else/And neighbour on neighbour, koumbaros(god-parent) on koumbaros/And brother looks on brother like Charon."

But the turbulent Mani described in that poem has subsided into a desolate silence. The main road built since the war transformed the old ways. Now the last signs of the vendetta visible to the traveler are the gaunt decaying stone towers in every village from which rival clans only a century ago attempted to exterminate one another.

WOMEN

Sit in a public place in Greece and the world—men, women and children—will pass you by. But watch more closely and you may begin to feel that this is not the women's world. They pass across this public stage bearing the signs of their errands—a tray of food for the baker's oven, or swollen shiny plastic bags of shopping, or with one or two well-dressed children in tow. Enter stage right, exit stage left. Their real drama is elsewhere. Even those who pause to chat lack the lordly confidence of the men whose every gesture reveals their certainty that they are running the show.

So where is the women's world? Are they kept in the wings, handing out the props and shifting furniture? Or are they performing in another arena? One where the crowds are not so big, perhaps, but where the rewards are enough to live on?

What it means to be a woman in Greece depends very much on which woman. Where does she live, is she married, how old is she, how well off is she? Above all, what choices can she make? Clearly the life choices for a woman of eighty have been very different from those confronted by her granddaughter. But different in which ways; and are there, along with new choices, new constraints?

The life-style of old: The old woman of eighty or ninety, who spends the winter months curled on the corner of a striped divan near the stove and emerges in the summer to sit on a stool on balcony or doorstep, carries memories of a life punctuated by war and

political turbulence. As she dandles her grandchildren and great-grandchildren she is certain that the one thread that runs through all external events is family. But while she has a powerful sense of continuity, which, no doubt, she tries to instil into the generations that follow after, she lives in a world where the very substance of life has been transformed. If, as is likely, she started life in a small village (the cities and major towns all expanded during the course of this century), she will have seen the peasant's daily *aghóna* (struggle) in the fields transmuted into something more like a regular day's work. Women's labor in the fields is still a very significant part of the Greek economy (and it is, in the '80s, beginning to be recognized by the formation of farming-women's organizations with the encouragement of the PASOK government). But it is unlikely to be the intensively heavy work which broke down the health of women in the early part of the century and, very often endangered their babies too. The coming of the "*traktér*," the pride of the farming man, bedizened with necklaces like a favorite horse, has freed women's bodies for lighter labor.

Today's great-grandmother sees younger women able to spend more time in or near the house. In the traditional view a woman without a house is as incomplete as a house without a woman. Within the broader horizons of the modern woman a house may seem a paltry kingdom to inherit, especially if it is one box in a concrete block. But until the present day the link between the woman and the house has been a constant, varying according to economic and ideological constraints. Those wealthy merchants' houses of the 18th and 19th centuries which can still be seen in towns such as Kastoria and Siatista, were decorated inside with a painted profusion of flowers, fruit and friezes of wide rolling countryside. They were gilded cages for the women whose lives were passed within them.

It is commonplace that political repression is often replicated in relations between the sexes. While Greece was under Turkish rule—and in northern areas this period extended until 1912, well within living memory—Turks restricted Greeks and Greek men restricted Greek women. Christians and Muslims competed for the modesty of their women, that area of social relations which is so often the most immediately available source of insult between alienated communities. Notable incidents of Turkish oppression took the form of acts against women (many a female saint owed her martyrdom to a pasha whose attentions she resisted); but the constraints of modesty imposed on women were not simply measures to protect them against tyranny. Women represented, and still in many ways represent, the vulnerable interior of the family. Men's honor is at stake defending it.

The oldest women today often fret at the immodest dress of young women, tapping their wrists with the side of a hand to show where sleeves should end and drawing a line halfway down their chests to show how far the excesses extend. Clothes are certainly strongly symbolic in Greece (of youth or age, social conformity or eccentricity, joy or mourning) but maybe in their reading of the messages of dress, the critics in the older generation disregard the less visible constraints which still have force for many young women—particularly the fact that an unmarried woman is, theoretically, answerable to her father if there is anything about her comportment of which he disapproves.

A woman's relationship to her house, to its physical fabric, affects her whole life. In many areas of Greece (broadly speaking, the south and the islands) there has traditionally been the expectation that the family of a woman who is about to be married will provide a house as well as some furniture and other goods or property. The dowry has strongly affected women's marriage chances and in addition the balance of male and female children in families has been critical for economic success or failure. Sons have sacrificed their inheritance to dispose of their sisters; women have been driven to the brink of suicide as their market value plummets in a family crisis.

Attempts are now being made to limit the power of these expectations, and the dowry is technically illegal. In northerly areas the normal pattern is the reverse: it is the man's family which expects to provide a house, or house room, for each new couple. Traditionally families extended as the sons married and brought their wives to the parental house where they were subject to the often tyrannical rule of the *petherá* (mother-in-law) who had no doubt suffered at the hands of her own *petherá* when she was the new "bride." As families began to expect more comfort and privacy and, it is said, became less willing to "have patience" with each other, it became normal for only the latest married son to remain at home. Now it is the norm for a new house or flat to be made available for the new couple. But in these cases it is still most likely to be the mother-in-law who will keep a supervisory eye on the household management and child-rearing practices of her son's wife.

The house—a woman's showcase: Once a woman is established in her own house, she can exhibit her worth through the objects in it. As a visitor to a Greek house, you may be shown into the *salóni*, and the shutters may be thrown open in your honor so that every item in the room sucks up light like a sponge. The furniture gleams with a limpid varnish, the mirror-backed cabinet is filled with phalanxes of glasses of every category. There are glinting outposts of ornaments in every direction and, above, a formation of globes or crystal drops which defies both gravity and any creeping invasion of darkness at the room's edges. The challenge to the housewife is clear; every speck of dust which is allowed to settle will be reflected back as two. But all is under her control. Her banner is raised victoriously on every side. Every item of furniture is dressed overall with a festive array of fabrics embroidered, crocheted, tasseled and trimmed. They are crisply ironed and draped just so, pressed so that their corners hang precisely at the midpoint of the table edges, or pushed into ripples by heavy vases.

The visitor who is left alone for a little longer, while the "Kyría" goes to make coffee in her back kitchen, may begin to dwell upon the stitches, the accumulated moments of womens' hours and days—subtly toned flowers in blues and reds and gold, silky green leaves, intricately counted patterns of crosses involving many handfuls of colors from the haberdasher's glass topped drawer, encrusted edges, patient repetitions in the millions of tugged loops of a crocheted curtain. It is the crystallization of many moments, calm moments, anxious moments, stitches drawn between sighs—of boredom, hope or resignation. Or more often, stitches shared with groups of neighbors, patterns borrowed from friends, hems and tassels wrought to the sound of laughter and gossip and never far from the clink of coffee cups.

Greek women's handiwork is no mere pastime. It is bound closely to the traditional sense of woman's role and destiny. A young girl learns to sew so that she will be marriageable. These skills symbolize, obscurely, all that she must be. The bride must show that she has the wherewithal to "dress" the house, all the ornamental and comfortable fabrics which will line the nest of marriage. The usually impressive accumulation of fabrics and furnishings is brought to the new house with some ceremony—in the past on the backs of a string

of well laden mules, now more often in a truck which creeps through village or neighborhood with the horn sounding and shouts of merriment issuing from the back. In viewing the goods, other women typically express admiration for the bride's "golden hands" and there is a strong sense that it is more than her skill that is being displayed. She has laid out her virtue before them. In the cities or wherever money is more available than time it has become customary for more and more items to be purchased. But handwoven fabrics were prized even when they were more common and today mothers and grandmothers hand on to their daughters items which probably lay in their own dowry chests, shrouded in the whiff of camphor, all their married lives.

Housework is, of course, a kind of display and in Greece the performance is almost always virtuoso. In both towns and villages many tasks are appropriately done in public view—hanging the washing, beating rugs, airing bedclothes, taking food to the bakeries to be cooked and shopping. A woman's work is manifested to the world. And although the house is a private realm it is opened to visitors; the worst would be assumed of a housewife who never opened her doors to her neighbors. A woman makes her command over the physical things of life apparent to all. Seeing a woman washing a dusty public pavement, early in the morning, doubled over and using a tiny handmade broom, seeing her whitewashing the steps with the sole purpose, it might seem, of enabling them to be made dirty so that they can again be cleaned, one might be inspired to ask, why does she enslave herself in this way? Older houses are not built or furnished for convenience and many tasks are performed with a frequency disproportionate to their laboriousness.

There is more than one answer and more than one demand for this symbolic tax from women. Firstly, they are restoring order against the natural state of dirt and disorder that would otherwise take over. As each housewife sweeps the road in front of her house and whitens the trees and paving stones, she marks a territory where harmony is restored, where, in religious terms, that family has printed the stamp of redemption upon the fallen world. Correspondingly, grace is manifested in material things—if the bread rises well and the vegetables grow plump the family would seem (both to themselves and to others in the community) to be enjoying the protection of God and the saints.

Almost every house or flat has, somewhere, its saints who inhabit a quiet niche along with fragile dried leaves or flowers from a bygone festival, a phial of holy water from a place of pilgrimage, and the quickly faded wedding crowns of artificial twigs. It is part of the process of caring for the house to attend to the icons. Icons need light. A small glass filled with water and olive oil with a floating wick provides a steady golden bud of flame. These ancient and simple lamps may be replaced by an electric bulb (do the saints blink at the lurid aquarium green?) for every day. But at a time of crisis, and before a major festival, the woman of the house cleans and fills the little oil lamp, and fits a new pink wick, and maybe sets similar flames burning before the icons in a local church or roadside shrine. Women take responsibility for the family icons. They say the prayers and visit churches. "*Eméis plirónoume*" they say: "We women pay."

On the other hand, the reverse, secular, side of this coin is marked with the same price. Given that in Greek society, moral status is thought to be *visible*, every housewife, every individual, is vulnerable to the remarks of others. Even for those supported by a modern political ideology it is difficult to stand against a norm set by peers and neighbors.

It is the bearing of children which brings a woman to her full status. It would be difficult to exaggerate the importance given to marriage in Greece. The feeling that there is no more appropriate mode of living for an adult of either sex is prevalent, and it is widely assumed that monks and nuns who explicitly reject it must have been disappointed in love. The fact that marriage is essential for a complete life is symbolized by the ritual in which

chance of marriage.

Having married, a woman finds the pressure is relaxed. Momentarily. The next anxiously awaited event is of course pregnancy. This anxiety may be forestalled if a bride is already pregnant. This has been common in some areas as much in the past as today, while elsewhere a woman's protest: "My Dad will kill me!" has not always been an exaggeration. Pregnancy outside engagement has always been a serious matter in every part of Greece. Now that the concept of engagement is becoming less formal (the families may at first have a simple verbal understanding, rather than exchanging rings and gifts, or, even less formally, the young people may come to an understanding by themselves) there is both greater flexibility in sexual matters and

a young adult who dies unmarried must be dressed in wedding clothes and, in a poignant ceremony, is "married" in the coffin with a single wedding crown.

Marriage and the woman's worth: The pressure for women to marry is intense. They are given less time to do so than men; an unmarried woman in her late twenties is a matter for concern to her relatives whereas a man can acceptably retain his "freedom" (unmarried people are always described as "free") until forty or so. Women who choose not to marry have to confront the stubborn belief that they are single not through their own choice but of necessity. Circumstances have proved too much for them, runs the typical interpretation, with the result that they have missed their

greater scope for misunderstandings.

Although childbearing is their fulfilment, Greek mothers often talk of the suffering involved in having children. They don't just mean the pains of childbirth, either. They expect to suffer anxiety on the child's behalf from its first breath until it is safely married. They share this suffering with the *Panagia*, the Virgin Mary, who is the model of womanhood explicitly offered by Greek Orthodoxy, and whose sufferings on behalf of her son are remembered during the course of the Church's year. Women are "Eves," caught in the trammels of human sexuality and only redeem themselves by bearing, as the Virgin Mary did, a child.

Motherhood means nurture. The mother

gives substance to her child while she is pregnant and the process does not stop there. Mothers tend to feed their children with great anxiety (a reason sometimes given for preferring bottle-feeding is that "at least you can see what it has eaten"). Unfortunately many a Greek child is aware of this and exploits the mother's sensitivity on this matter. The degree of a mother's love for her family can be represented by the effort she puts into preparing food. If she produces boiled macaroni day after day she will be aware that she is skimping. The favorite dishes—*dolmádhes, pastítsio*, and *pítta* for example—take hours to prepare and involve a number of different processes. A *hortópitta* even requires that the cook should wander the fields in search of the right kinds of weeds.

While the ideal of motherhood is nurturing, ideally a mother should train her family to fast—that is to control the types of food they eat at certain times in order to achieve religious purity. Fasting is regarded quite flexibly these days in many households, with the consequence that women often casually enquire what other families are eating—so that their standards are neither higher nor lower than the average. Strict fasting means abstention from meat, all animal products and oil. Special dishes (*ladherá*) are made with oil and vegetables as a kind of intermediary level of restraint. There are women, mostly old, whose faces light up as they say, during a fast period, "Not a drop of oil have I eaten, not a drop ...", who take their gift of abstention to the Vespers every evening and appear to enjoy a peaceful detachment from physical needs. These women may be viewed with suspicion by the less devout and the irreligious, lest they start to use their piety as a ground for judging others. For families there is a balance of opposing values to be maintained for to make children fast more than is generally thought to be necessary is a denial of mother love.

Upon death: A woman's care of the other members of the family extends to everyone in it but is concentrated especially on those who are most helpless—children and the dead. Care for the dead also, paradoxically, involves the preparation of food. But it is in fact a kind of reversal of the nurturing process. During life a person needs to build up the body for life and health. After death it becomes necessary to let the body melt, unburdening the soul and purifying the person ready for ultimate resurrection. By giving food away to other families a woman helps the dead person she is caring for to lose, symbolically, unwanted flesh. On the five "Soul Saturdays" in the year black-clothed women can be seen in cemeteries all over Greece. They busy themselves with candles, or polishing the marble plaques around the graves, but most importantly, they take foil-wrapped bundles of food and, like children on a picnic, they swop with their neighbors—a piece of cake for a piece of *loukoúmi* (a Turkish delight) and the special kind of wheat porridge known as *kóllyva* for a long ribbed biscuit. Such food is accepted with the words "May God forgive." It is an orgy of giving, each woman going away with a package as big as the one she brought. If for any reason a woman is unable to fulfil her duties towards the dead she is quite likely to see the person in dreams. When she ceases to experience such dreams the dead person no longer needs her care.

Changed values: The pattern of expectations and fulfilment with regard to women's lives has changed little over most of the 20th century. Until very recently what had changed was the nature of the materials with which a woman expressed her commitment to the family and its continuity. Clothes are now shop-bought, foods are richer, household furnishings often have an electrical plug attached. Today both old and new values coexist—the importance of being a wife and mother with the importance of being able to earn a good income. And it might be added that provision for the combination of the two roles is not worse than in many other European countries—especially given the usually reliable support of a young woman's mother in the background. What was and has remained important has been the need for a woman to know that she has value. Where a woman's dowry has been external to herself she has been able to feel, once she is married, a solidity and security in relation to her husband. Where her value has been symbolized by the trivia of household furnishing she has still had a means of display and self-presentation. Now more substantial though less visible qualities are being appreciated—education, competence out in the world, the quality of being a *drastiria*, a "woman of action." But these new values do not necessarily mean freedom, and certain visible indicators of a woman's character—the way she dances, what she drinks, whether she smokes—are still given weight. Most of all, a woman is still expected to be linked to a family.

This is the most shocking thing about

as a joke or an insult but which Greek city women take in their stride) and even a seat in a *kaffaneio*. Acceptance of such "privileges" simply makes overt the peculiar position that a foreign woman is necessarily in.

Women are likely to respond to the visiting anomaly with a barrage of questions: "*Mamá, babá, zoun?*" ("Mom, Dad, are they alive?"); "*Adélfia?*" ("Brothers and sisters?"); and, pointing to the ring finger of the right hand, "*Andras?*" ("Don't you have a husband?"). These are not routine polite enquiries but are attempts to clarify what is, for them, the most important thing about a person—the link with family responsibilities.

The traveler can conduct herself as she wishes. She can allow herself to be placed in the sexually free category or emphasize that

foreign women in Greece. Women traveling in Greece are often a little unnerved by the separation of men's and women's worlds. Add to this the rather obvious attentions from men which foreign women attract in areas accustomed to tourism and the female traveler is left wondering how she is viewed by local people.

"Pseudo-men": Because Greek fathers and brothers have traditionally been the guardians of female sexuality (the assumption being that individuals of either sex are not all that good at saying "no" on their own account) women who evidently have freedom of movement and economic independence are thought likely to be unconstrained in other ways. In this they resemble men. Foreign women are often given small chances to be "pseudo-men," offered cigarettes or strong drink (offers which women from small and traditional villages would take

she's a nice family girl. But, powerful as these stereotypes are, there is no need to be pushed into either. There is such a strong sense of "how *we* do things" that there is a corresponding streak of open-mindedness in most Greeks, ready to accept that in your country you do things differently.

This acceptance of other values is having to be exercised more and more within the Greek family, between generations. The family's sphere of interests was once visibly contained within its own four walls and its fields. Now it is interpenetrated by the world, by television, by education, by its members' movements throughout Greece and further afield. But it represents, still, the front line of contact with the real moral issues of human weakness, human needs and mortality. This is where women are at work.

Xenomania/ XENOPHOBIA

As a small country Greece has always had to contend with the *Xénos*, the foreigner. Whether as invader or just as visitor, the *Xénos* has had a big impact on the Greek conception of self. A *Xénos* isn't simply a non-Greek, he or she might be a Greek from another town. In the past when a woman married a man from over the mountain she married a *Xénos*. The songs sung at her wedding were often laments wishing her well in the "after life." Departure for another village and departure for another world were equated. The *Xénos* who carried her off was viewed with as much suspicion as any foreigner. Even today in many places the Athenian is almost as much a *Xénos* as the punk rocker on his package tour from England. But whereas fifty years ago xenophobia was the predominant sentiment, today its flip side, xenomania, is by far more prevalent.

Tourism has been on the rise since the early sixties. During the dictatorship (1967–1974) foreigners were encouraged to buy property tax-free. And although Pasok, the socialist government in power since 1980, certainly doesn't patronize foreigners to the same extent, their policies show that they recognize tourism as Greece's number one industry. In 1985 tourism by itself brought in almost as much money as all other industries combined — from olive oil to scuba masks to large scale machinery.

But xenomania is not without its problems; in many ways Greece was not prepared for such expansion in the tourist industry. A baker and his wife on Ámorgos who can earn three times their salary by renting out rooms to foreigners during the summer may not think too much about the aesthetics of the port or the influx of less traditional mores when they decide to add some guest rooms to the family house. And although the wife may complain when her husband starts running after blond Swedes (see Kamáki) or when her kids start demanding products she has never heard of like Coppertone tanning lotion the casual relationship between a fast expanding tourist industry and her family's whims may not be deeply explored. And even if she does blame the tourists she depends on them for her family's livelihood. *Xénos* has clearly become a much more ambivalent term now that it pivots freely between "phobia" and "mania." One moment the tourist is the one to thank for the new road and the relative high standard of living and the next the tourist is the one to blame for sex and drugs and rock and roll.

What is particularly interesting about Greek tourism is the way it attends to the foreigner's particular material needs but still obstinately refuses to accommodate the foreigner's different pace of life. A trendy hotel in Hydra may serve all the right cocktails in its bar but the owner will absolutely refuse to get up before ten to fix breakfast. Obviously according to him no one who is anyone gets up that early. He hasn't taken into consideration that a trendy German may not have the same sleeping habits as a trendy Greek.

The speed with which Greece has become the vacation paradise for all of Europe means that until recently it was more equipped for backpackers than the clientele of luxury liners. But this is slowly changing as Greeks realize that it needs to attract this latter group in order to profit from tourism. Tourists can look forward to more and more varied services. And also perhaps to a less manic reception, neither xenophobia nor xenomania but xenophilia.

Yoghurt

Most visitors to Greece rave about the yoghurt. Rich, thick and creamy in its commercial form or tart and slippery in the *spitiko* (home-made) version it is a much more substantial food than the watery yoghurt you find in other countries. For this reason the American habit of "drinking" a yoghurt for lunch is completely unfathomable to a Greek. Yoghurt is neither a beverage nor a meal. It has its own peculiar culinary function. Like parentheses it separates the meal from the rest of daily activities. It cleans the palate. Meals often start with a plate of *tsatsiki* (a delicious thick spread of yoghurt, cucumber and garlic) or finish with a bowl of yoghurt smothered in the region's honey and walnuts. Whether as a preface or a finale to a meal the yoghurt's smooth consistency helps digestion. In general yoghurt is regarded as soothing. In fact in Greek when the sea is calm they say it is 'like yoghurt'. In recent years England has begun importing Greek yoghurt to pacify holiday makers when they return to dreary Britain after two weeks of Mediterranean sun and sea. Once upon a time tourists brought back pockets full of pebbles and shards as momentos of their trip, now they can forego the fuss: a quick trip to the corner deli provides all the ingredients for a real Greek *tsatsiki*. Although the Delta and Fage yoghurt available barely resembles its tangy, crusty *spitiko* counterpart, a good imagination can still conjure up the smell of thyme and oregano and the distant bells of sheep and goats scampering across a mountainside.

ZORBA

Nobody has done more for the image of the earthy, passionate, impulsive Hellenic hedonist than Hollywood's ethnic chameleon, Anthony Quinn. Nikos Kazantzakis may have invented Zorba but only Quinn could dance that lusty rogue of a peasant into the hearts of millions. Kudos must go, too, to Director Eli Kazan, who captured in stark black-and-white the austerity—of social mores no less than of mountains and architecture—of a highland Cretan village.

Though most foreigners know him as "Zobra the Greek," the original novelistic version is entitled *Aléxis Zorbás*—that adjective ("the Greek") Kazantzakis would have found quite superfluous. Readers of the Greek novel know he couldn't be anything else. In fact, it's clear that Zorba was a real person, hailing—some say—from a small town on the Macedonian peninsula of Chalcidice, whom the author met when Zorba came to work on Crete.

He may have been mortal once, but Zorba has acquired mythic qualities. He's a modern stereotype, perhaps, but with a long lineage. European elites long regarded peasants as "noble savages" close to home, and romantic literature and travelers' accounts abound with rustic peasants dancing their troubles away. In Greece, there's a special twist; the peasants' "wild" dances and "discordant" music gets likened to ancient Dionysian revels. Yet however trivialized they have become, Zorba and his predecessors represent quite sober explorations of a very old philosophical problem in Greece: the power of passion and the limits of reason. It's a problem not confined to the ancients, nor to European philosophers grounded in that classical tradition. It has also been a core issue of Orthodoxy, whose rational, worldly power has always coexisted with the most mystical of theologies. This abstract, otherworldly faith flourished in the sensuous landscape of Kazantzakis' native Crete.

Kazantzakis was preoccupied with spiritual questions all his life. Though he eventually left the Orthodox Church, there is no doubt that his own personal conflicts over sex, as well as his literary themes, come from early religious experiences. His novel about Zorba explores the problem of body and soul which always obsessed him. "The Boss"—who many say was really Kazantzakis himself—is an intellectual trapped in a world of words. He keeps himself from sin by repressing all feelings of desire for forbidden things. But he is totally unable to act. The Boss' paralysis finds its antithesis in Zorba, who confronts his desires—for food, for wine, for the charms of women—naturally, even defiantly. Kazantzakis may be forgiven his hint of romanticism, for the rude peasant here is not just noble, but wise. It's the scholar who needs to be taught by Zorba, the unlettered laborer who "knows himself."

It's somehow apt that for most of us today, Zorba is a celluloid, not a literary, figure. Words are not Zorba's *forte*. For all his pearls of earthy wisdom (laced with Quinn's exclamations in superbly accented Greek) Zorba knows the limits of words. When something profound happens—as when his daughter dies—Zorba must dance! Be it ecstasy or sorrow, Zorba seems to say, the body is better at translating the ineffable. Much the same message emerges in the film "Never on Sunday," as Melina Mercouri, playing the whore-with-a-heart-of-gold, dances joyously at quayside with eager young sailors. How else can she get that stuffed-shirt scholar, Homer, a Greek-American estranged from his own roots, to understand what life's about?

Zorba, Melina, Dionysus, the dancing Greek—reincarnated under tourism in fanciful, distorted guises which sell everything from package holidays to tape cassettes—still express something about what it means to be Greek: about dramatic self-assertion before a skeptical public, about the pleasures and tensions of sociability, about passion and control. If foreigners barely understand what dancing, feasting, even smashing plates, mean to Greeks, we nonetheless find the exuberance we see there irresistible. For in Zorba and the rest we discern a spontaneity and collective *bonhomie* lost in the anonymity of our own more industrialized societies. Greeks and foreigners alike keep Zorba alive, because Zorba is "good to think with"—not just about Greeks, but about ourselves.

Hotel Grande Bretagne
ATHENS

**Tel.: Automatic Direct - Dial System 3230-251/9,
3250-701/9 (72 lines) Reservations: 3225-312
Telex: (21) 9615 Cables: HOTBRITAN**

*The oldest and most famous hotel in Athens, linking the elegance of
the past with the modern comfort of the present –
For over a century the favourite meeting place of international
celebrities.
400 spacious rooms all with private baths, the majority redone
in sumptuous marble; now equipped with minibars, color T.V.,
"news-at-a-glance", piped music and Video;
25 private suites – the latest "The Presidential" – all decorated
with rare antiques –
Fully air-conditioned and centrally heated –
Restaurant, cocktail bars, the internationally famous "G.B. Corner"
with its late night service –
Banquets and conference facilities –
Ballroom internationally known for the splendour of its receptions –*

Guide in Brief

Traveling to Greece   312
Travel Information   313
Getting Acquainted   313
Tourist Information   315
Health and Emergencies   315
Transportation   315
Communications   318
News Media   319
Festivals and Seasonal Events   319
Sports and Recreation   321
Cultural Activities   324
Nightlife   325
Accommodations   326
Dining Out   327
Survival Greek   330
Further Reading   333
Appendix   336
  Restaurants   336
  Tourist Police Phone Numbers   337
  Accommodations Listing   338
  Airline Offices   345
  Embassies and Consulates   347
  Tourist Offices Overseas   349
  Museums and Sites   350

Art/Photo Credits   356

Index   358

Traveling to Greece

By Air: Greece has good air connections with all five continents and is serviced by numerous international airlines. There are different ways of flying at a much lower cost than the standard airline ticket (APEX, stand-by, last-minute seats, "bucket shops"), and you may want to inform yourself of the different possibilities, and of their related advantages and disadvantages, before buying a ticket. The great majority of airline passengers traveling to Greece make **Athens Hellenikon Airport** their point of entry. If you are flying with Olympic Airways you will arrive at the **West Air Terminal.** All other airlines service the **East Air Terminal.** Between the two terminals there is taxi service, and buses with departures every 20 minutes.

Between central Athens and Hellenikon there are various connecting services. A **taxi** ride from the West Terminal to Athens (Syntagma/Omonia) should cost approximately 400 drs. and will take roughly 30 minutes. From the East Airport it should cost approximately 500 drs. and will take slightly longer. There's a fee of 15 drs. per bag as well.

Bus service is much cheaper and works well if you're not in a rush. Between the West Terminal and Syntagma, the Olympic Airways bus runs every half hour for 100 drs. and the blue city bus #133, which is considerably slower, for 30 drs. Between the East Terminal and Syntagma the yellow Express Bus #18 runs every 20 minutes for 80 drs.

Between Piraeus and the East-West Terminals, the yellow Express Bus #19 runs to Akti Tzelepi for 80 drs., right to the port center. The same journey by taxi costs roughly 500 drs. from the West Terminal and 350 drs. from the East.

By Sea: By far, the majority of visitors entering Greece by sea do so from the west, that is from Italy. You can catch a boat to Greece from Venice, Ancona, Bari and Otranto, but the most regular service is from Brindisi. Daily ferry lines (somewhat less frequent in the low-season) connect Brindisi with the three main western Greek ports: Corfu, Igumenitsa and Patras. Corfu is a nine-hour trip; Igumenitsa 11 hours; and Patras 16 to 18 hours, depending on whether it is a direct boat or one making stops in Corfu and Igumenitsa. Igumenitsa is the ideal port of call for those setting off to see central-western Greece. Patras is best if you want to head directly to Athens or into the Peloponnese. Regular buses and trains connect Patras and Athens (four hours by bus). If you plan to take your car with you on the boat you should make a reservation well in advance. Otherwise, arriving a few hours before the departure time should suffice, except during peak seasons when booking in advance is advisable.

Italy and the west, however, are by no means the only provenance for Greece-bound sea travelers. Southward, boats connect Alexandria and Piraeus once every 10 to 15

VOYAGE PITTORESQUE

days; eastward, boats run weekly between Haifa, Limassol and Piraeus, and once every five days between Volos, Cyprus and Syria, not to mention the numerous crossing-points between the East Aegean Islands and the Turkish coast; northward, frequent boats connect Piraeus and Istanbul, and in the summer boats run twice a month between Odessa (USSR) and Piraeus.

By Land: From Europe via Yugoslavia. The overland route from northwestern Europe to Greece is a long one—some 1900 miles from London to Athens. It is a rather arduous and impractical travel option if you're just trying to get to Greece for a brief vacation, but it can be an interesting trip if you make the journey a part of your vacation. By car there is an E route that runs through the interior of Yugoslavia, entering Greece just above Thessaloniki. There are also inexpensive bus services, like the famous Magic Bus, which connect Athens and Thessaloniki with many European cities—a three and a half day trip from London. The various trains that you can take from northwest Europe will take about as long as the bus, will cost considerably more, but may get you to Greece feeling more intact. Hitching to Greece is also a possibility, though hitching through Yugoslavia is reported to be difficult.

From Asia via Turkey. If you are traveling to Greece from Asia you'll pass through Istanbul and cross into Greece at the Evros River. The recommended route is by car or bus. The road is good and the journey from Istanbul to Thessaloniki takes approximately 15 hours; various bus companies run the route. The train has the mythic appeal of running the route of the old Orient Express, but unless you're a great train fan the travel time may be prohibitive: some 25 hours from Thessaloniki to Istanbul. The Thessaloniki-Istanbul trip crosses the fascinating region of Thrace: a fine adventure if you have the time and the spirit to hitchhike through it.

Travel Information

Passports and Visas: With a valid passport citizens of Western Europe, the United States, Canada, Australia and New Zealand can enter Greece and stay in the country for up to three months. No visa is necessary. To stay longer than three months you must obtain a permit from the Aliens Bureau in Athens (9 Halkondili St.). Citizens of other countries should contact the nearest Greek embassy or consulate with regard to visa requirements.

Customs: According to Greek Customs you are allowed to bring into the country duty-free: all used personal belongings (clothes, camping gear, etc.); foodstuffs and beverages up to 10 kilos; 200 cigarettes or a comparable amount of tobacco; 1 liter of distilled spirits or wine; and two packs of playing cards(!).

You may also bring one of each of the following: a camera and film; a movie camera and film; a projector; a pair of binoculars; a portable musical instrument; a portable radio, phonograph or tape recorder; a bicycle; and sports gear (such as skis, tennis rackets, etc.).

You may bring $150 worth of new articles duty-free (excluding electronic devices) provided they are intended for your personal use or as gifts, but not for resale.

It is prohibited to import narcotics, medicine (except limited quantities prescribed by a licensed physician for your own use), explosives, weapons and (yes, that's right) windsurfers—unless a Greek national residing in Greece guarantees it will be re-exported.

For other specific restrictions regarding the importation and exportation of such things as animals, plants, shotguns, pleasure craft and antiquities contact the nearest Greek embassy, consulate or Tourist Organization.

Currency and Exchange: An unlimited amount of foreign currency and traveler's checks may be brought into Greece. However, if you plan to leave the country with more than $500 (or an equivalent in other currency) in bank notes you must declare that sum upon entry into Greece. Each traveler is permitted to import and export no more than 3,000 Greek drachmas.

All banks and most hotels are authorized to buy foreign currency at the official rate of exchange fixed by the Bank of Greece. Though it's safer to carry most of your currency in traveler's checks, it is convenient to carry a limited sum in US dollars. On those occasions when you can't find a place to cash checks you'll usually find a Greek who is interested in changing drachmas for dollars.

Getting Acquainted

Climate: The Greece seen in tourist posters is a forever warm and sunny place. And it is, by European standards, warm and sunny. But this picture does not do justice to Greece's considerable climatic variety. The north and inland regions have a "modified continental" climate, meaning that the winters are quite cold and summers very hot. In Yanina and Thessaloniki, for example, snow and freezing temperatures are not uncommon. In the mountain regions winters are even more inclement. The southern islands, most of the Peloponnese and the Attic Peninsula conform more to the traditional Mediterranean image: a long season of sun and warmth extending roughly from mid-April to mid-October. But here too the winters are cool and rainy.

In general, late spring (April–June) and fall (September–October) are the best times to visit. During these periods you'll find mild to warm temperatures, sunny days and fewer tourists. In July and August you'll find Greece at its sultriest and most crowded. Still, millions of tourists seem to prefer the heat and the company, choosing this period for their vacation in Greece.

Clothing: If you visit Greece during the summer months you'll want to bring lightweight, casual clothing. Add a sweater or jacket to this and you'll be prepared for the occasional cool night breezes. Lightweight shoes and sandals are ideal for Greece in the summer, but you'll also want to bring a pair of comfortable, already broken in walking shoes. If you plan to do any hiking in the mountains or on the islands bring lightweight hiking shoes. A hat or scarf is also highly recommended for protection from the intense midday sun. In general both Greeks and tourists dine in casual dress. You'll only need formal dress if you plan to go to fancy establishments, casinos, formal affairs, etc. If you visit Greece during the winter months bring the same kind of clothes you would wear during spring in the northern part of the United States or central Europe: that is, be ready for rainy, windy days and temperatures ranging between 40 and 60 degrees fahrenheit (3°C–16°C).

While in Greece be aware of the social significance of the way you dress, and of how the Greeks perceive it. Greece, like any other country, has a set of codes, both stated and implicit, which defines the socially acceptable range of attire. The Greeks will not expect you as a tourist to dress as they do. In certain places and regions, however, you will encounter requirements or conventions concerning the way you dress. To enter a church, men must wear long pants and women, sleeved dresses. Often these will be provided for you at the church entrance if you do not have them. Not complying with this code will be taken as insulting irreverence on your part. Nude bathing is another activity which merits discretion. Nude bathing is legal on very few Greek beaches, though socially acceptable on many. The main rule-of-thumb is this: if it is a secluded beach and/or a beach that has become a commonly accepted locale for nude bathing you probably won't be bothered by, nor offend, anyone.

Lastly, you may need to conform to the socially acceptable dress code depending on the region you are in. On Mykonos, for example, male and female tourists alike will shock no one by wearing shorts, a swim-suit or going-bare-chested in most public places. But this same dress will be severely alienating if worn in a mountain village in Epirus or Crete or in any other area less accustomed to tourists. The best approach is to observe what people around you are wearing and to dress accordingly.

Time Zone: Greek time is two hours ahead of Greenwich Mean Time. So, when it is noon in Greece it is 10 a.m. in London, 5 a.m. in New York, 8 p.m. in Sydney.

Like the rest of the Common Market, the clock is advanced one hour during summer to give extended daylight hours.

Electricity: 220 AC is the standard household electric current throughout Greece. This means that appliances from the United States require converters. Greek outlets and plugs are different from both American and most European types, so you'll probably need an adapter as well.

Banking and Business Hours: All banks are open to the public from 8 a.m. to 2 p.m. Monday through Friday. Some banks close half an hour earlier on Friday. In heavily touristed areas, however, you may find banks open additional hours and on the weekends for currency exchange.

The schedule for business and shop hours is somewhat more complicated. Business hours vary according to the type of business and the day of the week. The main thing to remember is that businesses generally open at 8 a.m. and close on Monday, Wednesday and Saturday at 2.30 p.m. On Tuesday, Thursday and Friday **most** businesses close at 1.30 p.m. and reopen in the afternoon from 5.00 p.m. to 8.30 p.m.

You'll soon learn that schedules are flexible in Greece (both in business and personal affairs). To avoid disappointment, allow yourself ample time when shopping and doing business. That way you may also enter into the Greek spirit of doing business, in which a good chat can become as important as the matter of business itself.

Public Holidays

New Year's Day—January 1

Epiphany—January 6

Shrove Monday, First Day of Lent

Feast of the Annunciation/
   Independence Day—March 25

Labor Day and Flower Festival—May 1

Good Friday

Orthodox Easter

Assumption of the Holy Virgin—August 15

"Ohi Day," National Holiday—October 28

Christmas Day and Boxing Day—
   December 25–26

Credit Cards: Many of the better established hotels, restaurants and shops accept major credit cards. The average pension or *taverna* does not, however. Inquire before making your purchase.

Tipping: Most restaurants and *tavernas* add a 15 percent service charge to the bill, so a tip is not normally expected. When service has been particularly good it is customary to leave some small change on a plate for the waiter.

Just as important as any such gratuity, however, is your appreciation of the food you eat. Greek waiters and restaurant owners are often gratified and proud when you tell them you like a particular dish.

Tourist Information

If you would like tourist information about Greece before or during your trip, write, call or visit the nearest **Greek National Tourist Organization** known as the G.N.T.O., or E.O.T. in Greece. There are 15 regional G.N.T.O. offices located across the country. (*See* Appendix for listing.)

The most complete G.N.T.O. office is centrally located in Syntagma Square in Athens at this address:

E.O.T., Information Desk, National Bank of Greece, Syntagma Square, 2 Karageorgi Servias St., Tel: (01) 322-2545, 323-4130.

The Greek Tourist Police, located in most large cities, can also be helpful in providing you with information about hotels and other

services. They can also help you address a wide variety of travel-related questions and problems (*See* Appendix).

For information and assistance related to motoring contact **ELPA**, the Greek Automobile Association, which grants the same help to members of home-country auto clubs as it does to its own members:

ELPA, 2-4 Messogion St., Athens Tower B (779-1615) and 6 Amerikis St., near Syntagma (363-8632).

Health and Emergencies

Greece does not have any serious diseases apart from those that you can protract in the United States or the rest of Europe. Citizens of the United States, Canada and United Kingdom do not need any health immunizations to enter the country.

The drinking water in Greece is safe.

In Greece there are certain pharmacies which are open outside normal shop hours and which work on a rotating basis. If you need a pharmacy at one of these times you can find out which ones are open either by looking at the card in your nearest pharmacy's window (which gives details on 24-hour pharmacies) or by consulting a local newspaper in which this information is given.

In case of a medical emergency requiring hospital treatment in Athens—call 166. If for some reason this fails, call the local tourist police—171 in Athens; for elsewhere see listing in Appendix. They should speak English and will have information as to which hospitals have emergency facilities.

The Greek health system will be bewildering to the tourist who needs to make use of it, particularly in an emergency. Perhaps most important in emergencies is to find a competent speaker of both Greek and English who can make the necessary maneuverings for the patient's safety and inform you of what is going on. If you're entirely helpless, try calling your embassy. US citizens can call the "**emergency**" number 721-2951 in Athens.

Transportation

Boats: It's hard to imagine a trip to Greece without a boat trip. Nearly every island in the Greek seas can be reached by one kind of boat or another, be it a large car ferry, small passenger boat or fisherman's *kaiki*. Pireus is the nerve center of the Greek ferry network, and chances are you'll pass through it at least once.

In general, you can get information on ferries at the port police (in Pireus and most other ports), known as the *limenarhio* in Greek, at most NTOG offices and at certain travel agents. The *limenarhio* has the most complete and up-to-date information. The NTOG bureau in Syntagma Square in Athens offers a weekly schedule which should be checked for accuracy. And when you inquire at a travel agent be aware that they sometimes will inform you only of the ferry lines with which they are affiliated. In the high-season the routes are numerous and it's worthwhile looking around before purchasing your ticket. It's also advisable not to purchase your ticket too far in advance of the boat's scheduled departure: very rarely do tickets for the boat ride actually sell out; more frequently there will be changes in schedules and you're left trying to get a refund. It's also possible to buy tickets on board and, though, it is sometimes more expensive, it's a last-minute alternative.

When you board your vessel in Pireus, be sure you're on the right boat. With the number of last-minute changes, delays etc., it's possible to get on a boat headed to some other destination, or one not stopping at your chosen island.

All the above invokes this suggestion: be flexible when traveling the Greek seas. Apart from schedule-changes, a bad stretch of weather can keep you island-bound for as long as the wind blows. Strikes too occasionally are called during the summer, usually lasting a few days. However, when they do occur, there's usually advance notice given in the news media.

If you're traveling by car, especially during the high season, you'll have to plan somewhat further ahead. This is because during the peak season, some lines are booked for many weeks in advance. Also if you want to book a room for an overnight trip during the high-season, it's a good idea to book ahead. Otherwise gamma class—also known as deck, tourist, third—is the classic, cheap way to voyage the Greek seas. There's always a space of one sort or another—in community with an international multitude, singing around a guitar, passing a bottle around, under the stars. And if the weather turns bad you can always go inside to the lounge, snack bar or some quieter hallway corner.

Apart from the major network of ferries there is also a whole informal sub-network of fishing boats that can get you to smaller, more remote islands. Sometimes these boats cater to tourists, advertising their services in the harbor. Other times, if your destination is especially obscure, you'll have to ask around.

At the other end of the naval spectrum, you'll find scheduled hydrofoil service to certain islands on the "Flying Dolphins." These connect Pireus with most of the Argo-Saronic region (Aegina, Poros and many other ports, as far as Monemvasia) as well as Volos with the Northern Sporades (Alonissos, Skiathos, Skopelos etc.). This is the executive way to island hop: the hydrofoils are more than twice as fast as normal ferries and twice as expensive. You'll get there quickly but unless you get one of the few available spaces aft, you'll have to weather the somewhat bumpy ride in a seat inside.

Domestic Airlines: Olympic Airlines is the exclusive operator of domestic air routes in Greece. Most areas of the country are well-connected by air routes to and from Athens. A few routes run directly out of Thessaloniki and Heraklion as well. As traveling across the land and sea is half the fun of being in Greece, you'll probably choose to fly as an expedient because you want to cross an unusually great distance in a rush (Thessaloniki and Rhodes or Heraklion, for example). Flights are considerably more expensive than boats, buses and trains (two and a half times more on the average), though still cheap as compared to domestic flights in other countries. The flight between Thessaloniki and Athens costs less than $30.00. You can book tickets at any Olympic office. Fare information and timetables are available at most NTOG offices and many hotels. For information and reservations by phone, call: 9616161.

Buses: A vast network of bus routes spreads across Greece, called KTEL. KTEL is a privately run syndicate of bus companies whose buses are cheap, generally punctual and will take you to almost any destination that can be reached on wheels. Among Greeks it's the most popular way of traveling, so you'll have good company. KTEL buses often have a distinct "personal touch"—many drivers also own the bus (or have some other "familial" stake in it), decorating and treating the bus with great care. They're proud of the bus and of the way they drive it.

The most important thing to note about KTEL is that in larger cities there will be different bus stations for different destinations. Traveling from Thessaloniki to Halkidiki, for example, you'll leave from one station, and to Ioanina, from another.

An additional bus service is that of **OSE**, the state railway organization. This is a much more limited service and runs only the major routes.

City Buses: Nearly every city bus in Greece has a coin-operated ticket machine inside it. A ticket costs 30 drs. Have exact change ready, as the driver won't have any to give you.

In Athens you can also get around by the metro. Since there is only one line running from Piraeus to Kifissia, there are a lot of places it can't take you. For certain trips, however, such as from Piraeus to central Athens, it can be quite convenient.

Trains: The best thing about rail travel in Greece is the price; it is even less expensive than taking the bus. Otherwise the Greek rail service known as **OSE**, is quite limited, both in the areas it reaches and frequency of departures. Greek trains are also quite slow and, unless you are doing the Athens-Thessaloniki run overnight in a couchette, you'll probably find the bus more convenient.

You can speed things up by taking an express train for a small surcharge. If you're on a tight budget you can really cut costs by taking the train round-trip, in which case there's a 20 percent reduction.

Taxis: Taxis in Greece, especially in Athens, is a subject that merits a guide book to itself. It may well be that your taxi "experience" in Greece will figure among the most prominent memories of your vacation. Perhaps the Greek taxi experience is best divided into three stages for analytical purposes.

First: getting a taxi. It's nearly impossible at certain times of the day, and probably worst before the early afternoon meal. When you hail a taxi, try to get in before stating your destination. The drivers are very picky and often won't let you in unless you're going in their direction. If you have to say it, say it loudly and clearly (and with the right accents) as they may well otherwise just pass you by. If you see an empty taxi, run for it, be aggressive. Otherwise you'll find that some quick Athenian has beaten you to it.

Second: the ride. Make sure the taxi meter is on when you start out, and not on "2"— that's the double-fare which is only permitted from 1 a.m. to 5 a.m. Once inside you may find yourself with company. Don't be alarmed. It is traditional practice for drivers to pick up two, three even four individual riders, provided they're going roughly to the same area. In these cases, make a note of what the meter-count is. In fact, because taxis are so cheap they end up functioning as a

mini-bus service. Here too is often where the fun begins. Packed in with a Greek mother with her shopping bags overflowing with groceries, a chic Kolonaki businessman and a radical bohemian university student, you may find yourself in the middle (literally) of some rather interesting conversations. If, however, you are alone you may find yourself chatting with an ex-seaman who tells you a few yarns from his days in the United States, or perhaps with a driver who speaks no English at all.

Third: paying up. If you've traveled with company make sure you aren't paying for that part of the trip that happened before you got in. Otherwise the meter will tell you the straight price which may be adjusted according to the following tariff regulations:

Minimum Fare	DRS 110
Fare Starts at	25
Rate per km. Inside City Limits	23
Rate per km. Outside City Limits	39
Waiting Time, Per Hour	240
Surcharge from Railway Stations, Airports, Seaports, International Bus Stations	30
Night Hours: 5–6 a.m., Surcharge	30
1–5 a.m.—Tariff "2"	Double Day Rate
Baggage over 10 kgs. Each	30

Some drivers will quote you the fair price, others will try to rip you off. If the price is clearly above the correct price, don't hesitate to argue your way, in whichever language, back down to a normal price.

In recent years various Radio Taxi services have started up in Athens. They can pick you up within a short time of your call. These taxis, however, are often more expensive than the regular ones.

Driving: Having a car in Greece enables you to get to a lot of otherwise inaccessible corners of the country. As a tourist you will be able to drive for up to four months without having to pay Greek road taxes. When you enter the country with your car it will be "written into" your passport. This entry will state that you are not allowed to leave the country without your car. If for some reason you want to leave without your car, you are obliged to have it "sealed" and withdrawn from circulation before your departure. **Warning:** this process can be very complicated and time-consuming, and a real problem if you have to leave in a rush.

It is recommended that visiting foreign motorists possess an international driver's license. These are available through the auto club in your home country, or, in Greece from **ELPA**, the Greek Automobile Touring Club.

Greek traffic control and signals are basically the same as in the rest of continental Europe. However, the actual practise of Greek driving has little in common with driving in Frankfurt or Oslo. Translate Zorba on wheels, if you will. A red light is often considered not so much an obligation as a suggestion. Greece has the highest accident rate in Europe after Portugal, so—drive defensively! Also, Greece now has a mandatory seat belt law. If you don't wear it you risk getting tagged with a considerable fine.

Renting a Car: Renting a car in Greece is relatively expensive in comparison with other European countries. Prices vary according to the type of car, season, and length of rental and do not include local taxes and duties which can add to about 18 percent of the bill. Payment can generally be made with major credit cards. An International Driver's License (see above) is usually required and you must be at least 21 years old. A few recommended firms in Athens are: **Hertz**, (tel. 922-0102/03/04); **Avis**, (tel. 923-8822 or 922-3760); **Hellascars**, (tel. 323-3487). You can also make reservations through the **Association of Car Rental Enterprises** in Athens, 314 Syngrou Ave., Kallithea (tel. 951-01). If you're a member of your home country's automobile club, chances are you're automatically granted full services from ELPA. For information call: 779-1615 (in Athens).

Renting Motorcycles, Bicycles, Scooters: On most Greek islands and in many mainland tourist areas you'll find agencies that rent small motorcycles, bicycles and various types of scooters. On the islands these are certainly the way to go. For a reasonable price they give you the freedom to wander where you will. For longer periods, rates are cheaper. Before you set off make sure the "bike" of whichever sort actually works. Ask to take it for a test spin down the street. Otherwise you may get stuck with a lemon or, worse, they may hold you responsible for its malfunctioning when you return it. Above all, be careful. More than one vacation in Greece has been ruined by the bumps, scratches and bruises of a moped accident.

Chartering a Yacht: Chartering a yacht is one of the more exotic ways of island-hopping in Greece. It is by no means cheap, although renting a boat with a group of friends may not far exceed the price of renting rooms every night for the same amount of people.

Depending on your nautical skills and your taste for autonomy you can either take the helm yourself or let a hired crew do so for you. There are over 1,000 yachts available for charter in Greece, all of which are registered and inspected by the Ministry of the Merchant Marine. For more information about chartering a yacht in Greece contact:

The Greek Bareboat Yacht Owners Association, 56 Vas. Pavlou Street, Kastella-Piraeus (tel. 452-5465).

The Hellenic Professional Yacht Owners Association, 43 Freattydos Street, Marina Zea, Pireaus (tel. 452-6335).

The Greek Yacht Brokers and Consultants Association, 36 Alkyonis Street, P. Phaliron, Athens (tel. 981-6582).

Cruises: If you'd like to leave the planning and sailing and cooking in someone else's hands, then a cruise may be just the thing you want. A score of different Aegean Sea cruises are available, some limited to Greek territory, others ranging as far as Venice and Port Said. Their length also varies considerably, from a one day jaunt in the Argosaronic Gulf to a 14-day tour of the east Mediterranean. The names of cruise companies offering Mediterranean and Greek Island cruises are listed below. For more information see a travel agent.

Chandris Cruise; Cycladic Cruises; Epirotiki Lines; K Lines-Hellenic Cruises; Hellenic Mediterranean Lines; Intercruise LTD.; Mediterranean Sun Lines; Sun Line Cruises; Viking Yacht Cruises.

Communications

Postal Services: Greek post offices are officially open Monday to Friday from 7:30 a.m. to 7:30 p.m. and on Saturday until 1:00 p.m. In practise, however, the hours are much more restricted. Certain sections within the post office, such as Registered Letters and Parcel Collection, may close as early as 1:30 p.m. Some regional post offices are closed by mid-afternoon. So, if you want to get something done at the post office, it is advisable to do it in the morning.

Postal rates are subject to fairly frequent

change so you'll do best to inquire at the post office. Stamps are available at the post office, and from many kiosks (*periptera*) and hotels for a slight surcharge. If you want to send a parcel from Greece remember **not** to wrap it until a post office clerk has inspected it. Some post offices will then provide you, for a fee, the necessary materials to wrap it up. Otherwise you'll have to bring your own wrapping paper, string, scissors etc. If you're sending home bought goods, get the store to do it for you. Sending a package from Greece can be an exasperating experience.

Letters can be sent Post Restante to any post office. Bring your passport when you go to pick up mail.

Telegrams: Telegrams can be sent from the OTE (see below). There are at least four different types of cables that you can send: the regular cable; the urgent cable which costs twice as much; the greetings telegram, again twice as much; and the letter telegram.

Telephones: Most kiosks have phones, and this usually is the most convenient way to make a local phone call. A call costs five drs. There are also coin phones, usually red, that may be found in coffee shops, hotels, restaurants and kiosks as well. And in certain places you'll also find phone booths—the blue ones for local calls, the orange for long distance.

You can also make long distance calls from any one of the many kiosks, which have metered phones. However, a call from a kiosk will cost somewhat more than from the state phone company, OTE. Still, sometimes getting to the local OTE is such a hassle that you'll find the 15–20 percent additional charge worth it. Many hotels also have these metered phones.

Most sizeable Greek towns and cities have an OTE office where you can make long distance calls and send telegrams. Some in the larger cities are open 24 hours-a-day, others from 7:30 a.m. to 11:30 p.m.

For a listing of the area codes of major Greek cities *see* Appendix.

News Media

The Press in English: There are two main English language publications which provide news and information for tourists and residents in Greece—*The Athens News* (a daily newspaper), and *The Athenian* (a monthly magazine). *The Athens News* contains a smattering of world news taken from wire services,

Greek news coverage, advertisements and other announcements, and an often bizarre rubric, "From the Police Files." *The Athenian* has articles on various aspects of life in Greece (politics, culture, travel) and useful information on what is happening in Athens. The "Athens Organizer" is a centerfold with a fairly comprehensive list of useful telephone numbers and services. A newer magazine, *30 Days: Greece This Month*, is another monthly magazine worth mentioning, with a more specialized focus on Greek political and business life. All three of these publications are available at most kiosks in downtown Athens and in other areas of Greece frequented by tourists.

Radio and Television: ERT 1 and ERT 2 are the two Greek state radio channels. ERT 1 is divided into three different "programs." First (728 KHz) and Second (1385 KHz) both have a lot of Greek popular music and news, some foreign pop and occasional jazz and blues. Third Program (665 KHz) plays a lot of classical music. ERT 2 (98 KHz) is much like the first two programs.

News can be heard in English, French, German and Arabic on the First Program at 7:40 a.m. every day of the week; in English twice a day on ERT 2 at 2:00 p.m. and 9:00 p.m. The BBC World Service offers news on the hour (plus other interesting programs and features). The best short wave (MHz) frequencies on which to pick up the BBC in Athens are: 3:00–7:30 a.m. GMT—9.41 (31 m.). 6.05 (49 m.). 15.07 (19 m.); 7:30 a.m.–6:00 p.m. GMT—15.07 (19 m.); 6:30 p.m.–11:15 p.m. GMT—9.41 (31 m.). 6.05 (49 m.). U.S. Armed Forces Radio (AFRS) operates 24 hours a day at 1594 KHz and 1484 KHz with news on the hour.

There are two state-owned and -operated television channels in Greece—**ERT 1** and **ERT 2**. These channels often transmit American and English movies and programs which, conveniently for the English-speaking viewer, are not dubbed, but rather carry Greek subtitles.

Festivals and Seasonal Events

(Partial Listing of Festivals)

January 1	Feast of St. Basil: All over Greece.
January 6	Epiphany—Blessing of the waters: All over Greece.

January 8	"Gynaecocracy"—men and women switch roles: Villages in the areas around Komotini, Xanthi, Kilkis and Serres (village of Monoklissia).		litary parades in major cities.
		Christmas season	All over Greece. Little children sing carols door-to-door for a small gratuity.
February–March (the three weeks before Lent)	Carnival season: All over Greece. Some villages with celebrations of special interest are: Naousa, Veria, Kozani, Zante, Skyros, Xanthi, Hios (Mesta, Olimbi), Galaxioi, Thebes, Poligiros, Thimiana, Lamia, Kefalonia, Messini, Sohos, Serres, Agiassos (Lesvos), Karpathos, Heraklion, Amfissa, Efxinoupolis (Volos), Agia Anna (Evia), Rethimna, Patras.	December 31	New Year's Eve. More carols. Most of Greece plays cards on this occasion. Special celebration in the town of Hios.

(Seasonal Events)

		April–October	Sound and Light. Performances in Athens at Acropolis; in Corfu at Old Venetian Castle; Rhodes at Palace of the Nights. Evenings.
Shrove Monday	Beginning of Lenten fast. Picnics ·in the countryside. Kite flying: All over Greece.	May–October	Rhodes. Theater, concerts, dance, etc.
March 25	Independence Day—anniversary of the day Bishop Germanos raised the standard of revolt against the Turks at Kalavrita in 1821: Military parades in all main towns.	May–September	Folk Dancing by the Dora Stratou Group at the Filopappus Theater.
		May	Folklore Festival at Elevsis.
		June–August	Heraklion. Concerts, theater, opera, etc.
Easter Cycle	Good Friday, Holy Saturday and Easter Sunday celebrated throughout Greece.	June–September	Athens Festival. Ancient drama, opera, music and ballet in the Herod Atticus Odeon.
April 23	Feast of St. George: Celebrated especially in Kaliopi (Lemnos), Arahova, Assi Gonia (near Hania) and Pili (Kos).	June	Rethymnon Wine Festival.
		mid-June–late-August	Lycabetus Festival. Theater performances in the Lycabetus Hill Theater.
May 1	Labor Day/Flower Festival—picnics in the countryside: All over Greece.	July–September	Epidaurus Festival. Performances of ancient drama in the open-air Epidaurus Theater.
mid/late-May	Anastenaria: Fire-walking ritual at Agia Eleni (near Agia Serres) and at Langada (near Thessaloniki).	July–August	Philippi and Thassos Festival. Ancient drama performances in the ancient theaters at Philippi and on Thassos.
August 15	Assumption of the Virgin: Festivals all over Greece. Major pilgrimage to island of Tinos.	mid-July	Dafnes Wine Festival (near Heraklion).
September	Cricket on Corfu.	late-July	Music Festival. On the island of Ithaca.
October 28	"Ohi Day"—anniversary of Greek defeat of invading Italian army in 1940 and Metaxas' response to the Italian ultimatum: "No." Mi-	August	Dodoni Festival. Ancient drama performances in ancient theater at Dodoni.

August	Epirotika Festival—Ioannina. Epirot cultural and artistic events.
August	Olympus Festival—near Katerini. Various cultural events in village of Litohoro and in the Platamona Castle.
August	Hippokrateia Festival—Kos. Various cultural events.
August	Rethymnon. Various cultural activities at the Venetian Fort.
mid-July–early -September	Dafni Wine Festival (near Athens).
early-July– mid-August	Alexandroupolis Wine Festival.
early- September	Thessaloniki Trade Fair.
October	Thessaloniki Dimitria Festival. Theater, music, ballet, etc.

Information and tickets for many of the above events can be obtained from the: **G.N.T.O. (E.O.T.) Festival Office**, 2 Spirou Miliou Arcade, (entrance from 4 Stadiou St.), Tel: 322-1459 or 322-3222, Ext. 240.

Sports and Recreation

Greece offers a wide variety of possibilities for sports and recreation. The following is a partial listing of these activities and where you can do them.

Water Skiing: You'll find facilities for water skiing at: Vouliagmeni (on the coast southeast of Athens); Agrinio (Lake Trihonida); Volos; Edessa (Lake Vegoritida); Ioannina; Thessaloniki; numerous locations on Corfu; Hania, Crete; Elounda, Crete; Kithera; Mitilini; Porto-Heli; Poros; Rhodes; Skiathos; Gerakina, Halkidiki; Kalithea, Halkidiki; Halkida; Hios.

Sailing: Numerous locations in Greece have sailboats for rent. There are sailing schools, housed in the naval clubs of the following cities: Athens (Paleo Faliro); Thessalniki; Corfu; Volos; Syros; Kalamata; Alexandroupolis.. Further information can be obtained from: the **Sailing Federation**, 15A Xenofondos Street, Athens, (tel. 323-5560, 323-6813).

Windsurfing: You'll find windsurf boards for rental at many popular Greek beaches, and at all the beaches run by the G.N.T.O. For information: the **Hellenic Windsurfing Association**, 7 Fil Filelinon Street, Athens, (tel. 323-0068, 323-0330).

Fishing: Where can't you catch a fish in Greece? In the villages of most islands you will find boats and fishing tackle for hire. If you'd like some suggestions contact: the **Amateur Anglers and Maritime Sports Club**, Akti Moutsopoulou in Piraeus, (tel. 451-5731) or the **Piraeus Central Harbormaster's Office**, (tel. 451-1311).

Diving: Greece is **not** the place to come to for scuba diving: submarine activity with diver's breathing apparatus is forbidden in all Greek waters (seas, lakes and rivers), with the aim of preserving the nation's cultural heritage of submerged antiquities. However, mask and snorkel are permitted and can add a whole other dimension to your swimming in Greek waters.

Tennis: You'll find tennis facilities at the tennis clubs in the following cities: numerous athletic clubs and centers in Athens; Glifada; Kalamaki; Thessaloniki; Patras; Corfu; Heraklion; Hania; Larissa; Ioannina; Rhodes; Halkida; Volos; Alexandroupolis; Serres; Agrinio; Katerini; Veria; Kavala; Trikala. Many hotels and resorts have tennis facilities as well.

Golf: Greece is by no means a golfing country. Still, if you get the yen to tee-up try: The Glyfada Golf Course and Club, tel. 894-6820 (18 holes); The Afandou Golf Club, Rhodes, tel. (0214) 51225/6 (18 holes); The Corfu Golf Club, in the Ropa Valley, tel. (0661) 94220/1 (18 holes); The Porto Carras Golfcourse, near Neos Marmaras, Halkidiki, tel. (0375) 71381, 71221 (18 holes).

Health Spas: You'll find health spas with hydrotherapy in the following locations: Aedipsos, Evvia; Eleftheron, Kavala; Kaiafa, Illia; Kamena Vouria, Fthiotida; Kyllini, Illia; Kithnos, Cyclades; Langada, Thessaloniki (also with mud baths); Lefkada, Ikaria; Loutraki, Corinth; Methana, Saronic Golf; Platistomo, Fthiotida; Smokovo, Karditsa; Therma, Ikaria; Thermopylae, Fthiotida; Vouliagmeni, Attica; Ipati, Fthiotida.

Skiing: Most Greek mountains have good snow cover for skiing from December to March with some of the higher mountains (Olympos, Parnassus and the Pindus) skiable until May. The following mountains have ski-lifts and are almost exclusively devoted to down-hill skiing, though there are also cross-country ski rental: Mount Vermio, Naoussa (chair-lift); Metsovo (chair-lift); Mount Pelion (chair-lift); Mount Parnassus (chair-lift); Mount Vitsi, Vigla Pissoderiou; Mount Vrondou, near Serres; Mount Dirfis, Liri; Mount Lefka Ori, Kallergi, Crete; Mount Mainalon, Ostrakina; Mount Olympus, Vrissopoules; Mount Pangeo, Kiladea Orfea; Mount Timfristos, Karpenissi; Mount Falakro.

For further information contact: the **Greek Skiing and Alpine Federation**, 7 Karageorgi Street, Athens, (tel. 323-4555).

Hiking and Mountain Climbing: Greece is a paradise for hikers and mountain climbers, with extensive trails and trail systems, mountain refuges (see chart), and expanses of mountains and forests untouched by the tourist masses. For information on trails, maps,.refuges and excursions contact the **Greek Alpine Club** in Athens at Eolou 68-70, (tel. 321-2429), with offices in most major towns in moun-

National Parks

Park	Location	Size	Geology	Flora	Fauna	Approach
Lake Mikri Prespa	Prefecture Florina NW Greek-Albanian Yugoslavian borders	4,650 Ha	Alluvial, calcareous gneiss, granite	Quercus macedonica, Juniperous excelsa	Waterfoul	Florina-Kastoria very good road
Samaria	Prefecture Hania-Crete (Lefka Ori)	4,850 Ha	Limestone, schist	Cupressus sp. Acer, Juniperus Olea oleaster, Platanus sp.	Cretan wild goat (curpa aegargrus cretica)	No road inside only trail network Pavilion at Xyloscalon
Parnassos	Prefecture Boetia-Phocis Phthiotis	3,513 Ha	Limestone	Abies, Ostrya, Junipers	Fox, wolf, squirrel	From Delphi or Amphiclia forest roads on the border. Ski center
Pindos (Valia)	Perivoli Grevenon Epiros	12,935 Ha	Serpentines, flysch, gabbro, fagus silvatica	Pinus nigra P. leucodermis boar, trout abies quercus	Ursus arcto wolf, wild goat	From Ioannina few roads impassable during winter
Olympos	All eastern slopes above Litochoron	3,998 Ha	Mostly limestone	Pinus nigra leucodermis, fagus	Wolf, fox, hare	Network of forest roads and trails. Metochi-Stavros-Prionia. Mountain refuges. Ski installations
Oeta	Prefecture Phithiotis	3,010 Ha with border zone 4,200	Sandstone formations and locally limestone	Quercus sp. fagus silvatica, castanea vesca P. nigra	Oeta wild goat, fox, wild boar, jackal, partridge	From Lamia foot trails. Mountain refuge
Mount Parnes	30 kms from Athens (Attiki)	3,812 Ha	Limestone, schist	Abies cephalonica, Ionica, P. halepensis Q. coccifera, arbutus unedo (broad leaf evergreen)	Hare, fox, jackal	Athens-Aghia Triada. Breeding reserve on game
Ainos	Cephalonia Island	2,842 Ha	Limestone	Abies cephalonica	Fox, hare, jackal	Patras by ferry to Sami, from there by road
Vicou Gorge	Zagoria Epiros	3,412 Ha	Limestone	Ocer, ostrya quercus sp.	Wolf, bear	From Ioannina to Monodendri

Ha = Hectare = 10,000 square meters

Mountain Refuges

The Greek Skiing and Alpine Federation has organized the following mountain refuge huts:

Mountain	Location	Altitude (Meters)	Capacity (Persons)	Information Telephone
CRETE				
Lefka Ori	Kalergi	1,680	40	(0821) 24647, Hania
Lefka Ori	Volikas	1,480	30	(0821) 24647, Hania
Psiloritis	Prinos	1,100	16	(081) 267110, Heraklion
PELOPONNESE				
Taigetos	Varvara	1,600	28	(0731) 22574 and 26444 Sparta
Parnonas	Arnomousga	1,450	35	As above
Panahaiko	Psarthi	1,500	50	(061) 273912 Patras
Panahaiko	Prassoudi	1,800	16	As above
Helmos	Pouliou Vrissi	2,100	16	323-4555 Athens
Ziria	Megali Vrissi	1,650	50	As above
Ziria	Portes	1,750	20	As above
Menalo	Ostrakina	1,540	24	(071) 21574 Tripolis
Menalo	(refuge)			(0756) 21227
CENTRAL GREECE				
Parnassus	Sarandari	1,900	20	323-4555 Athens
Parnes	Bafi	1,150	100	323-1867 Athens
Parnes	Varimbombi	600	12	246-9050 (refuge)
Iti	Trapeza	1,800	28	(0231) 26786 Lamia
Timfristos	Diavolotopos	1,840	40	(0237) 23102 Kaprenissi
Vardoussia	Pitimaliko	1,750	18	(0231) 26786 Lamia
Oxia	Karvounolaka	1,700	40	(0231) 26786 Lamia
Kitheronas	Petalo	1,000	50	554-6572 Eleusis
EUBOEA				
Dirfis	Liri	1,100	36	(0221) 25230 Halkida and (0228) 51285 (refuge)
THESSALY				
Pelion	Agriolefkes	1,350	80	(0421) 25696 Volos
Pelion	Zagora Hostel	1,600	16	As above
Ossa (Kissavos)	Kanalos	1,600	20	(0421) 220097 Larissa
Olympus	Spilios Agapitos	2,100	80	(0352) 21329 Litohoro and 21800 (refuge)
Olympus	Vrissopoules	1,900	50	323-4555 Athens
Olympus	Stavros	1,100	40	(031) 278288 Thessaloniki
Olympus	Profiti Elia	2,650	18	323-4555 Athens
MACEDONIA				
Pieria	Ano Milia	1,050	52	(0351) 23102 Katerini and 21284 (refuge)
Vermio	Seli	1,400	60	(031) 278288 Thessaloniki
Vermio	Seli	1,400	100	(0331) 26970 Veria
Vermio	Pigadia	1,450	60	(0332) 28567 Naoussa
Vermio	Vermio Hostel	1,400	18	As above
Vrondou	Lailias	1,500	60	(0321) 23724 Serres
Pangeo	Vlahika Klivia	1,500	25	(051) 23464 Kavala
Pangeo	Kilada Orfea	1,700	80	As above
Vitsi	Vigia Pissoderiou	1,650	60	(0385) 28008 Florina
Falakro	Bartiseva	1,150	20	(0521) 23054 (Drama) and 23049
Falakro	Kouri	1,400	16	(0521) 23054 (Drama)
Falakro	Horos	1,700	20	As above
EPIRUS				
Pindo Gamila	Diaselo Astrakas	2,639	28	(0651) 22138 Ioannina
Mitsikeli	Vrissi Paleohori	1,400	25	As above

tainous areas; the **Greek Skiing and Alpine Federation**, 7 Karageorgi Street, Athens (tel. 323-4555), the **Greek Touring Club**, 12 Politehniou St, Athens, (tel. 524-8601); and the **Federation of Excursion Clubs of Greece**, 4 Dragatsaniou St., Athens, (tel. 323-4107). Also refer to chart provided.

Cave Exploration: Greece is honey-combed with caves. Usually the local tourist police has information on where local caves are and how you go about visiting them. The following caves have facilities for public visitation: Koutouki, Peania, Attica; Perama, Ioannina; Drongorati, Kefallonia; Melissani, Andiparos, Cyclades; Glifada and Aleopotripa at Diros, Laconia; Kokkines Petres, Halkidiki.

Spectator Sports: Greece has a limited range of spectator sports. Soccer is the main one with matches played nearly every Sunday afternoon during the season. Check the local papers for information or contact the **Soccer Federation**, 137 Syngrou, Athens, (tel. 933-6410).

Basketball is becoming the second most popular sport in Greece after soccer and the national league competition is followed keenly. Check the local papers for information or call the **Basketball Federation**, 11 N. Saripolou Street, Athens, (tel. 824-5125, 822-4131).

Horse racing takes place at the **Faliron Racecourse** at the seaward end of Syngrou Avenue in Athens. There are races every Monday, Wednesday and Saturday at 6:30 p.m. For information call: 941-7761.

Cultural Activities

Museums, Archaeological Sites and Churches: The main question here is surely **which** museums, sites and churches to visit. Greece has such an abundance of them that in any one trip you'll just be able to see a fraction of what's available. In the Appendix are listed most of the museums and archaeological sites and a few of the interesting churches and monasteries. Numerous aspects of Greece's cultural heritage have been necessarily excluded from this listing (fortresses, most churches, arches, mosques etc.). However, with patience and an inquisitive eye you'll gradually discover them.

Libraries and Cultural Centers: In Athens there are two main cultural centers for those who speak English, the **British Council** and the **Hellenic American Union**. The British

Council in Kolonaki Square (tel. 363-3211) has a library with a wide range of books, periodicals and newspapers. It also sponsors occasional lectures, exhibitions and performances. It is open Mon.—Fri. 9:30 a.m. to 1:30 p.m. The Hellenic American Union, Massalias 22, 4th floor (tel. 363-7740) similarly has a library and sponsors various cultural events. It also runs several courses in Greek dance, film, language, literature etc. for foreign visitors. Open Mon.—Fri. 9:30 a.m. to 2 p.m.; Mon.—Thurs. 5:30 to 8:30 p.m.

In Thessaloniki there are also two main cultural centers for those who speak English, the **British Council**, on the corner of Egnatias and Vas. Sofias Streets (tel. 235236) and the **American Center**, in Mitropoleos St. just off Aristotelous Square (tel. 276347). Though somewhat more limited in scope, their activities are similar to those of the centers in Athens.

English Language Bookstores: Athens has numerous bookstores which carry books in English:

Compendium, Nikis 33, located just behind Syntagma Square, (tel. 322-6931).

Eleftheroudakis, Nikis 4, Syntagma, (tel. 322-9388).

Kakoulides—The Book Nest, Panepistimiou 25-29, Stoa Megarou Athinon, (tel. 322-5209).

Pantelides, Amerikis 11, (tel. 362-3673).

Lexis Bookshop, Emm. Benaki and Academisas 72.

Turtle Bookshop, Patriarcho Ioakim 24, Kolonaki. Books for children in English, French and Greek.

Theaters: Athens has an active theater life. As most productions are in Greek, however, there are limited options for the English-speaking tourist. Most productions in English take place during the various festivals. (*see* Seasonal Events).

You'll do best to check the English-language publications for up-to-date information.

One recent cultural initiative has provided some excellent productions of both modern and ancient drama in English in one of Greece's most striking open-air theaters—the "Stone Theater" (Petra Theater) in Petroupolis in the suburbs of Athens. During the summer, plays are produced under the auspices of the "Stones and Rocks Festival."

To experience the traditional Greek form of Karaghiozi shadow puppetry, visit the Karaghiozi Puppet Theatre in the Plaka, (tel. 322-4845), with performances every evening except Monday.

Music and Dance: A considerable part of the good music and dance performances takes place during the various festivals (*see* Seasonal Events). Besides these performances, however, there are still numerous events worth attending in both Athens and Thessaloniki. In Athens outstanding Greek and foreign musicians often perform at the Lycabettus Theatre on Mount Lycabettus, not to mention the larger concerts that take place in the soccer stadiums. Opera can be seen at the Olympia Theater performed by the Lyriki Skini (the National Opera Company). In Thessaloniki performances of music, opera, dance and theater take place at the State Theater of Northern Greece. In both Athens and Thessaloniki the cultural institutes (Goethe, British Council, French) sometimes sponsor interesting events. For listings of popular Greek and *rembetika* music *see* section on Nightlife.

Athens has an active dance scene with ballet, folk, modern, jazz and experimental dance troupes. The various troupes are: The Athens Ballet; The Contemporary Dance Group of Haris Mandafounis; The Small Dance Theatre of Lia Meletopoulou; The Ilanga Dance Theatre; Bouri; The Hellenic Chorodrama; The Young Dancers and Choreographers of Katerina Rodiou; The Dance Theatre of Nafsika; The Hellenic Ballet of Rene Kabaladou; the Dora Stratou Group.

Greek Music: Greece has incredible music— or, rather, musics, ranging from folk to "light popular," *rembetika* to Byzantine chanting, **Theodarakis** and **Hazidakis** to **Dionisios Savopulos** (*see* Byzantine Chants, Rembetika and Theodarakis etc. in the Cultural Dictionary).

In the folk area keep your ear tuned to the great regional variety which still exists today. Crete has one of the richest traditions, characterized by the *lyra* (fiddle), *laouta* (lute) and *santouri* (hammer dulcimer). Epirus is also notable, characterized by the extensive use of the *klarino* (clarinet) and an extraordinary, disappearing tradition of polyphonic singing. *Nisiotika* is the general name for "island music" which has its own sound, style and instruments, varying from island group to island group (the Ionian, Cycladic, Dodecanese etc.).

If you want to explore the world of *rembetika* listen for these greats: Vassilis Tsitsa-

nis, Markos Vamvakaris, Sotiria Bellou, Kazantzides, Papazoglou, Papaioanou, and Tsaousakis. The best single introduction to *rembetika*, however, still remains the six-volume collection "The History of Rembetika" from EMI.

Little introduction is required for Mikos Theodorakis and Manolis Hazidakis. You'll hear their songs on every bus, boat and plane in Greece. In a very different vein is the folk-rock hero Dionisios Savopulos. Dipping into the Greek well of Byzantine and Asia Minor melodics he draws out a unique style of contemporary folk-rock music. Another recent group which, working out of the Greek folk tradition, produces a distinctly contemporary music is **Himerini Kolimvités** (with an album by the same name from Lyra Records in Greece).

Cinema: Going to the movies in Greece during the summertime is a special pleasure and not to be missed. Nearly all the movie theaters that run in the summer (the others shut down) are open-air—sometimes tucked among apartment buildings whose tenants watch the film from their balconies, while in other areas, perched on a seaside promontory under rustling palm trees, stars and the moon (on Aegina, for instance). The tickets are cheap and soundtracks are in the original language. It's also a great way to beat the dogday heat of high-summer in Greece.

Nightlife

Metropolitan "nightlife" in Greece, which is to say in Athens and Thessaloniki, can be roughly divided into four categories: bars; live music clubs with jazz and rock; discoteques; and *boites*, *tavernas* and clubs with live Greek music. It should be noted first, however, that for most Greeks, the *taverna* remains the most popular site for a night-out; where you pass an evening eating, drinking and, sometimes, singing with your *parea* (*see* Cultural Dictionary). In fact, locales with live Greek music are almost always *tavernas* with an additional set-up for music. In general younger Greeks frequent the bars, music clubs and discoteques, while the locales for popular Greek music are more favorable among the older generations.

In Athens the weekly *Athenorama* has an extensive listing of all the various locales and events. If you really want to find out what's going on in the city, ask a Greek friend to help you check out the listings. For information on the local music scene you can also inquire at

Pop 11 record shop, Skoufa 15, Kolonaki. However, do take note that during the late summer (July-August) many of these locales close down.

In Athens (a sampler)

Bars: Some of the more exciting ones you might want to try are:
Glamorous—Akamandos and A. Pavlou 1, Thission; **Papakia**—Iridanou 5, Athens; **Ramba**—D. Vassiliou 14, Neo Psychico; **Time Pub**—Trikoupi and Akti Moutsopoulou 58, Zea, Pireaus.
Predominantly gay bars include: **Rocambole**—Epicharmou 1, Plaka; **Vagelis**—Tholou 9, Plaka; and **Yannis**—Tholou 18, Plaka. One of the few bars with a sizeable lesbian patronage is **Sirius**—Haritos 43, Kolonaki.

Live Music Clubs (jazz and rock): For live rock clubs try: **Tiffany's**—Adrianou 134, Plaka; **Skiachtro**—Panourgia 12, Delfinario, Kastella; and **Podilatissa**—Fthiotidos 68, Ambelokipi, which alternates performances of jazz, blues, soul and rock.
For live jazz clubs try **The Half Note**—Michalokopoulou 56, Llissia; and **Tzaz**—in Rangava Square, off Thespidos Street in Plaka.

Discos: Try: **Disco 14**—Kolonaki Square; **Paramount**—Soutsou, Kolonaki; **Mad Club**—Lissiou, Plaka; **ABC**—Patission 177, Amerikis Square; **Vido Disco**—Syngrou 255. Two predominantly gay discos are **Jacare**—Tholou 13, Plaka and **Why Not?**—Hill 3, Plaka.

Live Greek Music (tavernas, boites, clubs): Three good *boites* with performances of varying kinds of Greek popular music are on Tholou Street in Plaka: **Apanemia** at #4, **Esperides** at #6 and **Sousouro** at #17.
A few *tavernas* where you'll usually hear music are: **O Pontos**—corner of Achileos and Terpsitheas, near Omonia; **Kortsopon**—Pireos 68, beyond Keramikos; and **To Arkadi**—Thivon 50, opposite the Pan Athenaikos football stadium.

Rembetika Clubs: Some of the better ones in this category are:

Anatoli, Dimosthenous 62 Kallithea, (tel. 959-3696). Cold plates. Opens 9:30 p.m. Closed Wednesday.

Kouasimodos, Tsakalof 13, (tel. 361-8339). Full menu. Music begins at 10:30 p.m.

Closed Monday.

Moratorium, L. Katsoni 11, end of Ippokratous at Alexandras, (tel. 644-8115). Assorted cold plates and appetisers. Open at 10 p.m. Closed Wednesday.

Pigi Tou Rembetikou, Ag. Glikerias 11, Galatsi, (tel. 292-1820). Full menu. Open 10 p.m. Go early or call for reservations.

Rembetiki Nichta, Formionos 102, Pangrati, (tel. 766-9903). Complete menu. Open 9:30 p.m. Closed Wednesday.

Rembetiki Istoria, Ippokratous 181, (tel. 643-0474). Cozy neighborhood place.

Frankosyriani, Arachovis 57, Exarchia. Nikos Argyropoulos featured. Homemade assorted cold plates. Music begins at 10:30 p.m. Closed Tuesday. Lots of Markos Vamva karis songs.

In Thessaloniki

Pubs

De. Facto, 17 P. Mela St.

Time Out, 6 N. Foka St.

Mandragovas, 98 Mitropoleos St.

Sante, 70 Mitropoleos St.

Penny Lane, 8 M. Iosif St.

Discos

Amnesia, near Airport (only during summer)

Smeraldo, near Airport

Accommodations

The most widespread type of accommodation in Greece is the pension or cheap hotels, where you can still find a decent room at reasonable rates. Besides these, there is also a wide range of other possibilities, from the deluxe hotels to pension rooftops. In the Appendix you'll find a sampling of different categories of hotels in Athens and Thessaloniki.
On the islands and in many parts of the mainland another kind of cheap lodging is

renting private rooms (*domatia*). These are rented out by local residents at prices controlled by the tourist police. In general, when looking for any kind of accommodation, the tourist police can be of considerable help. If you're in a fix you can inquire at their office. If you'd like to make a reservation or arrangement in advance call them and they'll often be able to help you out (*see* listing in Appendix).

Greece has a number of youth hostels for which you officially need a youth hostel card, however, you can often buy one on the spot or just pay an additional charge. There are youth hostels in: Athens; Mycenae; Nafplion; Olympia; Patras; Delphi; Litochoro; Thessaloniki; Corfu; Santorini; and on Crete at Aghios Nikolaos, Hania, Heraklion, St. Basil (Rethymnon) and Sitia. There are also accommodations at the YMCA and YWCA in both Athens and Thessaloniki.

A large portion of the tourists who come to Greece usually decide to "rough it" in one form or another. Those who want to camp at organized campsites with facilities will find hundreds of them all over Greece, some run by the NTOG, some by the Greek Touring Club, and many privately. The most beautiful campsites in Greece, however, are usually the ones you find on your own. While in most places it is officially illegal just to lay out your sleeping bag or pitch a tent, if you're discrete you'll rarely be bothered. That means, asking permission if you seem to be on private property, avoiding "unofficial" campsites set up in popular tourist areas, and, **always** leaving the place looking better than when you came.

Monasteries and convents can often provide lodging as well for travelers. Mt. Athos of course has a long tradition of this hospitality (for men). Certain other monasteries in Greece also welcome overnight visitors on a more informal basis. If you've found a monastery that does accept overnight guests, realize that you'll have to dress (no shorts) and behave accordingly. The doors may closed as early as sunset and some kind of donation may be expected.

There are two other special kinds of accommodations in Greece worth mentioning: mountain refuges run by the various Greek mountaineering clubs and traditional settlements run by the NTOG. Mountain refuges can range from a small 12-bed ski hut where you need to bring your own food and supplies to 100-bed lodges where all meals are provided (*see* listing in Sports and Recreation). The traditional settlements are villages recognized by the Greek government as forming an important part of the national heritage. Buildings in these villages have been restored and set up by the NTOG for tourist use. At the moment there

are eight such villages with others to be restored and developed in the future. These houses and villages are, in their different ways, strikingly beautiful, and highly recommended for a week or month retreat in rural Greece.

The NTOG traditional settlements are:

Oia (Santorini), Paradosiakos Ikismos Oias, Oia, Santorini, Greece, tel. (0286) 71234.

Makrinitsa (on Pelion Mountain), Xenia Hotel, Portaria Village, tel. (0421) 25922.

Vizitsa (on Pelion Mountain), tel. (0423) 86373.

Mesta (on Chios Island), Paradosiakos Ikismos, Mesta, Hios, Greece.

Psara Island, tel. (0251) 27908.

Fiskardo (on Kephalonia Island), Paradosiakos Ikismos, Fiskardou, Fiskardo, Kephalonia, Greece, tel. (0674) 51398.

Kapetanakos Tower (Areopoli, Mani), tel. (0733) 51233.

Papingo, Zagorochoria (Epirus), tel. (0653) 25087/(0651) 25087.

Reservations can be made either through the above addresses or by writing directly to:

Greek National Tourist Organization, EOT Dieftynisi Ekmetalefseos, 2 Amerikis Street, Athens 10564, Greece.

Dining Out

Eating out in Greece is above all a social affair. Whether it be with your family or your *parea*, that sacred circle of friends, a meal out is an occasion to celebrate, a time for *kefi*. This may have something to do with the fact that eating out in Greece continues to be affordable and popular, not something restricted to those who have American Express cards. And the predominance of the *taverna*, that bastion of Greek cuisine, reflects this popularity. These casual eating establishments have more or less the same style and setup throughout Greece, and the menu too is more or less similar. Which is to say no frills, no packaging which tries to convince the "consumer" that this *taverna* is different from the others, special, distinct. The place, and your being there, is somehow taken for granted: you eat the good food at Yanni's or Yorgos', you enjoy yourself, and you don't pay an arm and a leg for it.

This is the general background for eating out in Greece against which we find, of course, considerable variation. The *taverna* is by no means the only kind of eating establishment. You'll also encounter: the *éstiatório*, the restaurant as we usually think of it—fancier and more polished than the *taverna*, with linen tablecloths and higher prices; the *psistaría*, a barbecue-style restaurant which specializes in lamb, pork or chicken on a spit; the *psarotavarna* which specializes in fish; the *ouzerí* which is mainly an establishment for drinking, but which also serves *mezédes*, snacks, of various types; the *gyros* stand with *hiro* sandwiches and *souvláki*, sometimes a sit-down place with salads.

There's also considerable regional variety in Greek cuisine and you should keep an eye out for those specialties of the house which you haven't seen before. Another thing you'll quickly learn in Greece is how strikingly different the same dish can be when it is prepared well or prepared badly, for example, a *melatsanasalata* or stuffed tomatoes. It's therefore worthwhile shopping around for your *taverna* (especially in heavily touristed areas), asking the locals what they suggest, walking into the kitchen to look at the food (a customary practise), instead of getting stuck with the tourist trap which spoils your appetite for *moussaka* for the rest of the trip.

Here are few notes about Greek eating habits. In Greece the main meal is eaten at midday, between 1:30 p.m. and 2:30 p.m. and is usually followed by a *siesta* break lasting until 5:00 p.m. The evening meal can either be another full meal, or an assortment of *mezedes*. This is usually eaten sometime between 9:00 p.m. and 11:00 p.m. (Breakfast in Greece is rather meager, usually consisting of bread, butter, jam and coffee.

Greeks never simply "go out drinking." Even if an evening involves heavy drinking of retsina or ouzo, these will always be accompanied by food—an inveterate habit which minimizes the effects (and after-effects) of the alcohol. When it comes to ordering your wine, check to see if they serve wine from the barrel (ask for chima). This is the inexpensive local stuff which varies from town to town. Otherwise you can choose among the various bottled wines, some of the better Greek labels being: Rotonda, Cambas, Boutari, Calliga. *Aspro* is white, *mavro* is red, and *kokkinelli* is rose.

Some *tavernas* you'll find do not have menus, or have menus without prices. It's a good idea to inquire with the restaurateur how much things cost before you eat them. And, as mentioned above, you can always find out what dishes they serve by walking into the kitchen.

The list below is a partial listing of some of the more popular foods you'll find on your travels.

In the Appendix you'll find a sampling of eating establishments in Athens and Thessaloniki.

Hors d'oeuvres and dips—usually eaten as appetizers with *psomí*—bread

Kdokithákia—deep-fried zucchini

melitsánasálata—eggplant dip

rossikisaláta—cold potato salad, lots of mayonnaise

táramasaláta—fish roe pate/dip

tzaziki—yoghurt/cucumber dip, heavily garlicked

Vegetables

anginária—artichokes

arakádes—peas

bámies—okra

dolmádes—stuffed grape leaves

fasolákia—snap beans

horiátiki—olive, feta cheese, onion, cucumber and tomato salad

hórta—steamed wild greens

koukiá—horse beans

maróuli—lettuce

patzária—beets

yemistés—stuffed tomatoes or peppers

yígantes—large haricot beans

Various Meats

Note the following terms: *psitó*—roasted; *sti soúvla*—barbecued on the spit; *tiganitó*—fried; *sto foúrno*—baked; *skáras*--grilled; *vrastó*—boiled; *kapnistó*—smoked.

arni—lamb

biftéki—"beefsteak"

brizóla—pork or beef chop (*chirinó* or *moschári* respectively)

keftédes—meatballs

kokorétsi—stuffed innards roasted on the spit

kotópoulo—chicken

loukaniká—sausages

mialó—brain

paidákia—lamb chops

sikotákia—grilled liver

souvláki—chunks of pork or lamb roasted on the spit or fried

Various Dishes, Soups and Specialties

avgolémono—chicken stock thickened with egg and lemon

fasoláda—bean soup

moussaká—eggplant and ground lamb casserole with white sauce

pastítsio—macaroni casserole

patsás—tripe stew, sold at special patasas stands

salingária—snails fried in oil and herbs

stifádo—any kind of stew, stewed meat

souzoukákia—baked meat rolls

yiorvoulákia—meat-and-rice balls

Seafood

astakoś—lobster

bakaliáros—cod

galéos—shark "steak"

garídes—shrimp

glóssa—sole

gópes—small, fried fish

kalamária—squid

ksifías—swordfish

ktapódi—octopus

péstrofa—trout

sinagrída—red snapper

soupiés—cuttlefish

Desserts

Rarely will you find dessert served where you eat dinner. You'll find sweets instead at *zachariplastía* (sweet shops—*see* Special Feature) and some *galaktopolía* (dairy stores). One sweet you'll sometimes served at *tavernas* is halvá.

baklavá—fillo dough leaves, honey, nuts

bougátsa—sweet custard pie

galaktoboúriko—a heftier custard pie, less common

kataifí—chopped nuts wrapped in shredded wheat with honey

krema—plain custard

loukoúmi—Turkish delight

moustalevriá—grape pudding, usually in fall

rizógalo—rice pudding

Other Snacks

kalambóki—roast corn on the cob, sold on the street

kastaná—roast chestnuts, sold on the street

kouloúria—sesame-sprinkled "pretzels"

kreatópita—meat pie

spanakópita—spinach pie

tirópita—cheese pie

tost—toasted sandwiches sold at "tost" stands

Drinks

bira—beer

kokkinélli—rose wine

krasí—wine

mávro—red

me to kiló, or *híma*—wine by the kilo., local

neró—water

retsína—resin-flavored wine

óuzo—anise-flavoure liqueur

rakí—grape-crush brandy

tsípouro—basically like raki

Coffee, Tea

Greeks generally drink their coffee and tea with lots of sugar. An essential phrase for those who like their hot drinks without sugar is—"*horís záhari*," literally, "without sugar." Tag this phrase at the end of whatever drink you are ordering: for example, "nescafé *horís záhari*." You can also ask for your drink "*sketos*" which means the same thing in a slightly less emphatic way. If you like some sugar ask for "*métrio*" medium amount of sugar. If you love sugar say nothing and they'll probably dump a few teaspoons into whatever you're drinking. "*Me gála*" means "with milk."

nescafe—freeze-dried coffee. In warmer weather you may want "frapé," cold nescafé mixed in a shaker.

elenikó café—Greek coffee, boiled and served with the grounds in the cup. If you want a large cup of it ask for "*diplós*." *Elenikó café* is also known as "*turkikó café*" but this sometimes provokes patriotic objections.

tsai—tea either with milk or with lemon, "*me limóni*"

kamomíli—camomille tea

tsái tou vounóu—mountain tea. Tea made with any one of various mountain herbs such as sage. Not easy to find.

Other Useful Words

aláti—salt & *pipéri* (pepper)

boukáli—bottle

potíri—glass

piroúni—fork

koutáli—spoon

mahéri—knife

katálogo/lista—menu

to logaviasmó—the bill

Survival Greek

"Survival Greek" is actually a misleading title for this section, for it is possible to "survive" in Greece just knowing English. Greeks have seen so many English-speaking tourists and have such strong connections with the English-speaking world (through emigration, the media, education) that you're always bound to find Greeks that can understand your basic utterances. This section isn't so much about survival as it is about beginning to bridge the gap between you the alien tourist and the native Greek, about being perceived as a *ksenos*, a foreigner or guest, instead of a *tourista*. Greeks put great stock in their language and are highly responsive to the efforts of foreigners who try to learn it. Precisely because Greeks so effusively appreciate your efforts, Greek can be one of the most gratifying European languages to learn. With a little study and practise on your part and you too may soon be met with the stock praise: "*P'oss émathes tósso kalá ta ellenikå?*" That is, "how did you learn Greek so well?"

The following is a listing of some words and phrases that may be useful to you. You'll also want to carry a pocket-sized English-Greek-Greek-English dictionary with you. For those who actually want to study Greek, a few textbooks and dictionaries are listed at the end of this section.

A α (*alfa*) 'a' as in fat

B β (*vita*) 'v' as in voodoo

Γ γ (*gama*) gutteral 'g' sound except before an 'e' or 'i' sound when it sounds like a 'y' in you

Δ δ (*dhelta*) hard 'th' as in the

E ε (*epsilon*) 'e' as in sell

Z ʒ (*zita*) 'z' as in zebra

H γ (*ita*) 'i' as in machine

ⓝ θ	(*thita*) 'th' as in thick	
Ι ι	(*iota*) 'i' as in machine	
Κ κ	(*kappa*) 'k' as in kiss	
Λ λ	(*lamdha*) 'l' as in light	
Μ ν	(*mi*) 'm' as in mouse	
Ν ν	(*ni*) 'n' as in night	
Ξ ξ	(*xi*) 'ks' sound as in extra	
Ο ο	(*omikron*) 'o' as in oat	
Π π	(*pi*) 'p' as in pet	
Ρ ρ	(*ro*) 'r' as in rent	
Σ ϛ ς	(*sigma*) 's' as in sit	
Τ τ	(*taf*) 't' as in tax	
Υ υ	(*ipsilon*) 'i' as in machine	
Φ φ	(*fi*) 'f' as in fish	
Χ χ	(*hi*) 'ch' sound, like German 'ch' in nicht	
Ψ ψ	(*psi*) 'ps' as in psychology	
Ω ω	(*omega*) 'o' as in oat	

Diphthongs

ΑΙ αι	like 'e' in sell
ΑΥ αυ	'av' or 'af' sound
ΕΙ ει	both like 'i' in machine
ΟΙ οι	
ΕΥ ευ	'ev' or 'ef' sound
ΟΥ ου	'oo' sound
ΓΓ γγ	'ng' sound as in angle
ΓΚ γκ	hard 'g' sound if at beginning of word; 'ng' if in middle
ΜΠ μπ	'b' sound as in Bugs Bunny
ΝΤ ντ	'd' sound at beginning of word; hard 'th' sound if in middle

Basic Expressions

yes	*né*
no	*óhi*
okay	*en dáksi*
please	*parakaló*
thank you	*efharistó*
(very much)	*para polí*
excuse me	*signómi*
it doesn't matter	*dhen pirázi*
it's nothing	*típota*
certainly	*málista*
good day	*káli méra*
good evening	*káli spéra*
good night	*káli níhta*
goodbye	*addio*
Greetings!/ "health to you"	*yá sou, yá sas*—plural or formal
Greetings!/"rejoice"	*hérete*
bon voyage	*kaló taksídhi*
welcome	*kalós ílthateh*
good luck	*kalí tíhi*
How are you?	*ti kánis, ti kánete*—plural or formal
fine, well (in response)	*kalá*
so so (in response)	*étsi kétsi*
pleased to meet you (very much)	*hárika (poli)*
I also, me too	*kai egó*
Have you…?	*éhete…?*
Is there….?	*éhi….?*
How much does it cost?	*póso káni?*
It's (too) expensive	*íne (polí) akrivó*
How much?	*póso?*
How many?	*pósa?*
Do you have a room?	*éhete éna domátio?*
Can I…?	*bóro na…?*
When?	*póte…?*
Where is…?	*póu ine…?*
From where…?	*ápo póu…?*
Where are you from?	*ápo póu iseliste?*—sing./formal
What is your name?	*pos se/sas léne?*—sing./formal
Do you speak English?	*milás/miláte angliká?* (sing./plural-formal)
Do you understand?	*katálaves?*
What time is it?	*tí ora íne?*
What time will it leave?	*ti ora tha fígi?*
I don't…	*dhen* + verb
I want	*thélo*
I have	*ého*
I am/we are	*íme/ímaste*
I understand	*katalavéno, katalávo*
I pay	*pliróno, ploróso*
I go	*piyaíno, páo*
it must/I must	*prépi na*

I need a—	*hriázome ena/mia—*	village	*horió*
today	*símera*	spring	*pigí*
tomorrow	*ávrio*		
yesterday	*hthes*	**Numbers**	
now	*tóra*		
here/there	*edhó/ekí*	1	*énna/mía*
near/far	*kondá/makriá*	2	*dhío*
small/large	*mikró/megálo*	3	*tría/tris*
less/more	*ligótero/perisótero*	4	*téssera*
quickly	*grígora*	5	*péndhe*
slowly	*argá, sigá*	6	*éksi*
good/bad	*kaló,oraío/kakó*	7	*eptá*
warm/cold	*zestó/krío*	8	*oehtó*
shower with hot water	*douz me zestó neró*	9	*ennea*
hotel	*ksenodhohío*	10	*dhéka*
bed	*kreváti*	11	*éndheka*
key	*klidhí*	12	*dhódeka*
room (with a window)	*domátio (me*	13	*dhekatría*
	paráthiro)	14	*dhekatéssera*
entrance	*ísodhos*	etc, until 20	
exit	*éksodhos*		
toilet	*touleta*	20	*íkosi*
women's	*ginekón*	21	*íkosi énna*
men's	*andrón*	30	*triánda*
store	*magazí*	40	*saránda*
kiosk	*períptero*	50	*penínda*
open/shut	*aniktós/klistós*	60	*eksínda*
What time does it	*ti ora anígi/klíni?*	70	*evdhomínda*
open/close?		80	*ogdhónda*
post office	*tahidromío*	90	*ennenínda*
stamp	*grammatósima*	100	*ekató*
letter	*gramma*	150	*ekatopenínda*
envelope	*fákelos/postcard*	200	*diakóssia*
	kárta	300	*triakóssia*
telephone	*tiléfono*	400	*tetrakóssia*
bank	*trápeza*	1000	*hília*
bakery	*fournos*		
embassy	*presvia*		
consulate	*proksenion*	**Days of the Week**	
marketplace	*agorá*		
pharmacy	*farmakío*	Monday	*deftéra*
doctor	*yatrós*	Tuesday	*tríti*
hospital	*nosokomío*	Wednesday	*tetárti*
police	*astinomia*	Thursday	*pémpti*
station	*stathmós*	Friday	*paraskeví*
stop (on a bus)	*stási*	Saturday	*sávato*
bus/train	*leoforío/tréno*	Sunday	*kiriakí*
automobile	*aftokínito*		
boat	*karávi, vapóri*		
petrol station	*benzinádhiko*	**Untranslatable Words**	
bike/moped	*podílato/móto-*		
	podílato	*kéfi* to be in good spirits, having a good time	
on foot	*me ta pódhia*	with your *parea*	
ticket	*isitírio*		
road/street	*dhrómos/ódhos*	*paréa* one's group of close friends, your	
beach	*paralía*	"gang" (see cultural dictionary)	
church	*eklisía*		
ancient ruins	*arhéa*	*kaimós* is in a sense the opposite of *kefi*, one's	
center	*kéntro*	life-suffering, sadness	
square	*platía*		
sea	*thálassa*	*palikári* a good fellow (honorable, brave,	

intelligent etc.); a rough synonym is *levendi*

filótimo adjective meaning literally "love of honor"

mángas a "toughie," a "cool dude," macho

re short for *moré*, baby, kid, dummy; a word thrown in when addressing another person, a buddy in that typically male Greek rough-affectionate manner

malákas literally "masturbator"; often combined with *re* (*re malákas*); can be directed to friends affectionately or to others more antagonistically

paidhiá "the boys," fellows, guys

alítis a bum, roughly the opposite of *palikári*

lipón well, so, now then

élla! Come! Come on!

oríste(?) Can I help you?

po po po! Well well! What have we here!

ópa! Look out!; also, at a music *taverna* for example, "way to go!," "all right!" etc.

The Language of Gestures: Greek is a gestural language; you don't speak it with your hands in your pockets or with your head still. The body and its movements are signs which form an integral part of the communicative process. You can learn this aspect of Greek only through close observation. Two of the most common of these gestures are those indicating 'yes' and 'no'. 'No' is often communicated by jerking the head and chin up and back sharply. This is often a very slight movement. Sometimes, in fact, only the eyebrows or eyes make this upward gesture. The gesture indicating 'yes' is a rather gentler one, a slow downward angling of the head.

Texts for Learning Greek

Farmakidhes, Anne. *A Manual of Modern Greek*. New Haven: Yale Univ. Press, 1983, 2nd ed.

Rassias, John and Peter and Chrysanthi Bien. *Demotic Greek*. Hanover, NH and London: University Press of New England, 1983.

Sofroniou, S.A. *Modern Greek*. New York: David McKay and London: Hodder & Stoughton, 1983.

Stone, Tom. *Greek Handbook*. Athens: Lycabettus Press, 1982. (a handy emergency phrase book)

Further Reading

Ancient History and Culture

Bowra, Maurice. *The Greek Experience*. London: Weidenfeld and Nicolson, 1957.

Burn, A.R. *The Pelican History of Greece*. Harmondsworth: Penguin, 1966.

Dodds, E.R. *The Greeks and the Irrational*. Berkeley and Los Angeles: U. of California Press, 1951.

Finley, M.I. *The Ancient Greeks*. Harmondsworth: Penguin, 1963.
The World of Odysseus. New York: Viking Press, 1954.

Graves, Robert. *The Greek Myths*. Harmondsworth: Penguin Books, 1986.

Hammond, N.G.L. *A History of Greece to 322 B.C.* Oxford University Press, 1965.

Kerenyi, K. *The Gods of the Greeks*. London: Thames and Hudson, 1951.
The Heroes of the Greeks. London: Thames and Hudson, 1951.

Kitto, H.D.F. *The Greeks*. Harmondsworth: Penguin, 1951.

Pollitt, J.J. *Art and Experience in Classical Greece*. Cambridge: CUP, 1972.

Renfrew, Colin. *The Emergence of Civilization: The Cyclades and the Aegean in the Third Millennium B.C.* New York: Simon and Schuster, 1970.

Thompson, George. *Aeschylus and Athens*. London: Lawrence and Wishart, 1980.

Vernant, J.P. *Myth and Thought*. London: Routledge & Kegan Paul, 1983.

Byzantine History and Culture

The Alexiad of Anna Comnena. Trans. by E.R.A. Sewter Harmondsworth: Penguin, 1969.

Michael Psellus: Fourteen Byzantine Rulers.

Harmondsworth: Penguin, 1966.

Runciman, Steven. *Byzantine Style and Civilization*. Harmondsworth: Penguin, 1975.

Sherrard, Philip. *Byzantium*. New York: Time-Life Books, 1966.

Talbot Rice, David. *The Art of the Byzantine Era*. London: Thames and Hudson, 1963. *The Byzantines*. London: Thames and Hudson, 1962.

Modern Greek History and Culture

Alexiou, Margaret. *The Ritual Lament in Greek Tradition*. Cambridge: Cambridge U. Press, 1974.

Beaton, Roderick. *Folk Poetry of Modern Greece*. Cambridge: Cambridge U. Press, 1980.

Campbell, John. *Honor, family and patronage: a study of institutions and moral values in a Greek mountain community*. Oxford: Oxford U. Press, 1964.

Clogg, Richard. *A Short History of Greece*. Cambridge: Cambridge, 1979.

Danforth, Loring H. and Tsiaras, Alexander. *The Death Rituals of Rural Greece*. Princeton: PUP, 1982.

Du Boulay, Juliet. *Portrait of a Greek Mountain Village*. Oxford: Clarendon Press, 1974.

Eudes, Domenique. *The Kapetanios: Partisans and Civil War in Greece, 1943–1949*. NY and London: Monthly Review Press, 1972.

Fourtouni, Eleni. *Greek Women in Resistance*. New Haven: Thelphini Press, 1986.

Friedl, Ernestine. *Vasilika: A Village in Modern Greece*. New York: Holt, Rinehart and Winston, 1962.

Herzfeld, Michael. *Ours Once More: Folklore, Ideology and the Making of Modern Greece*. Austin: University of Texas Press, 1982.

Mackridge, Peter. *The Modern Greek Language*. Oxford: Oxford U. Press, 1985.

Matthews, Kevin. *Memoirs of a Mountain War, Greece: 1944–1949*. London: Longman, 1972.

McNeill, William. *Metamorphisis of Greece Since World War II*. Oxford: Blackwell, 1982.

Mouzelis, Nicos P. *Modern Greece: Facets of Underdevelopment*. London: MacMillan Press, 1978.

Papandreou, Andreas. *Democracy at Gunpoint*. Harmondsworth: Penguin, 1972.

Sarafis, Marion. *Greece: From Resistance to Civil War*. Nottingham: Spokesman, 1980.

Tsoucalas, Constantine. *The Greek Tragedy*. Harmondsworth: Penguin, 1969.

Woodhouse, C.M. *Modern Greece: A Short History*. London: Faber and Faber, 1984.

Ancient Greek Literature

Aeschylus. *The Oresteia*. Trans. by Robert Fagles. New York: Viking Press, 1975.

Aesop. *Fables of Aesop*. Trans. by S.A. Hanford. Harmondsworth: Penguin, 1954.

Aristophanes. *Lysistrata/The Acharnians/ The Clouds*. Trans. by A.H. Sommerstein. Harmondsworth: Penguin, 1973.

Aristotle. *The Nicomachean Ethics*. Trans. by Martin Ostwald. Indianapolis: Bobbs-Merrill, 1962.

Grene, David and Lattimore, Trans. by David *Greek Tragedies* (3 Vols.). Chicago: U. of Chicago Press, 1968.

Hesiod. *Theogony*. Trans. by Norman Brown. Indianapolis: Bobbs-Merrill, 1955.

Herodotus. *The Histories*. Trans. by A.R. Burn. Harmondsworth: Penguin, 1972.

Homer. *The Iliad*. Trans. by Robert Fitzgerald. New York: Anchor Books, 1975. *The Odyssey*. Trans. by Robert Fitzgerald. New York: Anchor Books, 1963.

Plato. *The Republic*. Trans. by H.D.P. Lee. Harmondsworth: Penguin, 1955. *The Symposium*. Trans. by Walter Hamilton. Harmondsworth: Penguin, 1951.

Sappho. Trans. by Mary Barnard. Los Angeles: U. of California Press, 1958.

Thucydides. *The Peloponnesian Wars*. Trans.

by Crawley. New York: Modern Library, 1951.

Trypanis, Constantine. *The Penguin Book of Greek Verse*. Harmondsworth: Penguin Books, 1971.

Modern Literature by Greeks

Barnstone, Willis (ed.). *Eighteen Texts: writings by contemporary Greek authors*. Cambridge: Harvard UP, 1972.

Cavafy, C.P. *Collected Poems*. Trans. by Edmund Keeley and Philip Sherrard Princeton: Princeton U. Press, 1975.

Dalven, Rae (trans.). *Modern Greek Poetry*. (anthology). New York: Russell and Russell, 1971.

Elytis, Odysseus. *The Axion Esti*. Pittsburgh: U. of Pittsburgh Press, 1974.
Selected Poems. Trans. by Edmund Keeley and Philip Sherrard. London and NY: Viking Penguin, 1981.

Friar, Kimon (trans). *Modern Greek Poetry*. (anthology). New York: Simon and Schuster, 1973.

Karapanou, Margarita. *Kassandra and the Wolf*. Trans. by N.C. Germanacos. New York: HBJ, 1976.

Kazantzakis, Nikos. *Zorba the Greek*. New York: Simon and Schuster/Touchstone, 1971.
Christ Recrucified (The Greek Passion). New York: Simon and Schuster/Touchstone, 1981.

Haviaris, Stratis. *When the Tree Sings*. New York: Simon and Schuster, 1979.
The Heroic Age. New York: Penguin, 1985.

Makriyannis, Yannis. *The Memoirs of General Makriyannis, 1797–1864*. London: OUP, 1966.

Myrivilis, Stratis. *The Schoolmistress with the Golden Eyes*. London: Hutchinson, 1964.

Ritsos, Yannis. *Ritsos in Parentheses*. Trans. by Edmund Keeley. Princeton: Princeton U. Press, 1979.
Yannis Ritsos: Selected Poems. Trans. by Nikos Stangos: Penguin, 1974.

Papadiamantis, Alexandros. *The Murderess*.

Trans. by Peter Levi. London: Writers and Readers, 1983.

Politis, Linos. *A History of Modern Greek Literature*. Oxford: Clarendon Press, 1973.

Seferis, George. *Collected Poems*. Trans. by Edmund Keeley. Princeton: PUP, 1981.

Sikelianos, Angelos. *Selected Poems*. Princeton: PUP, 1979

Siotis, Dino (ed.). *Ten Women Poets of Greece*. San Francisco: Wire Press, 1982.

Taktsis, Costas. *The Third Wedding Wreath*. Trans. by John Chioles. Athens: Hermes Publishers, 1985.

Tsirkas, Stratis. *Drifting Cities*. Trans. by Kay Cicellis. New York: Alfred Knopf, 1974.

Vassilikos, Vassilis. *Z*. New York: Farrar, Strauss and Giroux, 1968.

Foreign Writers and Greece

Andrews, Kevin. *Athens Alive*. Athens: Hermes Press.
The Flight of Ikaros. Harmondsworth: Penguin, 1984.

Durrell, Lawrence. *Prospero's Cell*. London: Faber and Faber, 1945.
Reflections on a Marine Venus. London: Faber and Faber, 1953.
Bitter Lemons. London: Faber and Faber, 1978.

Fowles, John. *The Magus*. London: Cape, 1977.

Gage, Nicholas. *Eleni*. London: Collins, 1983.

Levi, Peter. *Hill of Kronos*. New York: Penguin, 1984.

Miller, Henry. *The Colossus of Maroussi*. New York: New Directions, 1958.

Renault, Mary. *The Last of the Wine*. London: Sceptre, 1986.

Greenhalgh, Peter and Edward Eliopoulos. *Deep into Mani*. London: Faber and Faber, 1985.

Special Travel Books and Guides

Constantine, David. *Early Greek Travellers*

and the Hellenic Idea. Cambridge: CUP, 1984.

Dubin, Marc. *Greece on Foot*. Leicester/London: Cordee, 1986.

Durrell, Lawrence. *The Greek Islands*. New York: Viking Press, 1978.
Mani: Travels in Southern Greece. Harmondsworth: Penguin, 1984.

Holst, Gail. *Road to Rembetika*. Athens: Denise Harvey, 1975.
Theodorakis: Myth and Politics in Modern Greek Music. Amsterdam: Adolf Hakkert, 1980.

Huxley and Taylor. *Flowers of Greece and the Aegean*. Chatto and Windus, 1971.

Leigh Fermor, Patrick. *Roumeli: Travels in Northern Greece*. Harmondsworth: Penguin, 1984.

Melas, Evi. *The Greek Islands*. Exeter: Webb and Bower, 1985.
Temples and Sanctuaries of Ancient Greece: A Companion Guide. London: Thames and Hudson.

Millard, Anne. *Usborne Pocket Guide to Ancient Greece: Everyday Life in Greek Times*. London: Usborne, 1981.

Pausanias. *Description of Greece* 2 vols. Trans. by Peter Levi. Harmondsworth: Penguin, 1979.

Petrides, Ted. *Greek Dances*. Athens: Lycabettus Press, 1975.

Sfikas, George. *The Mountains of Greece*. Athens: Efstiadis, 1979.
Trees and Shrubs of Greece. Athens: Efstiadis, 1978.
Wild Flowers of Greece. Athens: Efstiadis, 1976.

Spencer, Terence. *Fair Greece Sad Relic*. London: 1974.

Stoneman, Richard (ed.). *A Literary Companion to Travel in Greece*. Harmondsworth: Penguin, 1984.

Stubbs, Joyce. *The Home Book of Greek Cookery*. London: Faber and Faber, 1963.

Stavroulakis. *Cookbook of the Salonikan Jews*. Athens: Lycabettus, 1985.

Tsigakou, Fani-Maria. *The Rediscovery of Greece*. London: Thames and Hudson, 1981.

Appendix

Restaurants

Athens

Gerofinikas, Pindarou 10, (tel. 362-2719, 363-6710). Cosmopolitan Greek cuisine with Istanbul specialities included. Fresh fish, eggplant puree, lamb with artichokes and tantalizing sweets. Open lunch and dinner.

Bajazzo, Ploutarchou and Dinokratous, Kolonaki, (tel. 729-1420). Unique creations which combine nouvelle cuisine and traditional Greek dishes. "Festival of Seafood," "Dialogue of veal with green apple and mushrooms" and marvelous desserts such as the "Floating Mountain" meringue, "Black Forest Torte," cranberry cake and white chocolate mousse. Full wine list. Expensive by Greek standards but cheap by world-wide standards for innovative, high-quality food. Bird's Bistro with informal menu and bar upstairs. Reservations necessary. Open for lunch on Mon.–Fri. 12 p.m.–4 p.m., and for dinner Mon.–Sat. 8 p.m. to 2 a.m. Closed Sunday.

Kostoyiannis, Zaimi 37 (Pedion A'reos), Exarchia, (tel. 821-2496). Large selection of appetisers. Main dishes include rabbit stifado and quail. Good spiced quince with whipped cream and walnut cake for dessert.

Prunier, Ipsilantou 63, Kolonaki, (tel. 722-7379). French cuisine in romantic setting.

Comilon, Polyla 39, Ano Patissia, (tel. 201-0592). Unusual appetisers such as pork mandarin and Spanish tortilla. Very tasty paella and sangria. Cheesecake for dessert. Nightly from 8 p.m. Kitchen closes at 12:45 a.m. Closed Monday.

Markiza, Proklov 41 (Varnaya Square), Pangrati. (tel. 752-3502). Known for its Cypriot meat balls and onion pie.

Themistokles, Vas. Georgiou 31, Pangrati. (tel. 721-9553). Fine taverna fare in a nice garden.

Psara, Evechtheos and Erotokritou St. 16, Plaka. (tel. 3250-285). An old favorite with good seafood dishes tucked in quiet corner of Plaka.

To Omorfo, Ithakis St., 32, Halandri. (off Kifisias near the Athens Drive In). Good taverna food with a fireplace in the winter, garden in the summer; live music.

Terpsi, corner of Marmariotisis St. and Ethniki Antistaseos St. Halandri. Good taverna food.

Apotsos, Panepistimiou St. 10 (in the arcade). (tel. 363-7046). Classic Athenian lunchtime place; good food; great decor. Open only lunchtime. Closed Sundays.

Athinaikon, corner of Panepistimiou and Themistokleous. (tel. 322-0118). Another fine old "ouzeri". Open both lunch and dinner. Closed Sundays.

Namelesstaverna, corner of Mavromihali and Voulgaroktonou St., Exarchia. Cheap traditional food, garden. (along Mavromihali St. in Exarchia there are also a number of good tavernas).

Eden, 3 Flessa St., Plaka. (tel. 324-8858). Good vegetarian food; a nice change when you've had enough of standard taverna fare.

Note: for an extensive listing of *tavernas* and restaurants in Athens (including Spanish, Chinese, Italian, etc. cuisine) *see The Athenian* weekly magazine.

Thessaloniki

Olympos-Naoussa, 5 Vas. Konstantinou St., (tel. 275715).

Elvetikon, 42 Ayios Sofias St., (tel. 275521).

Stratis, 19 Vas. Konstantinou St., (tel. 234782).

Tiffany's, 3 Iktinou St., (tel. 274022).

Luxury Restaurants

Dionysius, Panorama, (tel. 941813).
Ted's House, 7 Mihalakopoulou St.—Aretsou, (tel. 427334).

Tavernas

Liopesi, Platia Navarinou.
Iordanis, 1 Venizelou St.—Panorama, (tel. 941138).
Klimataria, 34 P. Mela St., (tel. 277854).
Ta Nisia, 13 Koromila St., (tel. 285991).
I Folia Ton Filon Tou Falakra, 5 K. Melekinou, (tel. 210905).
Diagonios 13 P. Mela.

Ouzeris

Anapiros, 20 P. Nikolaou St., (tel. 238269)

Achileas, 17 Filikis Etairias St.

Corfu, 1 Stratigou Kazari St., (tel. 269109).

Patisseries

Agapitos, 57 Tsimiski St., (tel. 279107)

Ellinikon, 209 Vas. Olgas St., (tel. 411133).

Hatzifotiou, 37 P. Mela St. (tel. 232166).

Greek Tourist Police Telephone Numbers
(with the area codes of main Greek cities)

Athens	(01) 171 and 8221-721
Aegina	(0297) 22-391
Agrinion	(0641) 23-381
Alexandrupolis	(0551) 28-424
Argostolion (Kefalonia)	(0671) 22-200
Arta	(0681) 27-580
Ayios Nikolaos	(0841) 28-156
Delphi	(0265) 82-200
Edessa	(0381) 23-355
Halkis	(0221) 24-662
Hania	(0821) 24-477
Heraklion	(081) 283-190
Hios	(0271) 26-555
Hydra	(0298) 52-205
Igumenitsa	(0665) 22-302
Ikaria	(0275) 22-222
Ioannina	(0651) 25-673
Itea	(0265) 32-222
Kalamata	(0721) 23-187
Kalambaka	(0432) 22-813
Kamena Vourla	(0235) 22-425

Kassandra	(0374) 22-204,
Kastoria	(0467) 22-696
Katerini	(0351) 23-440
Kavala	(051) 222-905
Kea	(0288) 21-200
Kerkira	(0661) 30-669
	and 30-265
Kithnos	(0281) 31-201
Korinthos	(0741) 23-282
Kos	(0242) 28-227
Lamia	(0231) 23-281
Larissa	(041) 227-900
Lefkas	(0645) 92-389
Loutra Edipsou	(0226) 22-456
Loutra Kaiafa	(0625) 31-706
Loutra Kilinis	(0623) 96-267
Loutra Smokovu	(0443) 61-204
Loutrakion	(0741) 42-258
Mesolongion	(0631) 22-555
Methana	(0298) 92-463
Mitilini	(025) 22-776
Mykonos	(0289) 22-482
Nafplion	(0752) 27-776
Nea Moudania	(0373) 22-100
Olympia	(0624) 22-550
Parga	(0684) 31-222
Paros	(0284) 21-673
Patras	(061) 220-902
Pireus	(01) 4523-670
Pirgos	(0621) 23-685
Poros	(0298) 22-462
Preveza	(0682) 22-225
Rethimnon	(0831) 28-156
Rodos	(0241) 27-423
Samos	(0273) 27-404
Serres	(0321) 22-001
Sitaia (Crete)	(0843) 24-200
Sparta	(0731) 28-701
Spetsai	(0298) 73-100
Spilaia Dirou (Mani)	(0733) 522-000
Thassos	(0593) 22-500
Thessaloniki	(031) 522-589
Tinos (Andros)	(0283) 22-255
Tripolis	(071) 223-039
Volos	(0421) 27-094
Vouliagmeni	(01) 8946-555
Xylokastron	(0743) 22-331
Zakinthos	(0695) 22-550

Accommodations

Athens

CATEGORY DE LUXE

Acropole Palace, 51, Patission St., 104 33 Athens, (tel. 5223851-7, tlx. 21-5909). Blt. 1930, Ren 1981, Open Jan.–Dec., Number of rooms: Sglb 40, Dblb 47, Stes 18, Airconditioned throughout, 2 bars, restau-

rant, roof garden, night club, convention facilities, transfer service available from several points in Athens.

Amalia, 10, Amalias Avenue, 105 57 Athens, (tel. 3237301-9, tlx. 21-5161). Blt. 1961, Open Jan.–Dec. Number of rooms: Sglb 6, Dblb 92, Stes 1. Airconditioned throughout, central heating, bar, restaurant.

Astir Palace, Vass. Sophias & El. Venizelou corner, 106 71 Athens, Syntagma Square. (tel. 36443112 [8 lines], tlx. 22-2380, Cbl. Astirathen). Blt. 1983, Open Jan.–Dec. Number of rooms: Sglb 10, Dblb 38, Stes 28, VIP Stes 2. Fully airconditioned, 4 channel audio system in all rooms and public areas, Apokalypsis gourmet restaurant, Asteria coffee shop, Athos bar, all rooms with TV and video, newstand, sauna, health care, beauty parlor, conference and banquet facilities.

Athenaeum Inter-Continental, 89-93, Syngrou Avenue, 117 45 Athens, (tel. 9023666, tlx. 22-1554). Blt. 1982, Open Jan.–Dec. Number of rooms: Dblb 630. Airconditioned throughout, central heating, 2 bars, 3 restaurants, swimming pool, convention facilities with simultaneous translation in 4 languages and closed circuit TV, automatic dialing, color TV in all rooms with in-house movies, secretarial service, valets, health studio, bank facilities.

Athens Chandris Hotel, 385, Syngrou Avenue, 175 64 P. Phaleron, (tel. 9414824-6, tlx. 21-8112, Cbl. Chandrotel-Athens). Blt. 1977, Open Jan.–Dec., Number of rooms: Sglb 50, Dblb 300, Stes 22. Airconditioned throughout, central heating, 2 bars, 2 restaurants, Four seasons Restaurant A-la-carte also for non-residents, coffee shop, room service, conference rooms, ballroom fantasia, swimming pool snack bar restaurant, parking facilities, free shuttle service between Hotel-Syntagma Sq.

Athens Hilton, 46, Vass. Sofias Avenue, 106 76 Athens, (tel. 7220201-9, tlx. 21-5808, Cbl. Hiltels). Blt. 1963, Ren 1974, Open Jan.–Dec. Number of rooms: Dblb 480, Stes 24. Airconditioned throughout, 3 bars, 5 restaurants, swimming pool, convention facilities, secretarial service, aut. dress cleaning.

Athens Holiday Inn, 50, Michalakopoulou Street, 115 28 Athens, (tel. 7248322-29, tlx. 21-8870). Blt. 1979, Open Jan.–Dec. Number of rooms: Dblb 200. Airconditioned throughout, central heating, American bar, restaurant, coffee shop, discotheque, bowling, meeting and banqueting facilities up to 500 persons, parking, Bistro Greek.

Caravel, 2, Vass. Alexandrou Avenue, 161 21 Kessariani, (tel. 7290721-29, 7290731, tlx. 21-4401). Blt. 1975, Open Jan.–Dec. Number of rooms: Sglb 100, Dblb 316, Stes 55. 3 bars, 3 restaurants, roof garden, indoor & outdoor swimming pools, room service, 24-hour coffee shop, all hotel operations fully computerized, conference facilities, conventions and other professional group events, easy distance of business and sightseeing center.

Grande Bretagne, Syntagma (Constitution) Square, 105 63 Athens, (tel. 3230251-9, 3250701-9 [72 lines] tlx. 21-9615, 21-5346, Cbl. Hotbritan). Blt. 1862, Ren 1962, Refurbished 1981, Open Jan.–Dec. Number of rooms: 450 rooms, plus 25 suites from Junior to Presidential. Airconditioned throughout, central heating, 2 bars, 3 restaurants, 24-hour room service, convention & function facilities.

King George, 3, King George Street, 105 64 Athens, (tel. 3230651-61, tlx. 21-5296, Cbl. Geking). Blt. 1936, Ren 1978, Open Jan.–Dec. Number of rooms: Sglb 60, Dblb 80, Stes 10. Airconditioned throughout, central heating, bar, restaurant, room service, convention facilities, transfer service available.

Ledra Marriott Hotel-Athens, 115, Syngrou Avenue, 117 45 Athens, (tel. 9525211, tlx. 22-1833, Res. direct line 9324642). Blt. 1983, Open Jan.–Dec. Number of rooms: 258, Stes 25. All rooms with individual climate control, airconditioning, radio, color TV, in-room movies, minibar, 24-hour room service, direct dial telephone with message light, rooftop swimming pool, hydrotherapy pool, bar, coffee shop, cocktail and lobby lounge, poolside bar, 3 restaurants, conference rooms, ballroom, pre-function space outside ballroom, audiovisual equipment.

Park, 10, Alexandras Avenue, 106 82 Athens, (tel. 8832711-19, tlx. 21-4748, Cbl. Parxente). Blt. 1976, Open Jan.–Dec. Number of rooms: Sglb 15, Dblb 111, Stes 20. Airconditioned thoughout, central heating, coffee shop, Pizzaria, roof garden, swimming pool, congress hall, room service, gift shop, beauty parlor, garage.

N.J.V. Meridien Athens, Vass. Georgiou A' & Stadiou Sts., 105 64 Athens, Syntagma Sq., (tel. 3255301 [9 lines], tlx. 21-0568, 21-0569). Blt. 1980, Open Jan.–Dec. Number of rooms: Sglb 30, Dblb 124, Stes 28. Airconditioned throughout, central heating, bar, restaurant, room service, all rooms with mini bar, color TV & video.

Royal Olympic, 28, Diakou Street, 117 43 Athens, (tel. 9226411-13, 9220185, tlx. 21-5753, Cbl. Roytel). Blt. 1968, Open Jan.–Dec. Number of rooms: Sglb 35, Dblb 262, Stes 8. Airconditioned throughout, central heating, bar, restaurant, room service, convention facilities, transfer service available.

St. George Lycabettus 2, Kleomenous Street, Dexameni, Kolonaki, 106 75 Athens, (tel. 7290711-19, tlx. 21-4253, Cbl. Mantzotel). Blt. 1973, Open Jan.–Dec. Number of rooms: Sglb 21, Dblb 128, Stes 5. Airconditioned throughout, central heating, bar, restaurant, room service, swimming pool, convention facilities, bank facilities, roof garden, hairdressing, grill room with panoramic view to Acropolis.

CATEGORY A

Astor, 16, Kar. Servias Street, 105 62 Athens, (tel. 3255555, 3255111, tlx. 21-4018, Cbl Hotelastor). Blt. 1964, Ren 1983, Open Jan.–Dec. Number of rooms: Sglb 32, Dblb 98, Stes 3. Airconditioned throughout, central heating, bar, restaurant, room service.

Attica Palace, 6, Kar. Servias Street, 105 62 Athens, (tel. 3223006-8, Res 3237905, tlx. 21-5909). Blt. 1962, Open Jan.–Dec. Number of rooms: Sglb 9, Dblb 69. Airconditioned throughout, central heating, bar, restaurant, room service, snack bar.

Divani-Zafolia Palace, 19-23, Parthenonos Street, 117 42 Athens, (tel. 9229650-9, 9229151-5, tlx. 21-8306, Cbl Dizafotel). Blt. 1977, Open Jan.–Dec. Number of rooms: Sglb 27, Dblb 159, Stes 7. Airconditioned throughout, central heating, bar, restaurant taverna, swimming pool, convention facilities.

Electra Palace, 18, Nikodimou Street, 105 57 Athens, (tel. 3241401-7, tlx. 21-6896). Blt. 1973, Open Jan.–Dec. Number of rooms: Sglb 20, Dblb 100. Airconditioned throughout, central heating, bar, restaurant, room service, swimming pool.

Golden Age, 57, Michalakopoulou Street, 115 28 Athens, (tel. 7240861 [9 lines], tlx. 21-9292, Cbl Goldenage). Blt. 1975, Open Jan.–Dec. Number of rooms: Sglb 18, Dblb 96, Stes 8. Airconditioned throughout, central heating, bar, restaurant, cafeteria, taverna, room service.

King Minos, 1, Pireos Street, 105 52 Athens, (tel. 5231111-18, tlx. 21-5339). Blt. 1964, Ren 1980, Open Jan.–Dec. Number of rooms: Sglb 56, Dblb 122. Airconditioned throughout, central heating, bar, restaurant, room service, convention facilities, transfer service available.

Olympic Palace, 16, Filellinon Street, 105 57 Athens, (tel. 3237611, tlx. 21-5178, Cbl Olpallas). Blt. 1960, Ren 1965, Open Jan.–Dec. Number of rooms: Sglb 26, Dblb 70. Airconditioned throughout, central heating, bar, restaurant, room service, convention facilities.

CATEGORY B

Acadimos, 58, Akademias Street, 106 79 Athens, (tel. 3629220-9). Blt. 1962, Ren 1975, Open Jan.–Dec. Number of rooms: Sglb 19, Dblb 104. Central heating, bar, restaurant, room service.

Acropolis View, 10, Galli & Webster Streets, 117 42 Athens, (tel. 9217303-5, tlx. 21-9936). Blt. 1971, Open Jan.–Dec. Number of rooms: Sglb 3, Dblb 20. Airconditioned throughout, central heating, bar, restaurant, roof garden.

Adrian, 74, Adrianou Street, 105 56 Athens, (tel. 3250454, 3221553, 3250461). Blt. 1962, Ren 1976, Open Mar.–Oct. Number of rooms: Sglb 22. Airconditioned throughout, central heating, bar, roof garden.

Alfa, 17, Chalkokondyli Street, 104 32 Athens, (tel. 5243584-7). Blt. 1960, Ren 1984, Open Jan.–Dec. Number of rooms: Sglb 9, Dblb 79. Central heating, bar, restaurant, room service.

Arethusa, Metropoleos & Nikis Street, 105 63 Athens, (tel. 3229431-9, tlx. 21-6882). Blt. 1971, Open Jan.–Dec. Number of rooms: Sglb 16, Dblb 72. Airconditioned throughout, central heating, bar, roof garden, restaurant, room service.

Athens Center Hotel, 26, Sofokleous & Klisthenous Streets, 105 52 Athens, (tel. 5226110-19, tlx. 21-4488, Cbl Centerotel). Blt. 1976, Open Jan.–Dec. Number of rooms: Sglb 13, Dblb 123. Airconditioned throughout, central heating, bar, restaurant, roof garden, room service, parking facilities.

Athens City, 232 Patission Street, 112 56 Athens, (tel. 8629115-6). Blt. 1985, Open Jan.–Dec. Number of rooms: Sglb 6, Dblb 31, Stes 3. 40 Bedrooms & stes. with 2 channel music, also rooms with TV & video, bar airconditioned, snack bar, 24 hours room service, parking facilities.

Athinais, 99, Vass. Sophias Avenue, 115 21 Athens, (tel. 6431133, 6441815, 6461682, 6431240, tlx. 21-9336, Cbl Athinotel). Blt. 1976, Open Jan.–Dec. Airconditioned throughout, central heating, bar, snack bar, restaurant, roof garden, room service.

Atlantic, 60, Solomou Street, 104 32 Athens, (tel. 5235361-6, tlx. 21-5723). Blt. 1960, Ren 1972, Open Jan.–Dec. Number of rooms: Sglb 41, Dblb 117. Airconditioned only in double rooms, central heating, bar, restaurant, room service.

Balascas, Liossion & Epirou Streets, 104 39 Athens, (tel. 8835211-5, tlx. 21-0618). Blt. 1978, Open Jan.–Dec. Number of rooms: Sglb 14, Dblb 69. Airconditioned throughout, bar, restaurant.

Christina, 15, Petmeza & Kallirois Streets, 117 43 Athens, (tel. 9215353-7, 9215342-4, tlx. 21-9304). Blt. 1975, Open Jan.–Dec. Number of rooms: Sglb 13, Dblb 80. Airconditioned throughout, central heating, 2 bars, snack bar, restaurant.

Dorian Inn, 15-17, Pireos Street, 105 52 Athens, (tel. 5239782, 5231753-7, tlx. 21-4779, Cbl Hoteldorian). Blt. 1974, Open Jan.–Dec. Number of rooms: Sglb 5, Dblb 112, Stes 29. Airconditioned throughout, central heating, 2 bars, restaurant, room service, swimming pool, convention facilities, roof garden, direct dial telephone system.

El Greco 65, Athinas Street, 105 52 Athens, (tel. 3244553-7, tlx. 21-9682, Cbls Grecotel, Apriltd). Blt. 1958, Ren. 1980, Open Jan.–Dec. Number of rooms: Sglb 17, Dblb 75. Several rooms airconditioned, central heating, bar, restaurant, room service, snack bar, cafeteria.

Eretria, 12, Chalkokondyli Street, 106 77 Athens, Kaningos Square, (tel. 3635311 [10 lines], tlx. 21-5474). Blt. 1966, Ren. 1980, Open Jan.–Dec. Number of rooms: Sglb 7, Dblb 49, Stes 7. Airconditioned throughout, central heating, bar, restaurant, room service, cafeteria.

Grand, 19, Patission Street, 104 32 Athens, (tel. 5243156-9). Blt 1975, Open Jan.–Dec. Number of rooms: Sglb 8, Dblb 91. Airconditioned throughout, central heating, bar, restaurant, room service, convention facilities.

Ilissos, 72, Kallirrois Avenue, 117 41 Athens,

(tel. 9215371, 9223523-9, tlx. 21-0537). Blt. 1980, Open Jan.–Dec. Number of rooms: Sglb 16, Dblb 80. Airconditioned throughout, central heating, bar, restaurant, cafeteria, room service, convention facilities.

Ionis Hotel, 41, Chalkokondyli Street, 104 32 Athens, (tel. 5232311 [4 lines], 5230413 [4 lines], tlx. 21-8425, Cbl Ionishotel). Blt. 1977 Open Jan.–Dec. Number of rooms: Sglb 10, Dblb 92. Airconditioned throughout, central heating, 2 channel music in the rooms, bar, restaurant.

Palladion, 54, El. Venizelou Avenue, 106 78 Athens, (tel. 3623291-5). Blt. 1907, Ren 1974, Open Jan.–Dec. Number of rooms: Sglb 1, Dblb 57. Rooms airconditioned, central heating, bar, room service.

Pan, 11, Metropoleos Street, 105 57 Athens, (tel. 3237817, tlx. 22-1911, Cbl Panhotel). Blt. 1960, Ren 1984, Open Jan.–Dec. Number of rooms: Sglb 6, Dblb 46, Stes 8. Public rooms and most of rooms airconditioned, central heating, snack bar, room service.

Plaka, 7, Kapnikareas Street, 105 56 Athens, (tel. 3222096-8, tlx. 22-1020. Cbl Plakotel Athens). Blt. 1960, Open Jan.–Dec. Number of rooms: Sglb 11, Dblb 56. Airconditioned throughout, central heating, bar, restaurant, room service.

Titania, 52, El. Venizelou Avenue, 106 78 Athens, (tel. 3609611-9, tlx. 21-4673, Cbl Titanotel). Blt. 1976, Open Jan.–Dec. Number of rooms: Sglb 42, Dblb 333, Stes 21. Rooms fully airconditioned with private baths, radio music, 2 channels in all rooms, TV sets on request, restaurant with greek specialities and international dishes, snack bar, piano cocktail lounge "Taboo" in the roof garden, convention facilities, garage for 400 cars, shopping center.

Xenophon, 340, Acharnon Street, 111 45 Athens, (tel. 2020310-24, tlx. 21-5294). Blt. 1970, Open Jan.–Dec. Number of rooms: Sglb 22, Dblb 164. Airconditioned throughout, central heating, bar, restaurant, room service, convention facilities, garage, parking facilities, transfer service available.

CATEGORY C

Achilleus, 21, Lekka St., 105 62 Athens, (tel. 3233197, 3225826).

Achillion, 32, Ag. Konstantinou St., 104 37 Athens, (tel. 5225618).

Albyon, 20, Akominatou St., 104 37 Athens, (tel. 5231137, 5223058).

Alma, 5, Dorou Street, 104 31 Athens, (tel. 5240858-9).

Ami, 10, Iras Street, 117 43 Athens, (tel. 9220820).

Apollon, 14, Deligiorgi Street, 104 37 Athens, (tel. 5245211, 5245214).

Arias, 20, Karolou Street, 104 37 Athens (tel. 5228527-9).

Aristidis, 50, Sokratous St., 104 31 Athens, (tel. 5223881, 5223923).

Artemission, 20, Veranzerou Street, 104 32 Athens, (tel. 5230524, 5230036, 5234959).

Astra, 46, Deligianni Street, 104 39 Athens, (tel. 8213772).

Athinea, 9, Vilara Street, 104 37 Athens, (tel. 5243884-5, 5245737).

Attalos, 20, Athinas Street, 105 54 Athens, (tel. 3212801-3).

Capri, 6, Psaromilingou Street, 105 53 Athens, Koumoundourou Sq., (tel. 3252085, 3252091).

Carolina, 55, Kolokotroni Street, 105 60 Athens, (tel. 3220837-8).

Crystal, 68, Kolonou & Achilleos Sts., 104 37 Athens, (tel. 5231083).

Delph, 21, Ag. Konstantinou Sq., 104 37 Athens, (tel. 5222751, 5226549).

Economy, 5, Klisthenous Street, 105 52 Athens, (tel. 5220520-2).

Elite, 23, Pireos Street, 105 52 Athens, (tel. 5221523, 5223610)

Epidavros, 14, Koumoundourou St., 104 37 Athens, (tel. 5230421).

Evropa, 7, Satovriandou Street, 104 31 Athens, (tel. 5223081).

Fivos, 12, Petta Street, 105 58 Athens, (tel. 3220142-3).

Florida, 25, Menandrou St., 105 53 Athens, (tel. 5223214, 5239712).

Helicon, 3, Dorou Street, 104 31 Athens, (tel. 5221695, 5228428).

Hera, 9, Falirou Street, 117 42 Athens, Makriyanni area, (tel. 9235618, 9236682).

Jason, 3, Nikiforou Street, 104 37 Athens, (tel. 5248031-3).

Imperial, 46, Metropoleos Street, 105 63 Athens, (tel. 3227617-8).

Kalypso, 34, Epikourou Street, 105 53 Athens, (tel. 3251451-2).

Keramikos, 30, Keramikou & Iassonos Streets, 104 36 Athens, (tel. 5247631, 5247443).

Kissos, 6, Mezonos Street, 104 38 Athens, (tel. 5243011-3).

Kronos, 18, Ag. Dimitriou Street, 105 54 Athens, (tel. 3211601-3).

Lido, 2, Nikiforou & Zinonos Sts., 104 37 Athens, (tel. 5248211-4).

Marina, 13, Voulgari Street, 104 37, Athens, (tel. 5224769, 5229109).

Medoussa, 4, Evripidou Street, 176 74 Kallithea, (tel. 9426216).

Minion, 3, Mezonos Street, 104 38 Athens, (tel. 5234222-3).

Morfeus, 3, Aristotelous Street, 104 32 Athens, (tel. 5234601).

Museum, 16, Bouboulinas Street, 106 82 Athens, (tel. 3605611-3).

Nafsika, 21, Karolou Street, 104 37 Athens, (tel. 5239381-3).

Nefeli, 16, Hyperidou Street, 105 58 Athens, (tel. 3228044-5).

Neon Kronos, 12, Assomaton Street, 105 53 Athens, (tel. 3251106-8).

Nestorion, 8, Pentelis Street, 174 64 Amphithea, (tel. 9425010, 9420272, tlx. 22-1427).

Niki, 27, Nikis Street, 105 57 Athens, (tel. 3220913-5, 3220886).

Olympia, 25, Pireos Street, 105 52 Athens, (tel. 5222429).

Omega, 15, Aristogitonos Street, 105 52 Athens, (tel. 3212421-3).

Orpheus, 58, Chalkokondyli Street, 104 32 Athens, (tel. 5224996).

Parnon, Tritis Septemvriou & Chalkokondyli Sts., 104 32 Athens, (tel. 5230013-14, 5235196).

Phedias, 39, Apostolou Pavlou St., 118 51 Athens, (tel. 3459511-5).

Pringhipikon, 27, Veranzerou St., 104 32 Athens, (tel. 5232376).

Rivoli, 10, Achilleos Street, 104 36 Athens, (tel. 5239714-6).

Roosvelt, 5, Favierou Street, 104 38 Athens, (tel. 5223413).

Sans Rival, 2, C. Paleologou & Liossion Streets, 104 38 Athens, (tel. 5248675, 5223431).

Stalis, 10, Akominatou Street, 104 37 Athens, (tel. 5241411-2).

Theoxenia, 6, Gladstonos Street, 105 77 Athens, (tel. 3600250).

Troikon, 20, Troias Street, 112 57 Athens, (tel. 8816695, 8217319).

Vienna, 20, Pircos Street, 104 31 Athens, (tel. 5225605-7).

Zinon, 3, Keramikou Street, 104 37 Athens, (tel. 5228811-13).

FURNISHED FLATS/HOTEL APARTMENTS

CATEGORY A

Ariane, 22, Tim. Vassou St., 115 21 Athens, (tel. 6466361-2, 6437302-4).

Ava, 9, Lyssikratous Street, 105 58 Athens, (tel. 3236618).

Delice, 3, Vass. Alexandrou Street, 115 28 Athens, (tel. 7238311-13).

Embassy, 15, Timoleontos Vassou St., 115 21 Athens, (tel. 6421152-4).

Kolonaki, 7b, Kapsali St., 106 74 Athens, (tel. 7213759, 7228412).

Lion, 7, Evzonon Street, 115 21 Athens, (tel. 7248722-4).

Perli, 4, Arnis Street, 115 28 Athens, (tel. 7248794-8, tlx. 21-5444).

CATEGORY B

Egnatia, 64, Tritis Septemvriou St., 104 33 Athens, (tel. 8227807).

Iokastis, HOUSE 65, Aristotelous St., 104 34 Athens, (tel. 8226647).

PENSIONS

CATEGORY A

Blue house, 19, Voukourestiou St., 106 71 Athens, (tel. 3620341).

CATEGORY B

Acropolis House, 6, Kodrou Street, 105 58 Athens, (tel. 3222344, 3244143).

Adam's, 6, Herefontos &Thalou Streets, 105 58 Athens, (tel. 3246582, 3225381).

Adonis, Voulis & 3, Kodrou Sts., 105 58 Athens, (tel. 3249737, 3249738).

Akron, 16, Theras Street, 112 57 Athens,

(tel. 8626220, 8626228).

Angela, 38, Stournara Street, 104 33 Athens, (tel. 5220216-7).

Antoniou, 232, Patission Street, 112 56 Athens, (tel. 8629841-2).

Apostolopoulos, 284, Patission & 5, Mistriotou Streets, 112 55 Athens, (tel. 2236375).

Aristofanis, 38, Aristophanous Street, 105 54 Athens, (tel. 3250872).

Athenian Inn, 22, Haritos St., 106 75 Athens, (tel. 7238097, 7239552).

Athens House, 4, Aristotelous Street, 104 32 Athens, (tel. 5240539).

Byron, 9, Vironos Street, 105 58, Athens, (tel. 3230327).

Dryades, 4, Dryadon Street, 114 73 Athens, (tel. 3602961, 3622881).

Elisabeth, 46, Arkadias Street, 115 27 Athens, (tel. 7775448).

Elli, 29, Heyden Street, 104 34 Athens, (tel. 8823487)

Feron, 43, Feron St., 104 40 Athens, (tel. 3632831-9, tlx. 21-5077).

George, 46, Nikis Street, 105 58 Athens, (tel. 3229569).

Heliki, 4, Enianos Street, 104 34 Athens, (tel. 8822560, 8810627).

Iokasti's House, 65, Aristotelous Street, 104 34 Athens, (tel. 8226647).

Iris, 8, Sorovits St., 112 52 Athens, (tel. 8647442, 8653222, 8654229).

Kirki, 40, Kefalinias Street, 112 57 Athens, (tel. 8235733).

Kypseli, 7, Skyrou St., 113 61 Athens, (tel. 8216232, 8213116, 8219898).

Lydia, 121, Liossion St., 104 45 Athens, (tel. 8219980, 8237952, tlx. 21-9786).

Myrtc, 40, Nikis Street, 105 58 Athens, (tel. 3227237, 3234560).

Nora, 38, Antiochias Street, 112 51 Athens, (tel. 8628876).

Odysseus, 39, Kimothois Street, 172 36 Athens, (tel. 9700571).

Oniro, 57, S. Trikoupi Street, 106 83 Athens, (tel. 8832731-3).

Patissia, 221, Patission St., 112 53 Athens, (tel. 8627511, 8627512).

Pnyx, 51, Apostolou Pavlou Street, 118 51 Athens, (tel. 3468859).

Remvi, 284, Patission & 3, Mystriotou Streets, 112 55 Athens, (tel. 2024124, 2231405).

Roy, 15, Rodou St., 112 52 Athens, (tel. 8615765, 8618763, 8610843).

Soudan, 47, Mavromichali Street, 106 80 Athens, (tel. 2605037).

Steyer, 123, Char. Trikoupi Street, 114 73 Athens (tel. 3615731).

Volcan, 10a, Ithakis Street, 113 61 Athens, (tel. 8815385).

Zorbas, 10, Gylfordou Street, 104 34 Athens, (tel. 8232543).

CATEGORY C

Amazon, 7, Pendelis Street, 105 57 Athens, (tel. 3234002-6).

Annabel, 28, Koumoundourou & Satovriandou Sts., 104 37 Athens, (tel. 5243454).

Argo, 25, V. Hugo Street, 104 37 Athens, (tel. 5225939).

Art Galery, 5, Erechthiou Street, 117 42 Athens, (tel. 9238376).

Athens Connections, 20, Ioulianou S., 106 82 Athens, (tel. 8213940).

Christ, 11, Apollonos Street, 105 57 Athens, (tel. 3220177, 3234581).

Diana, 3, Kotsika Street, 104 34 Athens, (tel. 8223179).

Dioskouros, 6, Pittakou Street, 105 58 Athens, (tel. 3248165).

Greca, 48, Syngrou Avenue, 117 42 Athens, (tel. 9215626).

Inn Student, 16, Kydathineon St., 105 58 Athens, (tel. 3244808).

John's Place, 5, Patroou Street, 105 57 Athens, (tel. 3229719).

Kouros, 11, Kodrou Street, 105 58 Athens, (tel. 3227431).

Marble House, 35, An. Zini Street, 117 41 Athens, (tel. 9234058).

Milton, 4, Kotsika Street, 104 34 Athens, (tel. 8216806).

Paradise, 28, Mezonos Street, 104 38 Athens, (tel. 5220084).

Pella Inn, 104, Ermou Street, 105 54 Athens, (tel. 3250598).

Peter's, 32, Nikis Street, 105 57 Athens, (tel. 3222697).

San Remo, 8, Nissirou Street, 104 38 Athens, (tel. 5243454).

Thesseus, 10, Thisseos Street, 105 62 Athens, (tel. 3245960).

Tony's, 26, Zacharitsa Street, 117 41 Athens, (tel. 9236370).

Thessaloniki

CATEGORY DE LUXE

Makedonia Palace, Meg. Alexandrou Street, 546 40 Thessaloniki, (tel. 837520-9, 837620-9, tlx. 41-2162, 41-2164 Cbl Macepal). Blt. 1972, Open Jan.–Dec. Number of rooms: Sglb 44, Dblb 228, Stes 15. Airconditioned throughout, bar, restaurant, room service, congress facilities.

CATEGORY A

Capitol, 8, Monastiriou Street, 546 29 Thessaloniki, (tel. 516221, tlx. 41-2272). Blt. 1967, Open Jan.–Dec. Number of rooms: Sglb 35, Dblb 152, Stes 7. Airconditioned throughout, central heating, bar, restaurant, room service, convention facilities.

Electra Palace, 5a, Aristotelous Square, 546 24 Thessaloniki, (tel. 232221, tlx. 41-2590). Athens office: 5, Ermou Street, (tel. 3232104). Blt. 1972, Open Jan.–Dec. Number of rooms: Sglb 32, Dblb 93, Stes 6. Airconditioned throughout, central heating, bar, restaurant, grill room, room service, convention facilities.

Nepheli, 1, Komninon Street, 552 36 Panorama, (tel. 942002, 942024, 942068, 942080, tlx. 41-0357). Blt. 1967, Open Jan.–Dec. Number of rooms: Sglb 10, Dblb 55, Stes 5. Partially airconditioned, central heating, bar, restaurant, room service, roof garden, night club, convention facilities, parking.

Panorama, 14, Analipseos Street, 552 36 Panorama, (tel. 941123, 941266, 941229). Blt. 1969, Open Jan.–Dec. Number of rooms: Sglb 12, Dblb 35, Stes 3. Central heating, bar, restaurant, room service, channel music, cafeteria.

CATEGORY B

Astor, 20, Tsimiski Street, 546 24 Thessaloniki, (tel. 527121-5, tlx. 41-2655). Blt. 1973, Open Jan.–Dec. Number of rooms: Sglb 12, Dblb 72, Stes 6. Airconditioned throughout, central heating, bar, restaurant, parking facilities.

Capsis, 18, Monastiriou Street, 546 29 Thes-

saloniki, (tel. 521321-9, 521421-9, tlx. 41-2206, Cbl Capsotel). Blt. 1970, Open Jan.–Dec. Number of rooms: Sglb 33, Dblb 395. Aircondition optional, central heating, bar, restaurant, room service, swimming pool, convention facilities, discotheque, hairdressing, sauna, dress cleaning.

City Hotel, 11, Komninon Street, 546 29 Thessaloniki, (tel. 269421-30, tlx. 41-2208). Blt. 1972, Open Jan.–Dec. Number of rooms: 210 beds. Airconditioned throughout, central heating, all rooms with telephone & verandah, bar, cafeteria, TV lounge.

El Greco, 23, Egnatias St., 546 30 Thessaloniki, (tel. 520620-30). Blt. 1970, Open Jan.–Dec. Number of rooms: Sglb 18, Dblb 72. Airconditioned throughout, central heating, bar, restaurant, parking, automatic telephone service.

Metropolitan, Vass. Olgas & Fleming Streets, 546 42 Thessaloniki, (tel. 824221 [8 lines], tlx. 41-2380). Blt. 1979, Open Jan.–Dec. Number of rooms: Sglb 12, Dblb 99, Stes 8. Stes airconditioned, central heating, bar, restaurant, room service, olympic airways bus stop in front of the hotel, TV room, automatic outside telephone connection, parking facilities.

Olympia, Venizelou & 65, Olympou Streets, 546 31 Thessaloniki, 12km from the airport, (tel. 235421 [5 lines], 263201 [5 lines], tlx. 41-8532, Cbl Olympotel). Ren. 1980, Open Jan.–Dec. Number of rooms: Sglb 15, Dblb 100. Airconditioned throughout, central heating, bar, restaurant, cafeteria, fireplace, colour TV lounge, special halls for business or social events, car parking facilities.

Olympic, 25, Egnatias Street, 546 30 Thessaloniki, (tel. 522131-3). Blt. 1969, Ren 1975, Open Jan.–Dec. Number of rooms: Dblb 39, Dbln 13. Central heating, bar.

Palace, 12, Tsimiski Street, 546 24 Thessaloniki (tel. 270505, 270855, 238838, 225368). Ren. 1968, Open Jan.–Dec. Number of rooms: Sglb 33, Dblb 25. Central heating, bar, restaurant, room service.

Philippion, Kedrinos Lofos, 5km from the city center, (tel. 203320-22, tlx. 41-0210). Ren. 1979, Open Jan.–Dec. Number of rooms: Sglb 18, Dblb 70, Stes. 2. Central heating, bar, restaurant, coffee-shop, mini golf, pizzaria, swimming pool, night club, disco.

Queen Olga, 44, Vass. Olgas Avenue, 546 41 Thessaloniki, (tel. 824621 [10 lines]). Blt.

1969, Open Jan.–Dec. Number of rooms: Sglb 35, Dblb 113. Airconditioned throughout, central heating, bar, restaurant, room service, parking area.

Rotonda, 97, Monastiriou Street, 546 27 Thessaloniki, (tel. 517121-3, tlx. 41-2322, Cbl Hotel Rotonda). Blt. 1966, Open Jan.–Dec. Number of rooms: Sglb 16, Dblb 63. Airconditioned throughout, central heating, bar, restaurant, room service.

Victoria, 13, Lagada Street, 546 29 Thessaloniki, (tel. 522421-5, tlx. 41-2145). Blt. 1965, Open Jan.–Dec. Number of rooms: Sglb 9, Dblb 58. Partially airconditioned, central heating, bar, restaurant, room service.

CATEGORY C

ABC Hotel, 41, Agelaki Street, Sidrivani Square, 546 21 Thessaloniki, (tel. 265421 [5 lines], 221761, 279765, tlx. 41-0056). Blt. 1968, Open Jan.–Dec. Number of rooms: Sglb 15, Dblb 87, Stes 5. Partially airconditioned, central heating, bar, cafeteria & breakfast room with fireplace and airconditioning, stes. with A/C, color TV, mini bar, balcon.

Aegeon, 19, Egnatias Avenue, 546 30 Thessaloniki, (tel. 522921-3).

Amalia, 33, Hermou Street, 546 24 Thessaloniki, (tel. 268321).

Anessis, 20, 26th October St., 546 27 Thessaloniki, (tel. 515505-6).

Ariston, 5, Diikitiriou Street, 546 30 Thessaloniki, (tel. 519630).

Continental, 5, Komninon Street, 546 24 Thessaloniki, (tel. 277553).

Delta, 13, Egnatias Street, 546 30 Thessaloniki, (tel. 516321-7).

Emborikon, 14, Syngrou Street, 546 30 Thessaloniki, (tel. 525560).

Esperia, 58, Olympou Street, 546 31 Thessaloniki, (tel. 269321-5).

Haris, Oreokastron, (tel. 696174, 696198).

Grande Bretagne, 46, Egnatias Avenue, 546 25 Thessaloniki, (tel. 530735).

Madrino, 2, Antigonidon Street, 546 30 Thessaloniki, (tel. 526321-5).

Minerva, 19, Syngrou Avenue, 546 30 Thessaloniki, (tel. 530844).

Oceanis, 35, Nik. Plastira Street, Aretsou, (tel. 418870).

Park, 81, Ionos Dragoumi St., 546 30 Thessaloniki, (tel. 524121-4).

Pefka, Panorama, (tel. 941153, 941282).

Pella, 65, Ionos Dragoumi St., 546 30 Thessaloniki, (tel. 524221).

Rea, 6, Komninon Street, 546 24 Thessaloniki, (tel. 278449).

Rex, 39, Monastiriou St., 546 27 Thessaloniki, (tel. 517051, 517052).

Teleioni, 16, Ag. Dimitriou St., 546 30 Thessaloniki, (tel. 527825-6).

Thessalikon, 60, Egnatias Av., 546 27 Thessaloniki, (tel. 277722, 223805).

Vergina, 19, Monastiriou.St., 546 27 Thessaloniki, (tel. 527400-8).

PENSIONS

CATEGORY B

Athos, 20, Dagli Street, (tel. 266990).

Elizabeth Motel, 293, Monastiriou Street, 546 28 Thessaloniki, (tel. 515712-3).

Haris Motel, Micra, (tel. 417335).

Airline Offices

Most airline town offices are open Mon.–Fri. between 9 a.m.–5 p.m., the general sales agents offices are open also on Sat. between 9 a.m.–2 p.m. The Athens East Airport Central Exchange telephone number is: 96991.

There are direct buses to Athens East Airport Terminal departing from Athens Town Terminal 4, Amalias Avenue, every 20 minutes from 6 a.m.–12 a.m. Fare: 90 drs. including luggage. There are also direct buses to Athens West-East Airport Terminals from Piraeus departing from Piraeus Town Terminal, Akti Tzelepi, every 20 minutes, from 6 a.m.–12 a.m. Fare: 90 drs. including luggage.

Aeroflot (SU), 14, Xenofondos Street, near Syntagma Square, (tel. 3220986, 3221022).

Aerolineas Argentinas (AR), General Sales Agents: Link International Co. Ltd., 36, Voukourestiou Street, 106 73 Athens, near Syntagma Square, (tel. 3607936, 3609492).

Air Algerie (AH), 17, Filellinon Street, (tel. 3235504).

Air Canada (AC), 10, Othonos Street, Syntagma Square, (tel. 3235143, 3223206).

Air France (AF), 4, Karageorgi Servias Street, Syntagma Square, (tel. 3230501-6).

Air India (AI), 15, Omirou Street, near Syntagma Square, (tel. 3602457, 3603584).

Air Tanzania (TC), 233, Syngrou Avenue, 171 21 N. Smyrni, Oceanair Bldg., (tel. 9332951-2).

Air Zaire (QC), 16, Nikis Street, near Syntagma Square (tel. 3235738).

Air Zimbabwe (RH), 39, El. Venizelou Av., opp. the Athens University, (tel. 3239101-2).

Alia-Royal Jordanian Airlines (RJ), 4, Filellinon Street, Syntagma Square, (tel. 3241377, 3241342).

Alitalia (AZ), 10, Nikis Street, near Syntagma Square, (tel. 3244383-8).

Austrian Airlines (OS), 4, Filellinon Street, Syntagma Square, (tel. 3230844-46).

Balkan-Bulgarian Airlines (LZ), 23, Nikis Street, near Syntagma Square, (tel. 3226684, 3237547).

Biman-Airlines Of Bangladesh (BG), 15, El. Venizelou Avenue, near Syntagma Square, (tel. 3228089, 3241116 [5 lines], 3255061 [5 lines]).

British Airways (BA), 10, Othonos Street, Syntagma Square, (tel. 3222521 [9 lines]).

CP Air-Canadian Pacific (CP), 4, Karageorgi Servias Street, Syntagma Square, (tel. 3230344-7).

CSA-Czechoslovak Airlines (OK), 15, El. Venizelou Avenue, near Syntagma Square, (tel. 3232303, 3230174).

Cyprus Airways (CY), 10, Filellinon Street, near Syntagma Square, (tel. 3246965-7).

Eastern Airlines (EA), General Sales Agents: GOLDAIR Ltd. 15, El. Venizelou Avenue, near Syntagma Square, (tel. 3241116 [5 lines], 3255061 [5 lines]).

Egyptair (MS), 10, Othonos Street, Syntagma Square, (tel. 3233575-7).

El Al-Israel Airlines Ltd (LY), 8, Othonos Street, Syntagma Square, (tel. 3230116-8).

Ethiopian Airlines S.C. (ET), 25, Filellinon Street, near Syntagma Square, (tel. 3234275).

Finnair (AY), 16, Nikis Street, near Syntagma Square, (tel. 3255234-5, 3254831).

Gulf Air (GF), 23, Nikis Street, near Syntagma Square, (tel. 3226684, 3237547).

Iberia, Lineas Aereas De Espana (IB), 8, Xenofondos & Filellinon Sts., near Syntagma Square, (tel. 3245514-5).

Icelandair (FI), 6, Kriezotou Street, near Syntagma Square, (tel. 3632572, 3632443).

Interflug Gmbh (IF), 20, El. Venizelou Avenue, near Syntagma Square, (tel. 3624808, 3624809).

Iranair (IR), 16, El. Venizelou Avenue, near Syntagma Square, (tel. 3607611).

Iraqi Airways (IA), 23, Syngrou Avenue, (tel. 9229573, 9230236, 9233383).

Japan Airlines (JL), 4, Amalias Avenue, near Syntagma Square, (tel. 3248211-15).

Jat-Jugoslovenski Aerotransport (JU), 4, Voukourestiou Street, near Syntagma Square, (tel. 3236429, 3223675).

Kenya Airways Ltd (KQ), 5, Stadiou Street, near Syntagma Square, (tel. 3247000, 3245500).

KLM-Royal Dutch Airlines (KL), 22, Voulis Street, near Syntagma Square, (tel. 3242991-3, 3226011-3).

Korean Air (KE), General Sales Agents: Danae Chartering Ltd. 6, Psylla & Filellinon Streets, (tel. 3247511 [10 lines]).

Kuwait Airways Corp.–Kac (KU), 32, Amalias Avenue, near Syntagma Square, (tel. 3234506, 3234147).

Libyan Arab Airlines (LN), 3 Metropoleos Street, Syntagma Square, (tel. 3244816-9, 3247100).

LOT-Polish Airlines (LO), 4, Amalias Avenue, near Syntagma Square, (tel. 3221121, 3238638).

Lufthansa German Airlines (LH), 4, Karageorgi Servias Street, Syntagma Square, (tel. 3294-1).

Luxair (LG), 6, Kriezotou Street, near Syntagma Square (tel. 3603134, 3632572, 3632443).

Malev-Hungarian Airlines (MA), 15, El. Venizelou Avenue, near Syntagma Square, (tel. 3241116 [5 lines], 3255061 [5 lines]).

Mea-Middle East Airlines-Air Liban (ME), 10, Filellinon Street, near Syntagma Square, (tel. 3226911-5, 3235683-6).

Northwest Orient Airlines (NW), General Sales Agents: Link International Co. Ltd., 36, Voukourestiou Street, near Syntagma Square, (tel. 3604166-7).

Olympic Airways/Olympic Aviation (OA), Head Office: 96, Syngrou Avenue, 117 41 Athens, (tel. 9292111). Reservations (tel.

9616161 [60 lines], tlx. 21-5103, 21-5963). Ticket offices:

- 6, Othonos Street, (tel. 9292555 Int., 9292444 Dom).

- 96, Syngrou Avenue, (tel. 9292251, 9292333, Rate desk 9292341, tlx. 21-6488, Cbl Olympair).

- 3, Kotopouli Street, Omonia Square, (tel. 5237565-6, 9292217-20).

- 267, Kifissias Street, Kifissia, (tel. 8016119, 9292702).

- 2-4, Messoghion Avenue, (tel. 7759562-3, 9292701).

- 13, Athinon Street, Glyfada, (tel. 8944220). For Prepaid Tickets:

- 11, Mitropoleos Square, (tel. 9292257-8, 9292204, 9292482).

- Athens Hilton Hotel, (tel. 9292445).

- 27, Akti Miaouli, Piraeus, (tel. 4520968). Freight office: 98, Syngrou Avenue, (tel. 9292200 Int., 9292300 Dom). Town Terminal: 96, Syngrou Avenue, (tel. 9292251, 9292333, Rate desk 9229341). Hellinikon, West Air Terminal (tel. 9892111). Flight arrival/departure information (tel. 9811201-4, tlx. 21-5824, 21-5307). Airport East (tel. 9699317).

PAL-Philippine Airlines (PR), 15, El. Venizelou Avenue, near Syntagma Square, (tel. 3241116 [5 lines], 3255061 [5 lines]).

PAN AM-Pan American World Airways INC. (PA), 4, Othonos Street, Syntagma Square, (tel. 3235242, 3221721).

PIA-Pakistan International Airlines (PK), 15, El. Venizelou Avenue, near Syntagma Square, (tel. 3231931, 3241116 [5 lines], 3255061 [5 lines]).

Qantas Airways Ltd (QF), Filellinon & Nikis corner, near Syntagma Square, (tel. 3232792).

Royal Air Maroc (AT), 5, Metropoleos Street, Syntagma Square, (tel. 3244302-4).

SABENA — Belgian World Airlines (SN), 8, Othonos Street, Syntagma Square, (tel. 3236821).

SAS-Scandinavian Airlines System (SK), 6, Sina & Vissarionos Sts., near Syntagma Square, (tel. 3634444-9).

SAUDIA-Saudi Arabian Airlines (SV), 17, Filellinon Street, near Syntagma Square, (tel. 3244671-5).

Singapore Airlines Limited (SQ), 22,

Filellinon Street, Syntagma Square, (tel. 3239111-8).

South African Airways (SA), 4, Karageorgi Servias Street, Syntagma Square, (tel. 3229007, 3237857).

Sudan Airways (SD), 44, Amalias Avenue, near Syntagma Square, (tel. 3244716/7).

Swissair (SR), 4, Othonos Street, Syntagma Square, (tel. 3231871/5).

Syrianair (RB), 39, El. Venizelou Av., opp. the Athens University, (tel. 3238711-2).

Thai International (TG), 3-5 Lekka Street, near Syntagma Square (tel. 3243241-3).

Trans World Airlines Inc (TW), 8 Xenofondos Street, near Syntagma Square, (tel. 3236831).

TUNIS AIR - Societe Tunisienne De L'air (TU), 14, Xenofondos Street, near Syntagma Square (tel. 3220104-5, 3231973).

Turkish Airlines (TK), 19, Filellinon Street, near Syntagma Square, (tel. 3246024).

VARIG-Brazilian Airlines (RG), 10, Othonos Street, Syntagma Square, (tel. 3226743, 3238685).

Yemenia-Yemen Airways (IY), 9, Patission Street, near Omonia Square, (tel. 5245912, 5220622).

Embassies And Consulates

Algeria: 14, Vass. Konstantinou & Eratosthenous corner, (tel. 7513560, 7518625, 7516204).

Arab Republic Of Egypt: 3, Vass. Sophias Av., (tel. 3618612-3).

Argentine: 59, Vass. Sophias Avenue, (tel. 7224753, 7224710).

Australia: 15, Mesoghion Street, (tel. 7757650-54).

Austria: 26, Alexandras Avenue, (tel. 8211036, 8216800, 8827520).

Belgium: 3, Sekeri Street, (tel. 3617886-7).

Brazil: 14, Filikis Eterias Square, (tel. 7213039, 7244434).

Bulgaria (People's Rep.): 2, Akademias St., (tel. 3609411-4).

Canada: 4, 1. Gennadiou Street, (tel. 7239511-9, 7239510).

Chile: 96, Vass. Sophias Avenue, (tel. 7775017, 7700272).

Colombia: 91, Marathonodromou Street, 154 52 P. Psychiko, (tel. 6474457, 6723057).

Costa Rica: 20, El. Venizelou Avenue, (tel. 3601377).

Cuba: 10, Davaki Street, 115 26 Erythros Stavros, (tel. 6925367, 6929895).

Cyprus: 16, Herodotou Street, (tel. 7237883, 7232727, 7239377).

Czechoslovakia: 6, G. Seferis Street, 154 51 P. Psychikon, (tel. 6710675, 6725332, 6713755).

Denmark: 15, Filikis Eterias Square, (tel. 7249315-7).

Ecuador: 6, Sotiros St., 185 35 Piraeus (tel. 4122361, 4115112).

Ethiopia: 10, Davaki Street, (tel. 6920565, 6920483).

Finland: 1, Eratosthenous & Vass. Konstantinou corner, (tel. 7519795, 7011775).

France: 7, Vass. Sophias Avenue, (tel. 3611663-5).

Gabon Republic: 22, K. Paleologou St., (tel. 5236795).

Germany Dem. Republic: 7, Vass. Pavlou St., 154 52 Paleon Psychikon, (tel. 6725160-3).

Germany Federal Rep.: 3, Karaoli & Dimitriou Street, (tel. 36941).

Honduras: 86, Vass. Sophias Av., (tel. 7775802, 7750170).

Hungary: 16, Kalvou Street, 154 52 Paleon Psychikon, (tel. 6714889, 6715515).

India: 4, Meleagrou Street, (tel. 7216227, 7216481).

Iran (The Islamic Republic Of): 16, Stratigou Kalari St., 154 52 P. Psychikon, (tel. 6471436, 6471783, 6471937).

Iraq: 4, Mazaraki Street, 154 52 P. Psychikon, (tel. 6715012, 6721566).

Ireland: 7, Vass. Konstantinou Av., (tel. 7232771-2).

Italy: 2, Sekeri Street, (tel. 3611723, 3611722).

Japan: Athens Tower, 2-4, Messoghion Avenue, (tel. 7758101-3).

Jordan (Hashemite Kingdom Of): 30, Pan. Zervou St., 154 52 Psyhiko, (tel. 6474161, 6474138).

Korea (South): 1, Eratosthenous & Vass. Konstantinou corner, (tel. 7012122).

Kuwait: 55, Al. Papanastassiou St., 154 52 N. Psychiko (tel. 6473593-5, 6724279).

Lebanon: 26, Kifissias Av., (tel. 7785158, 7704540).

Mexico: 5-7, Vass. Konstantinou Avenue (3rd floor), (tel. 7230754, 7232368).

Morocco: 14, Mousson Street, 154 52 P. Psychiko, (tel. 6474209-10).

Netherlands: 5-7, Vass. Konstantinou Avenue, (tel. 7239701-4, 7235159).

New Zealand: 15-17, An. Tsoha Street, (tel. 6410311-15).

Norway: 7, Vass. Konstantinou Avenue, (tel. 7246173-4).

Pakistan: 6, Loukianou Street, (tel. 7290214, 7290122).

Panama: 21, Vass. Sophias Avenue, (tel. 3631847).

People's Republic Of China: 2a, Krinon Street, 154 52 Paleon Psychikon, (tel. 6723282).

Poland (People's Rep.): 22, Chrissanthemon Street, 154 52 P. Psychikon, (tel. 6716917-18).

Portugal: 19, Loukianou Street, (tel. 7290096, 7290052).

Romania: 7, Emm. Benaki Street, 154 52 P. Psychikon, (tel. 6718020, 6712719).

Saudi Arabia: 71, Marathonodromou Street, 145 52 P. Psychikon, (tel. 6716911-3).

South Africa: 124, Kifissias & Iatridou corner, (tel. 6922125).

Soviet Union: 28, Nikiforou Litra Street, (tel. 6725235, 6726130).

Spain: 29, Vass. Sophias Avenue, Embassy (tel. 7214885, 7224242).

Sweden: 7, Vass. Konstantinou Avenue, (tel. 7224504-5).

Switzerland: 2, Iassiou Street, (tel. 7230364-6).

Syrian Arab Rep: 79, Marathonodromou St., 154 52 P. Psychikon, (tel. 6711604, 6725577).

Thailand: 23, Taygetou Street, 154 52 P. Psychiko, (tel. 6717969).

Tunis: 91, Ethn. Antistasseos Street, 152 31 Halandri, (tel. 6717590, 6529789).

Turkey: 8, King George B' St., (tel. 7245915-7).

United Kingdom: 1, Ploutarchou Street, (tel. 7236211-19).

United States Of America: 91, Vass. Sophias Avenue, (tel. 7212951-9, 7218400-1).

Uruguay: Embassy-Consulate: 1, Lycavitou Street, 1st floor, (tel. 3602635, 3613549).

Vatican: Embassy: 2, Mavili Street, 154 52 P. Psychiko, (tel. 6473598).

Venezuela: 112, Vass. Sophias Avenue, (tel. 7709962, 7708769).

Yugoslavia: 106, Vass. Sophias Avenue, (tel. 7774344, 7774355).

Zaire: 3, Digeni Griva Street, (tel. 6818925-7).

Tourist Boards

Greek National Tourist Organization Offices In The U.S.A. And Canada

Greek National Tourist Organization (Head Office), Olympic Tower, 645 Fifth Avenue, 5th Floor, New York, New York 10022, (tel. (212) 421-5777, tlx. 640125).

Greek National Tourist Organisation, 168 North Michigan Avenue, Chicago, Illinois 60601, (tel. (312) 782-1084, tlx. 283468).

Greek National Tourist Organization, National Bank of Greece Building, 31 State Street, Boston, Massachusetts 02109 (tel. (617) 227-7366, tlx. 940493).

Greek National Tourist Organization 611 West Sixth Street, Suite 1998 Los Angeles, California 90017 (tel. (213) 626-6696, tlx. 686441).

Greek National Tourist Organization 1233 Rue De La Montagne Montreal, Quebec H3G 1Z2, Canada (tel. (514) 871-1535, tlx. 05560021).

Greek National Tourist Organization 80 Bloor Street, Suite 406 Toronto, Ontario M5S 2V1 Canada (tel. (416) 968-2220, tlx. 06218845).

Greek National Tourist Organization Offices Abroad

Australia and New Zealand: Greek National Tourist Organization, 51-57 Pitt Street, Sydney N.S.W. 2000, (tel. 241-1663/4).

Austria: Griechische Zentrale fur, Fremdenverkehr, Karntner Ring 5, 1015 Vienna, (tel. 525317/8, tlx. 111816).

Belgium: Office National Hellenique de Tourisme, 62-66 Boulevard de I'Imperatrice, 1000 Brussels, (tel. 513-0206, 513-2712, tlx. 24044).

Denmark: Det Graeske Turistbureau, Vester Fartmagsgade 3, DK 1606 Copenhagen, (tel. 123063).

Finland: Kreikan Valtion Matkailutoimisto, Stora Robertsgatan 3-5 C38, 00120 Helsingfors, Helsinki 12, (tel. 607552, 607113).

France: Office National Hellenique de Tourisme, 3 Avenue de L'Opera, Paris 75001, (tel. 260-6534, tlx. 680345).

German Federal Republic: Frankfurt, Griechische Zentrale fur, Fremdenverkehr, Neue Mainzer Str. 22, 6 Frankfurt/Main 1, (tel. 236-561/2/3, tlx. 412034).

Hamburg, Griechische Zentrale fur, Fremdenverkehr, 2000 Hamburg 36, Never Wall 35, (tel. 366910, 366973).

Munich, Griechische Zentrale fur, Fremdenverkehr, Pacelli Str. 2, 8000 Munich 2, (tel. 222035/6, tlx. 528126).

Italy: Rome, Ente Nazionale Ellenico per il Turismo, Via L. Bissolati 78-80, 00187 Roma, (tel. 474-4249, 474-4301, tlx. 611331).

Milan, Ente Nazionale Ellenico per il Turismo, Piazza Diaz 1, (Ang. Via Rastrelli), Milan, (tel. 860-470, 860-477, tlx. 62331).

Japan: Greek National Tourist Organization, No. 11 Mori Building, 2-6-4 Toranomon, Minato-Ku, Tokyo 105, (tel. 503-5001/2, tlx. 2225529).

Netherlands: Griekse Nationale Organizatie Voor, Toerisme, Leidsestraat 13, NS Amsterdam, (tel. 254-212/3, tlx. 15465).

Norway: Den Greske Stats Turistbyra, Ovre Slottsgatan 15 B, 0157 Oslo 1, (tel. 426501/2, tlx. 74025).

Saudi Arabia: Embassy of Greece/Office of Tourism and Information, Madina Road, City Centre, P.O. Box 13262/Code No. 21493, Jeddah, (tel. 667-6280).

Spain: Oficina Nacional Helenica de Turismo, Alberto Aguilera 17, Madrid 15, (tel. 248-4889/90, tlx. 45796).

Sweden: Grekiska Statens Turistbyra, Birger Jarlsgaten 8 IV, 2 P.O. Box 5298, 10246 Stockholm 5, (tel. 210930, tlx. 10443).

Switzerland: Griechische Zentrale fur, Fremdenverkehr, Gottfried Keller Strasse 7, 8001 Zurich, (tel. 251-8487/8/9, tlx. 57720).

United Kingdom and Ireland: Greek National Tourist Organization, 195-197 Regent Street, London WIR 8DR (tel. 734-5997, tlx. 21122).

For all offices listed above, the cable address is "GRECTOUR" followed by the name of the city concerned.

In Mexico and South America the Greek National Tourist Organization is represented by the following governmental agencies:

Argentina: Embajada de Grecia, Avenida Pte. Rocke Saenz, Pena 547, Buenos Aires, R. Argentina.

Brazil: Embaixada da Grecia/Escritorio de Imprensa, Caixa Postal 12. .2604, SHI-SUL Ql 11 Conj. 01 Casa 11, Brasilia D-F.

Mexico: Embajada de Grecia, Paseo de las Palmas 2060, Colonia Lamas Reforma, Mexico, D.F. 11020.

Venezuela: Embajada de Grecia/Press Office, Avenida San Gabriel 60, Alta Florida, Caracas, Venezuela.

Museums and Sites

Athens

Acropolis Archaeological Site, (tel. 3210219). Open: Daily 08.30–17.00; Entrance fee: 300 drs. (including fee to the Museum).

Acropolis Museum, on the Acropolis, (tel. 3236665). Open: Daily 08.00–17.00, Closed on Tues. Entrance fee: 300 drs. (including fee to the archaeological site).

Ancient Agora Museum In The Stoa Of Attalos, Entrance from Thisson Sq., & 24, Andrianou St., (tel. 3210185). Open: Daily 08.00–17.00. Closed on Tues.; Entrance fee: 150 drs. (including fee to the archaeological site).

Athens City Museum, 7, Paparigopoulou Street, (tel. 3230168). Open: Mon; Wed; Fri. 0900–1330; Entrance fee: 100 drs.

Benaki Museum, Vass. Sophias Avenue, (tel. 3611617). Open: Daily 08.30–14.00, Closed on Tues.; Entrance fee: 100 drs.

Byzantine Museum, 22, Vass. Sophias Avenue, (tel. 7211027). Open: Daily 08.45–15.00, Sun. & Holidays 09.30–14.30, Closed on Mon.; Entrance fee: 200 drs.

Daphni Monastery, (tel. 5811558). Open: Daily 08.45–15.00, Sun. & Holidays 09.30–14.30; Entrance fee: 100 drs.

Epigraphical Collection, 1, Tossitsa Street, (tel. 8217637). Open: Daily 08.30–13.30, Sun. & Holidays 09.00–14.00, Closed on Tues. Admission free.

Jewish Museum of Greece, 36 Amalias St., (tel. 3231577). Open: Daily 09.00–13.00, Closed: Sat.

Museum of Cycladic and Ancient Greek Art, 4, Neofytou Douka St., (tel. 7249706). Open: Daily 10.00–16.00, Closed: Tues. and Sun.

Museum Of Greek Popular Art, 17 Kydathineon St., Plaka, (tel. 3213018). Open: Daily 10.00–14.00, Closed on Mon.; Admission free.

Hist. And Ethnological Museum, Stadiou St., (tel. 3237617). Open: Tue. to Fri. 09.00–14.00, Sat, Sun. 09.00–13.00, Closed on Mon.; Entrance fee: 100 drs. Admission free on Thurs.

Kaissariani Monastery, (tel. 7236619). Open: Daily 08.45–15.00, Sun. & Holidays 09.30–14.30; Admission free.

Kanellopoulos Museum, Theorias & Panos Sts., Plaka, (tel. 3212313). Open: Daily 08.45–15.00, Sun. & Holidays 09.30–14.30, Closed on Tues.; Sun. & Holidays the entrance fee is charged, Entrance fee: 100 drs.

Keramikos Museum, 148, Ermou Street, (tel. 3463552). Open: Daily 08.45–15.00, Sun. & Holidays 09.30–14.30 Closed on Tues; Entrance fee: 100 drs. (including fee to the archaeological site).

Keramikos Archaeological Site, Ermou & Pireos corner, (tel. 3463552). Open: Daily 08.45–15.00, Sun. & Holidays 09.30–14.30; Entrance fee: 100 drs. (including fee to the Museum).

Nat. Archaeological Museum, 1, Tossitsa St., (tel. 8217717). Open: Daily 08.00–17.00, Closed on Tues.; Entrance fee: 250 drs. (including fee to the exhibits from Thira & the Numismatic Museum).

National Gallery And Alexandros Soutsos Museum, 46, Vass. Sophias Avenue, (tel. 7211010). Open: Daily 09.00–15.00, 10.00–14.00, Closed on Mon.; Admission free.

Natural History, 13, Levidou Street, Kifissia, (tel. 8080254). Open: Daily including Sun. 09.00–13.00 & 17.00–20.00, Closed on Fri.; Sun. & Holidays the entrance fee is charged, Entrance fee: 30 drs.

Numismatic Collection, 1, Tossitsa Street,

(tel. 8217769). Open: Daily 08.30–13.30, Sun. & Holidays 09.00–14.00, Closed on Tues.; Admission free.

Roman Agora, End of Eolou Street, (tel. 3210185). Open: Daily 08.45–15.00, Sun. & Holidays 09.30–14.30; Entrance fee: 100 drs.

Temple Of Hephaistos And Ancient Agora, (tel. 3210185). Open: Daily 08.00–17.00; Entrance fee: 150 drs.

Temple Olympian Zeus, Olgas & Amalias Av., (tel. 9226330). Open: Daily 08.45–15.00, Sun. & Holidays 09.30–14.30, Entrance fee: 100 drs.

Theatre Of Dionyssos, D. Areopagitou Av., (tel. 3236665). Open: Daily 08.45–15.00, Sun. & Holidays 09.30–14.30; Entrance fee: 100 drs.

War Museum of Greece, Vass. Sophias Avenue, (tel. 7290543-4). Open: Daily 09.00–14.00, Closed on Mon.; LIBRARY Open: Tues.–Sat. 09.00–14.00; Admission free.

Piraeus

Maritime Museum Of Piraeus, Akti Themistokleous, (tel. 4516822). Open: Daily 09.00–12.30, Sun. & Holidays 10.00–20.00, Closed on Mon.; Tues. & Fri; admission free. Entrance fee: 100 drs.

Piraeus Archaeological Museum, 31, Char. Trikoupi Street, (tel. 4521598, 4518388). Open: Daily 08.45–15.00, Sun. & Holidays 09.30–14.30, Closed on Tues; Entrance fee: 100 drs.

Amphipolis

Archaeological Site, (tel. 051-224717). Open: Daily 08.45–15.00, Sun. & Holidays 09.30–14.30; Admission free.

Andros

Archaeological Museum, (tel. 0282-23664). Open: Daily 08.45–15.00, Sun. & Holidays 09.30–14.30; Closed on Tues. Entrance fee: 100 drs.

Museum Basil & Elisa Goulandris (Modern Art), (tel. 0282-22650). Open: Daily 10.00–13.00, 17.00–20.00, Closed on Tues.; Admission free.

Argos

Museum, (tel. 0751-28819). Temporarily closed; Entrance fee: 100 drs.

Chaironia

Museum, (tel. 0261-95270). Open: Daily 08.45–15.00, Sun. & Holidays 09.30–14.30, Closed on Tues.; Admission free.

Corinthos

Acrocorinth Archaeological Site, (tel. 0741-31443). Open: Daily 08.45–15.00, Sun. & Holidays 09.30–14.30; Entrance fee: 150 drs. (including fee to the Museum).

Museum, (tel. 0741-31207). Open: Daily 08.45–15.00, Sun. & Holidays 09.30–14.30, Closed on Tues; Entrance fee: 200 drs. (including fee to the archaeological site).

Crete

Ag. Nikolaos Museum, (tel. 0841-22462). Open: Daily 08.45–15.00, Sun. & Holidays 09.30–14.30, Closed on Tues.; Entrance fee: 100 drs.

Chania Museum, (tel. 0821-20334, 24418). Open: Daily 08.45–15.00, Sun. & Holidays 09.30–14.30, Closed on Tues.; Entrance fee: 100 drs.

Heraklion Archaeological Museum, (tel. 081-226092). Open: Daily 08.00–17.00, Closed on Mon.; Entrance fee: 200 drs.

Rethymnon Museum, (tel. 0831-29975). Open: Daily 08.45–15.00, Sun. & Holidays 09.30–14.30, Closed on Tues.; Entrance fee: 100 drs.

Aghia Trias Archaeological Site, (tel. 081-226092). Open: Daily 08.45–15.00, Sun. & Holidays 09.30–14.30, Closed on Fri.; Entrance fee: 100 drs.

Cnossos Archaeological Site, (tel. 081-231940). Open: Daily 08.00–17.00; Entrance fee: 200 drs.

Phaestos Archaeological Site, (tel. 0892-22615). Open: Daily 08.00–17.00, Entrance fee: 150 drs.

Gortys Archaeological Site, (tel. 081-226092). Open: Daily 08.45–15.00, Sun. & Holidays 09.30–14.30; Entrance fee: 100 drs.

Mallia Archaeological Site, (tel. 081-226092). Open: Daily 08.45–15.00, Sun. & Holidays 09.30–14.30; Entrance fee: 100 drs.

Tylissos Archaeological Site, (tel. 081-226092). Open: Daily 08.45–15.00, Sun. & Holidays 09.30–14.30, Closed on Mon.; Entrance fee: 100 drs.

Other Archaeological Sites, (tel. 081-226092). Saint Titus, Gournia, Open: Daily 08.45–15.00, Sun. & Holidays 09.30–14.30; Admission free.

Heraklion Harbour Fortress (Koules), (tel. 081-286228). Open: Daily 08.45–15.00, Sun. & Holidays 09.30–14.30; Entrance fee: 100 drs.

Delos

Archaeological Site, (tel. 0289-22259). Open: Daily 08.45–15.00, Sun. & Holidays 09.30–14.30; Entrance fee: 200 drs. (including fee to the Museum).

Museum, (tel. 0289-22259). Temporarily closed.

Delphi

Archaeological Site, (tel. 0741-31207). Open: Daily 08.45–15.00, Sun. & Holidays 09.30–14.30; Entrance fee: 150 drs. (including fee to the Museum).

Museum, (tel. 0265-82313). Open: Daily 08.00–17.00, Closed on Tues.; Entrance fee: 200 drs.

Dion — Pieria

Archaeological Site, (tel. 0351-53206). Open: Daily 08.45–15.00, Sun. & Holidays 09.30–14.30; Entrance fee: 100 drs. (including fee to the Museum).

Museum, (tel. 0351-53206). Open: Daily exc. Mon., Wed. 08.45–15.00, Closed on Tues.; Entrance fee: 100 drs. (including fee to the archaeological site).

Egina

Temple Of Aphaia, (tel. 0297-32398). Open: Daily 08.45–15.00, Sun. & Holidays 09.30–14.30; Entrance fee: 100 drs.

Museum, (tel. 0297-22637). Open: Daily 08.45–15.00, Sun. & Holidays 09.30–14.30, Closed on Tues. Entrance fee: 100 drs. (including fee to the temple of Apollo).

Elefsis

Museum, (tel. 5546019). Open: Daily 08.45–15.00, Sun. & Holidays 09.30–14.30, Closed on Tues.; Entrance fee: 100 drs. (including fee to the archaeological site).

Epidavros

Archaeological Site & Museum, (tel. 0753-22009). Open: Daily 08.00–17.00, Closed on Tues.; Entrance fee: 200 drs.

Eretria (Evia)

Archaeological Site & Museum, (tel. 0221-62206). Open: Daily 08.45–15.00, Sun. & Holidays 09.30–14.30, Closed on Tues.; Entrance fee: 100 drs.

Filippi

Archaeological Site, (tel. 051-516470), Open: Daily 09.00–17.00, Sun. & Holidays 10.00–17.00; Entrance fee: 150 drs.

Museum, (tel. 05-516261). Open: Daily 08.45–15.00, Sun. & Holidays 09.30–14.30, Closed on Tues.; Entrance fee: 100 drs.

Kerkyra

Archaeological Museum, (tel. 0661-30680). Open: Daily 08.45–15.00, Sun. & Holidays 09.30–14.30, Closed Tues.; Entrance fee: 100 drs.

Museum Of Asiatic Art, (tel. 0661-23124). Open: Daily 08.45–15.00, Sun. & Holidays 09.30–14.30, Closed on Tues.; Entrance fee: 100 drs.

Kos

Museum, (tel. 0242-28326). Open: Daily 08.45–15.00, Sun. & Holidays 09.30–14.30, Closed on Tues.; Entrance fee: 100 drs.

Castle, (tel. 0242-28326). Open: Daily 08.45–15.00, Sun. & Holidays 09.30–14.30, Closed on Tues.; Entrance fee: 100 drs.

Restored Ancient Dwelling, (tel. 0242-28326). Open: Daily 08.45–15.00, Sun. & Holidays 09.30–14.30; Entrance fee: 100 drs.

Asclepieion And Other Archaeol Sites, (tel. 0242-28763). Open: Daily 08.45–15.00, Sun. & Holidays 09.30–14.30; Entrance fee: 100 drs.

Lesvos

Eressos Archaeological Museum, (tel. 0251-22087). Open: Daily 08.45–15.00, Sun. & Holidays 09.30–14.30, Closed on Tues.; Admission free.

Mytilini Archaeological Museum, (tel. 0251-22087). Open: Daily 08.45–15.00, Sun. & Holidays 09.30–14.30, Closed on Tues.; Entrance fee: 100 drs.

Milos

Archaeological Site & Museum, (tel. 0287-21620). Open: Daily 08.45–15.00, Sun. & Holidays 09.30–14.30, Closed on Tues.; Entrance fee: 100 drs.

Catacombs, (tel. 0287-21620). Open: Daily 08.45–14.30; Sun. & Holidays 09.30–14.30; Entrance fee: 50 drs.

Mykine

Archaeological Site, (tel. 0725-27502). Open: Daily 08.00–17.00; Entrance fee: 200 drs.

Mystras

Archaeological Site, (tel. 0731-25363). Open: Daily 08.45–15.00, Sun. & Holidays 09.30–14.30; Entrance fee: 200 drs. (including fee to the Museum).

Museum, (tel. 0731-25363). Open: Daily 08.45–15.00, Sun. & Holidays 09.30–14.30, Closed on Tues.; Entrance fee: 150 drs (including fee to the archaeological site).

Nafplion

Museum, (tel. 0752-27502). Open: Daily 08.45–15.00, Sun & Holidays 09.30–14.30, Closed on Tues.; Entrance fee: 100 drs.

Palamidi Fortress, (tel. 0752-28036). Open: Daily 10.00–16.30, Sun. & Holidays 10.00–15.00, On March 25 remains open. Entrance fee: 100 drs.

Popular Art Museum, (tel. 0752-28379). Open: Daily 09.00–13.00 & 17.00–19.00, Closed on Tues.; Admission free.

Nemea

Museum, (tel. 0746-22739). Open: Daily 08.45–15.00, Sun & Holidays 09.30–14.30, Closed on Tues.; Entrance fee: 100 drs.

Olympia

Archaeological Site, (tel. 0624-22517). Open: Daily 08.45–15.00, Sun. & Holidays 09.30–14.30; Entrance fee: 200 drs.

Museum, (tel. 0624-21529, 22742). Open: Daily 08.45–15.00, Sun. & Holidays 09.30–14.30, Closed on Tues.; Entrance fee: 200 drs.

Historical Museum of Olympic Games, (tel. 0624-25572, 22596). Open: Daily 08.45–15.00, Sun. & Holidays 09.30–14.30, Closed on Tues.; Entrance fee: 100 drs.

Olynthos (Chalkidiki)

Archaeological Site, (tel. 0373-21862). Open: Daily 08.45–15.00, Sun. & Holidays 09.30–14.30; Admission free.

Oropos

Amphiaraion Museum, (tel. 0295-62144). Open: Daily 08.45–15.00, Sun. & Holidays 09.30–14.30, Closed on Tues., Entrance fee: 100 drs. (including fee to the archaeological site).

Ossios Loukas

Byzantine Monastery, (tel. 3213571). Open: Daily 08.45–15.00, Sun. & Holidays 09.30–14.30; Entrance fee: 100 drs.

Patmos

Monastery Of St. John-Vestry-Library, (tel. 0241-21954). Open: Daily 08.45–15.00, Sun. & Holidays 09.30–14.30; Admission free.

Pella

Archaeological Site, (tel. 0382-31160, 31278). Open: Daily 08.45–15.00, Sun. & Holidays 09.30–14.30; Entrance fee: 100 drs.

Museum, (tel. 0382-31160, 31278). Open: Daily 08.45–15.00, Sun. & Holidays 09.30–14.30, Closed on Tues.; Entrance fee: 100 drs.

Pylos

Museum, (tel. 0723-22448). Open: Daily 08.45–15.00, Sun. & Holidays 09.30–14.30, Closed on Tues.; Entrance fee: 100 drs.

Nestor's Palace, near Pylos, (tel. 0723-31358). Open: Daily 08.45–15.00, Sun & Holidays 09.30–14.30; Entrance fee: 100 drs.

Ramnous

Archaeological Site, (tel. 0294-93477). Open: Daily 08.45–15.00, Sun. & Holidays 09.30–14.30; Admission free.

Rodos

Acropolis-Theatre-Stadium, (tel. 0241-27674). Open: Daily 08.45–15.00, Sun. & Holidays 09.30–14.30; Admission free.

Museum, (tel. 0241-27674). Open: Daily 08.45–15.00, Sun. & Holidays 09.30–14.30, Closed on Tues.; Entrance fee: 200 drs.

Palace Of The Knights, (tel. 0241-27674). Open: Daily 08.45–15.00, Sun. & Holidays 09.30–14.30, Closed on Tues.; Entrance fee: 200 drs.

Perimetre Of The Medieval Walls, (tel. 0241-27674). Open to visitors accompanied by a guide on Mon. and Sat. afternoons. Visitors should gather in the courtyard of the Palace of the Knights. Open: 15.00–17.00; Admission free.

Camiros Excavations, (tel. 0241-27674). Open: Daily 08.45–15.00, Sun. & Holidays 09.30–14.30; Entrance fee: 100 drs.

Acropolis Of Ialyssos, (tel. 0241-27674). Open: Daily 08.45–15.00, Sun. & Holidays 09.30–14.30; Entrance fee: 100 drs.

Acropolis Of Lindos, (tel. 0241-27674). Open: Daily 08.45–15.00, Sun. & Holidays 09.30–14.30; Entrance fee: 200 drs.

Decorative Collections, (tel. 0241-27674). It is open to the public on Mon., Wed. and Fri. from 09.00–13.00; Entrance fee: 100 drs.

Samos

Hera Temple — Archaeological Site, (tel. 0273-61177). Open: Daily 08.45–15.00, Sun. & Holidays 09.30–14.30; Entrance fee: 100 drs.

Vathy Museum, (tel. 0273-27469). Temporarily closed.

Pythagorion Museum, (tel. 0273-61400). Open: Daily 08.45–15.00, Sun. & Holidays 09.30–14.30, Closed on Tues.; Admission free.

Efpalinion Orygma, (tel. 0273-61400). Open: Mon., Thu., Sat. 10.00–12.00; Admission free.

Samothraki

Archaeological Site, (tel. 0551-41474). *Dorion: Doric* marble temple dated 260 B.C. *Arsrnoeion*. Circular construction dating 288-281 B.C. Open: Daily 08.45–15.00, Sun. & Holidays 09.30–14.30; Entrance fee: 100 drs.

Museum, (tel. 0551-41474). Open: Daily 08.45–15.00, Sun. & Holidays 09.30–14.30, Closed on Tues.; Entrance fee: 100 drs.

Santorini (Thira)

Museum, (tel. 0286-22217). Open: Daily 08.45–15.00, Sun. & Holidays 09.30–14.30, Closed on Tues.; Entrance fee: 100 drs.

Archaeological Site, (tel. 0286-22217). Well preserved ruins of the ancient town (Theatre, agora, temple, site of athletics, government-house, fortifications, private house, tombs of achaic and classical periods, early Christian relics). Open: Daily 08.45–15.00, Sun. & Holidays 09.30–14.30; Admission free.

Akrotirion Thiras Archaeological Site, (tel. 0286-81366). Open: Daily 08.45–15.00, Sun. & Holidays 09.30–14.30; Entrance fee: 150 drs.

Sikyon

Archaeological Site, (tel. 0742-28900). Ruins of the town's walls, the Stadium, the Gymnasium, the Sacred Spring, the Bouleuterion, the temple of Artemis and the theatre are well preserved. Open: Daily 08.45–15.00, Sun. & Holidays 09.30–14.30; Admission free.

Museum, (tel. 0742-28900). Open: Daily 08.45–15.00, Sun. & Holidays 09.30–14.30, Closed on Tues.; Admission free.

Sounion

Archaeological Site, (tel. 0292-39363). Open: Daily 09.00 till Sunset, Sun. & Holidays 10.00 till Sunset; Entrance fee: 150 drs.

Sparti

Museum, (tel. 0731-25363). Open: Daily 08.45–15.00, Sun. & Holidays 09.30–14.30, Closed on Tues.; Entrance fee: 100 drs.

Thessaloniki

Archaeological Museum and Treasures Of Ancient Macedonia (Vergina Findings), (tel. 031-830538). Open: Daily 08.45–15.00, Sun. & Holidays 09.30–14.30, Closed on Tues.; Entrance fee: 200 drs (both Museum & Vergina findings).

Folklore Museum, 68, Vass. Olgas St., (tel. 031-830591). Open: Daily 09.00–14.00, Closed on Tues.; Admission free.

Saint George (Rotonta), (tel. 031-213627). Temporarily closed.

Crypt Of Saint Dimitrios, (tel. 031-270008). Open: Daily 08.45–15.00, Sun. & Holidays 09.30–14.30; Admission free.

The White Tower — Byzantine Museum, Vass. Konstantinou St. Open: Daily 09.00–14.00, Closed Tues.

Thive

Museum, (tel. 0262-27913). Open: Daily 08.45–15.00, Sun. & Holidays 09.30–14.30, Closed on Tues.; Entrance fee: 100 drs.

Tiryns

Archaeological Site, (tel. 0752-27502). Open: Daily 08.45–15.00, Sun. & Holidays 09.30–14.30; Entrance fee: 100 drs.

Vergina

Archaeological Site, (tel. 031-830538). Open: Daily 08.45–15.00, Sun. & Holidays 09.30–14.30; Entrance fee: 100 drs.

Volos (Nea Anchialos)

Archaeological Site, (tel. 0421-25285). Open: Daily 08.45–15.00, Sun. & Holidays 09.30–14.30; Entrance fee: 100 drs.

Vravrona

Museum, (tel. 0294-71020). Open: Daily 08.45–15.00, Sun. & Holidays 09.30–14.30, Closed on Sun.; Entrance fee: 100 drs (including fee to the archaeological site).

Archaeological Site, (tel. 0294-71020). Open: Daily 08.45–15.00, Sun. & Holidays 09.30–14.30; Entrance fee: 100 drs (including fee to the Museum).

ART/PHOTO CREDITS

Cover	David Beatty
3	David Beatty
4/5	David Beatty
6/7	David Beatty
8/9	David Beatty
10/11	Michele Macrakis
12/13	David Beatty
14	David Beatty
16	Amanda Eliza Weil
17	Amanda Eliza Weil
18	Eileen Tweedy
19L	By Courtesy of Benaki Museum
19R	By Courtesy of Benaki Museum
20	Margot Granitsas
22L	By Courtesy of Ashmolean Museum
22R	By Courtesy of Ashmolean Museum
23	G P Reichelt
24	Paul Herrmann
25	By Courtesy of Cyclades Museum
26	David Beatty
27L	By Courtesy of Ashmolean Museum
27R	By Courtesy of Ashmolean Museum

29	By Courtesy of Byzantine Museum
31	Amanda Eliza Weil
33	Eileen Tweedy
34/35	Karen Van Dyck
37L	Ethiniki Pinakothiki
37R	Ethiniki Pinakothiki
38	Karen Van Dyck
40	Spiros Meletzis
41L	Karen Van Dyck
41R	Karen Van Dyck
42	Karen Van Dyck
44/45	By Courtesy of Princeton University Library
46	By Courtesy of Ashmolean Museum
48	By Courtesy of Ashmolean Museum
50	Karen Van Dyck
52	By Courtesy of Ashmolean Museum
53	By Courtesy of Princeton University Library
54	By Courtesy of Ashmolean Museum
57	By Courtesy of Ashmolean Museum
58/59	Amanda Eliza Weil
60	Michele Macrakis
61	Amanda Eliza Weil
62	G P Reichelt
63	Amanda Eliza Weil
64	Susan Muhlhauser
65	David Beatty
66L	Margot Granitsas
66R	David Beatty
68	G P Reichelt
69	Amanda Eliza Weil
70	David Beatty
71	Michele Macrakis
72	Michele Macrakis
73	Michele Macrakis
74	Amanda Eliza Weil
75	Amanda Eliza Weil
76	David Beatty
77L	Michele Macrakis
77R	Michele Macrakis

78	David Beatty
79	David Beatty
80	Susan Muhlhauser
81	Susan Muhlhauser
82	Barbara F Gundle
83	Amanda Eliza Weil
85	Michele Macrakis
86/87	Michele Macrakis
88/89	Tony Stone Worldwide
90/91	Tony Stone Worldwide
92/93	Michele Macrakis
94	Tony Stone Worldwide
96/97	By Courtesy of Ashmolean Museum
100	Amanda Eliza Weil
101	Amanda Eliza Weil
102	Amanda Eliza Weil
103	Michele Macrakis
104L	Amanda Eliza Weil
104R	Fay Zika
105	Ethniki Pinakothiki
106	Tony Stone Worldwide
107	Dieter Lotze
108	Amanda Eliza Weil
109	Amanda Eliza Weil
110L	Michele Macrakis
110R	Amanda Eliza Weil
111	Amanda Eliza Weil
112	Amanda Eliza Weil
113	Amanda Eliza Weil
115	Fay Zika
118	Michele Macrakis
119	Michele Macrakis
120	Barbara F. Gundle
121	Michele Macrakis
122	Fay Zika
123L	Fay Zika
123R	Aliki Govrdomichalis
124	Fay Zika
125	Fay Zika
126	Karen Van Dyck
127	Karen Van Dyck
128	Margot Granitsas
129L	Michele Macrakis
129R	Gaetano Barone
131	By Courtesy of Victoria and Albert Museum
132/133	Tony Stone Worldwide

135	Paul Herrmann	184/5	David Beatty	241L	Tony Stone Worldwide
136	Michele Macrakis	188	Dieter Lotze	241R	Karen Van Dyck
137L	Tony Stone Worldwide	189L	Susan Muhlhauser	242L	David Beatty
137R	Susan Muhlhauser	189R	Susan Muhlhauser	242R	Amanda Eliza Weil
138	Paul Herrmann	190	Amanda Eliza Weil	243	David Beatty
139	Susan Muhlhauser	191	Amanda Eliza Weil	244	David Beatty
140	Michele Macrakis	192	David Beatty	245	David Beatty
141	Tony Stone Worldwide	193	David Beatty	246	David Beatty
142	Margot Granitsas	194	Margot Granitsas	247	David Beatty·
143	Barbara F. Gundle	195	Susan Muhlhauser	248	David Beatty
144	By Courtesy of Benaki Museum	196	Amanda Eliza Weil	249	David Beatty
		197	Dieter Lotze	250	David Beatty
145	Barbara F. Gundle	198	Susan Muhlhauser	251	David Beatty
148	Tony Stone Worldwide	199L	Dieter Lotze	253	David Beatty
149L	By Courtesy of Benaki Museum	199R	Amanda Eliza Weil	254/255	David Beatty
		200	Amanda Eliza Weil	258	Barbara F. Gundle
149R	Tony Stone Worldwide	201	Dieter Lotze	259	Jens Schumann
150	David Beatty	203	Dieter Lotze	260	Michele Macrakis
151	Dieter Lotze	204/205	Tony Stone Worldwide	261	G P Reichelt
152	Susan Muhlhauser	208L	P. Petrolpoulous	262	G P Reichelt
153	Susan Muhlhauser	208R	Michele Macrakis	263	Jens Schumann
154	Susan Muhlhauser	209	Ben Nakayama	264	Jens Schumann
155L	Ethiniki Pinakothiki	211	Amanda Eliza Weil	265L	G P Reichelt
155R	Susan Muhlhauser	212	Susan Muhlhauser	265R	Barbara F. Gundle
157	Susan Muhlhauser	213	Amanda Eliza Weil	266	G P Reichelt
158/159	Tony Stone Worldwide	214	P. Petrolpoulous	267	Amanda Eliza Weil
160	Susan Muhlhauser	215	David Beatty	268	Barbara F. Gundle
162	Michele Macrakis	216	P. Petrolpoulous	269	Margot Granitsas
163	Amanda Eliza Weil	217	P. Petrolpoulous	273	Amanda Eliza Weil
164	Michele Macrakis	219	Jen Schumann	274	Michele Macrakis
165L	Amanda Eliza Weil	222	David Beatty	275	Michele Macrakis
165R	Michele Macrakis	223	David Beatty	277	Jane Cowan
166	By Courtesy of Ashmolean Museum	224	David Beatty	278	Amanda Eliza Weil
		225L	Susan Muhlhauser	279	David Beatty
167	Tony Stone Worldwide	225R	David Beatty	280	Michele Macrakis
168	Tony Stone Worldwide	226L	David Beatty	281	Amanda Eliza Weil
169L	Gaetano Barone	226R	Susan Muhlhauser	287	David Beatty
169R	Susan Muhlhauser	227	Susan Muhlhauser	289	Amanda Eliza Weil
170	By Courtesy of Ashmolean Museum	228L	Susan Muhlhauser	291	By Courtesy of Pinacotheque Nationale de Goica
		228R	Susan Muhlhauser		
171	Gaetano Barone	229	Susan Muhlhauser		
174	Tony Stone Worldwide	230	David Beatty	293	Jane Cowan
176	Michele Macrakis	231	David Beatty	295	Amanda Eliza Weil
177	Michele Macrakis	232	Michele Macrakis	299	Michele Macrakis
178	Michele Macrakis	233	David Beatty	303L	Barbara Gundle
179	Tony Stone Worldwide	234	David Beatty	304L	David Beatty
180	Amanda Eliza Weil	235	David Beatty	305	Amanda Eliza Weil
181	Michele Macrakis	236/237	Xaritatos	306L	David Beatty
183	Karen Van Dyck	240	David Beatty	307	Amanda Eliza Weil
				310	Amanda Eliza Weil

Backcover Pictures: David Beatty (top right corner); David Beatty (Bells); Courtesy of Ashmolean Museum (Beehives); Michele Macrakis (Beaches); Courtesy of Ashmolean Museum (Treasures); Amanda Eliza Weil (Travelers); Tony Stone Worldwide (Temples); Michele Macrakis (Oranges); David Beatty (Olivegroves); Susan Muhlhauser (Orthodoxy); Amanda Eliza Weil (Sisters); Eileen Tweedy (Sailing); Amanda Eliza Weil (Salads).

Spine (from top to bottom): Courtesy of Ashmolean Museum; Amanda Eliza Weil; Michele Macrakis; David Beatty; David Beatty.

INDEX

A

Abdera, 114
About, Edmond, 162
Accommodations, 326-327
   list of, 338-345
Achaea, (Peloponnese province), 28, 31, 187, 197
Achaean League, 28
Acharnés, 258
Achladi, 218
Acronyms, (Cultural Dictionary), 272
Acropolis, (in Athens), 164, 168-170, 175
   Agorá, 169
   Erechtheion, 168-169
   Kerameikos Cemetery, 170
   Parthenon, 168
   Propylaia, 169
   Stoá of Attalos, 169
   temple of Athina Nike, 169
   Theater of Dionysos, 169
   Thisseion temple, 169
Aegean Islands, 21, 221-234
   early history, 221
   Latin influence, 221
   Persian invasion and influence, 221
   population movement and exchange, 221
Aegina, 17, 25, 175-178
   abandonment of, 17
Aéri, 244
Aetolian nation, 22
Afáia, Temple of, 178
Afrodite, Spring of, 155
Agamemnon, King, 21
Agathopes, 218
Aghia Paraskevi, 234
Aghiassos, 234
Aghii Theodori, monastery, 199
Agii Theodori, (church), 171
Agio Apostoli, Church of, 230
Agios Giorgos, (church), 229
Agios Isodoros, 234
Agricultural Bank, 70
agricultural estate, 70
Agrínio, 140
Aháta, 244
Aheron, 47
Ahiropiitos, Church of, 103
Aigion, 187
air travel, see transportation
Airline Offices, (list of), 345-347
Akritas, Cape, 202
Akrotiri, archaeological site, 213
Alaja Imaret, mosque, 104
Albanians, 17, 32
"Alexander the Great," (Greek coffee house), 83
Alexander's Greece, 27
Alexandria, (Greek poet), 95
Alexandroupolis, 114
Ali, Ibrahim, 32
Ali, Mehemet, (his house), 110
Ali Pasha, the "Lion of Ioannina," 32
Aliákmon, (the longest river in Greece), 129-130
alóni, (threshing-ground), 262

Alónisos, (island), 149
Alónisos, (town), 149
Alpine Club, (in Athens), 155
Amfipolis, 109
Ámfissa, 140
amphitheater, (Ioannina), 122
Anargirios and Korgialénios College, (on Hydra), 182
Anavatos, 231
ancient drama festival, (in Epidauros), 182
andrismos, (the Greek version of "machismo" in the islands), 77
Andros, 218
Anghelaki-Rooke, Katerina, (poet), 176-177
Angistri, 175
Angistri, (beach), 178
Ano Meria, 216
Ano Poli, 104
Ano Siros, 218
Ano Vathy, 224
Antiparos, 214
Antiquities of Athens, (1700 c. book by architects Stuart and Revett), 53
Ápella, 244
Apollo, temple of, 175, 185
Apollo Belvedere, 54
Aráhova, 137
Arcadia, (Peloponnese province), 187
Arcadian mountains, 188
Archaeological Service, Greek, 150
Archaeological Museums,
   Aegina, 175
   Chóra, 228-229
   Epirot, 120
   Samos Island, 224
   also see complete list of, 350-355
   also see different listings under individual names
archaeological sites,
   see under individual listings
   also see list of, 350-355
archaic period, 24
architecture, styles of,
   Byzantine, 100, 167, 171, 198
   Cycladic, 207
   cross-in-dome form, 104
   folk architecture on Tínos, 209
   Italian-designed neoclassical mansions on Syros, 218
   on Santorin, 214
   Roman, 102
   Turkish, 110, 224
archontiká, (mansion or lord's manor), 122, 128, 179, 182
Arditos, (the hill of), 165
Areopolis, 201
Argalásti, 156
Argenti, Phillip, (historian), 229
Argenti Ethnographic and Folklore Museum, 229
Argive plain, 190
Argo, (Jason's ship), 147
Argolis, (Peloponnese province), 187, 189
Argos, 188
Argosaronic islands, 175-182
Argostóli, 144
Aristi, 125
aristocracies, 22
Aristotle, 22, 26, 80
Armenians, 32
Arna, 201
Árta, 141
Artemis at Brauron, Sanctuary of, 172

Artemis, Sanctuary of, 152
artists' colony, 179
Arundel Collection, 51
Arvanitovlachs, (tribal group), 63
Asclepius, Sanctuary of, (God of Healing), 56
Ashmolean Museum, 51
Asklepíon, 243
Aslan mosque, 120
Asómatos, Church of, 258
Áspri Pétra, 242-243
Assumption of the Virgin Mary, 46
Astakós, 141
Astrákas, Hut, 126-127
Astros, 197
Athénes Ancienne et nouvelle, (early account of Athens by Saint-Georges), 51, 55
Athens, 22, 24, 27, 79-83, 161-172, 175
   ancient Greece, 22, 24, 27
   city streets, 163-164
   early history, 161
   modern Athens, 79-83, 161
   night movies, 167
   society today, 162-163
Athens Museum, City of, 172
Athens' National Archaeological Museum, 213
Athens School of Fine Arts, 179-180
Athina, (goddess), 47
Athina, My Grandmother, (excerpt from this collection of short stories written by Greek author Costas Taktsis), 84
Athinás Street, 80, 83
Attic drachma, (coin), 28
Attica, 21, 24, 27
Atticus, Herodes, 28, 47
Athicus (Herodes) Streets, Athens, 165
Averof, (the famous Greek warship), 181
Averof, Evangelos, 122
Averof Street, (Ioannina), 120
Avgonima, 231
Avlis, 152
Ayi Dimitrios, monastery, 199
Ayia Marína, 175, 178
Áyia Paraskeví, (church), 154
Ayia Rúmeli, 265
Ayia Sophia, Church of, 103
Ayiá Yianni, 156
Ayios Galas, 231
Áyios Lavréndis, 156
Ayios Nikólaos Kasnitzi, (church), 130
Ayi Anargiri, (the oldest church in Kastoría), 129
Áyos Nikólaos, (resort in Crete), 258
Ayos Nikólaos, (monastery), 154
Ayos Stéfanos, (monastery), 153-154

B

Babin, Jacques, 50
backpacking,
   Pindos Range, 126-127
   on Paros, 214
   the Cyclades, 207
Balkan Wars, 37, 68, 147, 181
"Barbarous", (origination of), 47
Barbayiorgos, (popular image of the Rúmeliot), 136
Barthes, Roland, 62

Bassai, 197
Baths of Helen, (healing springs), 187
Batsi, 218
Beloi, 124
Benaki Museum, 172
"Berati", (Greek folk dance), 61
Bezesten, (a six-domed covered market in Salonika), 104
bird sanctuary, 130
Bishop of Tríkala, 121
black-figure painting, 24
boat travel, 315-316
Bocher, 55
Boeotian, plains, 68
Bouboulína, (Greece's national heroine), 182
bougátsa (famous Greek cream pastry), 120
Bourtzí, the islet, 192
Bouverie, James, 55
Boy's Naval Training School, 181
Brecht, Bertolt, (playwrite), 117
Bulgars, 31
bureaucracy, (early politics), 70
Burgundian de la Roche, 30
Buses, 316-317
Butterfly Valley, (Rhodes), 242
Byron, Lord, (early foreign traveler), 51, 140, 144, 162, 172
Byzantine art and architecture, at Chios, 231
  at Kastoría, 129
  at Mount Athos, 107
  Panayia Ayiogalousenas Church, 231
  at Poros, 231
  also see, individual listings and museums and sites, 350-355
Byzantine Church Music, (Cultural Dictionary), 272-273
Byzantine Museum, (Athens), 172
Byzantine rule, 30-31
  effect of crusaders, 31
  fall of, 31
  invasion of Slavs, 30

C

Caesar, Julius, 187
caique, (a fishing boat), 75, 149, 175
Candia, (Iráklion), 49
Cape of Ayia Marína, 178
Cape Soúnion, 172
Capodistria, (first president), 191
Capuchin, maps, 55
Capuchin, priests, 51
Castle of St. Nicholas, 241
Catharsis, 80
Cellarius, Christoph, (author), 49
centaurs, (mythical creatures), 156
Center Union, party, 42
Central Greece, 147-156
Cephalonia, 144
Chain Tower, 102
Chalcidice, Peninsula, 108
Chalkis, 151-152
Chandler, 50-51, 53, 55-56
changing values, (in Greek culture), 82-83
Chanía, (capital of Crete), 260-262
  architecture, 261
  excursions from, 261-262
  restaurants and tavernas, 261
Charioteer, (at Delphi), 138
Cháris of Lindos, (sculptor), 240
chiflik, (a large track of land under hereditary ownership), 68, 72

chiflikia, Turkish, 76
Chios, 17-18, 32, 221-222, 227
  beaches, 234
  depopulation, 222, 228
  early history, 227-228
  festival, 234
  Kastro fortress, 228
  mastic production, 229-230
  Turkish invasion, 221
  Turkish savagery, 17
Choniates, Michael, (Archbishop), 30
Chóra, 216, 228-229, 250
  medieval castle at, 250
chora, (main town), 207
Christianity, 28, 30, 63, 68, 111-112, 199
  the beginning of, 111-112
churches,
  see under individual listings
Cicero's lament, 49
Citadel of Ali Pasha, 119
city culture, 79-83
  changing values, 82-83
  developing country syndrome, 82
  education, 82
  employment, 81
  industry, 81
civic breakdown, (ancient Greece), 26
civilization, early, 21
class hierarchy, (island culture), 76
Claudis, Emperor, 26
climate, 313
Coffee, (Cultural Dictionary), 273-274
coins, (used in early trade), 28, 175
Colonels, The, 42
Colossus, the, (one of the Seven Wonders of the World), 240
'The Colossus of Marousi', (a book by Henry Miller), 180
Communications, (services for the tourist), 318-319
Communist Party, 40
Confederation of Dilos, 25
Conference of London, (1829), 33
Constantine, (emperor), 28
Constantinople, 30
conurbations, 22
convents,
  Galaták, 151
  also see individual listings
Corbusier, Le (a modern architect), 207
Corfu, 32, 76
Corinth, 25-26, 28, 187
  ancient ruins, 187
  history of, 187
Corinthia, (Peloponnese province), 187
Crete Island, 256-268
  boat trips, 266
  bus travel, 267
  climate, 256
  ferry to, 256
  food, 267-268
  history of, 257-258
  mountain hiking on, 261-266
  population, 257
  villages and towns, 257
Chronicle of a City, (a novel by Prevelákis), 260
Crusades, 30-31
Crusius, Martin (a German scholar), 49

Cultural Activities, (list of), 324
Cultural Center, (at Delphi), 138
"cultural club,", (Epirus), 117-118
Cyclades Islands, 76, 207-208
  archaeological finds, 207
  architecture, 207
  geography, 207-208
  history, 207
Cyllene, mountain range, 187
Cyrus, 24

D

D'Azeglio, 61
Daphni, Monastery, 171
Darius, (Cyrus'son), 24
The "Dark Ages", 21-22
death-masks, (golden), 191
Delagrazia, 218
Delectables, (Cultural Dictionary), 274-275
Deliyiannis, Theodore, 36
Delphi, 135, 137-138
depopulation,
  abandonment of Samos (15th c.), 17
  effects of the world slump on (1893), 36
  evacuation of Aegina (896), 17
  exdos from Chios (1821), 17
  Greece and Turkey exchange (1923), 18, 112
  Jewish settlement in Salonika, 105
  in current times, 17-18
  in the northeast Aegean islands, 221
  Turkish attack on Corfu and the Peloponnese, 32
Dervenakia, 189
Despotate of Epirus, 119, 141
developing country syndrome, 82
Diakofti, bay of, 249
dialects,
  East Greek, 21
  West Greek, 21
Diapháni, 243
Diaspora, Greeks, 69
Didimotiho, 114
Dilos, 50, 209
  archaeological site at, 209
Dining Out, 327-330
Dion, (Macedonian site), 56, 101
Dionisios the Dog Sophist, 121
Dionysus, Theater of, 55
Dodecanese Islands, 239-252
  British rule, 239
  German occupation, 239
  Italian colonialists, 239
  Turkish rule, 239
  unification with Greece, 239
Dodona, (Epirus' main archaeological attraction), 47, 121
Dorian, Lake, 105
dolmádhes, (Greek food), 61
Donoussa, 216
dópyi, ("of this place"), 72
Dorian, tribes, 17, 21
dowry house, 73-74
Drakei, 226
Drakiá, 156
Drakólimni, 127
Duchy of Athens, 30
Dürres, 141

E

early travelers,
  Chandler, 50-51, 53, 55-56

Giraud, 51, 55
Guys, 51, 56
Nointe, 51, 54
Spoon, 50-53, 55-56
Tournefort, 50, 53, 55
Vernon, 54, 55
Winckelmann, 51, 54
Wheler, 50-53, 56
Wood, 50, 53, 55
Eastcourt, Sir Giles, 55
Easter, (tradition on Kalymnos), 77
economies, (island), 76
Edessa, 130
Edipsós, 152
Edirne, (Turkey), 114
education,
in Athens, 82
on Kalymnos, 79
Eftánisa, (Greek for Ionian Islands),
142
Egyptians, 21
Eleni, (book and movie), 119
Elfsis, 50
Elis, (Peloponnese province), 187
Elonis, Monastery of, 198
Embassies and Consulates, 347-349
emigration, mass,
see, depopulation
employment, (Athens), 81
Ephesus, 56
Epidauros, 180, 187, 192-193
Epidauros, Sanctuary of, 191
Epirus, 19, 30, 117-122
archaeological site, 121
architecture, 117
coastal region, 118
economy, 117
geography, 118
history, 117
modernization, 117
Eptahorio, 128
Ermoúpolis, 18, 218
Erotokritos, (Cretan verse-romance),
78
ethnos, (kingdom), 22, 27
Etuscans, 21
Euboea, (second largest island in
Greece), 150-151
Euplinius, Tunnel of, 223-224
Euripus Channel, 151
European principalities, 75
Evangelistria, monastery, 199
Evil Eye, (Cultural Dictionary), 275-
276
Evros, plain, 114
Evzone Guard, 165
exodus, mass
see, depopulation

F

Falasárna, 263
family life, (traditional), 64
farmers, (island), 76
federations, 28
Fengari, Mount, (Mount Moon), 114
Fermor, Patrick Leigh, (travel-
writer), 61
ferries, see,
transportation
festivals,
festival of the bull, 234
in Olýmpoi, 246
Olympic Games, 196-197
on Lévros, 234
Sarakatsanides Feast, 65
Shos Carnival, 108

St. George's Day, 137
Theater at Epidauros, 192
also see Festivals and Seasonal
Events
Festivals and Seasonal Events,
(listing of), 319-321
Féstos, (Minoan settlement), 258
Festos, (palace), 21
Fetiye Mosque, 120
Filákio, 260
Filárimo, 242
filótimos, (to "love honor"), 65
Finch, Sir John, 54
Finikia, 218
Fira, (island capital of Santorin), 212
Firostefani, 213
Flea Market, (Athens), 164
flokatis, 65
Florira, 130
Fokas, Nikephoros, 106
Folegandros, 216-218
beaches, 217
geography, 216
population, 216
restaurants, 217
"folklorismos," 61
food, 217-218, 234, 249, 262, 267-
268
fortresses,
Corinth, 187
Didimotiho, 114
Kastro, 228
Monemvasia, 198
Nauplia, 191
also see fortresses under individual
listings
Fourmont, (abbé), 52
foustanélla, (a pleated skirt), 136
Fowles, John, (author), 79, 182
Franco's Bar, (Fira), 212
Frankocástelo, 266
French Revolution, (influence on
Greek nationalism), 33
Frés, 263
frescoes, 104, 114, 124, 130, 154,
172, 199, 213, 230, 241, 258, 263
"Friendly Society," (a secret
organization), 32
Friends or Paréa, (Cultural
Dictionary), 276-278
frontistiria, (private tutorial schools),
82
Frosíni, Kýra, (mistress of Ali
Pasha's son), 120
fur industry, (in Kastoria), 130

G

Galatáki, 151
Galatás, 180
Galaxídi, 138-139
Galerius, Arch of, 102
Galerius, Caesar, 102
Garrion, 218
Genoese, 18
German, occupation, 39
Gerolymin, 202
Gía, 243
Gikas, (the painter), 179
Gingilos, mountain, 265
Giraud, Consul, 51, 55
Glóssa, 148
GNP, 82
Golden Fleece, 147
Gorge of Imbrós, 266
Gorge of Samaría, 264-266
hiking on, 264-266

Górtyn, (Minoan settlement), 56,
258
Gothic invasions, 28
Goulandris Museum, (in Athens),
172, 207
Grafitti, 278-279
Grambúsa, island, 263
Grammos-Vitsi, 129
Grand Metéoron, (monastery), 153-
154
Great Lavra, (monastery), 106
Great Panathenea, (festival), 23
Greeks,
Orthodox, (arrival of, from
Turkey), 18
also see different tribes under
individual listings
Greek Orthodox Church, 32, 64
groin-vaulting, 130
guerrilla fighters, 136
Guys, Pierre-Augustin, 51, 56
Gypsies, 70, 112, 193
Gytheion, 200-201
bazaar at, 201
people of, 201

H

Hades, 47, 141
Hadrian, (Philhellene emperor), 28,
170
Halépa, 261
Hamza-bey Jami, mosque, 104
health or hot springs,
Baths of Helen, 182
Edipsós, 152
Kámena Vourla, 152
in general, 321
also see different listings under
individual names
health regulations, 315
Helen's Gold, 55
Helicon, 47
hellene, (a progressive Greek), 83
Hellenic, culture, 24, 30, 119, 135
"Hellenic Ideal," 50
Hellenikon Airport, (Athens), 83
Hellenistic age, 28
helots, (serfs), 26
Hera, temple to, (at Olympia), 196
Herakles, 47, 188, 190
Hereford Cathedral, 49
Hermes, statue, 196
Herodotus, 24, 121, 197
highway robbery, 18
hiking,
see backpacking
see mountain climbing
Hinitsa, 182
Holomon, Mount, 109
Holy Apostles, Church of the, 104
Holy Virgin Cloister, 179
Homer, 155
Homer, Stone of, 231
Homeric, (pirates), 18
Hora Sfákion, 266
Horitianá, 263
hórta, a wild grass, 267
Hospitality, 280-281
hotels, see accommodations
House of the Lion Hunt, 101
House of Parliament, (location of),
83
House of Tsamados, 180
Hydra, (island), 178-180
Hydriot Archives, 180

I

Iálysos, 239
Iconoclast Controversy, 103
Icons, 281-282
Ierá Odós, (the Sacred Way — Athens), 167-168
Ierápetra, 258
Iliad, Homer, 21-22
"imero", (the cultivated sponge), 251
industrialization, 38
Igumenitsa, 118, 142
industry, (Athens), 81
International Fair, in Salonika, 105
Ioannides, Dimitrios, 43
Ioannina, 119-122
Ionian, (people), 21
Ionian colonies, 21
Ionian Islands, 142-144
  Cephalonia, 144, 197
  Corfu, 143-144
  Itháki, 144, 197
  Kithira, 142
  Lefkáda, 144
  Zante, 142, 197
Ionian revolt, 24
Ionic Confederacy, 221
Ios, 216
Isihast Debate, 103
island culture, 74-79
  class hierarchy, 76
  Easter, 77
  education, 79
  music, 78-79
  women, 77-79
Isthmus of Corinth, 180
Istiéa, 152
Italian, invasion (during W.W.I.), 39
Itéa, (port of) 138
Itháki, 144

J

Janissaries, (Sultan's professional army), 63
Jason of Pherae, (Thessalian tyrant), 27, 47, 147
Junta, 282-283

K

Kaisariani, monastery, 165, 171
Kakoyannis, Mihalis, (film maker), 179
Kalamaria, 105
Kalamas River, 119
Kalamata, 202
Kalamáta, (Crete) 261
Kalathénes, 263
Kalávria, 181
Kalavrian League, (a religious association), 181
Kalikratés, 266
Kalpaki, (battle site location), 124
Kalymnians, 61
Kalymnos, 76, 250-252
  sponge diving, 250-252
Kamáki, 78, 283-284
Kambi, (the Greek plains), 67
Kámena Vourla, 152
Kámiros, 239, 242
Kampos, 228-229
Kanaris, Admiral, 232

Kanzantzídhis, (popular Greek singer), 61
kapetans, (great rebel leaders), 67
Kapheneia, (Greek coffee house), 83
Kapodístrias, Ioánnis, (first governor of Aegina), 33, 175
Kara Aly, tomb of, 229
Karaghiozis, (the traditional puppet show), 136,298, 299,300
Karagunides, (tribal group), 63
Karantína, 175
Kari, 234
Kariadi, (the Old City of Kastoría), 129-130
Karístos, (port of), 151
Karlovassi, 225
  Old Karlovassi, 225
  waterfront, 225
  Middle Karlovassi, 225
  New Karlovassi, 225
Kárpathos, 243-247
  traditional houses, 245
  family life in villages, 245-246
  traditional dress, 246
  main annual festival in Olýmpoi, 246
Karpenísi, (district of), 140
Karvounis, Mount, 225
Kassandra, 109
Kastanea, 226-227
Kastanies, 114
Kastéli, 263
Kastoriá, 32, 125-129
Kastoria Lake, 129
Kástro, (fortress in Epirus), 120, 217, 228
Katara Pass, 122
Kavála, 110-112
Kazantzákis, (Greek novelist), 61
Kea, 218
Kemal, Mustafa, 38, 105
  birth place of, 105
Kepesovo, 124
Keramoti, 111
Kerkis, Mount, 226
Kérkyra, see Corfu
Kilis, 105
Kimi, 150
King George I, 36
Kingfisher days, 84
Kinolos, 218
Kipi, 124, 127
Kipselis (of Corinth), 23
Kiriakosélia, 263
Kíthira, island of, 142, 202
KKE, communist party, 43
Klarino, (Epirot clarinet), 118
Klephts, (bandits or thieves) 22-33, 67, 136
Klisúra, gorge, 140
Knights of St. John, 240
Knossos, (late Minoan palace), 21, 258
Kokinókastro, 149
Kokkari, 225
Kolimbarión, 263
Kolokotrónis, (hero of the Greek War of Independence), 83, 190
kolóna, (column), 175
Kolona, hill of, 175
Komotini, 112-114
  Maronia arhaeological site, 114
Konitsa, 125
Korais Library, 228-229
Koronia, Lake, 108
Kos, 77, 242-243
  archaeological sites, 242-243
  Neolithic settlement, 242-243

Kosmadei, 226
Kotes, ("hens"), 77
Koudeika, 226
Koufonissia, (islands), 216
Koukounariés, (beach on Skiathos), 148
Krávara, (region), 139
Krista, 258
Kunduriotis, Admiral Pavlos, 179
Kutsovlachs, (tribal group), 61, 63, 122
Kyato, 187
Kyrapanagiá, 244

L

Laconia, (Peloponnese province), 187, 198, 202
Lafonisos, 264
Lagada, gorge, 202
Lagadia, 195
lakes,
  Pambiotis, 119, 121
  Vegoritis, 130
  Trihonis, 141
  also see lakes under individual listings
Lambrakis, George, 42
Lamia, 140
Langadas, 108
  Thracian ritual on May 21, 108
language, 248-287
  for the tourist 328-333
Lassithi Plain (on Crete), 67, 258
Lato, Doric city of, 258
Laurion, 25
laúto, (musical instrument), 78
Lefkáda, 144
Lefkes, 215
Lemonodassos, (forest of lemon trees), 193
Leonidion, 197-198
Lepetimnos, Mount, 234
Lévros, 222, 232-234
  early occupation, 232
  lesbian presence, 232-233
  artists' culture, 232
  archaeological museum, 233
Levidi, 195
Levktra, 26
Lia, (village in Morgana), 119
Liberal Party, 37
Lidoríki, (stone village), 139
Ligourio, 192
Limen, 111
Limenaría, 111
Limni, 151
Limnos Meston, 230
Limonári, (beach on Skópelos), 148
Linariá, 150
Líndos, 239, 241
lingua franca, 83
Lion of Amfípolis, 109
Litóchoron, 155
Lixúri, 144
Logothétis, Castle, 224
Logothétis, General, 224, 228
London Society of Dilettanti, 52, 54
Loutráki, 148
Loutro, 265

M

Macedon, 17-18, 24, 27
Machriráchi, 156
Madamados, 234

The Magus, (a novel by John Fowles), 182
Mahéri, 263
Mainalon, (mountain), 195
Mainalon range, 194
Makrinítsa, 156
Makriyánnis, General, 139
Malea, Cape, 202
Malía, (Minoan settlement), 258
Malmsey, or Malvoisie, (dark fruity Greek wine), 198
Mandráki, 241, 242
Manges, (petty criminals), 80
Mani, the, 18-19
Mansion of Admiral Tombazis, 179
Mantinia, 193-194
Manziker, 30
Mappa Mundi, 49
Marathi, 216
Marathokampos, 226-227
Marathon, 24
Marias, 66
Maronia, 114
Marpissa, village, 216
Marpunda, 149
Mask of Agamemnon, 55
Matapan, 202
Matapan, Cape, 201, also known as Cape Tenaron
Megalo, 125
Megalopolis, 197
Megas Ialos, 218
Mégas Lakkos, 127
Mehemet II, Sultan, 31
Mala, Pavlos, (tomb of), 130
Memmius, (Roman consul), 28
Ménetes, 244
mercenaries, 22, 26-27, 31
merchant community, early, 32
Merchant Navy Training School, 180
Mesklá, 262
Mesolóngion, 140
Messenia, (Peloponnese province), 187, 197
Messenian Gulf, 201
Mesta, 229-231
Metamórphosis, *see* Grand Metéoron
Metaxas, (fascist dictator), 38, 69
Metéora, 153
Méthana, 182
metsovitiko, (a smoked yellow cheese), 123
Metsovo, 119, 122
Miaulis, Andreas, (a Greek hero), 179
migrations and invasions, 17-18
also see specific listings for further information
Mikró Pápingo, 125, 126-127
Miliá, 148
Miliés, 156
Military Harbour, (Aegina), 175
Miller, Henry, (author of '*The Colossus of Marousi*'), 180
"millet", (religious community), 32
Milopótamos, 156
Milos, 218
Minoans, 21
Minotaur, 21
Mistras, (Byzantine holy place), 31, 199
Mítikas, (the top of Mount Olympus), 156
Mitilini, 233-234
Mitropolis, (Athens), 163

mizithra, (a white, soft, saltless cheese), 123
modernization, (conflict in Epirus), 117
Molyvos, 234
monasteries, *see* under individual listings
Monastery of Áyios Nektáros, 178
Monastery of Áyos Nikólaos, 121
Monastery of the Mavrotissa, 130
Monastery of Ósios Lukás, 136
Monastery of Panayia Hrisoleóntissa, (Aegina) 178
Monastery of Panayis Zoodóhos Pigi, (Virgin of the Life-Giving Spring — located in Poros), 181
Monastery of Pantaleímon, 121
Monastery of Prusós, 140
Monastery of Revelations, 250
Monastery of St. Paraskevi, 124
Monastiraki, (Athens), 163
Monémvasia, the ''Gibraltar of Greece''), 198
Moni, 175
Moni, (beach), 178
Moni Stomiou, 125
Moni Vrondiani, 225
mono-cropping, 69
Monodendri, 124, 127
Morea, (alternate name for Peloponnese in early times), 189
Morgana, 119
Moria, 234
moriés, (mulberry trees), 189
Mórnos reservoir, 140
Morosini, 55
Mosaics, 101-102, 136
Mount Athos, (Holy mountain), 106-107, 109, 136
monastic community at, 106
history of, 106
Cenobite monasteries, 106
Idiorrhythmic monasteries, 106
museum at, 107
Mount Díksio, 242
Mount Dikti, (Crete), 256, 258
Mount Fríkion, 152
Mount Gamila, 125, 127
Mount Hymettus, 165
Mount Ida, (on Crete), 67, 260
Mount Kertis, 226
Mount Lycabettus, 164
Mount Mitsikeli, 119, 121
Mount Olympus, 47, 155-156
Mount Oros, 175
Mount Ossa, 154
Mount Pangeon, 110
Mount Parnassus, 67, 137
Mount Parnes, 165
Mount Parthenion, 188
Mount Pélion, 156
Mount Pendeli, 165
Mount Simvolon, 110
Mount Smolikas, 128
Mount Tímfristos, 140
Mount Tomaron, 121
Mount Velúhi, (Timfristos), 136
Mount Vion, 128
Mount Voras, 130
mountain climbing,
Mount Kertis, 226
Pindos Range, 126-127
Mount Olympus, 155-156
on Crete, 261-266
in general, 322, 324
mountain men, 64, 66
Mountain Refuges, (list of), 323

mountain settlements, (early), 63
mountains, *see* under individual listings
Movies, 287-288, 325
multiple dwellings, (Athens), 79
Municipal Museum, (Ioannin), 120
museums and sites, (list of), 350-355
music, (islands), 78-79
Muslims, 18, 38, 63, 68, 112, 113
miniority Pomaks, 112
in Komotini, 113
Mussolini, 124
Mycenae, 190
Mycenaean Gallery, (Athens), 172
Mykale, Cape, 223
Mykonos, 208-211
geography, 208
beaches, 209
tourist season, 208
discos and bars, 209
mythology, 21, 114, 147, 156, 187, 188, 190-191, 209, 216
Legend of Theseus, 21
Polyphemus, 114
Tantalos, 187
people of Tiryns, 188
origination of Nemean games, 190
walls at Tiryns, 190-191
Mycenaen, 191
on Dilos, 209

N

Nakromantion, (the oracle of the dead), 47, 142
Namean, plain, 190
Namedays, 288-290
Naoussa, 215
nascent handicrafts industry, 69
National Archaeological Museum, (Athens), 172
National Liberation Front, (''EAM'' in Greek), 40
National Museum, at Athens, 191
National Park, (Athens), 165
National Park, (Zagorahoria), 125
National Parks, (list of), 322
National Theatre of Greece, 193
nationalism, 32, 36, 62, 68
Nauplia, first capital of Greece, 189-191
Naval Museum, (Hydra), 182
Navarino, 33
Navarinon, Bay, 202
also called the Bay at Sphacteria
Navarinu Square, (Salonika), 102
Návaktos, 139-140
Naxos, 216
Nea Moni, monastery, 231
Neapolis, 125
néfos, (smog), 80
Negades, 124
Negropon, *see* Euboea
Nektários, 'Ayios, (Anastásios Kefalás: 1846-1920), 178
Nemea, 189
"Neon", (Greek coffee house), 83
Nestos, River, 112
New Democracy, (conservative party), 43
New Ionia, (in Athens), 80
New Smyrna, (urban Athens), 80
News Media, 319
Nikephoros, Fokas, the Byzantine Emperor, 30

nightlife, 326
Nikea, 30
nikokirá, (house-mistress), 78
nikokyróules, ("the little housewives"), 74
Nikópolis, 141-142
níos, (the word for island), 187
nisiotika, 78
Nointe, Marquisde, (early French ambassador in Constantinople), 51, 54
Nymphs, (the hill of), 165

O

Observatory, (in Athens), 165
Odeon Galerius Palace Complex, 102
Odysseus, 144
Odyssey, Homer's, 21
Oia, 213
Old Harbor, (*Spetses*), 182
Olympia, 196
Olympic games, 165, 196-197
   ancient site of, 196
   museum of, 196
   origination of, 196
   site of modern games, 165
Olýmpoi, 246
   annual festival at, 246
Olympio, (Ioannina), 120
Olympus, 47, 154-155
Ómalos, 264
Omonoia, Square, (Athens), 83, 163
oracle, (at Delphi), 138
Oral Tradition, 291-295
Orchomenus, 194
Orei, 152
Orestiada, 114
Ormos Marathokampos, 227
'Ossios David, Church of, 102
Óthon, 244
Ottoman Greece, 31-33, 68, 75, 123
Our Greek Folk Songs, (television program), 61
oúzo, production of, 234

P

Pagase, 147
Palamas, Archbishop of Salonika, 104
Palamidi, (Mycenae's citadel), 191
Palatia, (plateau), 181
palioánthropo, (a dirty old man), 71
Palladian, 193-194
Pambiotis, Lake, 119, 121
Panagia Church, 217
Panagia Evangelistra, (shrine), 209
Panayia, 111
Panayia Armáta, (celebration in honor of Greece's national heroine, Bouboulína held on Hydra), 182
Panayia Glikofiloussa, Church of, 234
Panayia Kumbelidiki, (church), 130
Panayía Véra, Church of, 258
Pandrossou, Street (Athens), 164
Panhellenic Socialist Movement, ("PASOK"), 43, 62, 71, 74
Panochorió, 247
   local government, 247
Panorama, 105
Panormítis, monastery of, 250
Papanastasíou, Alexandros, (Prime Minister of the Republic in 1924), 195
Papandreou, Andreas, (Prime Minister of Greece), 197
Papandreou, George, 42
papas, (the priest), 52
Pápingo, 125
Parga, 47
Park of Freedom, (Athens), 166
Parnassus, 47
Parnon, range, 199
Paros, 214-216
   beaches, 215
Parthenon, 24
Pasha, Ali, (the "Lion of Ioannina"), 119
Pasha of Vallona, 32
passports, visas and customs, 313
Patmos, 250
Patras, (Peloponnese port city), 187, 197
patronage, (political), 71
Pausanias, (travel writer 2nd C.), 28, 48-49, 53, 188, 193-195, 200
Peace of Nikias, (the), 26
Peirene, spring of, 188
Peisistratos, (tyrant), 23
Pelagos, (island), 149
Pelion, 148
Pella, (Macedonian site), 101
   House of the Lion Hunt, 101
Peloponnese, 17, 19, 21, 22, 30-31, 187-202
   arrival of the Albanians (1338), 17
   arrival of the early settlers, 21
   settlement by the Dorians, 21
Peloponnesian League, 25-26
Peloponnesian War, 26, 175, 200, 202
Penta lofos, 128
People's Square, (Ioannina's central square), 120
Perama, (cave), 122
Perdika, 175
Pergamum, 56
Pericles, language, 17
Periptera, 295-296
Peristéra, (island), 149
Persian, empire, 24
Persian Wars, 175
Petra, 234
Petralona, Cave of, 109
Phanariots, (aristocratic families), 33
philhellenism, 32
Philip of Macedon, 27
Philippi, 100, 101
   Roman ruins at, 111
philoksenia, love of strangers, 268
Philopappus, (the hill of), 164
Phoenicians, influence of, 21-22
Pigádia, 244
Pindar, the poet, 197
Pindos Mountains, 21, 62, 119, 147
Pinios River, 153
Pipéri, 149
Piraeus, 175
Piraeus Archaeological Museum, (Athens), 172
pirates and piracy, 17, 18, 32, 63, 150, 181, 217
Pirgi, (limestone "Towers"), 125
pismatiká, 78
Pithio, 114
pitiusa, (pinetree island), 182
Plaka, (district in Athens), 80, 161
Plataea, (land victory at), 25
Platamónos, 156
Platanos, 226
Plethon, Gemistos (a Greek philosopher), 199
Plomari, 234
Pnyx, 164
Pococke, (author), 50
poets
   Kálvos, Andréas, 144
   Foscolo, Ugo, 144
   Solomós, Count Dhionisios, 140, 144
   Pindar, 197
   Ritsos, Yannis, 182, 198
   Seferis, George, 215
   also see, poets under individual listings
Poliriniá, 263
polis (city-state), 21-22, 26, 28, 30
politics, 36-43
   the early democracy, 36
   formation of political parties, 36-43
   Metaxas' dictatorship, 38
   joining NATO, 41
   prosperity during the 50s and 60s, 41
   the colonels, 42
   student protests, 43
Poliyiros, 108
Polycrates, King, 223
Polyphemus' Cave, 114
Pondi, (refugees from the Black Sea), 72
Pondios, 62
population, 15, 17-18, 22, 37-38
   exchange (1923) 18, 38
   explosion, 22
   emigration, 22
   effect of Balkan Wars, 37
Populist Party, 38
Poros, 180
Porto Heli, 182
Poseidon, Sanctuary of, 181
Poseidon's, temple, 172
Potamia, 111
Potidea, 108
Potidea Canal, 109
pottery, 24
prehistoric, archaeological sites, cave of Petralona, 109
   in Áspri Pétra on Kos, 242-243
Prespa Lakes, 130
Préveza, 141
Priene, 56
Protestantism, 52
protests, student, (during the 70s), 43
Psara, 232
Psilorítis, 256
Public Holidays, (list of), 315
purdah, 65
Pylos, (the city of old Nestor from Homer's *Odyssey*), 202
Pyrgi, 229-230
Pyrgos, 226
Pyrrhus, (Epirot king), 122
Pythagoras, 223
Pythagoreio, 223

Q

Queueing, 296

R

raki, (local liquor), 262
Récit de l'état présent de la ville d'
Athenes (1674), (first modern
account of Athens by Babin), 50
red-figure painting, 24
religion, 23-24
religious and ethnic communities,
(early), 61
religious pilgrimage, (to Tínos), 209
Rembetika, 297-298
rembetiko, music, 80, 298-299
resinato, wine, 32
resistance, movement, 39
Restaurants, (list of), 336-337
Réthimnon, 258, 260
Revett, Nicholas, 53
Rhodes, 239-242
in ancient times, 239-241
archaeological sites, 242
Rhodes, City of, 239-241
architectural variety, 239
ancient times, 239
Roman influence, 240
fortress Castle of St. Nicholas, 241
Christian influence, 241
Rhomaioi, (citizens of the eastern
part of the Roman Empire), 135
Rion, 139
Ritsos, Yannis, (one of Greece's
greatest poets), 182, 198
Rodopi, Western and Eastern, 113
Roger of Sicily, (Norman ruler), 30
Roman Empire, (ancient greece),
28, 30
romanios, (a Greek of traditional
learning), 83
Roumlouki, (a refugee vilage), 71,
73
rousfeti, ("string-pulling"), 71
Royalist Government, 37
Rúmeli, 135-142
Rupel, Pass, 105

S

St. Andreas, (patron saint of Patras),
197
St. Athanasios, basilica of, 124
St. Catherine, Church of, 104
St. Demetrius, Church of, 103
St. Elias, Church of, 104
Saint-Georges, Guillet de, 51
St. George's Day festival, (in
Aráhova), 137
Saint George, Church of, 102
St. Nicholas Orphanos, Church of,
104
St. Nikodemos, (church), 171
St. Nikólaos, (church), 124
St. Peter, the Athonite, (early
monk), 106
Salamis, 25, 175
naval victory at, 25
Sálona, (the castle), 140
Salonika, (the second largest city in
Greece), 31, 98-105
ancient city, 98-100
Ano Poli, 104
city tour, 101
International Fair, 105
Islamic influence, 104
rail travel from, 105
Roman ruins, 102
the Great Fire of 1917, 100

Sámos, 17-18, 221-227
abandonment of, 17
archaeological site, 223-224
Architecture, 224
beaches, 225
mountain climbing, 226
Turkish invasion, 221
Samothrace, 114
sanctuaries,
Artemis, 56, 152
Asclepius, 56
Epidauros, 191
Poseidon (Poros), 181
also see under individual listings of
sites
Santorin, (also known as Thíra),
209, 212-214
archaeological finds, 213
architecture, 214
beaches, 214
geography, 212
night life, 213
restaurants, 212
santouri, (musical instrument used
on the islands), 78
Sarakatsanides, (tribal group), 17,
63, 108, 117
Sarakatsanides Feast, 65
Sarandaporos River, 128
Saronic Gulf, 25, 175
Sarti, 109
sculptors, 24, 178
Seferis, George, (the Nobel prize-
winning poet), 150, 215
Selcuk, 56
Selimiye, Mosque, (16th C.), 114
Seneca, 28
Serbs, 31
serf population, 22, 26
Serifos, 218
Serres, 108
panayiri (fair), 108
services, (Athens), 81
settlers, early, 21
Sfakopigádi, 263
shadow puppet theater, 298-300
sheepherders, (Peloponnese), 189
Siatista, 128
Siderounta, 230
Sifnos, 218
Sigri, 234
Sikaminia, 234
silver mines, 25-26, 172
Sími, 247
Simi harbor, 76
Sithonia, 109
Skála, 250
Skala Eressos, 234
Skiátho, (island), 148
skiing, (snow), 108, 195, 321-322
Skinoussa, 216
Skópelos, (island), 148
Skyros, (island), 150
Skyros, (town), 150
Slavs, 17, 30
Smyrna, 55
socialist government, (influence of),
67
Society of Dilettanti, 52, 54
Socrates, 27
Sofias Avenue, (Athens), 166
Sohos, 108
carnival in February, 108
Solomós, (national poet), 140, 144
Solon, (aristocrat),23
Soufli, 114
Souvala, 175
Spahi, (warrior), 68

Sparta, 24, 175, 199-200
ancient ruins and modern, city,
199-200
Spatherei, 226
Sperhios Valley, 140
Spetses, 182
Sphacteria, Bay, 202
also called Navarino Bay
sponge, diving and fishing, 247,
250-252
Spoon, Jacob, 50-53, 55-56
Sporades, Northern, (islands), 147-
152
sport and recreation activities, (list
of), 321
squatting, 68
Stabo, 48
Stackelberg, Baron, 19
Stadíou Street, 83
Stadium, (in Athens), 165
Stáfylos Cove, (beach on Skópelos),
148
Stavró, 261
Stayira, 109
Stines, (Athens), 49
Stoicism, 28
stone masons, of Lagadia, 196
Strátos, 141
Strefi, (the hill of), 165
Strophyliá, 151
Strymonic, Gulf, 109
Stuart, James, 53-55
subashi, (police chief),32
Sulla, (Roman conqueror), 152
Summer lovers, (a Hollywood movie
filmed on Santorin Island), 213
Syntagma Square, 83
Syros, 218
architecture, 218
museum, 218
seaside towns, 218

T

Ta Vaporia, (The Boats), 218
Taïgetos (mount), 200, 202
Taïgetos, range, 199
Taktis, Costas, (contemporary Greek
writer and author), 84
tanneries, (ta tabákika), 140
t'arhéa, (the ancient remains), 135
ta'vli, 147
Taxiarchi, (church),130
Taxiarchon, Church, 234
Tegea, 193
annual fair, 193
temples,
Apollo, 175, 185
Afáia, 178
Apollo at Bassai, 197
also see different temples under
individual listings
Temple of Artemis, (one of the
Seven Wonders of the Ancient
World), 56,152
Temple of Olympian Zeus, 170
Tenaron, Cape, 201, also known as
Cape Matapan
Teos, 56
Thasos, 25, 111
theater, at Epidauros, 192-193
theaters, 324-325
Thebes, 26-27, 30
Theodorakis, 300-301
Theognis, (poet) 23
Theologos, 112
sanctuary of Pan, 112